Earnest Endeavors

George Rublee, ca. 1930

Earnest Endeavors

The Life and Public Work of George Rublee

Marc Eric McClure

Contributions in American History, Number 202
Jon L. Wakelyn, Series Editor

PRAEGER

Westport, Connecticut
London

Library of Congress Cataloging-in-Publication Data

McClure, Marc Eric, 1966–
Earnest endeavors : the life and public work of George Rublee / Marc Eric McClure.
p. cm.—(Contributions in American history, ISSN 0084–9219; no. 202)
Includes bibliographical references and index.
ISBN 0–313–32409–3 (alk. paper)
1. Rublee, George, 1868–1957. 2. Political consultants—United States—Biography 3. Lobbyists—United States—Biography. 4. United States. Federal Trade Commission—History. 5. United States—Economic policy—To 1933. 6. Intergovernmental Committee on Refugees. 7. Jews—Germany—Migrations—History—20th century. 8. Refugees, Jewish—History—20th century. I. Title. II. Series.
E748.R895M33 2003
973.91′092—dc21 2003051750

British Library Cataloguing in Publication Data is available.

Library of Congress Catalog Card Number: 2003051750
ISBN: 0–313–32409–3
ISSN: 0084–9219

First published in 2003

Praeger Publishers, 88 Post Road West, Westport, CT 06881
An imprint of Greenwood Publishing Group, Inc.
www.praeger.com

Printed in the United States of America

The paper used in this book complies with the Permanent Paper Standard issued by the National Information Standards Organization (Z39.48–1984).

10 9 8 7 6 5 4 3 2 1

Copyright Acknowledgment

All photos courtesy of the Rublee Family Estate.

Contents

Acknowledgments vii

Abbreviations ix

1 Introduction 1

2 Foundations (1868–1892) 5

3 "Latent Possibilities" (1892–1908) 23

4 "Who Is George Rublee?" (1909–1911) 49

5 "Garibaldi's Expedition" (1912) 65

6 "The Most Assiduous and Persistent and Tireless Lobbyist" (1913–1914) 85

7 "An Ideal Public Servant" (1914–1916) 105

8 "A Vision as Mystical and Inspired as That of the Holy Grail" (1917–1919) 135

9 "A Man of Mystery . . . with No Definite Work" (1919–1929) 171

10 "Dwight Morrow's Colonel House" (1930) 197

11 The "Detached, Friendly Sage" (1930–1938) 219

12 The "Gaunt Prophet" (1938–1939) 247

13 Conclusion (1940–1957) 283

Selected Bibliography 287

Index 297

An unnumbered photo essay follows page 63

Acknowledgments

I would like to extend special appreciation to George and Ellen MacVeagh Rublee of Washington, D.C., for access to the Rublee Family Papers, for two memorable visits to Crossways in 1995 and 1996, and for numerous other contributions toward this work. Doug Brown, archivist at Groton School, has since 1995 been very helpful both in providing access to George Rublee's correspondence in the Endicott Peabody Papers and in providing several works on the history of the school. Charles Horsky (1910–1997) was also exceptionally kind to allow me to copy Rublee's correspondence at Covington and Burling law firm in Washington, D.C. A special thanks goes to Wallace Dailey, director of the Theodore Roosevelt Collection in the Houghton Library at Harvard University, for his generous help with the Progressive Party Papers. Funding for a number of research trips was made possible through the Alfred D. Chandler Jr. Traveling Fellowship from the Harvard Business School, the Herbert Hoover Presidential Library Association, and the English–Speaking Union Washington chapter.

I would also like to thank William Becker for his many efforts on my behalf in directing my dissertation at George Washington University and also Charles Herber, James Hershberg, and Peter Klarén for their thoughtful analysis of parts of this work. I also would like to thank Donald Pickens, William Kamman, and Bullitt Lowry (1934–2002) for guidance in my first effort to treat George Rublee while at the University of North Texas. Finally, I want to thank my wife, Rachel, and my mother, Kaye, for many years of support, encouragement, and patience, without which this work would not have been possible.

Abbreviations

AMTC	Allied Maritime Transport Council
DMP	Dwight W. Morrow Papers, Amherst College
FTC	Federal Trade Commission
FRUS	*Papers Relating to the Foreign Relations of the United States*
German Documents	*Documents on German Foreign Policy, 1918–1945*, Series D (1937–1945)
GR	George Rublee
GRP	George Rublee Papers
GSA	Groton School Archives
HBS-Lamont	Thomas Lamont Papers and Diaries, Baker Library Special Collections, Harvard Business School
Hearings I	*Hearing Before a Subcommittee of the Committee on Interstate Commerce, United States Senate, Relating to the Fitness of the Members of the Federal Trade Commission, February 25 and 26, 1915*
Hearings II	*Hearing Before a Subcommittee of the Committee on Interstate Commerce, United States Senate, Relating to the Fitness of the Members of the Federal Trade Commission, Part II, March 3, 1915*
HHPL-Pre-Com	Herbert Hoover Presidential Papers, Pre-Commerce Correspondence, Herbert Hoover Presidential Library
HHPP	Herbert Hoover Presidential Papers, Herbert Hoover Presidential Library
HLS-Hand	Learned Hand Papers, Harvard Law School Special Collections

HLS-Hudson	Manly O. Hudson Papers, Harvard Law School Special Collections
HRP	Horace Rublee Papers
HU-PPA	Progressive Party Archives, Houghton Library Special Collections, Harvard University
HUA	Harvard University Archives
JBR	Juliet Barrett Rublee
JBR-Dartmouth	Juliet Rublee Papers, Baker Library Special Collections, Dartmouth College
LBP	Louis Brandeis Papers, Brandeis Law Library, University of Louisville
LNC	London Naval Conference
LNC records	U.S. Department of State, Record Group 43, International Conferences, Records of the London Naval Conference
Pearson Papers	Drew Pearson Papers, Lyndon B. Johnson Presidential Library
RBP	Robert P. Bass Papers, Baker Library Special Collections, Dartmouth College
TRP-LoC	Theodore Rooselvelt Presidential Papers, U.S. Library of Congress
WWP-LoC	Woodrow Wilson Presidential Papers, U.S. Library of Congress
Yale-Acheson	Dean Acheson Papers, Sterling Library Special Collections, Yale University
Yale-House	Edward House Papers and Diaries, Sterling Library Special Collections, Yale University
Yale-Leffingwell	Russell Leffingwell Papers, Sterling Library Special Collections, Yale University
Yale-Lippmann	Walter Lippmann Papers, Sterling Library Special Collections, Yale University

1

Introduction

A number of years ago, while perusing Walter Langsam's 1940 *The World Since 1914*, I happened upon a brief section describing the effort of George Rublee to devise a plan for the emergency emigration of Germany's Jewish population following the 1938 German-Austrian anschluss.[1] I was unfamiliar with the history of Rublee's effort coming out of the Evian conference and was intrigued with what appeared to be his surprising partial success in winning at least some German cooperation on a plan for orderly Jewish emigration. Interested in Rublee's identity, I soon learned that he was but an obscure historical figure. Although he appeared in a number of historical monographs on disparate subjects, I found that there was no general treatment of his life. Researching a little further, I learned that Rublee had agreed to an interview with the Columbia University Oral History Office in 1951, and so I sent for a transcript of his memoir. What I read captivated me. I found Rublee a compelling and attractive personality and perceived in his life story a remarkable and dramatic effort to make a meaningful public contribution. Then early in my historical training, I soon realized that specialization in the profession rendered Rublee an unlikely subject for historical scholarship. Involved in domestic economic and political reform during the Progressive Era, questions of war economy and inter-Allied cooperation during World War I, and disjointed international missions throughout the interwar period culminating in his effort on behalf of German Jews in 1938, Rublee transcended traditional historical categories. Upon locating and obtaining access to Rublee's hitherto undisturbed papers at the Rublee family home in Cornish, New Hampshire, I decided to make a treatment of his public work both the focus of my research and the catalyst for my studies in history.

George Rublee (1868–1957) was a man of middle-class origins steeped in republican virtues who, owing to a gifted intellect, opportunity, and conviction, managed to make a series of significant public contributions between 1910 and 1940. Trained as a lawyer but more interested in the humanities and public policy, Rublee had a limited interest for the financial world in which he excelled. Instead, he sought opportunities to contribute to the search for solutions to some of the political and economic problems of the distressed and turbulent period in which he lived. Modern, tolerant, and adaptive, Rublee read widely and listened intently in an effort to understand the issues confronting the Western democratic-capitalist system. Especially interested in social and economic problems stemming from the emergence of big business, Rublee formed friendships with like-minded progressive lawyers and journalists who sought to contribute to the formation of enlightened public policy. Beginning in 1910, Rublee took an active role in helping to develop progressive policies on the state and national level, first as counselor to Governor Robert Bass of New Hampshire and then as adviser to Theodore Roosevelt and the Progressive Party during the 1912 presidential campaign. In 1914 Rublee managed to take control of the direction of the nation's antitrust policy and served on the Federal Trade Commission from 1915 to 1917, seeking to set it on a productive and useful course.

Upon America's entry into war in 1917, a then moderately nationalistic Rublee became fixated on the problem of a swift conversion to a war economy and the importance of coordinating the Allies' transportation systems to make the most economical use of available shipping. Owing to his interest and grasp of the shipping and supply crisis, Rublee was chosen to represent the United State on an inter-Allied body in London, the Allied Maritime Transport Council, beginning in January 1918. Working in London with progressive American and European technical experts, Rublee became a committed internationalist and worked to expand U.S. cooperation with Allied bodies throughout 1918 and during the armistice period. Frustrated in those efforts, especially as a result of the counterdesigns of then food administrator Herbert Hoover, Rublee throughout the interwar period sought to expand U.S. commitments to Europe and to increase American cooperation with progressive international organizations. Interested in improving U.S.–Latin American relations, Rublee worked as an adviser to Ambassador Dwight Morrow in Mexico from 1928 to 1929 and served as adviser to Colombian president Enrique Olaya Herrera from 1931 to 1933. Between those two assignments Rublee acted as legal counsel to the American delegation at the 1930 London Naval Conference, during which he worked to mitigate against U.S. political isolation from Europe. Owing to his accumulated international experiences, including his influence in Latin American and European circles and acclaim as a financial expert and skilled negotiator, Rublee was selected in 1938 to direct a U.S.-led effort to locate havens of refuge for German Jews.

Rublee's involvement in these varied endeavors had a unifying theme—an interest in humanity and a desire to improve the domestic and international political system by sustaining those economic structures that were beneficial and discarding or transforming those that were corrupt or socially destabilizing. His views were, of course, colored by his own experiences, but his mind was open enough and his experiences broad enough that he rejected little out of hand. Indeed, his independence and openness to varying points of view prevented him from adopting a narrow "elitist reformer" outlook despite a heavy dose of that viewpoint during his formative years. With a classical-oriented education, professional training in law, a background in journalism, an understanding of economic, financial, and monetary systems, and a lifelong interest in politics, society, and human relations, Rublee was usually able to grasp the significant trends and events challenging the Western world and to discern beneficial policy changes. That the tumultuous period in which he lived adopted a middle course between an antiliberal socialism and laissez-faire capitalism only after agonizing upheavals and widespread suffering is an indication that Rublee did not win controlling influence over the issues. Failing that, he was able to achieve economic policy changes leading toward a regulated market economy and helped shape the foundations of Eastern Establishment internationalist policy through his broad associations and through his formative influence on Dean Acheson, for whom Rublee was a mentor. Although Rublee did not succeed in preventing the upheavals that attended this period, he did live to see a number of the views he championed dominate Western thinking, and he did have some influence in shaping post–World War II U.S. policy.

When Rublee was successful in altering the course of public policy as it developed, it was owed to a tenacious drive that emerged once his passion was engaged. When aroused by the opportunity to effect a meaningful change, Rublee's unyielding determination led him to heroic efforts and allowed him to hazard unconventional, even daring methods to win a contest. Owing to his influential relations on Wall Street and his association with leading journalists, publishers, and labor leaders and with progressive members of both the major political parties, Rublee was a resourceful and resilient competitor who did not shrink from openly or surreptitiously challenging industrial magnates, senators, and even presidents for control of public policy. His ability to survive such contests was often the result of thoughtful strategy and quiet influence.

In February 1888, at age nineteen, George Rublee made the following observation in a sophomore theme paper at Harvard College: "It has been the fate of many men to achieve moderate eminence in their lifetime, then to lapse into comparative obscurity, and at last gradually to gain a permanent and shining place in the House of Fame."[2] Rublee's observation regarding the revival of interest in the nineteenth-century English poet Thomas Hood may well bear some similarity to Rublee's own eventual place in American history. Although during his lifetime Rublee was highly regarded for his public work, since his death in 1957 he has indeed lapsed into deep obscurity. Since commencing my work on Rublee in 1994, I have found only one or two historians who readily knew something of Rublee's work, and I suspect that only a handful of historians have any idea about the scope of his involvement in national and world affairs. While this study of Rublee does not aim to elevate him to a "House of Fame," it does attempt to fully document the important and varied contribution that he made to America history during the first half of the twentieth century. Whether or not his place will be "permanent and shining" will depend on other historians' reaction to Rublee's efforts to alter the course of momentous world events.

This work, detailing George Rublee's public contribution, relies overwhelmingly on original research in primary documents, many of which are unpublished. In addition to government documents in various Washington-area archives, sources for this study include the presidential papers of Theodore Roosevelt, Woodrow Wilson, Herbert Hoover, and Franklin Roosevelt; the papers of Dean Acheson, Edward House, Arthur Bliss Lane, Russell Leffingwell, Walter Lippmann, and Henry Stimson at Yale University; the papers of James Barr Ames, Charles Eliot, Edwin Gay, Learned Hand, Manly O. Hudson, and Thomas Lamont at Harvard University; the papers of Herbert Hoover, Hugh Wilson, and Lewis Strauss at the Hoover Presidential Library; the papers of Endicott Peabody at Groton School; the papers of Dwight Morrow at Amherst and Robert Perkins Bass at Dartmouth College; the papers of Louis Brandeis and Stephen Wise at Brandeis University; the papers of Drew Pearson at the Lyndon B. Johnson Presidential Library; and the papers of George Rublee, Horace Rublee, and Juliet Barrett Rublee, on loan from the Rublee family in Washington, D.C., and those of George Rublee and Dean Acheson—now inaccessible—at Covington and Burling law firm in Washington. Finally, of great importance to this study is Rublee's 300 page oral memoir recorded by Columbia University's Oral History Office in 1951. Owing to his secretive style, it is essentially the existence of the memoir that has preserved George Rublee from utter obscurity.

NOTES

1. Walter Consuelo Langsam, *The World Since 1914* (New York: Macmillan Company, 1940), 863-864.

2. George Rublee, "Hood," 22 February 1888, George Rublee Papers (from Crossways, Cornish, New Hampshire).

2

Foundations (1868–1892)

Although it is possible to move directly to an examination of George Rublee's public contributions with little consideration of his formative influences, there is much value in understanding the professional and intellectual developments of his youth that were central to his ability to play a role in the development of U.S. domestic and foreign policy. His father's experiences as a newspaper publisher and minister to Switzerland were a profound influence on Rublee's interest in domestic and foreign issues, and his own attachment to European civilization through his course of study and various travels played a key role in not only shaping his own internationalist outlook but also making him capable of working effectively on international governmental bodies. His attainments as a corporate lawyer, his knowledge of domestic politics and international relations, and his understanding of the role of the news media in the political process were also crucial to the work he would perform. A number of intellectual and personal attributes were likewise central to his achievements. His reticence, scholarly bearing, and ease in high society were important in establishing Rublee as a man of influence, and his religiously inspired interest in public service gave him both the initiative to strive for what he believed to be good and the will to continue working toward that good despite suffering repeated defeats. An understanding of these and other aspects of his formative years is pertinent to understanding how and why George Rublee was able to make a wide-ranging contribution to important episodes in American history from the administrations of Woodrow Wilson to Franklin Roosevelt.

According to George Rublee, the two greatest influences on his life were his father, Horace Rublee, and Endicott Peabody, founder and headmaster of Groton School. George Rublee's progressive outlook on politics and his understanding of political parties and the role of journalism were mostly shaped by the experiences and convictions of his father. Endicott Peabody charged Rublee with a deep commitment to public service and served as a lifelong mentor, spiritual counselor, and friend. Writing to Peabody in January 1898, Rublee attested to the influence of these two men on his life: "I really care more about being useful to humanity than I do for anything else, and my father and you have helped me most to that end."[1] Owing to their heavy influence on his life, a study of Rublee must begin with a study of these two men.

Although George Rublee would become a prominent Eastern Establishment figure, he was not patrician by birth. Horace Rublee was born on a modest Vermont farm in 1829 and moved with his family to Sheboygan Falls, Wisconsin, at age eleven, where the family secured virgin farmland when the territory of Wisconsin was just being cleared of its Native American population. According to family lore, Horace's mother was the "first white woman in that part of the country."[2] Though deprived of a formal education, at a young age Horace Rublee "developed a fondness for books and pleasure for study," and he managed to prepare himself rather well in literature, history, and political thought.[3] In 1849, at age twenty, Horace made the momentous decision to leave the family farm and move to Madison, Wisconsin, where he entered the university only recently established there. Lacking an independent income to devote himself solely to his studies, Horace Rublee worked part-time as a librarian for the state legislature and also as a legislative reporter for the *Madison Argus*, a paper aligned with the Democratic Party. After a few years, Horace, finding that he had a natural talent for journalism and a passion for politics, quit the university to become an editorial writer for the *State Journal*, the leading paper in Madison and one devoted to Whig policies in support of banks, business, and a return to public virtue in politics. According to one of his peers in the newspaper business, "the farmer lad, Horace Rublee, like Horace Greeley, became a journalist by natural selection. He had a marked aptitude for the profession." Not long after joining the *Journal*, the owners of the paper promoted Horace to editor. From that position he became one of the most influential newspapermen in the Midwest.[4]

As the 1850s progressed, Horace Rublee became energized by the great political contests of the day, particularly the question of slavery as it related to regional antagonisms stemming from the fugitive slave laws and the development of the western territories. Following the disintegration of the Whig Party in the wake of the 1854 Kansas-Nebraska Act, Horace Rublee joined fellow Wisconsin Whigs at Ripon, Wisconsin, on 20 March 1854 to found the Republican Party. Horace was a leading force in the formation of the new party and was elected chairman of the party's central apparatus, the Republican State Central Committee, a position he would retain for the better part of the next thirty years. As chairman he organized and led numerous campaigns for local, state, and national positions, including taking a "prominent part in the great political campaign of 1856, the election of Lincoln in 1860, and the remarkable controversy among Republicans" of Wisconsin in which he worked to end "all favor of the states' rights doctrine."[5]

Horace Rublee was an idealist who wanted to see the new party restore virtue and honorable conduct to politics. With others he sought to protect the party from being tainted and corrupted by the conventional spoils system. Carl

Schurz, later the renowned civil service reform advocate, in a letter to Horace in November 1862 affirmed that he agreed with Horace's "sentiments as to those qualities our man in the Senate *ought*" to possess so as "to avert that danger" of raising "corrupt men to places of power and influence."[6] E. Daniels, another Wisconsin party leader, had expressed a similar reform vision for the party in a letter to Horace two years earlier:

> For the future I look away from these old political bruisers who think that all political work means gambling for the spoils, I look to the young men just coming into political life with...their boyish enthusiasm for what is good and true and honorable yet upon them. For them the Republican party opens a grand entry into the arena of politics, replete with the prizes worthy of the noblest capacity to be won not by trickery but by manly devotion to freedom and the interest of the country.[7]

It was to men such as Schurz and Daniels that Horace Rublee was closest in the party, and together they worked to advance civic virtues within it. Had Horace been in the United States during the presidency of Ulysses Grant, he may well have joined in the rebellion of the Liberal Republicans who broke with Grant in the 1872 election, making civil service reform their central issue. As it turned out, Horace was at the time representing the Grant administration in Europe and took no apparent part in the schism.

After fourteen years of waging political battles and running the *Journal*, at age forty Horace Rublee's health was suffering, and he sought less strenuous work in the diplomatic service. In 1869 President Grant named him minister to Switzerland, a post he would hold until 1876.[8] On 7 July 1869, George Rublee, the youngest of three children, celebrated his first birthday in London, where the family stopped en route to Switzerland. Spending most of his first eight years in Europe gave George an attachment to European civilization and an interest in European political affairs that would stay with him throughout his life. While he lived in Switzerland, Europe experienced dramatic events that both touched upon his father's work as minister and set the stage for the turbulent world affairs through which he would live and operate. Chief among these momentous events was the1870 Franco-Prussian War, which led to the unification of the German Empire and the tumultuous and tragic Paris Commune. From these fault lines Rublee would live to see the collapse of Western European civilization and the climatic upheavals of the century-old struggle between capital and labor.

Although Robert Ferrell in his authoritative work *American Diplomacy: A History* reserves special disdain for the Grant administration's "inept" appointments to the diplomatic service, Horace Rublee must stand out as a notable exception.[9] Although his appointment was certainly related to his political influence, Rublee's work as an editor and his understanding of the role of newspapers in shaping public opinion allowed him to make a significant contribution as America's minister to Switzerland, especially in regard to the *Alabama* claims. His work on behalf of the United States in this inflammatory international dispute demonstrates that Horace Rublee brought resourcefulness and competence to his mission. Although George Rublee was but a toddler when his father took an active part in shaping the course of an international event, his father's activities were a model for the sort of work he would later undertake, and it is likely that he learned important lessons from his father's experiences, later conveyed to him.

The contest between the United States and Great Britain known as the *Alabama* claims dealt with the damage that the CSA. *Alabama* and its sister ships inflicted on northern shipping during the Civil War. Although the British government maintained that the sale of these warships to the Confederate states was legal because they were not outfitted with armaments, the United States government maintained that ships were contraband and that the British were responsible for damages resulting from the illegal sale. The argument between the two countries began during Andrew Johnson's administration when Secretary of State William Seward demanded that Great Britain pay compensation for the direct and indirect damages that the *Alabama* and its sister ships had caused. After several years of wrangling, an 1871 treaty between the United States and Great Britain authorized the creation of an international tribunal to arbitrate the contest. The tribunal was to meet in Geneva, Switzerland, and was composed of neutral experts from Italy, Brazil, and Switzerland, as well as one representative each from the United States and Great Britain. The American representative was the eminent Charles Francis Adams.[10]

Having arranged for the tribunal to settle the issue, the contest between the United States and Great Britain soon shifted to the news media, where each attempted to shape European public opinion, apparently in hopes of influencing the panel's judgment. Owing to his proximity to the court and his rich background in journalism, Horace Rublee soon found himself drawn into the international contest as the two powers continued their struggle through the press. According to John Bancroft Davis, Secretary of State Hamilton Fish's principal assistant for the claims, British newspapers struck first and warranted a rebuttal. In January 1872 Davis wrote to Horace from Paris asking for his assistance. Davis explained that the "British Press is opening upon our case with a vigor and combination that prove inspiration. Under the circumstances we have no choice but to defend ourselves in the same way."[11] Davis believed that the British were "especially aiming to influence opinion in diplomatic circles, with a view of affecting the Portuguese and Italian arbitrators unconsciously themselves." Davis complained that "to a certain extent they have succeeded for the moment," but he hoped to win back ground with a counteroffensive. Davis cautioned, however, that "it is a delicate thing to undertake to discuss the merits of our case through the press, and could only be justified by the freedom with which the British press have allowed it to be attacked." Davis believed that such delicate work required a great amount of time and skill, and he complained that "I am so occupied that I cannot prepare articles—even if it were proper for me to do so. ...Perhaps you may be willing to give a helping hand yourself in this direction—or at least to supervise what may be done by others."[12]

Horace evidently welcomed the task and soon submitted a scheme for carrying out a campaign that Davis found "judicious and sound." In the following months Horace drafted articles that were circulated in leading papers in Europe, especially those of France and Switzerland, and that answered British attacks on the American case. In February Davis praised Horace for his articles and for the letters with which he had kept the America commission aware of shifting European opinion: "What you have done and are doing has been of great value, and we all hope here that you will keep at it."[13]

As the tribunal neared convening, Horace was called upon to carry out evermore sensitive work. When Horace let the American commission in Paris know of a rumor circulating against the American position in Swiss circles, Davis explained the United States version of the particular issue and asked Horace, "without seeming to do so," to let the American view "reach headquarters, where I doubt not the [British] lie has already gone." Horace was again called on to perform a bit of clandestine diplomacy just prior to the opening of the tribunal in Geneva in June. On June 3 Davis warned that "the Treaty is going to collapse this week" because "our British cousins" intend to "prevent a court from being present." Davis insisted, "We have got to make one or two [arbitrators] move to [require] a quorum to adjourn. One of these two must be Stäimpfli [of Switzerland]. I rely upon you to quietly make sure that he is at Geneva on the 15th no matter what happens." How Horace acquitted himself of these missions is nowhere evident, but it is clear that the American claims commission had a great deal of confidence in his abilities and that he made some contribution to the success of the *Alabama* claims.[14] For many historians the claims are a turning point in Anglo-American relations, after which there was fairly steady improvement as the two nations found similar interests in world affairs. Strained relations would continue, however, throughout Horace's lifetime and through most of George's, whose own efforts would be directed at establishing an Anglo-American alliance in the twentieth century.

Although Horace Rublee's work on the *Alabama* claims was the most noteworthy of his mission, other issues are worthy of mention as they reflect on George Rublee's political orientation. In 1871 the Grant administration instructed Horace to raise the issue of a gold standard with Switzerland. Great Britain had been championing a monometallic gold standard throughout most of the century, and the Grant administration, keen on encouraging British investment in the United States., supported the adoption of an international gold standard. The French, however, had succeeded in 1865 in drawing Belgium, Switzerland, and Italy into a Latin Monetary Union, which preserved the bimetallic system.[15] In his capacity as minister, Horace Rublee became an early advocate of the gold standard as he advanced the cause of the monometallic system in Switzerland. His work in Europe affected his view on the subject thereafter. Upon his eventual return to the United States in the summer of 1876, Horace was offered the chairmanship of the Wisconsin Republican Party. Horace, however, would accept the position only if the party would agree to change the ambiguous stand it had taken on so-called soft money in its platform.

With a great number of people in Wisconsin, especially farmers, attracted to the Greenback Party's arguments in favor of fiat money, the Republicans had soft-pedaled the issue. Horace, now a staunch advocate of sound money and an international gold standard, forced the party to make "honest money the prominent issue of the campaign" and led the contest himself, writing numerous articles and delivering speeches in defense of sound monetary policy. According to a later editorial in the *Sentinel*, as a result of Horace's efforts "Wisconsin, which had been included in the list of doubtful states, was redeemed for the Republican party and became known throughout the land as one of the most stalwart of all states in support of honest money."[16] The battle over the greenback was but the first of a series of political contests in which principally debt-ridden farmers and small producers sought relief through inflationary policies. That contest would continue into George Rublee's adulthood, and he would play a role in reforming the system in an effort to address westerners' complaints while maintaining easterners' sound money policy. It is likely that Horace's interest in, and understanding of, complex monetary issues, as they relate to national and international economies, contributed to his son's aptitude for the subject.

Although the Rublee family was French Huguenot in origin, Horace Rublee evidently had a strong affinity for German cultural traditions and was drawn to German communities both in Wisconsin and in Switzerland. While serving in Geneva, he became especially taken with the solid republican virtues that he identified in the workings of the German-dominated Swiss Confederation. During his years in Switzerland, Horace witnessed a historic contest in which a progressive Swiss middle class sought to "enlarge the field of federal authority" with the goal of reducing the "prerogatives of cantonal power" and thereby the power of conservative aristocrats.[17] Horace was impressed with the Swiss progressive impulse and wrote a lengthy summary of the successes of the movement to Secretary Hamilton Fish in 1874. Horace's letter praising Swiss politics must have been somewhat painful for himself to write and for Fish to read given the scandals surrounding the Grant administration and the general decline in civility and virtue in American politics since the Civil War. Rublee was especially interested in Switzerland's innovative political devices such as the initiative and referendum that were adopted in its federal constitution to aid the forces of progress and democracy. These same devices would soon be popular among liberal reformers and populists in the United States. Interestingly, the depiction Horace offers of the Swiss political system seems to be a model for Robert La Follette's so-called Wisconsin Idea, developed more than twenty years later. It may be that Horace carried home to Wisconsin political ideas that matured with La Follette's generation; certainly, the similarities are strong, and Rublee and La Follette were friends.[18] Rublee's passionate report on Swiss politics is also of interest because it offers a clear demonstration of the political tradition in which George Rublee was raised.

Horace's report to Fish summarized several successful political seasons in Switzerland. As he witnessed the enactment of various bills in the federal legislature, Horace was "most favorably impressed by the sound, healthy, normal, upright, vigorous, republican character" of the proceedings. Horace found that a bill was first "carefully drawn up" by a commission made up of "competent persons," who included "practical men and men of theory, experienced lawyers, men versed in legislation, and one or more leading professors from Swiss universities." When a bill is "finally drawn up, it is published, accompanied by a message from the federal council explaining its provisions in detail, and giving reasons for their adoption. The people then, in their turn, subject it to criticism." Rublee found that groups as diverse as "law societies, teacher's societies, [and] commercial unions" then publicly debated the merits of the proposed legislation. Horace noted that the public vetting strengthened the process: "[W]hen the bill is presented for action...it is pretty certain to be already a well digested measure, and public opinion in regard to it is very thoroughly known." Horace admitted that although the "procedure may be a little cumbrous and complicated, ...it affords a strong security against the evils of hasty legislation." Moreover, "it enlists popular interest in legislation and gives to the individual citizen a deeper sense of his influence and his responsibilities in connection with the government."[19]

In a passionate conclusion to what might in another's hands have been a dull consular dispatch, Horace proclaimed the glory of the Swiss republic and a progressive approach to politics:

> The interest manifested in the legislative changes now taking place extends to all classes. The country appears to have the hearty co-operation of its best and wisest citizens, and these seem to be moved not by a mere desire to fill a conspicuous place in the eyes of the public, or to associate their names with some prominent measure, but by sincere wish to aid in determining and achieving what is really for the true welfare of the State.
>
> At a time when, in some European countries, very anomalous forms of government have assumed the republican name, it is gratifying to observe that there is at least one European state in which republicanism is both properly understood and properly practiced, and where a government of the people, and by the people, unites, with as large a measure of individual liberty as exists in any organized community, all the advantages of order and stability, of careful and judicious legislation, of economy in the administration and justice in the execution of the laws, to as high a degree as can be found in any country upon the earth.[20]

This vision of a virtuous, enlightened republic appears to mirror the political ideals of Liberal "Mugwump" Republicans and their progeny, Progressive Republicans, of whom Horace and George Rublee are a good example.[21] Both the father and the son had great faith in humankind's ability to improve society through the application of reason to public policy and through a revival of moral conduct in politics. Commissions made up of technical experts and social scientists would figure prominently in their schemes for improving political life. Coming as he did from the Liberal Republican tradition, for George Rublee public service would be the highest calling, and an enlightened public policy would be the enduring vision.

While Horace Rublee decided to remain in Switzerland throughout the Grant administration, Wisconsin Republicans were anxious for him to return and take up his position of leadership. E. W. Keyes, who served as chairman of the Wisconsin party in Horace's absence, demanded in July 1874, "How much longer are you going to stay on foreign shores: why don't you come home?" Keyes believed it was "passing strange" that Horace could "content [him]self there, so far away from everything that is of interest," and warned that he could lose his "identity as an American." "I say to you Rublee, come home! For Christ's sake come home!"[22]

Whereas Horace Rublee does not seem to have been in danger of losing his identity as an American, George Rublee definitely was—and, in fact, had. Upon his return to the United States at age eight George spoke English, French, and German equally well and found that American children his age regarded him "as a sort of foreigner" for having "lived in Europe so long."[23] Furthermore, the Rublees did not immediately settle upon their return to America but instead bounced around among the cities of Madison, Boston, New York, and Milwaukee, as Horace worked first with Boston's Commercial Advertise and then entered negotiations for the editorship of the *Atlantic Monthly.* Ultimately, however, he returned to Milwaukee to become editor and part-owner of the *Sentinel*. George Rublee, who when he left Switzerland had been "interested in poetry and good books," appears to have suffered academically as a result of years of continuous change. After a year at Quincy Hall in Boston, George studied with a German clergyman in western New York in the summer of 1878 and then moved with his mother and his brother, William, to England, where William attended Cambridge and George studied in a "Swedenborgian school."[24] After a year in England, George lived with his mother at a health resort in Dansville, New York, where, according to him, he "ran wild and nearly lost the faculty for studying."[25] Although Rublee would soon overcome this scholastic setback, it may be that his later renowned reticence took shape in these years of extended isolation from children his own age and much of his time spent with adults. Coupled with his European background and ideological makeup, this early isolation from his peers may also have contributed to Rublee's independent spirit and eventual willingness to work with the progressive element of either party, Democrat or Republican.

While George may have suffered some from the repeated relocations, the experience made him especially attached to his father, who, though often absent, sought to keep alive in his son an interest in literature, history, and politics. Horace had some success in that regard, for at age eleven George reported that he was reading such works as "Higginson's history of the United States" and had his father searching for "a life of Napoleon Bonaparte," which he wanted "very much."[26] At age thirteen George would note in a letter to his father that he had just finished Richard Green's *A Short History of the English People,* which he found "the most interesting history that I have ever read."[27] Having become rather bookish, the next year at Phillips Academy at Exeter, following yet another move, Rublee would complain that, although his older roommate was "a very nice good sort of a boy," he was "not very literary in his tastes."[28]

Nevertheless, Horace Rublee had reason to become seriously concerned about his son's education in the winter of 1884, when, after a good start at Exeter, George became discouraged, stopped studying, and became interested only in sports. George would soon be sixteen, and his father feared that he hadn't many opportunities left before his path would become rather fixed for good or ill. As fortune would have it, Horace, who was looking for a new situation for his son, learned from Harvard president Charles Eliot about the opening of a new school at Groton, Massachusetts. Horace soon wrote to the school's founding headmaster, Endicott Peabody, to learn more about the new program.[29] Peabody replied promptly and asked in turn for the particulars of George's academic record. Horace admitted that George's "education thus far has been rather desultory" owing to having "changed his school every year" but asserted that his son was likely "more intelligent than the average boy his age, as he has read a great deal outside his studies." Horace was sure that George was "capable of making rapid progress" if his "interest is aroused." At the moment, however, his son was "very fond of play and much addicted to lawn tennis, baseball, etc."[30] Despite his mixed academic record, George Rublee was accepted into Groton and was entered in the fourth of six forms in 1884, the first year of the school's existence. As Rublee later recalled, Groton was "a sort of last chance," and he was determined to make the best of it.[31] Endicott Peabody's Groton School was something entirely new and different for George, and it is difficult to overstate the profound impact the place had in shaping the course of his life. After years of moving from school to school with long periods of separation from his father, Rublee found at Groton "truly a common life, like that of a large family each member of which seeks to help the other."[32] The inspiration was clearly Peabody's, whom Rublee in a sophomore theme paper at Harvard described as "a man of great firmness, infinite patience, tact, executive ability, and...a loftiness of spirit seldom found." Peabody's "deepest concern was not in regard to scholarship," but rather "the problem which absorbed his whole soul was the problem of maintaining in his school that ideal of high thinking and simplicity of life which would be the beginning of a steadfast, earnest, Christian manhood." What made Groton so special, according to George, was that "the controlling principle which underlies the whole system of the school...is the principle of love."

Rublee, who considered himself something of an authority on schools, believed that it was a lack of "spontaneous" and "genuinely felt" compassion "which detracts from the usefulness, and impairs the success of most of the schools in this country."[33] For Rublee, this "spirit of love" at Groton made "the boys feel that the headmaster and his assistants are their friends as well as their teachers, and are sincerely striving for their good." This feeling was achieved in part because "outside of hours, master and boy drop all formality and meet upon the broad plane of good-fellowship and friendship." Further, "the masters join in all the out-door sports and athletic games...and yet in school maintain their dignity and authority unimpaired." The headmaster on "winter evenings...reads aloud in his study, whither all may go who care to listen." Rublee believed that "by such methods as these the death blow has been dealt to that traditional antagonism which is supposed to exist between boys and their teachers." Although Rublee was something of a religious skeptic before attending Groton, he found the approach to spiritual development there to be important to the atmosphere of loving support and to be "singularly wise" in its approach to religion.[34] Rather than "being encouraged to put on an unreasoning and sanctimonious goodness which surrenders at the first encounter with actual temptations," at Groton "the boys are taught the folly of sin, and the speciousness of it" and are encouraged "to realize the reasonableness of decency in life and thought, and the blessed reward of a living faith in God."[35]

Rublee responded enthusiastically to the friendly and relaxed environment at Groton and made a dramatic turnaround. Clearly able and gifted, Rublee apparently needed a more nurturing environment than he had found at other schools. Much later in life he recalled that the atmosphere at Groton was central to his success in academics: "It stimulated me tremendously; I can't tell you how it affected me. I had some knowledge of good books because I'd lived with my father and we had read together. So the masters were interested in me and I suddenly became a scholar."[36] Rublee soon mastered Greek to the extent that by the Christmas vacation of 1884 he scored a ninety-five on Yale's entrance examination in Homer. Encouraged by his successes, George began to pour himself into his school work: "I worked harder there, I think, with more enthusiasm and more success than I ever have since."[37]

Scholarship, however, was not the only facet of a boy's life at Groton. The school's original announcement stated, "Every endeavor will be made to cultivate manly, Christian character, having regard to moral and physical as well as intellectual development."[38] The practical application of this statement was that sporting events played an important role in a Groton boy's development. This aspect of Groton life appealed to Rublee as well. Not only was he fond of sports, he excelled at them. Ultimately reaching a height of six feet four inches, Rublee entered Groton at sixteen already over six feet and had natural athletic ability.[39] This interest and skill soon translated into a leadership opportunity for Rublee when he was selected as the first captain of Groton's baseball team, or "The Nine," as they were called.[40]

Rublee's sudden scholastic and athletic success and popularity after years of mediocrity made his short time at Groton something of a surreal experience and left his memory of those days permanently golden-hued. While Rublee would maintain an exceptionally strong emotional attachment to Groton throughout his life, the school responded with equal enthusiasm to him, making the name George Rublee legendary. Frank Davis Ashburn, in his work *Fifty Years On: Groton School, 1884–1934*, notes that Rublee "seemed to be a being apart." "Although listed as a fourth former in the first catalogue, in the second he emerges as an entire sixth" and became the sole member of the first graduating class. The name "George Rublee" stands alone on the first of a series of wooden panels that surround the old lecture hall listing the names of each graduating class down to the present.[41] Rublee became famous among Groton graduates for his various feats in school, both athletic and academic, and later for his public work. In *Fifty Years On*, Ashburn, in remarking upon Rublee earning ten honors on his entrance examinations at Harvard, notes that Rublee in so doing made a good name for Groton and secured a place in the school's hall of fame: "There were giants in the earth in those days, and there is no question that Rublee was one of them. …It was a good omen and a typical Rublee performance that he, the first Grotonian to enter college, took ten honors in his Harvard entrance examinations."[42] At Harvard Rublee continued to do well, and Groton was pleased when the "first graduate" won "high scholastic fame as a freshman at Harvard."[43] Secretary of State Dean Acheson, a 1911 Groton graduate and a protégé of Rublee in some respects, would recall that "[f]or me George Rublee began as a tradition—his name carved in lonely eminence on an oaken panel…, appearing again in the gymnasium as the captain of every team, and in the folklore of the place as the winner of prizes, the setter of standards."[44] Another noted Grotonian, Ellery Sedgwick, editor of *Atlantic Monthly*, remarked in 1946 on the "distinguished and useful life" that Rublee had lived and observed that Groton "began with George Rublee" and had "never done so well since."[45] Groton School and Rublee seem to have done well by each other, and the circumstances that brought the two together appear now fortuitous; the school found for itself a "character of the most intriguing sort" who distinguished himself and acted as a role model for subsequent generations of students and alumni, and Rublee, who would have no children and whose wife was perpetually in search of a raison d'être, found something that he could cherish and derive satisfaction from throughout his life and that, at a crucial time in his development, had afforded him an opportunity to excel.[46]

Rublee left Groton a profoundly different person. Although Horace Rublee had instilled in George an interest in politics and civic virtue, Endicott Peabody elevated the idea of public service to that of a religious duty. Under the influence of Peabody, Rublee, who returned to Groton repeatedly throughout his freshman year at Harvard, had something of a conversion experience in March 1887. In a letter to Peabody on 24 March Rublee equated sinfulness with an interest in self-promotion and expressed a deep commitment to public work as an expression of his confirmation in the Christian faith. He wrote:

> It is through you and Mr. Billings that I have been brought to a partial realization of the love of Christ for all mankind and me, and of the littleness of all else compared with that. By your help I have been led to despise my old life and my former aspirations; your hand has broken a rift in the thick clouds of my sinfulness, through which a single ray of pure light has pierced and fallen on my soul. …Oh, what shall I say to those who have given me the possibility of such a hope? A whole life devoted to nothing else and spent in service could not repay the debt I owe to you and to Groton school, every member of it.[47]

George believed that "[c]ontemplation will always bring back these past Sundays at Groton as the most precious of my life, and will envelop them with a halo of sanctity which none others can ever possess." At Harvard in October 1887, George wrote his first sophomore theme paper, entitled "What Shall I Do When I leave College?" The paper reflected his recent views concerning public service and his notion of a life well lived: "Merely selfish existence for me is, I hope, in my case a thing gone by; and life, as a responsibility is just beginning to reveal itself to me. I see all about me a world of progress, in which there is nothing stable; ...and where the tendency is towards gradual amelioration. Unless I succeed in becoming an active factor in the execution of this grand plan, I must consider my presence on the earth a misfortune."[48] George explained that "until about a year ago I had intended to study law" because "I had a vague idea the profession depended upon the intellect" and because "I knew that some of the men engaged in it reaped rich harvests in the fields of fortune and fame." Owing to a "new interpretation" of life, "wrought largely by the influence of the school where I prepared for college," George had decided that teaching rather than the practice of law was the better path for him. Nevertheless, there were several aspects of the teaching profession that, he confessed, made him resist committing to it. In addition to the modest salaries that "make it a matter of self-sacrifice for an able man to accept a position," he worried about the public disdain for teachers in America: "The mass of men barely conceal their contempt for school-teaching, as a profession which no man with a competence would adopt voluntarily; and look upon it as a refuge for those weaklings who from a lack of energy or of prudence are unable to battle successfully with the world."[49]

George was further concerned that "the love I bear to my old school fascinates me; and I am afraid I should not be so willing to devote myself to a life of work in another place." Arguments in favor of law came from friends who argued that George had "no right to live without the means to provide decently for" himself and family and that he would have "just as fine an opportunity to make [himself useful to his] generation in the pursuit of law as in school." Although at the beginning of his essay George related that he was "inclined to accept" a position at Groton that seemed to await him if he wished it, he concluded the piece saying, "My mind is not made up, and I do not yet know what I shall do."[50] The question of whether to pursue a life in academe or in law would plague Rublee for the next five years and would nag at him through much of his life. Hedging, George decided in 1887 to study the classics, which would allow him to teach or go on to study law after graduation. Despite playing baseball and joining several clubs at Harvard, George took the highest second-year honors in classics, and he went on to graduate magna cum laude in 1890.[51]

One of the most important aspects of Rublee's experiences at Harvard was the friendships he made there. His undergraduate and graduate college friends from Harvard included Herbert Croly, Phillip Littell, Norman Hapgood, Walter Weyl, George Santayana, John Bass, Joseph Cotton, Louis Dow, Learned Hand, and Edward Burling. All of these friendships proved to be lifelong, and several would be vital to his public work. One intriguing view of Rublee as a friend comes from Judge Learned Hand, who later remarked on Rublee's notoriety as a man of influence. According to Hand, Rublee exercised a curious domination (I cannot use any other word) over a number of us. As I look back on it, I am a little surprised that this should have been so; for although he had very distinguished abilities, he had his way more by the impress of his personality than by the force of his reasoning. I cannot remember many occasions in which we fought it out with a give and take. Perhaps that was the reason why he had so much influence as he did; he imposed upon us by a background of certainty that made us yield. It was as if he had capacities beyond ours.[52]

A friend from later in life, the Morgan banker Thomas Lamont, offered a less intimate portrait of Rublee but one equally helpful in getting an idea of the impression he made on others:

What one does not always find in…excellent men, but which could be found in George Rublee in superlative degree, are the qualities of modesty, self-effacement, generosity of heart, complete candor, simplicity, kindliness. All those qualities showed in George's benevolent countenance and lovely smile. I have never known a man whose face so perfectly mirrored the beauty of his character. Yet, with all his sweetness, there was plenty of spice. He could never have achieved so greatly in the world of affairs had he not been a strong man of unswerving will.... He was no pushover. He was a rock of Gibraltar. And what a sense of humor he had, with what a witty turn of phrase he could expose the pomposities of fraud. That twinkle in his eye was always with him—once in a very great while, a merrily malicious twinkle, but much more often a twinkle of unuttered laughter.[53]

To whatever faculty he owed it, George Rublee was a man of great personal influence. Although some found in him "an elusive detachment, an aloofness even in the midst of involvement," Rublee had an attractive quality that he used to his advantage.[54] Rublee, however, had less confidence in himself than did those he impressed. Writing to his fiance in 1898, he felt it necessary to warn her, "Among some very kind people there is a sort of impression that I am the possessor of an exceptional mind. That is not the fact and I do not want you to believe it."[55]

Nevertheless, although when he graduated Harvard at age twenty-two George was not yet "a rock of Gibraltar," he already had developed attributes that were distinguishing. He had rather refined social tastes and was evidently quite keen on maintaining an elevated standard of living (likely the greatest obstacle to his committing to a teaching career). George seems to have picked up these tastes from his mother, Katherine Hopkins Rublee, who came from a family well established in law and politics in Illinois and Wisconsin. While Katherine was intent on maintaining a well-appointed home at nearly all costs, Horace evidently needed much less for his satisfaction. For instance, upon learning of Katherine's plan to buy him an expensive birthday present one year, Horace complained to George that "a new set [of studs] either of gold or diamonds would not add a particle to my happiness."[56] Although George's letters indicate that he was more attached to, and inspired by, his father than his mother, it was a matter of some significance that he leaned in his mother's direction in regard to social tastes. This refinement would give him a certain necessary quality that allowed him to enter and operate in the most elite American and European social circles during his lifetime. A less fortunate attribute he shared with his mother was periodic bouts of depression, which, as George grew older, he experienced more frequently.[57]

Like many young men of his age and class, George set off on a yearlong European tour in August 1890, a few months after graduation. It was his first return to Europe since 1878. Carrying letters of introduction from his father, from Peabody, and from his Harvard Greek professor, Louis Dyer, George stayed with, or called, upon a number of European families in England, Switzerland, Italy, and France. Each of these encounters, it seems, led, in turn, to new names for him to call upon as he traveled around Europe. Although evidently much pleased with these new acquaintances, especially a Swiss couple to whom Peabody sent him, George seemed equally content to strike out on his own to explore the English lake country, the Swiss Alps, and the mountain lakes in northern Italy. Those days were usually spent on scenic mountain walks or in tennis matches and the nights spent reading various European works in German or French after an evening meal with fellow travelers.[58]

After two months traveling in remote mountain regions, George returned to the cosmopolitan centers of Western Europe for the winter, where he visited various museums, made friends in artist communities, and called upon sundry Europeans and Americans. At the beginning of October, George settled in Lausanne, Switzerland, where he became one of three pupils of a Messier Redl, whom Rublee described as an "old man over seventy" who knew "thirteen languages."[59] French was spoken at breakfast and dinner, and a "Hanoverian Fraülein" came to lunch to lead conversation in German. Writing in his journal not long after arriving in Lausanne in early October, George questioned his decision to settle with the Redls: "This is a very funny situation for me to be placed in. Here am I a young college graduate traveling for health and pleasure before beginning the work of life, settled in the family of an old tutor, and studying arduously, in fixed hours, as if I were beginning my school days!" Although unhappy with the schedule Redl forced upon him and irritated by the old man's sharp rebukes, George reminded himself, "I came to study French, and success in this life does not follow the man who allows pleasures not connected with the object he is pursuing to tempt him from it."[60] Despite his complaints, he managed many outings and had some pleasant moments when Mme. Redl invited young Swiss women his age for tea. On one occasion two sought to tell his fortune, one by reading his palm and the other through astrology. The results were generally on the mark. George recorded in his diary: "The two methods gave the same results in many things. All trials of this kind agree in finding it hard to describe me, and in predicting a troubled and various life for me. According to them my character is complex."[61]

At the end of October, George departed the Redls and moved on to Paris, a place that filled him with excitement and would become his favorite city. Owing to a letter of introduction from Louis Dyer, Rublee became the sole pupil of a Monsieur Chédieu, whom Rublee described as a "very fine old man who was a

Royalist and had had a certain position in literary circles in Paris." Chédieu's program of study was more to George's liking, allowing him time to absorb Paris. Throughout November and December he "went about very enthusiastically" in Paris taking in museums and lectures by day and theater and opera by night.[62] Although George mostly selected lectures on literature and art, he attended an address by Ernst Renan, famous for his modernist *Life of Jesus*, "chiefly out of curiosity to see the man." While he found that Renan's "enunciation was bad, and the lecture intolerably dull," George's own religious views would soon approach those of the French scholar.[63]

In early January 1891, Horace Rublee met George in Paris, and the two spent the remainder of the winter on a tour of the Mediterranean, stopping in Palestine, Jaffa, Beirut, Constantinople, and Greece. For George it was inspiring: "That was one of the most thrilling trips I've ever taken. I was full of enthusiasm about it with my classical training and...I was very happy to see those famous old lands."[64] The question at the end of the tour, however, was inescapable and was one that had plagued George throughout college—what was he to do with his life? George was still interested in teaching, but it seemed quite clear that his interests and tastes would be difficult to satisfy on a modest salary. Horace had for years thought his son should pursue law, believing that the profession would give him financial security and a preparation for politics, if that field figured in his future. By the end of the summer of 1891, George agreed to return to Milwaukee, where he would begin reading law with the general counsel of the Wisconsin Central Railroad. Rublee later recalled that this decision to study at a firm in Milwaukee, as opposed to attending a law school, was a mistake and was based on his interest in being near his father. The idea of studying law independently, which proved unprofitable, was abandoned in the early spring of 1892, and George returned to Europe, where he preferred to be.[65]

Upon his return to Europe, Rublee went immediately to Italy, where he lived and studied independently in the spring of his twenty-fourth year. He later remembered that time as one of the most enjoyable experiences of his life, as he spent his time traveling from inn to inn in rural Tuscany.[66] While still in Europe, Rublee received an invitation from Peabody in June to return to Groton to teach. After some hesitation, George refused the offer. The letter was exceptionally honest:

> Several reasons [have] influenced my decision. First comes one which causes me pain, but the truth of which I cannot deny. Instead of being a fairly mature person, possessing trustworthy knowledge of myself, as I believed a few years ago, I am in fact floundering about in a perfect chaos of undevelopment. My life is wholly unstable: the current of it flows in no certain direction, nor has it been gathered into one channel. Not a profitable position, nor a happy one; and certainly not one for a master at Groton School.[67]

George hoped that "it is a temporary stage and that I shall at last grow into a man and have done with all this puerility." Returning to Europe had been the result of "dreams, which after all were nothing but dreams." As he explained, "The intense interest and delight I have taken in art, a bright, fresh world for me, was almost dangerous; and I might easily have become a dilettante." The interest took hold of him first in Paris in 1890, and George confessed that "if I were to commence from the beginning again, I should strive to be an architect." That, however, could not be, and neither could he accept the position at Groton. Instead, he would make a second attempt at studying law: "If I do not alter my plans half a dozen times during the summer, I shall probably turn up at the Harvard Law School in the fall."[68]

At age twenty-four, George Rublee at last decided to turn away from his earlier interest in teaching and from his more recent passion for the arts and instead made a commitment to become a lawyer. It was not an easy decision for him and was based mostly on his interest in securing an income with which he could provide for himself and his family in a way that he believed fitting. It is worth noting that although Rublee felt that he was suffering from "a perfect chaos of undevelopment," he was incorrect in discounting his years of European travel and study as a waste of time. His interest in art, literature, and theater and his philosophical and scholarly demeanor, a natural trait enhanced by his European experiences, were important features in his attractiveness and in his ability to later move with ease in the highest European and American circles. The expertise that he would next gain, that of law, would complete his education and would prepare him to make a series of public contributions. Furthermore, through a series of fortuitous events the practice of law would allow him to return to Europe and pursue the life he most desired while still a young man.

NOTES

1. George Rublee [hereafter GR] to Endicott Peabody, 20 January 1898, Endicott Peabody Papers, Groton School Archives, Groton, Massachusetts [hereafter GSA].
2. George Rublee, "Reminiscences of George Rublee" (New York: Columbia University Oral History Research Office, 1972), 1.
3. *The Milwaukee Sentinel*, 19 October 1896.
4. Ibid., 19-24 October 1896.
5. Ibid., 19 October 1896.
6. Carl Schurz to Horace Rublee, 13 November 1862, Horace Rublee Papers (from Crossways, Cornish, New Hampshire) [hereafter HRP]. Emphasis in original.
7. E. Daniels to H. Rublee, 20 December 1860, HRP.
8. *The Milwaukee Sentinel*, 19 October 1896.
9. Robert Ferrell, *American Diplomacy: A History* (New York: W.W. Norton & Company, 1976), 9-10.
10. Ibid., 290-294.
11. John C. Bancroft Davis to H. Rublee, 1 January 1872, HRP.
12. Davis to H. Rublee, 7 January 1872; 11 January 1872; and 20 January 1872, HRP.
13. Davis to H. Rublee, 20 January 1872; and 11 February 1872, HRP.
14. Davis to H. Rublee, 29 January 1872; and 3 June 1872, HRP.

15. United States, Department of State, *Papers Relating to the Foreign Relations of the United States* (Washington: Government Printing Office, 1871) [hereafter *FRUS*], 872-875; and A.G. Kenwood and A. Lougheed, *The Growth of the International Economy, 1820-1990* (New York: Routledge, 1992), 104-106.

16. *The Milwaukee Sentinel*, 19 October 1896.

17. H. Rublee to Hamilton Fish, October 1874, *FRUS*, 1875, 1279.

18. Rublee, "Reminiscences," 79.

19. H. Rublee to Fish, October 1874, *FRUS*, 1875, 1279-1280.

20. Ibid., 1280.

21. Although Horace Rublee was out of the United States when the Liberals revolted from the Republican party in 1872, it is obvious that his political philosophies place him squarely in their camp. Incidently, with regard to the contentious debate over the place of Liberal Republicans in U.S. political history, I find myself in agreement with the more balanced conclusions of Gerald McFarland in his *Mugwumps, Morals & Politics, 1884 -1920* (Amherst: University of Massachusetts Press, 1975) rather than those of Richard Hofstadter in his *The Age of Reform* (New York: Vintage Books, 1955) or John Sproat in his *"The Best Men": Liberal Reformers in the Gilded Age* (New York: Oxford University Press, 1968). Unlike Hofstadter and Sproat, who argued that Mugwumps were "foolish, hypocritical, and self-righteous," McFarland found that these reformers were "simply sincere and morally concerned citizens" who adopted "a distinctive blend of [classical liberal] orthodoxy and reform," McFarland, *Mugwumps*, 3,174-175.

22. E.W. Keyes to H. Rublee, 14 July 1874, HRP. George Rublee, who left notes for posterity on his father's letters, noted that Keyes was a "a professional politician of the old style."

23. H. Rublee to Peabody, 20 July 1884, GSA; and Rublee, "Reminiscences," 3.

24. H. Rublee to Peabody, 20 July 1884, GSA.

25. Rublee, "Reminiscences," 4.

26. GR to H. Rublee, 4 April 1879, George Rublee Papers (from Crossways, Cornish, New Hampshire) [hereafter GRP].

27. GR to H. Rublee, 2 July 1882, GRP.

28. GR to H. Rublee, 17 September 1882, GRP.

29. H. Rublee to Peabody, 12 July 1884, GSA.

30. H. Rublee to Peadody, 20 July 1884, GSA.

31. Rublee, "Reminiscences," 4-5. When it began, Groton did not accept any students for the fifth or six forms, allowing those to be filled as the charter students progressed.

32. Rublee, "What a Good School Should Be," 17 April 1888, GRP.

33. Ibid.

34. George's early skepticism evidently stemmed from his father's own apparent agnosticism. As Reverend Judson Titsworth observed after Horace's death in 1896, "Mr. Rublee was lacking in what we call the conventional religious element." Nevertheless, Titsworth allowed that "if he lacked [religion] the ethics were there, and these are the substance of religion always." Undated news clipping, GRP.

35. Rublee, "What a Good School Should Be," GRP.

36. Rublee, "Reminiscences," 7.

37. Ibid., 8.

38. Frank Davis Ashburn, *Fifty Years On: Groton School, 1884-1934* (New York: At the Sign of the Gosden Head, 1934), 17.

39. H. Rublee to Peabody, 20 July 1884, GSA; and William Amory Gardner, *Groton Myths and Memories* (Concord: Rumford Press for Groton School, 1928), 21.

40. Ashburn, *Fifty Years On*, 20.

41. Author's visit to Groton School, May 1995.

42. Ashburn, *Fifty Years On*, 20.

43. Gardner, *Groton Myths,* 28.

44. Dean Acheson, *Morning and Noon* (Boston: Houghton Mifflin, 1965), 128.

45. Ellery Sedgwick, *The Happy Profession* (Boston: Little, Brown and Company, 1946), 52.

46. Quote from Dean Acheson, "George Rublee," in *The Groton School Quarterly* (Summer 1957(, 1.

47. GR to Peabody, 24 March 1887, GSA.

48. Rublee, "What Shall I Do When I Leave College?" 11 October 1887, GRP.

49. Ibid.

50. Ibid.

51. Groton Alumni Records, "George Rublee" folder, GSA.

52. Learned Hand to George Martin, 15 November 1957, Learned Hand Papers, Harvard Law School Special Collections, Harvard University, Cambridge Massachusetts [hereafter HLS-Hand].

53. Thomas Lamont, letter to the editor, *The Groton School Quarterly* (Summer 1957), 5.

54. Acheson, *Morning and Noon*, 128.

55. GR to Juliet Barrett, 6 February 1898, GRP.

56. H. Rublee to GR, 15 December 1895, HRP.

57. For Katherine Rublee's depressive tendency see GR to Peabody, 3 March 1887, 19 October 1887, 7 July 1895, and 26 August 1895, GSA.

58. GR, travel diary, 13 July through 6 December 1890, GRP; and various letters to Endicott Peabody, GSA.

59. GR, travel diary, 1 October 1890, GRP.

60. Ibid., 6 October 1890.

61. Ibid., 16 October 1890.

62. Rublee, "Reminiscences," 13; and GR travel diary, 26 October to 6 December 1890, GRP.

63. GR travel diary, 3 December 1890, GRP.

64. Rublee, "Reminiscences," 14.

65. Ibid., 15.

66. Ibid., 15-16.

67. GR to Peabody, 4 June 1892, GSA.

68. Ibid.

3

"Latent Possibilities" (1892–1908)

After spending the better part of two years moving freely around Europe, settling into law school was no easy matter for George Rublee. Being back at Harvard was a little disconcerting at first, and he found law "a terribly dull study" compared to his "recent and former interests." Despite a lack of enthusiasm and a belief that he lacked any particular talent for law, Rublee "worked hard at it" and gradually began "to see the thing." Nevertheless, when the examinations came at the end of the semester, he decided that he would give up law school if he was not successful. To his surprise he found that he "could write the answers without too much trouble," and he was amazed to find that his scores placed him second in his class. Rublee recalled that it was "a very great surprise to me and upset all my plans for giving up the law."[1] While he determined to continue for a second year, he confessed to Endicott Peabody, "I have very grave doubts of my ability to ever win a case."[2]

Although George had a difficult time readjusting to life at Harvard, he was happy to be closer to Peabody, on whom he relied repeatedly for guidance on temporal as well as spiritual matters. George's intellectual experiences since his confirmation in the Episcopal Church in 1887 had led him to question the very foundations of Christianity. Writing to Peabody in November 1892, he explained the difficulties he was having with the Christian faith. Although he believed that "Christ is a beautiful and marvelous example of goodness and obedience" and that "his character is an ideal and an inspiration," George confessed that "when he says that he is the Son of God and come to save the world, I do not know what he means. He speaks a mystery to me." George had reached modernist conclusions that had a humanist bent: "The universe is so vast and man such an insignificant part of it! I feel, though, that if God is and cares for us He will not blame us, if we are true and try to do right, even if we do not understand Him and the forces he employs. Indeed I believe we are not created capable of that understanding and it is not required of us."[3] Peabody would continue to engage George on spiritual issues and would seek to keep him focused on a life of service, perhaps thinking that through such work George's faith might be restored.

In the summer of 1893, as he had throughout college, Rublee lived in Milwaukee and worked with his father writing editorials for the *Sentinel.* In the fall he returned to Harvard Law School and completed a second successful year of study. During the summer of 1894, he passed Wisconsin's bar examination, and he considered not returning to Harvard for the third and final year of the program. Rublee believed that if he wished to practice law in Wisconsin, he had little reason to return for the last year, but he had begun to take an interest in New York and realized that he probably would need to complete the program to have a better chance of landing a job in a prestigious firm. Being "in great perplexity," George wrote to his old headmaster for advice. Peabody came from a distinguished New England family and was well connected in New York. For example, Peabody managed to secure financier John Pierpont Morgan as an original trustee of Groton. Peabody's advice to George was to complete the program at Harvard, after which he would attempt to help him secure interviews with prominent New York firms.[4]

After his graduation from Harvard Law School in June 1895, Rublee was at another crossroads in his life. His plan to go to New York was in jeopardy because his father had recently undergone throat surgery for cancer, and George believed that he should return to Milwaukee to be near his family. His plans were thrown in further disarray when he received a tentative offer to teach classes at Harvard Law School beginning in the fall of 1895. As Horace Rublee pointed out to his son, the offer showed that "in the judgement of the faculty of the school, your standing as a student is high." Horace released George from any obligation to return to Milwaukee but was cool about the teaching position. He pointed out that although it would "exempt [George] from the worry and strain of practice at the bar," it "offers no such pecuniary rewards as a successful lawyer may obtain." Horace admitted, however, that his close friend, Senator John Spooner of Milwaukee, approved of George taking the position at Harvard providing he could find a suitable firm in which to clerk.[5]

The offer to teach at Harvard came from Professor James Ames, dean of the Law School, and was contingent upon the trustees establishing a new professorship in international law, which would allow George to cover a course on carrier contracts. Turning, as always, to Endicott Peabody for advice, George explained the Harvard proposition: "The following year, if I liked teaching and my teaching were satisfactory, Mr. Ames said that the authorities would promote me to the position of assistant Professor. President Eliot, he said, was strongly in favor of having me take the place."[6] George had recently shared the stage with Charles Eliot and Columbia University president Seth Low at Groton's tenth-year anniversary celebration. Eliot, who appears to have known Horace Rublee for a number of years, seems to have been impressed with George's speech and took an active interest in him.[7] In addition to Eliot's support, George soon learned, somewhat to his surprise, that the law faculty "have a cordial desire that I should come back to the school" and "feel something like affection for me."[8]

Less than a month after Rublee's first letter to Peabody informing him of Harvard's tentative offer, Rublee wrote to notify his mentor that the proposed position had been withdrawn. Rublee had decided to accept the position and had arranged to work in a Judge Lowell's office in Boston, but the Harvard trustees decided to postpone the funding for another year, at which time the position might again be offered to George.[9] It was now midsummer of 1895, and Rublee was less sure of what to do than he had been in many years. In a letter to Peabody on 7 July 1895, his twenty-seventh birthday, George let it be known that his true interests remained elsewhere:

Now I am going to pass from the real to the ideal. You have at times inquired what sort of life I really desired to live. ...If I had a small income of my own I should go to Paris and study for several years with a view to taking the degree of Doctor.... I should strive in that time to acquire a thorough knowledge of classical literature and at the same time to learn to write. Then I should devote myself chiefly to historical work, particularly to the history of Italy in the Middle Ages and Renaissance. My aim would be to do for that period what Gibbon did for the decadence of the Roman Empire. At the same time I should perhaps attempt to write some different and lighter things.[10]

George believed that "this ideal of a life seems to me a good and an honorable ideal," and "it is the one thing to which my heart goes out. How I long for the calm, the repose, the happiness of a life given to such work!" The obstacle to his idea of a perfect life remained, however, the same: "But this is an ideal that cannot be realized, certainly at present, simply because I have not the income which I mentioned. I must work for a living."[11] Peabody replied sympathetically from England to George's letter and, encouraging him to make a go of it in New York, provided several letters of introduction for that purpose. George was not yet convinced that New York was the correct place for him, and he was still contemplating a move to Chicago, which would allow him to be closer to his family. But in the end he followed Peabody's advice and sought work in New York.[12]

By late September Rublee found a position at Lord, Day, and Lord, a distinguished New York law firm. On 28 September 1895, Rublee sent Peabody a letter to relate his success. In the note he copied a passage from a letter of recommendation from Dean Ames addressed to Lord, Day, and Lord. Ames' letter speaks of George's accomplishments and psychological makeup:

Mr. George Rublee tells me that you have some thought of giving him a place in your law office. There are very few graduates of the Harvard Law School of the last twenty-five years of whom I could write so high terms of commendation as I can of Mr. Rublee. He has impressed me as a man of singularly high character. His ability placed him among the best of the honor men. To me his personality is very attractive. I should not expect him to show himself a "hustler." Indeed he may at first allow a certain distrust of himself to hamper him. But I am confident that this objection, if it should manifest itself at all, would very soon disappear with experience in a busy office.[13]

Benefited by such a strong recommendation, Rublee had no difficulty securing the position. With the blessing of his family and approval of his mentor, Rublee moved to New York City in early October 1895.

Rublee had high hopes of at last settling down and applying himself to his profession. Unfortunately for George, the work that the firm gave him was not advanced but rather dull, and as a result he soon became disenchanted. Less than a month after his arrival, he wrote to Peabody to tell him of his dissatisfaction with his position. He explained that he had regrettably found that he "had the part of a sort of runner or errand boy," which was made all the more embarrassing when he was sent to a deliver a document to "none other than [Groton classmate] Nathaniel Thayer Robb," whose "position in the Manhattan [Trust] Company appears to be rather exalted." What's more, George found New York "less distinct and more artificial" than he had hoped and thought there was "a smaller possibility for growth and development" in New York than in Chicago. Since he felt "more like doing something for Chicago than…for New York," Peabody should "not be surprised [to] hear of my returning to the west."[14] An evidently concerned Peabody replied immediately, counseling George not to make any sudden changes but rather to allow time to adjust to New York. Horace wrote similarly in October and November, advising his son against a premature move and letting him know that his mother was "agitated" and feared that George was "making a great mistake."[15] Although Rublee secured an offer from a Chicago firm in November, he hesitated and remained in New York until December, unsure of how to proceed.[16] A letter from President Eliot in mid-December asking if George would be willing to teach either contract or finance law at Harvard in the spring as a replacement for Professor Samuel Williston added more confusion to the situation.[17] George let Eliot know on 17 December that he liked the idea of having "an experiment in teaching" but asked for more time to decide. Just after Christmas he accepted the position at Harvard but cautioned that "zeal and hard work are the only qualifications I am sure of possessing."[18]

In the spring of 1896 Rublee taught a large class of students and enjoyed the experience. As he later recalled, "[T]he students seemed to be satisfied," and it was "a very pleasant half year."[19] At the end of the semester Dean Ames offered him the position of assistant professor, but George was unable to accept it because Horace, now dying of throat cancer, was expected to live only a few months more. In a letter to President Eliot, George also explained that he had decided "not to abandon the practice of law without a somewhat longer experience than I have had."[20] It is likely that Horace's impending death rekindled George's concern about his own—as well as his family's—finances. He returned to Milwaukee in early summer and was able to be with his father during his last days. Horace Rublee died in October 1896, and George was left at yet another crossroads in his life. The co-owners of the *Sentinel* asked him to replace his father as editor, but he declined the offer. After some hesitation Rublee decided to move to Chicago, where a good friend, Edward Burling, practiced law and where he would be easily accessible to his mother. Burling, a spirited character from Wyoming, had become a close friend of Rublee's at Harvard Law School, as had Augustus and Learned B. Hand.[21]

In Chicago Rublee first joined a small, relatively new firm by the name of Lee and Lawrence but found that he had a "ridiculous" role that was no different from his work at Lord, Day, and Lord. After a few months, Burling and he decided to form their own partnership, Rublee and Burling (twenty years later Covington, Burling, and Rublee). They worked as assistants to Frank Lowden, later governor of Illinois, while they sought to establish their own clients. The two shared a flat together with Charles D. Norton, later a noted New York banker, and they all struggled to remain solvent. By the late spring of 1897, Rublee and Burling realized that they were going nowhere, so Rublee left Lowden's office and became a clerk at yet another firm in Chicago. His experiences in Chicago, like that of New York, were so far unsuccessful.[22]

At this point, George's life was not working out as he had hoped; he was thirty and was "rather at a loose end."[23] Depressed and frustrated, he turned yet again to Peabody for counsel. Writing in late October 1897, Rublee informed Peabody that he was thinking of giving up law: "I am not doing at all well in my profession & I think I shall soon have to make some sort of change, either form a new connection or undertake something new; for it is not only bad for me to be idle in an office in such a busy town as this, but further I can not afford it."[24] Rublee counted the newspaper business foremost in his options outside of law. Harvard chum Norman Hapgood was with the *Commercial Advertiser* and thought that George might find work on the paper as an editorial writer in New York. It was an option Rublee was considering, but he had not yet made up his mind.[25]

George's letter was a call for help; it was clear that his career was in dangerous decline. Although he could then not know it, his fortune was about to shift, and his life was about to take a dramatic—even fantastic—turn. The call to Peabody and a chance meeting on holiday at Lake Placid made all the difference in his life. In the fall of 1897 two new people came into his life with the power to alter its course: Victor Morawetz of New York City and Juliet Barrett of Chicago. Morawetz was a leading Wall Street corporate lawyer who was active in the merger movement that was then transforming American business; Juliet Barrett was a spirited and freethinking daughter of a wealthy Chicago industrialist who captivated and inspired George. Although the two entered his life at nearly the same moment, they answered very different needs; Juliet rekindled a hope in the pursuit of a worthy life, and Morawetz offered him the means to pursue it.

When Rublee wrote asking for help, Peabody apparently shared the circumstances of George's dilemma with Sherrard Billings, a master at Groton who remained a close friend of George's. Billings, seeking a better situation for the school's first graduate, contacted Victor Morawetz, a good friend of his who was making a fortune on Wall Street. Fortunately for George, Morawetz's practice was thriving, and he needed help. Through his second office in Chicago, Morawetz acted as general counsel for the Atchison, Topeka, and Santa Fe

Railroad, which was in receivership and which he was reorganizing. While the Chicago office promised "rapid promotion" if George did well there, Morawetz also needed a personal assistant in New York, where he was busy crafting the corporate trusts that J. P. Morgan and other investment bankers were financing. Following an interview with Morawetz in December 1897, George was offered whichever position he wished; he simply had to choose between New York and Chicago.[26]

Although George had concluded that acting as Morawetz's assistant in New York was more attractive because, as he explained, he would be "behind the scenes where [he] could observe the plans and acts of the leaders," leaving Chicago had recently become a difficult thing to do.[27] The problem in leaving was that he had fallen in love with twenty-two-year-old Juliet Barrett and was working to cause a corresponding feeling in her toward him. Juliet's interests and philosophy of life were lofty and corresponded closely to those that George held more closely before pursuing law. The two met on holiday at Lake Placid in New York in the late summer of 1897, and George, rather unusually, seems to have fallen for her immediately, as the two took walks together in "sunlit, beautiful, green woods" and floated "on the still water, beneath the glowing clouds, with the solemn mountains all around."[28] Giving what apparently was a premature profession of love at Lake Placid, it took George months to convince Juliet that he might be the one for her. Writing to her shortly after their meeting in August, George asked her not to fear that "any harm has come to me because I care so much for you" and explained that "[i]f you but knew how sad and barren life seemed to me before I met you," she would know that "nothing but good could come of such a feeling as mine."[29] Some months later, when their feelings for each other were more equal, George confessed that when he first met her, he knew that "the critical, decisive moment of [his] life had come":

> In so many lives there are latent possibilities of use which are not fulfilled. They seem to be experiments which are finally abandoned. I knew I might very likely be such an experiment, to be set aside and never completed, and that the time for deciding that question had arrived. Ever since then I have been in utter suspense, waiting to know what the decision would be, whether a miracle beyond my comprehension would happen and you would love me.[30]

Juliet would come to love him, and it would make a great difference in his life.

By late December the two had spoken privately, if hesitatingly, of marriage, but it was unclear how the relationship might progress. While, on the one hand, George was being offered new work with Victor Morawetz in either Chicago or New York, Juliet was scheduled to leave on a four-month grand tour of the Mediterranean with her family beginning in early January. With Juliet leaving Chicago for several months, George decided to travel to New York to learn more about the work Morawetz would have for him on Wall Street. Since he believed it was "an exceedingly grave decision I have to make, the gravest I ever had," he wanted to make the correct choice after so many fruitless beginnings.[31]

Although a relatively young thirty-eight when Rublee met him, Victor Morawetz was a leading lawyer in the new field of corporation law that was making possible the huge industrial combinations of the period. Like Rublee, Morawetz was a Harvard Law graduate whose career had also languished for two years following graduation as he searched for work in Chicago. In 1882, however, at age twenty-three, Morawetz produced a highly respected work entitled *A Treatise on the Law of Private Corporations Other than Charitable.* The work became an instant success, and in 1886 he produced a two-volume second edition, which Harvard Law School dean James Ames believed "was generally conceded to be the best treatise" on corporate law.[32] Morawetz's practice seems to have received a real boost after New Jersey's 1889 adoption of the general incorporation law and the 1895 *E. C. Knight* decision, which further undermined the Sherman Anti-Trust Act's usefulness in constraining economic concentration.[33] In the wake of these developments, lawyers such as Morawetz were being called upon to create exceedingly complex organizations and, in so doing, were traveling uncharted territory. Morawetz's book *On Corporations* had brought some order to the field, but the law continued to evolve at a rapid pace. George, who likely used Morawetz's treatise at Harvard, reported to Juliet, "In his kind [of work Morawetz] is, I think, probably the foremost lawyer in America, I mean in the law relating to bonds and railroads and in engineering financial operations."[34] As one of New York's foremost lawyers, leading industrialists such as John Pierpont Morgan and Andrew Carnegie regularly sought out his services. Earlier in the decade J. P. Morgan relied on Morawetz to create super–railroad systems in an effort to bring stability to the industry, which suffered a serious collapse in 1893 after years of overbuilding and subsequent debilitating competition. After he created them, Morawetz was asked to sit on the boards of the railroads that tied Morgan's systems together. Morgan also relied on Morawetz to create such new giant industrial concerns as the General Electric Company beginning in 1892.[35] In 1898 Morgan was on the verge of challenging Andrew Carnegie for a controlling consolidation of the steel industry, and Morawetz would soon be "smothered with work."[36]

After his January visit with Morawetz, Rublee was convinced that he should move to New York, where he would have much greater opportunity to advance as a corporate finance lawyer, a very lucrative line of work. Upon writing to Morawetz of his decision, the New York lawyer affirmed, "Your decision is, I believe, for the best—for both of us" and asked that George return as quickly as possible to New York.[37] Always mindful of his friends, George asked Morawetz to consider Edward Burling for the position in the Chicago office on the Santa Fe Railway reorganization, and he arranged for good friend Philip Littell to take the position offered to him on the *Commercial Advertiser*.[38]

George's situation in New York with Morawetz was a great departure from his previous experiences with other law firms. Writing to Juliet on 20 January, he related the highlights of his first day. Upon arriving in the office, he was given "the new mortgage of all the property of the Union Pacific Railway," which Morawetz "has just drafted, and said I might as well read it." The ninety-page document, it was thought, "would act as a good sedative for my nerves."[39] Morawetz, who believed that George was "more adapted to slide in near the top of the profession" rather than work his "way up from the bottom," evidently decided to take him on as a protégé.[40] As George explained,

> [Morawetz] took me out with him to lunch at the Lawyers Club. There and at other places he introduced me to sundry important persons. This he did by a little formula saying: "This is Mr. Rublee, who has come to help me practice law." The formula had an effect, as, on each occasion, the important person thereupon grasped my hand firmly and looked at me rather carefully. In the afternoon it was decided that I ought to join some clubs and that there must be no delay. So I met more important persons in committees and I don't know exactly what I did do nor what financial obligations to clubs I may be on the verge of incurring. For all I know I may be hopelessly insolvent.[41]

The next day, after lunch with Morawetz and the chairman of the Atchison Railroad, George got his first assignment, which was "to tell what will happen to the preferred stockholders, if a corporation called the General Electric Company reduces its capital stock by one half." George liked the work because it was "kind of a puzzle," but he was somewhat nervous about being asked to criticize "three other lawyers [who] have already given opinions." Marveling at Morawetz's confidence in him, George observed to Juliet: "As a German comedian kept saying in a play I have seen, 'it is to laugh.'"[42]

Although George denigrated his own capacities, Morawetz was quite satisfied with his work and soon had him involved in a number of demanding tasks. Morawetz also set him to reading various books on corporate finance, including Short's *Railway Bonds*, Noyes' *Thirty Years of American Finance*, and Morawetz's own *On Corporations*. By April Morawetz had George reporting on the "constitutionality of the proposed new Inter State Commerce Act," and in May he was asked to fashion "a supplemental mortgage of the Pecos Valley & Northeastern Railway," which was soon followed by drawing new leases for the Atchison, Topeka, and Santa Fe Railroad.[43] In June Morawetz asked George to help him with a new edition of his book, *On Corporations*. Although George believed it would be "a long, hard labor, as there has been a great development of the law of Corporations & thousands of corporation cases decided since the last edition," he knew that the work would help him learn "the law on the subject."[44] Of his work preparing the book George later recalled: "I used to go to the Bar Association in New York and use its great library. I went there almost every night, stayed there late, read and collected all the corporation cases of all the states of the union and also all the federal decisions in the Federal Report. It was a very long and arduous job and I made a note of each case..., what it decided and so forth."[45] The work made George exceedingly competent on the subject, so much so that by October he felt confident enough to reach "a conclusion opposed to" Morawetz's on a "question as to whether the United States Circuit Court here has jurisdiction of a certain case." As it turned out, George was correct, as he explained to Juliet: "[I]t was only a very simple matter. Mr. Morawetz had forgotten a circumstance."[46] Although the third edition of the book was never finished, owing to changes in both George's and Morawetz's life, the time George spent on the new edition was significant to his development as an expert on corporation law, which was of great importance in his later work to fashion a new national antitrust policy.

While George was at last progressing in his profession, his personal life had also taken a positive turn. His relationship with Juliet rekindled his humanitarian activism and renewed his commitment to perform some kind of public service. Writing to Peabody in January 1898, George let his old master know that "[m]y craving for a higher kind of life has increased[,] particularly during the time I was at Chicago." George believed that "the world has chief need of spiritually minded men who can deal sympathetically and understandingly with practical men of affairs." He related, "There are three men in Chicago who have power to do good, whose lives I think I have influenced for good." He added, "I only mention this to show that I am serious about wishing to be of service. I really care more about being useful to humanity than I do for anything else, and my father and you have helped me most to that end."[47] Although George pointed out that "I am not agnostic" because "[m]y faith in God and that good will prevail over evil is too positive for that," he confessed that he had not attended church in quite a while, explaining, "I do not think the effect of church going upon me is good." George, however, was prepared to accept that "I may be mistaken about church" and announced, "I will go regularly to any church here you may pick out for me & I will undertake to do any sort of philanthropic work that my circumstances will allow, that you will tell me."

Peabody soon sent George to see Dr. William Rainsford, who was rector of St. George's Episcopal Church in New York. Rainsford was an Irish-born theological liberal who challenged the church to place as much emphasis on serving the needs of the poor as it did in preaching the gospel. Rainsford came to St. George's in 1883, when the church was "struggling to survive in a decaying neighborhood."[48] With the financial and moral support of longtime member J. P. Morgan, Rainsford abolished the practice of pew rents that served as an obstacle to immigrants and transformed St. George's into an "institutional church." The church's services now encompassed both spiritual and secular activities, including youth clubs, "industrial classes, gymnasium classes, an employment agency, grocery department, dramatic society, [and] a clothing and tailoring department."[49] Rainsford's approach to Christianity was also especially modern and growing evermore undogmatic. He approved of leisure and sporting activities on Sundays and the use of alcohol in moderation as opposed to its complete prohibition, and he allowed dances to be held in church buildings so as to provide neighborhood youths an alternative venue to dance halls. His approach to Christian theology was equally liberal. He preached a humanistic gospel that "stressed the love of Jesus," the importance of service to one's neighbors, and the "symbolic nature of the creeds."[50] This was a theology that seems to have matched George's own views, and although George found Rainsford's sermons "a little theatrical" and complained that during them "he made altogether too much noise for his matter," he began attending St. George's regularly and began to see the Rainsfords socially. To George's surprise, upon offering himself for service, Rainsford soon put him to work teaching Sunday school classes. Although teaching "a dozen mischievous, unruly ragamuffins of about 14 years" was "not the sort of work" George had in mind when he offered himself for service, he accepted the assignment.[51] These "ragamuffins," as he explained to Juliet, were "children of poor people on the east side," whom he found "more mature and more intelligent in many ways than more fortunate boys." Determined to "be of some use to them," George bought them all a copy of *Treasure Island*, visited them at their homes, and found one of them employment at his firm as an errand runner.[52] The boy whom he helped get a job lived "in a rickety flat," and the family thought the four dollars he would earn a week at the law firm "a magnificent salary." Of his visit with the family George wrote, "The Booths are Irish, & very respectable, contented, agreeable people. I had a pleasanter call than is usual when I go in more fashionable society."[53]

Teaching Sunday school, going on social outings with the Rainsfords and Morawetz, and attending what appear to be most of the winter balls in New York that season seem to have helped keep George distracted during the months he had to wait for Juliet's return. Also helpful was seeing old college friends, especially Norman Hapgood, with whom he went regularly to the theater, and George Santayana. Describing these two men to Juliet, George observed that although Hapgood's "dramatic criticisms were attracting a good deal of attention," he believed that Hapgood "might do some other kind of work better." As for Santayana, who was returning to Harvard to teach philosophy, George believed he was "the cleverest man I have met" and praised him for being "a person who understands things, & not only understands, but can say what he thinks & feels, as [he] can, and I can't."[54]

Despite having old and new friends to occupy his mind, George had a rather difficult time awaiting Juliet's return. Making matters worse was that, owing to some confusion in the international postal system, he did not receive a letter from her for nearly six weeks after her departure. During that time he feared that she had lost interest in him, and he descended into a deep depression. Toward the end of that period, George wrote, "[i]f I don't before long hear something from you I am afraid I shall be discharged, which would in some respects be a pity, since our offices have just been enlarged by taking additional rooms, and my name has been painted up in large letters in various places in this building: but it is becoming more and more difficult to apply myself with any concentration to work."[55] For nearly six weeks George poured his heart into unanswered letters to Juliet that are a real window into his soul. Wanting her to understand how he operated, George explained that "the only way to get the best out of me is through the operation of my temperament," and he feared that he was not well suited for the practice of law, which he found rather uninspiring. He complained that, had he a different psychological makeup, he "might have learned to write agreeably or acquired some accomplishment, as I might have learned languages or read more books." Those achievements, however, "have not always seemed to me worth while and that is why my life so far has been so desultory." He explained that "nothing has ever seemed really worth while to me except when the stimulus, the inspiration to do it sprang from the thought that the doing would mean something to someone for whom I cared."[56]

Private observations though they may have been, this self-analysis is of benefit in understanding Rublee's often sporadic public work. In a later tribute to his mentor, Dean Acheson described Rublee's life as "a symphony...of alternating themes, one contented languor touched with melancholy, the other a passionate, almost demoniacal seizure which carried him to heights of brilliant and tireless effort." In closing the lengthy piece, Acheson, observed in wonder: "That George Rublee had gifts far beyond those given to most able men cannot be doubted. But why was he fully extended so intermittently? Why did his potentiality so often seem to elude him?"[57] George's letter to Juliet, full of pathos and honest reflection, points the way to answering Acheson's question. Rublee, it seems, was motivated to act only when he believed that he was somehow making a meaningful contribution. This quality would lead him, from 1910 to 1940, into many disparate, but passionate, crusades, the unifying theme for which was that they all aimed for the improvement of human life and human relations. This approach to public service seems also to reflect Horace Rublee's advocacy that public men be motivated "not by a mere desire to fill a conspicuous place in the eyes of the public...but by sincere wish to aid in determining and achieving what is really for the true welfare of the State."[58] Perhaps George's work would have seemed to him suspect if it were not motivated by the conviction that he was making a difference.

George's letters to Juliet during this period also reveal an intense interest in, and knowledge of, international affairs, an important qualification to his later work during World War I and the interwar period. His newspaper of choice in New York was the weekly *London Spectator*, which he believed "contains so much real information" and "is better, I think, than any of our papers." He thought it was good to read "English writers because there is an advantage in seeing things from different sides." In his spare time he also read such works as Otto von Bismarck's *Foundation of the German Empire*.[59] In a letter to Juliet on 22 February, George gave a sweeping review of world affairs that indicates the extent of his interest in, and understanding of international politics, as well as the pragmatism with which he approached the subject. Prophetically, he began:

> There are such a multitude of important events occurring everywhere, events which seem to portend changes and crises involving the vastest consequences. Never in my life before, I believe, has history or the promise of history, the making of it, been so interesting as it is now. And I think its interest will increase. We may live to see some great things done and we must understand and appreciate them if we can. Just consider how many problems there are which must soon be solved, no one knows how. First, there is, at our doors, this Cuban war which may involve us either in war with Spain or in a new policy of colonization. Then there is the eastern question, as to what is to be done with China and its great trade. There is the tottering Turkish Empire, which stands for the same reason why China stands, because the other countries can't agree on a division. Here are England & France quarreling about their respective rights in West Africa & the

Soudan and talking rather ugly on either side. England is carrying on a severe war in North West India & another in Ethiopia. There is the ever present chance of a row between England & Germany in South Africa, owing to the muss in the Transvaal. And now there is, too, a real danger of revolution and blood-letting & slaughter of Jews in France because a writer of rather high-colored novels has said that a Jewish Officer of the army was unjustly convicted of being a traitor. Every few days there is a riot in Austria because the people are dissatisfied with their government & jealous of each other. What is to be the outcome of all this fermenting?[60]

George ended his discourse with what could be described as the Eastern Establishment's creed, only there was not yet an Eastern Establishment: "To me one thing seems plain. It is that our country & England ought to be friends & help one another. We have the same instincts at bottom and, if we could depend upon one another, I believe we could hold our own against the rest of the world and that it would far better for humanity to have our race prevail."[61] Although in his advocacy of an international understanding with Great Britain George appears to be in agreement with Josiah Strong's views exalting Anglo-Saxon civilization, he was not exactly an Anglophile. In 1890, of the two English students studying with him at the home of M. Redl, he observed, "I like the people pretty well although they are English and I do not take to the English."[62] Nevertheless, he preferred the English to the French. Commenting on the Dreyfus affair and the slander trial of Émile Zola for his *J'accuse* article, to which he alluded in the 22 February letter, George observed, "Have you read about the trial of Zola? It has been the most extraordinary performance. If it were not for the seriousness of the possible consequences, it would be the most comic thing in the world. Put the court & all the people in it on a stage and add music by Sullivan or Reginald De Koven & we should have a surpassing opéra-boaffe. This trial gives me a lower opinion of French character than I ever had before."[63] Although George was disparaging of the French, he was equally critical of his fellow Americans, especially when it came to questions of international affairs. A week before America's declaration of war on Spain he wrote: "I am rather blue, too, about the prospect of war. War is a terrible calamity and this war seems so unnecessary."[64] He complained further, "It would be so very much better if such momentous questions could be decided by the exercise of human reason instead of by the influence of masses of ignorant men acting blindly under the sway of excitement & prejudice."[65] George was consoled by the thought that "[i]f there is a war I believe and hope it will be short."[66]

While many of George's letters touched upon such political and diplomatic issues, the one unending thread to all his letters was the question of his and Juliet's future life together. George made it clear from the beginning that he did not care for the practice of law: "When I am deep in a mortgage a sudden vision comes to me of a wide, summer field all green and blue & yellow with grass and flowers rustling beneath a mild wind. Such thoughts give a singular impression of the futility of the eager, noisy strife, the nervous excitement of life in a city like this, where buying & selling, eating and talking about one another seems to absorb human energies."[67] Although George believed that "[i]t is in our relations to other human beings that we fulfill the true purpose of our lives," he confessed that "I wish we could always live where we needed not to wear collars & could just be natural and unbothered. From that paradise we might make little excursions from time to time to watch the artificial people & their ways for amusement until the interest ceased and then back we should fly to our Arcadian refuge."[68] George's difficulty was that he could not afford an "Arcadian refuge." Making matters worse, it seemed that Juliet's father and brother thought that George was something of a gold digger, and although she was exceedingly wealthy, there was no indication that Juliet would bring any income at all with her to the marriage. Juliet lived on prestigious Lake Shore Drive in Chicago in a mansion complete with gymnasium, and her parents evidently envisioned her marrying someone of similar wealth.[69]

The presumption that George was attempting to marry Juliet for her money led him in one letter into something of a tirade against the social customs of the wealthy. He complained:

> It has been a prevalent idea in this country which is fast expiring, that a man should spend his life from early boyhood on in toiling to amass a fortune; that as soon as he has laid the foundations thereof[,] he should marry, beget a family, neglect his wife & children, but at any cost keep them in luxury & idleness without knowledge either of the difficulties or opportunities life presents. Why this idea has seemed so praiseworthy is a little hard to perceive, but it has been, with a little tawdry disguise, put before young men as an ennobling and inspiring one. It has done a great deal of harm. It has made men dull, coarse, ignoble and it has made women frivolous, vulgar and shallow.
>
> For my part I believe that the notion of there being virtue in a man's supporting a woman without her making any contribution is an unconscious survival from the period when men regarded women as inferior creatures, necessary for the satisfaction of their passions, good to trifle with & indispensable to the creation of families, but not to be considered as companions or in any real sense equals. Society was organized on such principles for a long period. Then, of course, men supported women just as they did their horses & dogs.[70]

George argued that the constraints placed on wealthy daughters that forced them to marry only wealthy men was an idea that "among intelligent people in the East…has about disappeared." He complained further that "the theory that a man should wait until he has plenty of money before wanting a woman to marry him is a good theory for a clock which goes on quietly till it comes to the hour and strikes." He believed that "[a] man who could regulate himself so satisfactorily would not be capable to know what love meant" and added, "I did not fall in love with you because I wanted to marry, but because I could not help myself."[71]

George had concluded that the two could live in comfort on about $4,000 a year, which he could earn by writing articles for the *Commercial Advertiser* and teaching courses at the Columbia Law School in addition to his work with Morawetz.[72] He had also begun, on Morawetz's advice, to buy as much Atchison, Topeka, & Santa Fe stock as he could in hopes of making a speculative income. George promised Juliet that "[i]n a boarding house we shall never dwell," but the two could afford on his income to "take two or three rooms, & quest for our meals in Bohemia." He argued, "We should be absolutely free to do as we pleased and the want of luxuries would not weigh upon either of us."[73] George's rather romantic views of a Bohemian life in New York and his arguments for a modern marriage—evidently reflecting Juliet's own inclinations—finally won the day, and the two became engaged in late October 1898 and were married in Chicago in early January 1899.

It is not clear how long George and Juliet were required to "quest for their meals in Bohemia." In the first year or so after their marriage, Juliet's father came through, giving her $40,000 worth of bonds in his Barrett Manufacturing Co.[74] Although in a letter that George wrote during their engagement he claimed that "[i]t is more fun to have a little money than it would be to have a great deal" and that "[t]here is nothing in the world that I want in addition to what I have," within a year of their marriage George and Juliet were investing heavily in the stock market on margin. Throughout the first year of his work in New York, Morawetz had advised George to invest in preferred shares of the Atchison Railroad. George hesitated and watched the stock price rise from $24 to $67 per share over the course of the year without participating in the market. George and Juliet observed friends make small fortunes speculating in stocks, and, after incremental increases, they at last threw themselves completely into the market.[75] Although the Atchison's preferred stock had already experienced a strong ride on the New York Stock Exchange, its common stock was selling for about $20 and seemed destined to rise. George and Juliet, at first with the help of Morawetz and some friends, began buying as much stock on margin as they could. When they received the bonds from Juliet's father, they put them up as collateral and purchased more stock on margin. George later recalled that watching the market go up and down over the next year "was rather a bad atmosphere in some ways but there it was and I was much concerned about it."[76] With McKinley's reelection victory over Bryan in November 1900, the stock market experienced a "great surge" that continued until 9 May 1901, when the market collapsed. To their great fortune, George and Juliet sold their stocks at some point during the spring, when the prices were still high. Having bought so heavily on margin, they "emerged with about $250,000," a sum that seemed to Rublee "an enormous fortune."[77]

At age thirty-three, George Rublee was suddenly financially independent. The question before him was what to do now, continue as a lawyer on Wall Street and seek a truly enormous fortune or pursue the life he had abandoned nine years before when he left Europe to pursue law. Since 1899 George had been assisting Morawetz with J. P. Morgan's forays into the steel industry creating Federal Steel and National Tube and was interested in the work. In December 1900, Morgan bought out Andrew Carnegie to form America's first billion-dollar company, U.S. Steel. Morawetz was chiefly responsible for "drawing up the mortgages" and arranging the "complicated financial settlements" necessary to create the holding company.[78] Although George did not draft the legal documents, he acted as Morawetz's only assistant and was called upon to "go over them all, make suggestions, check things and so on" before they were passed on to Morgan's staff lawyers.[79] Rublee's participation in the creation of U.S. Steel further qualified him as an expert on corporate law and prepared him for his later work of creating the Federal Trade Commission.

George decided to stay with Morawetz throughout 1901, but once U.S. Steel was completed, they both began to reexamine their interests. Fortunately for George, Morawetz did not approve of working during the summer—unless there was an emergency reorganization—believing that "[w]hat one does during the summer is of the greatest importance in preparing one to work in the winter."[80] Although George and Juliet did allow themselves a lengthy vacation in Western Europe during the summer of 1901, it seems that they were unsure how to proceed with their lives and made few substantive changes. In July, a friend of George's from Milwaukee wrote to observe: "Your mother thinks you should alter your mode of living so as to conform to your enlarged means, and fears that the alteration will come hard to you and Juliet."[81] George soon received an offer from a cousin on his mother's side to join his brokerage firm, but he resisted the temptation.[82] By December 1901 George knew he wanted a change but was not yet sure what he wanted to do. Writing to Peabody on 31 December he observed, "The main point I see is that it would be well for me to stop trying to get more money and to clear out of Wall Street; but beyond this I have not reached any conclusion."[83] Peabody wrote back inviting George to take a teaching position at Groton, and although George found the idea of "dividing my time between teaching, study and writing" appealing, he made no commitment. George was interested in making some sort of contribution to society, but he seems to have been at a loss as to where he should begin. He was evidently surrounded by Social Gospel reformers at St. George's who were involved in all sorts of projects, but he seems to have been rather uncomfortable with their zealous approach and presumptuous attitudes. In 1898 he had confided to Juliet that he disliked some of the activists at St. George's because "[t]hey are so intense, at times" and are "sure that their interests are the only ones that can save the world." Further, he found that "[a]lmost all the people who are in earnest that I know, reformers, religious persons, artists, etc.—overdo their interests, get them out of proportion & adjustment to the rest of the universe." He thought they would do well to bear in mind the Greek maxim "Do nothing too much." While George wanted himself and Juliet to make a contribution, early in their relationship he had pointed out that "I don't think it wise for us yet to bother much over ethical ideas & schemes for doing good...We both want to do right & the opportunities will come."[84] Although in 1901 George took an interest in Seth Low's successful Anti-Tammany Fusion campaign, he otherwise does not seem to have found a role to play in the Social Reform movement.[85]

Sometime in 1902, however, George decided that he was most fit to make a contribution through the diplomatic service. Owing to his business experience and his long attention to international affairs and his years spent abroad, both as a child in Switzerland and as an adult traveling and studying, he believed himself qualified for some sort of position. In 1890 he had met Theodore Roosevelt in

New York when George's father came east and Roosevelt, then police commissioner, had paid Horace a visit. Recalling that Roosevelt "seemed to have much admiration for my father," George ventured to call on Roosevelt, who had become president in September 1901, following the assassination of William McKinley. As he later recalled, "I wanted to offer myself to do anything to be of assistance in the diplomatic service." Unfortunately, the interview did not go well. George found that Roosevelt was "shocked by the way I was going about this" and said that "[i]f I wanted a job—I would have to go into politics and work to earn" it.[86] Although George was at the time quite embarrassed by the episode and was surprised that Roosevelt seemed to consider diplomatic posts spoils for the political patronage system, he was likely a little irked when in 1906 Roosevelt sought out Willard Straight and other "bright young Ivy Leaguers to join the Foreign Service and drum up business for American companies abroad."[87]

Having failed in an effort to secure a diplomatic post and yet dissatisfied with work on Wall Street, George fell back on the idea of a life of writing. During the summer of 1902 George and Juliet returned to Europe, where they first spent two months enjoying the "out of door life" in Switzerland, taking "many glorious walks and climbs in the high mountains."[88] Writing to Peabody from Florence in October, George reported that "[t]he spell of Italy is as strong over me as ever" and admitted that the two considered settling in Florence, where George might "make a history of the Italian Commonwealths during the Renaissance with the emphasis on the political and human side." Yet, "for some cause which we are not quite able to explain to ourselves," George and Juliet were not ready to give themselves over to the émigré life. Instead, they determined to find "some place in American life that we might feel to be our own." George received an offer to become assistant general counsel for the Atchison Railroad while they were in Europe, and, after three months or so of vacationing, they decided to return to New York.[89]

Not long after returning to New York, however, Juliet's health broke down, and the two decided to travel to a spa in Carlsbad, then in Austria-Hungary, in the spring of 1903 to see a Swedish doctor who specialized in women's reproductive health. While Juliet went through a series of medical treatments throughout the spring and summer, George simply enjoyed life as best he could and returned to his former interest in tennis, entering tournaments (and winning some) in various places as the two traveled together. In the autumn of 1903, they followed Juliet's doctor back to Sweden, where the treatments continued with much success, although her condition rendered pregnancy an impossibility. While in Sweden, George began playing tennis at the royal tennis club outside Stockholm, where he became a regular tennis partner of the crown prince of Sweden, later Gustav V. Writing to Learned Hand, George reported, "The Crown Prince of Sweden, though past middle age, is mad about the game of lawn tennis and constantly plays in covered courts. Through my fondness for tennis I became acquainted with him and many other people who treated us very kindly."[90] George thought that Gustav looked "more like a college professor than like a king" and found that his "manners were perfectly democratic and pleasant," for "when I was his partner he used to pick up the balls for me when I served, as I did for him." George "called him 'Your Majesty' once in a while, but that was all."[91]

George and Juliet soon gave themselves over completely to the leisurely life of European high society and seemed to forget about their interest in finding their place in American life. Juliet had an American girlfriend in Stockholm who had married a Swedish architect and "who was acquainted with the artists and literary people." Through that couple George and Juliet met leading European painters and sculptors, including then-famous Anders Leonhard Zorn. They soon began to "be invited out to dinner." George, who had long been interested in architecture and art, later recalled it as "a lively and interesting period of my life." They soon had several invitations to country homes for the Christmas holidays and traveled with the prince's tennis club to a tournament given in the south of Sweden, where the royal family vacationed. Early in 1904 George and Juliet traveled to St. Petersburg and Moscow with the Russian sculptor Paul Troubetzkoy, and in the spring they worked their way south to the Riviera, where George continued playing in tennis tournaments. Although the two planned to remain longer in Europe, perhaps even another year, Juliet's father became seriously ill, and the two returned to America in the summer of 1904.[92]

While George mostly pursued a life of leisure and sports in Europe for more than a year, his experiences there were quite important to both his later diplomatic work and the development of his outlook on questions of political-economy. In addition to meeting a number of leading men in government circles, George must have become aware of the dramatic developments leading toward the creation of the welfare state in parts of Western and Central Europe.[93] Owing to economic distress from 1903 to 1905, Great Britain, for instance, was on the verge of adopting a number of new social programs, including workers' compensation and old-age pensions.[94] Labor unrest and radical socialist ideology led a number of countries to follow German chancellor Otto von Bismarck's effort to undermine support for socialism by building a paternalistic welfare state. The development of Rublee's political thought over the next seven years suggests that he was increasingly influenced both by his European experiences traveling as he did among aristocrats, artists, and intellectuals and by a continued attention to the development of European welfare legislation. He, too, would soon advocate social and economic reforms aimed at alleviating the suffering of European working-class poor, only his efforts would be directed at the millions of them who lived in the United States.

After spending several months in Chicago during the summer of 1904, George and Juliet returned to New York, where George again worked at Morawetz's office, which he found "always open to" him. Morawetz soon perceived that George was dissatisfied with life in the city and suggested the Rublees take a "cottage" at South Hampton, where they might find people more suited to their interests and still continue work in New York. Instead of South Hampton, George and Juliet accepted an invitation from Norman Hapgood to spend the summer in Cornish, New Hampshire, which was at the time a "center for artists and literary men."[95] Cornish, a rural community about twenty miles south of Hanover, boasted both beautiful landscapes and distinguished American residents. Included among the few hundred colonists were artists Augustus Saint-Gaudens, Thomas Dewing, and Maxfield and Stephen Parrish and men of letters Herbert Croly, Winston Churchill (the novelist) and Hapgood. The Cornish colony was established around 1885 as a simple place for Saint-Gaudens and his assistants "to work and lead an informal life," but by the turn of the century it was being called the "Athens of America" and was home to "painters, sculptors, decorators, novelists, journalists, playwrights, poets, critics, essayists, composers, musicians, theatrical performers, and patrons of the arts."[96]

In Cornish George and Juliet at last found both their "Arcadian refuge" and that "place in American life that we might feel to be our own." George was especially attracted to the place because there were "artists and writers but I believe I was then the only lawyer. Such a community was stimulating and interesting for me."[97] Juliet, who was interested in dance and art, was also happy, and George thought that she had "never found an environment that suited her so well."[98] The Cornish colonists created their own entertainment year-round, complete with masked balls and outdoor theater. Music also filled the summer nights as the colonists gathered for evening picnics to watch the sun set and the full moon rise.[99] A journalist writing in the *New York Daily Tribune* in 1907 described Cornish as "an atmosphere of modern antiquity" in which resided people who did not wish to create "a 'fashionable' summer resort, but rather to form there an aristocracy of brains."[100] Before the summer ended, George and Juliet decided to join the Cornish colony and began making plans to build or buy a home there.

George returned to work with Morawetz in the fall of 1905 but continued to be disenchanted with the work. It seems likely that being around Hapgood, Croly, and Churchill had reinvigorated his interest in public work. Returning to his earlier interest in the diplomatic service, George decided to return to Paris and take courses at the Ecole Libre des Science Politiques. Writing to Peabody in December 1905, Rublee explained that he intended to take "what the French, I think, call diplomatic history," as well as a course in international law. He was principally interested in learning "the method that scholars in France employ in the study of history."[101] Although George enjoyed the courses, he did not take them as seriously as he had intended. He ended up spending much time playing tennis and seeing such friends as George Santayana, who was giving lectures in Paris and who "spent a good deal of time going to small theatres and looking around odd places observing life in Paris." Letters of introduction from Barrett Wendell, noted Harvard English professor and Juliet's much older cousin, also led to further distractions for George as he and Juliet made the fashionable scene in Paris.[102]

George and Juliet returned to Cornish in the summer of 1906 and purchased the home that a wealthy Boston businessman had built for his wife, a painter interested in Cornish as an artists' colony. Although George called it a cottage,

"Crossways" was a rather large country home situated on beautiful New Hampshire acreage. The house was built around an immense hall upon which various ground and upper-floor rooms opened, giving the effect of a miniature Italian plaza. What had previously been a large art studio was converted into a library for George. There he could escape to read his eclectic works ranging from Greek tragedies and books on classical architecture to the latest publications on international affairs.[103] Crossways was regularly filled with close friends, many of whom eventually took up residence at Cornish, including lawyers Learned Hand and Edward Burling, journalist Philip Littell, and playwright and critic Walter Ayer.[104]

Crossways and the Cornish colony were truly George's Arcadian refuge. Writing to Peabody in September 1908, he related his perfect contentment with the place: "I love this beautiful country and my friends and neighbors here and I feel my home is here in a way that I never have felt about any other place."[105] It was a feeling that would endure. Forty years later he would observe, "Cornish has been a strong influence in my life because of my attachment for the peace and for the friends I made there. When I was far away the thought of Cornish was a cheering and sustaining influence."[106] Purchasing Crossways, however, stretched George financially because his "investments were not in good order," and, since he was "not willing to give up Cornish," he returned to work on Wall Street.[107]

Although the practice of law remained mundane for him, George was finding new inspiration through his friendships in Cornish. Herbert Croly and Norman Hapgood were both interested in shaping the course of American politics, Hapgood in his position as editor of *Collier's Weekly* and Croly through his book *The Promise of American Life*, published in 1909. Likely based on conversations begun at Cornish, Hapgood invited Rublee to write articles for *Collier's* beginning in January 1906. In the first article, "Government Rate-Making," George addressed the expanded powers that Theodore Roosevelt sought to give the Interstate Commerce Commission (ICC) through the Hepburn Act. Although in the article Rublee was especially interested in educating the public about the economic imperatives behind the seemingly unjust long-haul–short-haul rate differentials, the article is significant in revealing Rublee's skepticism about government commissions only eight years before his work to create the Federal Trade Commission.[108]

Rublee began the article by pointing out, "Agreement is unanimous that the public has so deep an interest in the railway system that it should be subject to supervision and regulation by the State." The only disagreement was "in regard to the method of correcting the evils that exist" in the system. Roosevelt's approach, he asserted, was to allow the ICC "first, to decide a given rate to be unreasonable" and then to "substitute for the condemned rate [one] deemed by the Commission to be reasonable." Rublee hoped to warn the public of the "magnitude of the power which such legislation would give the Commission" and "the illusory character of the provision for judicial review."[109] He cautioned:

[i]t does not seem to be generally understood that no review of the Commission's orders by a court can be effective if the power to fix specific rates is given to the Commission. In reducing a rate the Commission would exercise a legislative power within the limits prescribed by the Constitution. If the railroad affected by the Commission's order should appeal, the only question upon which the court could pass would be whether the reduction in rate would be so extreme as to deprive the railroad of its property rights and thus constitute a violation of the fifth amendment of the Federal Constitution.[110]

Rublee believed that a commission so authorized would possess "virtually autocratic power" because it would have "the functions of detective, prosecutor, and judge," and he asserted, "Human experience has shown the impossibility of securing a just and impartial performance of these various duties by the same persons."[111]

Rublee also believed, for various reasons, that a single group of men would be incapable of setting differential rates for the whole country. He asserted: "But imagine the position of a commission to which hundreds or perhaps thousands of such claims would be presented. How could any commission deal with them? Such work now occupies hundreds of highly paid traffic officials, but none of these deems himself competent to pass upon traffic matters except in the territory with which he is familiar."[112] Rublee argued that instead of giving the ICC "autocratic powers," the "present Interstate Commerce Act and its amendments, including the Elkins Act," should be enforced. These laws, he believed, contained measures that "render illegal virtually all those acts which are the grounds of complaint against railway companies." He suggested that instead of giving the commission "quasi-judicial function," Congress should provide the commission "an adequate number of special agents to enable the commission to investigate promptly and thoroughly alleged or suspected unlawful practices." Congress should also allow the commission to employ "special auditors" to examine the books of railway companies and should pass laws to prohibit "indirect preferences to shippers through the medium of private car lines, terminal roads, warehouses, elevators or other indirect methods." Additionally, the commission should be given adequate funds to "maintain all necessary suits" for the enforcement of laws. Finally, Rublee suggested that "it would probably be found advisable to create a special tribunal, consisting of circuit judges assigned for the purpose, to pass upon the reasonableness of rates when brought in question by the Commission."[113] Such judges should be well versed in economics and have some understanding of the business of railroads.

In October 1906 Rublee wrote a second article entitled "A Handicap to Business," in which he critiqued the national banking system and argued that inelasticity was the greatest defect in the nation's monetary system. In the article he sought to relate the essence of Victor Morawetz's plan to reform the nation's banking system and to make it intelligible to the readers of *Collier's*.[114] Although Morawetz's plan would become the basis for the Federal Reserve system in 1913, Rublee was an early advocate and was likely among the first to describe to the public the concepts behind what would eventually become the new banking and monetary system.[115] With his Milwaukee and Chicago background, which included membership in a Grange association, Rublee may have thought himself in a unique position to lessen the antagonism that existed between western Populists and eastern capitalists. He began his article noting, "In no other country having a mass of capital to be compared with ours do interest rates go up and down so far and at such short intervals as in the United States."[116] Rublee pointed out that although Western European countries' interest rates remained below 6 percent, in the United States they fluctuated annually from less than 2 to more than 50 percent. He also noted that in addition to "excessive fluctuations" there were in the United States "wasteful differences between interest rates in different parts of the United States at the same time." Pointing out that interest rates rise sharply the farther west one travels, Rublee observed that although "[w]e like to hear ourselves talk of the unbounded, measureless wealth of our Great West," he argued that exorbitant interest rates prevented the West from living up to its potential. Eschewing Populist arguments of class conflict, Rublee stressed that the annual interest rate fluctuations around harvest were not the work of rapacious eastern bankers but instead resulted from impersonal economic forces that could and should be mitigated. The problem leading to the grievous East–West variances was that "the people who control credit in the Eastern cities have no adequate facilities for judging competently the value of security offered by Western borrowers." What the United States needed, he argued, was a system that eased credit restrictions and brought the nation's banks into effective cooperation, for which the best plan that Rublee had seen was one "devised by Mr. Victor Morawetz, a distinguished New York lawyer and financier."

Rublee thought Morawetz's scheme laudable because it called for the creation of a "Joint Issue Department, governed by a Board of Managers, to be elected by the banks," which would be authorized to adjust reserve requirements of member banks "according to the state of [the nation's] financial conditions." Rublee believed that the ability to adjust reserve ratios according to the strength of the economy was "an excellent feature of the plan, as it provides machinery for exerting some measure of control over the existing credit, and consequently over the rates of interest." A second feature of Morawetz's plan that excited Rublee was his call for "the establishment of branches of the Joint Issue Department for different sections of the country." These branches would then organize subcommittees that would coordinate the movement of money and ensure bank compliance with national banking standards. Rublee believed that the regional branch oversight function would tend to remove the risks that New York bankers took note of when lending large sums of money to remote regions of the United States. Morawetz's system would thereby reduce both interest rate fluctuations and regional differentials.

Although Rublee did not describe the U.S. government's role in Morawetz's proposed national banking arrangement, he did suggest that the issue was a matter of national political concern. Rublee lamented that the "average man will not bother his head" about banking and monetary policy and feared that these would not be reformed until there was "public demand for improvement."

Rublee pointed out that under the existing system bankers had learned to "make huge speculative profits by foreseeing the fluctuations and anticipating their effect." Implying an expanded role for the federal government, Rublee concluded the article pointing out that "[r]elying entirely upon bankers and financiers to reform the currency is a little like expecting the owners of the old stage-coach lines, a few generations ago, to help the people get a railroad."

Although there is no way to measure the impact of Rublee's articles, they do indicate that he continued to sharpen his ideas regarding issues of political-economy. While his article on railroad rate differentials demonstrates some reluctance to place public policy in the hands of government commissions, Rublee's ideas on currency and banking reform demonstrate that he was moving toward what Herbert Croly would soon call New Nationalism. This approach to government, most fully articulated by Theodore Roosevelt in the 1912 presidential election, identified a positive role for the federal government in dealing with difficulties stemming from the modern urban-industrial system. Like other New Nationalist Progressives, Rublee would increasingly believe that, left unchecked, these systemic problems would soon lead to social revolution and debilitating upheaval. This notion of impending danger would lead Rublee and others to challenge so-called stalwarts from their own Republican Party who would allow no deviation from quasi-laissez-faire economic policies. It seems for these men government intervention in the economy was proper only if it benefited capitalists' interests. Although Rublee respected and rubbed elbows with such men every day in Manhattan, he increasingly recognized that the United States could not rely solely on the market for the distribution of goods and services. Moving stridently away from laissez-faire economic policy, progressives would soon call for government involvement in the economy over matters ranging from pure food to currency reform. Progressives such as Rublee would also recognize that sound public policy demanded expert advice and professional implementation. Rublee believed that "independent students of economics and other persons who have expert knowledge" of a subject should provide public leadership.[117] His 1906 *Collier's* articles were evidently a step toward offering such service, but he was anxious to do more as the pressures of the modern age continued to mount. Despite his growing anxiety he would have to wait a little longer.

Meanwhile, Rublee's fortieth birthday arrived with some misgiving. Writing to Peabody in September 1908 in a belated response to a birthday greeting, Rublee reported that he had formed a new partnership in New York with former Wisconsin senator John Spooner, a longtime family friend. Nevertheless, he expressed a continued hope in "getting really interested" in some worthwhile endeavor.[118] Although he could not know it, within a year a series of events would catapult him into the type of public work he had so long desired, and the seemingly disconnected experiences of his life since 1892 would prove central to his success. Rublee's work with Morawetz had given him intimate knowledge of the world of corporate mergers, allowing him to see both their benefit and detriment to the American political and economic system; his extensive experiences in Europe were of paramount importance to his ability to work effectively on international bodies for the next thirty years; and his knowledge of financial matters would be of great value in most aspects of his public work, ranging from his assistance to Governor Robert Perkins Bass in 1910 to his effort to save German Jews in 1938–1939. At age forty, George Rublee was poised and prepared to begin a long career in public service.

NOTES

1. Rublee, "Reminiscences," 16-18.
2. GR to Peabody, 12 September 1893, GSA.
3. GR to Peabody, 15 November 1890, GSA.
4. GR to Peabody, 16 September 1894, GSA; and Ashburn, *Fifty Years On*, 15.
5. H. Rublee to GR, 11 June 1895, GRP.
6. GR to Peabody, 13 June 1895, GSA.
7. Rublee, "Reminiscences," 18.
8. GR to Peabody, 7 July 1895, GSA.
9. Ibid. Rublee had likely arranged to work with the well-regarded U.S. 1st circuit Judge John Lowell, who was noted for being "[i]ndependent, learned and courteous as a U.S. judge" and for being "[p]articularly effective in commercial, marine and bankruptcy cases." He died in 1897. *Concise Dictionary of American Biography* (New York: Charles Scribner's Sons, 1964), 591.
10. GR to Peabody, 7 July 1895, GSA.
11. Ibid.
12. GR to Peabody, 26 August 1895 and 6 September 1895, GSA.
13. James Ames to Lord, Day and Lord. Transcribed in GR to Peabody, 28 September 1895, GSA.
14. GR to Peabody, 28 October 1895, GSA.
15. H. Rublee to GR, 10 October 1895 and 17 November 1895, GRP.
16. Ibid; 17 November 1895.
17. GR to Peabody, 31 October 1895, GSA.
18. GR to Charles Eliot, 27 December 1895, Harvard University Archives, UAI 5.150, Box 138B, Harvard University, Cambridge, Massachusetts [hereafter HUA].
19. Rublee, "Reminiscences," 20.
20. GR to Eliot, 27 April 1896, HUA.
21. Rublee, "Reminiscences," 20-21.
22. Ibid., 21-23.
23. Ibid., 23.
24. GR to Peabody, 26 October 1897, GSA.
25. Ibid.
26. Rublee, "Reminiscences," 23; and GR to Peabody, 20 January 1898, GSA.
27. GR to Peabody, 18 January 1898, GSA.
28. GR to Juliet Barrett, August 1897, GRP. Although George was regularly in the company of women, there seems to have been only one other in which he was seriously interested. That relationship seems to have been sabotaged by his mother, who, disapproving of the older woman's character, asked Endicott Peabody to intercede.
29. Ibid.
30. GR to Barrett, 2 February 1898, GRP.

31. GR to Barrett, 5 January 1898, GRP.

32. Quoted in Eric Chiappinelli, "Victor Morawetz," *American National Biography* (Cary, NC: Oxford University Press, 1998), vol. 15, 805.

33. See Glenn Porter, *The Rise of Big Business, 1860-1920* (Wheeling, IL: Harlan Davidson, 1973, 1992), 76-82.

34. GR to Barrett, 1 March 1898, GRP.

35. Alfred D. Chandler, Jr., *The Visible Hand: The Managerial Revolution in American Business* (Cambridge: Belknap Press of the Harvard University Press, 1977), 171-175; Chiappinelli, "Morawetz," 805; and Rublee, "Reminiscences," 25-26. Morawetz was a close friend of Francis Lynde Stetson, who was general counsel for J.P. Morgan. According to Rublee, "Stetson relied much on Morawetz and usually retained him in important matters for J.P. Morgan and Co."

36. Victor Morawetz to GR, 13 January 1898, GRP.

37. Ibid.

38. GR to Barrett, 20 January 1898 and 18 February 1898, GRP. In the letter, George confessed that "[e]ver since I arrived [in NY] Ned Burling has been much in my mind. I wish so much he had this chance with Morawetz instead of me. The work is so exactly suited to him & he would do it so much better than I can. I believe perhaps I can do something for him after a while. I don't want any mistake to happen in his career, for it might be such a good one." George would later introduce Burling to Judge Harry Covington and the three would establish one of Washington's most influential law firms.

39. GR to Barrett, 20 January 1898, GRP.

40. GR to Barrett, 4 April 1898, GRP.

41. GR to Barrett, 20 January 1898, GRP.

42. Ibid.

43. GR to Barrett, 22 April 1898, 10 May 1898, and 28 June 1898, GRP.

44. GR to Barrett, 19 June 1898, GRP.

45. Rublee, "Reminiscences," 31.

46. GR to Barrett, 3 October 1898 and 8 October 1898, GRP.

47. GR to Peabody, 20 January 1898, GSA.

48. Gardiner Shattuck, "William Stephen Rainsford," *American National Biography* (Cary, NC: Oxford University Press, 1998), vol. 18, 83.

49. "William Stephen Rainsford," *National Cyclopaedia of American Biography* (Ann Arbor: University Microfilms, 1967), vol. 42, 27; James Roark et al., *The American Promise* (Boston: Bedford Books, 1998), vol. 2, 804.

50. *National Cyclopaedia*, 27.

51. GR to Peabody, 22 March 1898, GSA. Rublee appears to have taught Sunday School at St. George's for about a year, after which he seems to have given up on his experiment with church involvement. Writing to Endicott Peabody in December 1899, William Rainsford complained about the "wholesale falling away from Church of our boys as soon as they leave college" and reported his disappointment with Rublee, who "seemed to promise so well," but who had "dropped the Sunday-School class" and church generally. Rainsford to Peabody, 18 December 1899, GSA.

52. GR to Barrett, 4 April 1898, GRP; and GR to Peabody, 22 March 1898, GSA.

53. GR to Barrett, 13 July, 1898, GRP.

54. GR to Barrett, 22 April 1898, GRP.

55. GR to Barrett, 11 February 1898, GRP.

56. GR to Barrett, 6 February 1898, GRP.

57. Dean Acheson, "George Rublee," *The Groton School Quarterly*, (Summer 1957) 3, 5.

58. H. Rublee to Hamilton Fish, October 1874, *FRUS*, 1875, 1280.

59. GR to Barrett, 8 June 1898, GRP.

60. GR to Barrett, 22 February 1898, GRP.

61. Ibid.

62. George Rublee, 1890 Travel Diary, 3 October entry, GRP.

63. GR to Barrett, 22 February 1898, GRP.

64. GR to Barrett, 8 April 1898, GRP.

65. Ibid.

66. Ibid.

67. GR to Barrett, 25 February 1898, GRP.

68. GR to Barrett, 6 October 1898, GRP.

69. GR to Barrett, 4 April 1898, GRP.

70. GR to Barrett, 14 October 1898, GRP.

71. Ibid.

72. GR to Barrett, 8 May 1898, and 10 May 1898, GRP.

73. GR to Barrett, 7 October 1898, GRP.

74. Rublee, "Reminiscences," 28.

75. GR to Barrett, 19 October 1898; and Rublee, "Reminiscences,"27-28.

76. Rublee, "Reminiscences," 28.

77. Ibid., 29. $250,000 in 1901 would be worth about $4,500,000 in 2003.

78. Rublee, "Reminiscences," 33. It is likely that this is the work that led Robert La Follette to later identify Morawetz as "one of the eighty odd men . . . constituting the money trust." See Norman Hapgood to Edward House, 28 December 1914, Edward House Papers, box 55, folder 1722, Yale University Archives, Sterling Library Special Collections, Yale University [hereafter Yale-House].

79. Rublee, "Reminiscences," 33-34.

80. GR to Barrett, 4 April 1898, GRP.

81. Philip Littell to GR, 23 July 1901, GRP.

82. Rublee, "Reminiscences," 30.

83. GR to Peabody, 31 December 1901, GSA.

84. GR to Barrett, 5 June 1898, GRP.

85. GR to Peabody, 29 September 1901, GSA.

86. Rublee, "Reminiscences," 35-36.

87. Ron Chernow, *The House of Morgan: An American Banking Dynasty and the Rise of Modern Finance* (New York: Simon & Schuster, 1990), 134.

88. GR to Peabody, 19 October 1902, GSA.

89. Ibid.

90. GR to Hand, 21 July 1904 (erroneously dated 1909 on typescript), HLS-Hand, box 107, folder 1.

91. Rublee, "Reminiscences," 36-39.

92. Ibid., 40-43.

93. Among George's and Juliet's photographs from this period are ones taken at an outdoor meeting of the Socialist party in a northern European country. GRP.

94. Daniel T. Rodgers, *Atlantic Crossings: Social Politics in a Progressive Age* (Cambridge: Belknap Press of Harvard University Press, 1998), 230-231.

95. Rublee, "Reminiscences," 43-46.

96. John H. Dryfhout, "The Cornish Colony," *A Circle of Friends: Art Colonies of Cornish and Dublin* (Durham, NH: University of New Hampshire, 1985), 34; Author's interview with Ella Poe Burling, 14 December 1994, Washington, D.C; and Gerald Gunther, *Learned Hand: The Man and the Judge* (New York: Alfred A. Knopf, 1994), 172.

97. Rublee, "Reminiscences," 46-47.

98. GR to Peabody, 26 September 1905, GSA.

99. Dryfhout, "The Cornish Colony," 40-41, 52.

100. Ibid., 39-40.

101. GR to Rublee, 2 December 1905, GSA.

102. Rublee, "Reminiscences," 49.

103. Author's recollections of Crossways visit, May 1995 and June 1996, and various conversations with George and Ellie Rublee in Washington and New Hampshire.

104. With the exception of Burling, all of these men would be founders of Croly's *The New Republic.*

105. GR to Peabody, 16 September 1908, GSA.

106. Rublee, "Reminiscences," 46.

107. Ibid., 52.

108. Rublee's assertions regarding the economic soundness of long-haul/short-haul rate differentials are supported in Albro Martin's *Enterprise Denied: Origins of the Decline of American Railroads, 1897-1917* (New York: Columbia University Press, 1971).

109. George Rublee, "Government Rate-Making," *Collier's Weekly*, 6 January 1906, 21.

110. Ibid.

111. Ibid.

112. Ibid.

113. Ibid.

114. See Victor Morawetz, *The Banking and Currency Problem in the United States*, 2nd ed. (New York: North American Review Publishing Co., 1909).

115. V. Morawetz to Edward House, 5 January 1927, box 82, folder 2769, Yale-House. In the letter Moratwetz explains his role in the creation of the Federal Reserve system.

116. George Rublee, "A Handicap to Business," *Collier's*, October 1906, 17.

117. Ibid.

4

"Who Is George Rublee?" (1909–1911)

After years of lauding the importance of public work but not finding anything suitable or inspiring, in 1910 George Rublee suddenly found himself at the storm center of the insurgent revolt of progressive Republicans against conservatives in their own party. Although the conservatives staunchly opposed any government encroachment into the market economy or business place on behalf of the urban working poor, the progressives increasingly believed that the deplorable conditions of millions of predominantly immigrant workers pointed toward social revolution. While in all parts of the country reformers were working toward change on various levels, George Rublee joined a small cadre of progressive New England lawyers and journalists who sought to intervene near the top of the political system to reach an accommodation between an entrenched capitalist class and an increasingly radicalized working class. All friends of Rublee, the group included journalists Norman Hapgood, Herbert Croly, and John Bass and lawyers Louis Brandeis, Joseph Cotton, Robert Bass, Learned Hand, Raymond Stevens, and Arthur Hill. Looking to developments in Great Britain and Germany, they advocated a third way between unrestrained quasi-laissez-faire economic liberalism and socialism. Although they often did not all agree on the same solutions and although their victories would be rather incomplete, their efforts were successful in finding a tentative accommodation that preserved both domestic tranquility and a dynamic free market economy within government-regulated-boundaries.

Whereas the social reform and purification movement had failed to arouse George Rublee to political activism, unrestrained logging in New Hampshire and other policies that squandered the nation's natural resources seem to have first motivated him to action. Sometime in 1909 Rublee joined the National Conservation Society and acted as its delegate to the Civic Federation's meeting in Washington in January 1910. While in Washington, Rublee was invited to join a number of his friends who were meeting to plan their course of action in a high-profile congressional hearing. The friends were Norman Hapgood, Gifford

Pinchot, John Bass, and Louis Brandeis. The matter they were discussing became known as the Ballinger-Pinchot controversy, nationally famous for further splitting the Republican Party between stalwarts and progressives and personally important for Rublee for marking his entry into the political arena.[1]

Hapgood, Pinchot, Bass, and Brandeis were all involved in the investigation surrounding Louis Glavis, a mid-level civil servant in the Department of Interior who in 1909 accused Interior Secretary Richard Ballinger of illegally clearing claims that his former business associates, the Cunningham Group, had made for coalfields in the Alaskan public domain. After Glavis brought the matter to President Taft's attention, Taft issued a public letter in September 1909 stating that he had "examined the whole record most carefully" and, having found no impropriety on Ballinger's part, authorized Glavis' termination from the Bureau of Forestry for "filing a disingenuous statement, unjustly impeaching the official integrity of his superior officers."[2] The matter might have ended there except that John Bass, a former war correspondent for the *Chicago Daily News* and a friend of Rublee's from Harvard Law School, interviewed Glavis in the fall of 1909 and presented his side of the story in an article that Hapgood published in *Collier's*. Although Bass' article, which gained national attention, did not directly accuse Ballinger of corruption, it charged that the Cunningham Group's claims were illegal and should be blocked as Glavis had argued. Soon after the article's publication Gifford Pinchot, chief of the Forestry Service in the Department of Agriculture and an outspoken Roosevelt holdover, publicly supported Glavis, and Taft soon found it necessary to dismiss him. A highly publicized contest between Pinchot and Ballinger ensued, further widening the rift that had been growing among Republicans regarding the extent to which Taft had or had not been carrying on Theodore Roosevelt's progressive policies.[3]

Because Ballinger had cleared claims to lands Roosevelt had removed from the public domain, the issue took on elevated importance. As Rublee soon explained to Endicott Peabody, the main question was whether Ballinger, "while pretending to favor conservation [had] been covertly trying to carry out the old plan of giving away the national resources to capitalists who want to use them for their own pecuniary profit."[4] Taft's support of Ballinger was something of a last straw for progressive Republicans, who with Democrats called for a congressional hearing to examine Ballinger's role in clearing the Cunningham Group's claims.[5] Although Hapgood might have been content to let Glavis sink or swim at the congressional hearings, having learned that Ballinger planned to sue the magazine for libel pending the hearings' outcome, Hapgood persuaded magazine owner Robert Collier to hire Louis Brandeis to represent Glavis. The case would be one of several that established Brandeis as the "People's Attorney."[6]

Rublee became interested in the Ballinger-Pinchot affair early on in the controversy and soon became deeply involved in the case. Likely owing to Hapgood's invitation, he joined the chief conspirators at Pinchot's home in Washington for their first strategy meeting in January 1910. While George likely made little contribution in the beginning, that meeting invigorated him, and he soon returned to Washington to attend the hearings. When not in Washington, Rublee began to meet with Brandeis and Hapgood at the Harvard Club in New York on Sunday evenings to discuss the case during Brandeis' commute between Boston and Washington. As a result of these ongoing meetings, Brandeis and Rublee, who had been only somewhat acquainted earlier, became close friends, and Brandeis began to rely increasingly on Rublee for assistance on the case.[7] As one Brandeis biographer noted, "A self-effacing person, Rublee was perfectly attuned to the needs of [Louis D. Brandeis]...[and] soon became LDB's right-hand man in Washington."[8]

The case against Ballinger got off to a slow start, and newspapers in the first few months tended to report rather negatively against Glavis and Pinchot, whose assertions Brandeis was having a difficult time proving. In March Rublee admitted to Peabody that "Pinchot is not himself a very good witness, partly" because he had little "personal knowledge concerning the acts which are alleged" against Ballinger and "partly because he is enthusiastic and not very exact, so that his statements are not always consistent."[9] The break they were hoping for in the case occurred when Brandeis at last located a clerk in the Interior Department who testified that President Taft had never actually investigated Glavis' charges, as the president had publicly maintained. Rather, the only investigation of Glavis' charges had been carried out by Ballinger himself, who also drafted the letter that Taft signed in September claiming that he had "examined the whole record most carefully."[10]

Although Brandeis, Rublee, and other Glavis supporters believed that this testimony, in conjunction with other evidence, was starting to make a convincing case against Ballinger, newspapers did not immediately share their enthusiasm. Rublee later recalled that the "very influential" *New York Evening Post* "had been reporting and commenting on the Glavis side of the case rather unfavorably." Rublee had known *Evening Post* owner Oswald Garrison Villard since Harvard and arranged a meeting with him in an effort to win the paper over. As Rublee recalled, "I knew Oswald Villard who owned the paper rather well and went to see him about this time. I impressed him a good deal with what I told him and he directed the editor to talk with me. I went over the testimony with him for two or three days, point by point, and he became converted completely to our side. He came out with a very strong editorial and came down to Washington to attend the hearings personally."[11] The *Evening Post's* support, according to Rublee, "turned the tide of publicity" by influencing the *Springfield Republican* and other papers supportive of the Taft administration to come out against Ballinger. The result, Rublee recalled, "was that the newspapers were generally changed over to our point of view."

Because Ballinger was ultimately exonerated by the congressional committee but resigned under public pressure, it is clear that Rublee's most important contribution to the case was in gaining the support of newspapers. Rublee's other notable contribution was in preparing and writing Brandeis' brief of the case. While in March Rublee reported that "Mr. Brandeis has asked me to assist him in writing the brief against Ballinger," by the time it was completed in June it was mostly George's work.[12] Writing to Peabody, he complained, "I am very busy about the brief which must be finished on June 12th—and I've got to do it all—I mean the writing of it."[13] Although Rublee was in the habit of writing briefs, the one against Ballinger ended up posing quite a strain. As he reported to Peabody, "A great mass of evidence is in the case. The record is about 5000 pages long—and it is a difficult matter to present." While in 1908 Brandeis had introduced what became known as the "Brandeis brief" in *Muller* v *Oregon*, for some reason he chose to rely on Rublee to write the Glavis brief.[14] As Brandeis explained to his brother, "Rublee did most of the writing & I supplied most of the 'scareheads' which are at times novelesque."[15] The 200-page document did reflect Brandeis' approach in *Muller*, in that rather than relying predominantly on legal precedents in the traditional fashion, the brief emphasized force of argument and presented an abundance of economic and financial statistics to bolster circumstantial evidence.[16] In the brief, Rublee emphasized that the charge against Ballinger was not that of fraud but rather "conduct contrary to the public interest and wrongful policies which would lead to the waste of public domain by over development and private greed."[17] Evidently satisfied with the brief, Brandeis sent it to a number of leading progressives. Forwarding a copy to Felix Frankfurter, Brandeis observed: "I am sending you…a copy of our brief in the Ballinger Case. If you find it good the credit is mainly due to George Rublee."[18]

Although in the end the joint congressional committee voted to clear Ballinger of misconduct, Ballinger resigned under public protest and was replaced with Walter Fisher, a friend of Rublee's who was "a Progressive and a Conservationist." Rublee believed that the entire ordeal was worthwhile because under Fisher's leadership the Cunningham coal claims were canceled, Glavis "was vindicated," and there were "stronger conservation policies in the west."[19] Whatever the merits of the effort, his participation in the Ballinger-Pinchot controversy was an important first step for George Rublee into the public arena.

Energized by the Ballinger affair, Rublee moved directly into another progressive–reactionary fray brewing at home in New Hampshire. Shortly after he moved to the state in 1906, Rublee had joined in the unsuccessful effort of a group of reformers known as the Lincoln Republicans to elect Cornish novelist Winston Churchill as governor of New Hampshire.[20] Rublee participated locally in Churchill's campaign, which denounced the control that the Boston & Maine Railroad exercised over the Republican Party and politics generally in New Hampshire. The Lincoln Republicans called for the restoration of popular democracy through a number of electoral reforms along the lines of Robert La Follette's "Wisconsin Idea." Those reforms included a direct primary law, the initiative and referendum, restrictions on campaign finance and lobbying, the direct election of U.S. senators, and a public service commission to regulate railroad and utility rates. Although Churchill generated considerable support and seemed sure to gain the nomination at the state convention, railroad-backed conservatives who controlled the convention apparatus allegedly resorted to fraudulent methods to secure their nominee. Despite the fact that, when counted, the "ballots cast for the candidates outnumbered the accredited delegates," Churchill lost the nomination, and the Lincoln Republicans were forced to wait four more years for reform.[21] While the episode served to increase the Lincoln Republicans' animosity for their conservative brethren and the Boston & Maine Railroad, it also served as a lesson for Rublee, giving him some preparation for the 1912 Republican Convention, at which he would work on a similar controversy regarding fraudulent delegates.

Invigorated by the fight against Ballinger and stalwart Republicans in Washington in 1910, George returned home to New Hampshire, where the Lincoln Republicans had geared up for a second effort to elect one of their own as governor. Writing to Peabody in August, Rublee announced that he was taking part in helping to elect progressive Republican Robert Bass as governor. George thought it would be "a lively insurgent campaign" because "[t]he B.&M. railroad and the old machine are opposing." He confirmed that "[m]y sympathy is with the insurgents generally: their ideas about legislation may be somewhat emotional and crude—but fundamentally they are right. In a democracy public officials must be responsible to the people and act for the people."[22] Rublee knew Robert Bass through both John Bass, his older brother, and Joseph Cotton, the young finance lawyer whom George brought into Spooner's firm in New York in 1908. They all had gone to Harvard College and Harvard Law School and were all smitten with the progressive bug.

Robert Bass was a Lincoln Republican and was first elected to the New Hampshire legislature in 1904 at age thirty-one. In 1906 he implemented tighter conservation policies as state forestry commissioner, and in 1908 he ran successfully for the state Senate on a reform platform that led conservative Republicans to oppose his campaign. In the spring of 1910 as a state senator he championed and won support for the passage of a direct primary law to take the nominating process out of the hands of party bosses, making New Hampshire the first eastern state to adopt that system. Capitalizing on the new direct primary law that he had helped to create, Bass redeemed Churchill's 1906 loss by defeating the Boston & Maine nominee in the Republican primary by a two-to-one margin and went on to win the general election in November 1910. Bass' election attracted national media coverage because he was the only successful Republican candidate for governor east of the Mississippi River and had run without support from the Taft administration. Bass instead ran as a progressive Republican with an endorsement from Theodore Roosevelt, recently returned from Africa and greatly irritated with the policies of his hand-chosen successor to the White House. Bass' election was a victory for insurgents everywhere and increased their momentum. It also confirmed for Taft what the Ballinger–Pinchot fight had demonstrated earlier in the year—that the game was afoot and that he could expect a progressive Republican challenger in the 1912 campaign.[23]

Bass' election meant new work for his close friends, Joseph Cotton and George Rublee, who had advised Bass throughout his 1910 campaign. Cotton, only thirty-five, graduated first in his class at Harvard Law School in 1900 and joined the office of Cravath, Henderson, and De Gersdorff, where he became a partner in 1906, an uncharacteristically quick advancement. Although engaged in the reorganization of railroads and the formation of public utilities and industrial corporations, Cotton managed to find time to edit and publish *The Constitutional Decisions of John Marshall* in 1906, a work reprinted into the 1960s. Having achieved much success during his first six years, Cotton resigned his newly earned partnership in 1907 with the idea of working independently but soon joined Rublee and Spooner, whose firm offered perfect freedom to pursue outside interests. In 1910 reform governor Charles Evans Hughes asked Cotton to work with New York's workers' compensation commission, the Wainwright Commission, in a pioneering attempt to establish a state-run disability insurance program similar to those created in Germany and Great Britain.[24]

During his successful 1910 campaign Robert Bass called for the adoption of an ambitious reform program that included a workers' compensation program, campaign finance reform prohibiting corporate contributions and requiring public disclosure of campaign expenditures, a public service commission to regulate and determine the reasonableness of utilities and railroad rates, child labor laws, and a permanent tax commission to fund these new programs and to equalize the tax burden in the state between individuals and hitherto under taxed corporations.[25] Between progressive Republicans and progressive Democrats, Bass had strong support in the General Court, the lower house of the New Hampshire legislature. With record-breaking speed, the General Court passed bills embodying the majority of Bass' campaign platform by early February 1911 and sent them up to the Senate, where they awaited action.[26]

While the General Court was busy passing bills, however, the Bass administration was moving into a showdown with the Boston & Maine railroad that threatened the success of Bass' reform package. Whereas the General Court was made up of several hundred members who represented every little town and village in New Hampshire, the Senate was made up of twenty-four men, fifteen of whom were identified with the railroad.[27] In addition to being generally hostile to Bass' progressive program, the Boston & Maine Railroad was determined to use its leverage in the Senate to get a legislative accommodation that it greatly needed—namely, the repeal of a twenty-year-old law that threatened the railroad's financial security. In 1889 the New Hampshire legislature had allowed the Boston & Maine Railroad (B&M) to consolidate various independent railroads within the state under the stipulation that the rates never be increased from those set in 1889. Although the railroad had lowered some commodity rates for large shippers since 1889, passenger rates and those for other commercial classes had risen considerably beginning in 1903. Since 1906 Democrats and progressive Republicans had been calling for the state to prosecute the B&M under the 1889 statue but had made no headway with conservative Republican governors, who were willing to accept the B&M's assertion that the railroad could not be operated without the rate hikes. Shortly after his inauguration, Bass called upon the legislature to create a special committee to examine the B&M's rate structure and to make a recommendation concerning the 1889 statute. To demonstrate his administration's commitment to reaching a decision in the public interest, Bass asked Louis Brandeis to act as counsel for the investigative committee. Brandeis, who was already prosecuting the B&M's sister railroad before the Interstate Commerce Commission at hearings in Boston, was pleased to have the opportunity to apply added pressure to Charles Sanger Mellen, president of the B&M and New Haven Railroad.[28]

Infuriated with the Bass administration and Brandeis, who was grilling his attorneys and managers in public hearings before the special committee, Mellen instructed his lieutenants in the New Hampshire Senate not to act on any of Bass' reform legislation until a bill was sent up from the General Court, which rescinded the 1889 statute. Because the New Hampshire Constitution allowed the legislature to sit for only three to five months every other year, time was running out on Bass to live up to his campaign promises. With his bills making no progress in the railroad-dominated Senate, toward the end of February Bass threatened to immediately begin prosecution of the B&M under the 1889 statue. In response, Mellen warned at a closed meeting of the special investigating committee that he would raise any rates that had been lowered in the past twenty years and that he would "draw a line around the State of New Hampshire and make no improvements there, [so] that the people would overthrow the existing administration" in the next election.[29]

While Rublee and Cotton had advised Bass on a number of issues and had authored the bill to create a workers' compensation program that was languishing in the Senate, they were both uncomfortable with what they perceived to be a "declaration of war on both sides."[30] Although they appreciated Bass' need to pressure Mellen, they were alarmed by his threat to enforce the 1889 rates, which was sure to provoke a strong response from Mellen. Writing together from their offices in New York at the end of February, Rublee and Cotton cautioned Bass about his approach. Leading off, Cotton warned: "If practically all the rates—even all the local rates—in New Hampshire are changed by lowering some and raising others, there will be an economic situation which for a few months during readjustment would be pretty nearly chaos, because no business man in New Hampshire could tell what his freight expenses were going to be."[31] Cotton was afraid that Mellen was "just about crazy enough...to do what he can to block legislation, stop plans for improvement in New Hampshire and curtail service." Cotton disagreed with Brandeis' view that Mellen was bluffing and that he would not "run amuck," because Cotton believed that "Mellen is under a great deal of pressure from Wall Street and Washington to break your legislation and 'teach the people in New Hampshire a lesson.'"[32] Agreeing with Cotton, Rublee suggested that Bass abandon the restoration of the 1889 rates and instead attempt to convince Mellen to allow the proposed new Public Service Commission to "investigate the whole rate situation and to make a report upon which the Legislature can decide whether...rates should be maintained or should be modified." Rublee believed that this approach "would be better for the State and for you than to have all your legislation fail and [risk throwing] the business of the state into the confusion" of unstable rates.[33] Rublee's support for a regulatory commission suggests that, in the five years since his 1906 article in *Collier's* regarding the Hepburn Act, his confidence in independent commissions had increased.

With the Bass administration and Mellen's men in no mood for compromise, Rublee decided to travel to Concord, where he might help break the logjam. Apparently, Cotton was more engaged in their legal practice, and Rublee seems to have been yearning, as usual, for more meaningful work. Juliet Rublee, writing to Learned Hand in the fall of 1910, had reported: "I think [George] is exceedingly blue about his work—and that delving away in law-books day after day, digging out material for other people to use, is boring him almost more than he can bear."[34] She pointed out, "For him to do really good work he has got to be interested. That both these things are possible was proved last year in the Ballinger case." Juliet thought that what he most needed was "a rather short and interesting case...where he would have all the responsibility and any blame or praise that might be attached to it."[35] Although such work would not come his way anytime soon, it nevertheless seems that George was most useful when he acted as counselor to men who wielded public authority, to inspire them and help them find solutions to daunting problems. The trouble that the Bass administration was having with the B&M was just the sort of situation in which Rublee could make a contribution. Being both a progressive and a finance lawyer with years of experience with railroads and an increasing interest in economic questions, Rublee spoke the language of both parties in New Hampshire and believed that he could accomplish something. While he could not then know it, in placing his foot on the train for Concord in early March 1911, Rublee began what would prove to be nearly a thirty-year career of breaking deadlocks and advising men of influence, himself almost always in the shadowy background.

Evidently, Rublee already had the basis of a solution in mind when he left New York. Shortly after arriving in Concord, he met with Bass, Brandeis, and the special legislative committee and suggested a solution that he thought was both fair to the railroad and in the public interest. He proposed that the B&M be authorized to collect its existing unauthorized rates for the next two years, in exchange for which the railroad would authorize its senators to pass the bill creating a public service commission. The new commission would be staffed with five experts in economics, three to be nominated by the railroad-controlled Governor's Council, who would over the course of the next two years thoroughly investigate the matter to determine on an economic basis whether or not it was in the interest of the state to allow the railroad to continue collecting the unauthorized rates. As part of the bargain, Rublee stipulated that if the commission found that the rates should be reduced, the B&M would have to refund the excessive rates charged to shippers over the course of the two-year investigation. Further, as part of the general agreement, the railroad could not raise any rates, regardless of whether they were beneath the legal maximum, until the investigation was completed. In this way the railroad would have a chance to convince a panel of experts that the rate hikes were justified and the state would escape dislocations in the economy and obtain its public service commission.[36]

Bass, Brandeis, and the five-member special legislative committee all agreed that Rublee's recommendation was reasonable, and the committee voted unanimously to report a bill to the legislature that embodied Rublee's proposal. One progressive Democratic member of the committee, Raymond B. Stevens, was at first skeptical of Rublee's allegiance. As he later reported, "I had seen very much of railroad influence: I had seen it work underground in so many ways that I was suspicious of Mr. Rublee when he appeared." Being wary, Stevens, who would become a lifelong friend and would figure prominently in some of Rublee's greatest public acts, "made a special investigation" on his own of Rublee, which he found "allayed all suspicion and gave me a feeling of a great deal of confidence in the man."[37]

Apparently at Rublee's suggestion, it was determined that Bass should send a special message to the legislature to accompany the bill coming out of the investigative rates committee. Owing to his being the author of the compromise, it was determined that Rublee was the one to write the special message. Reporting to Endicott Peabody on his year's work a little later, Rublee wrote: "I am sending a copy of Gov. Bass' special message to the Legislature. I wrote this message, but this is a fact which of course is not to be divulged."[38] He intended the message, delivered on 9 March to place "responsibility for failure to act where it belonged"—on the B&M and its supporters in the Senate.[39]

Rublee began Bass' message by chastising the Senate for its one piece of action thus far, that being its rejection of the bill sent up from the General Court that provided for the ratification of the Sixteenth Amendment to the U.S. Constitution, authorizing a federal income tax. Rublee asserted that the Senate had defied the will of the people because "[b]oth the Republican and Democratic platforms in the late campaign clearly directed the legislature to ratify the income tax amendment." Preparing the ground for support of the progressive legislation awaiting action in the Senate, Rublee continued:

> Such action not only alarms the citizens of the state who have confidently expected the general court to enact the laws so emphatically and unmistakably demanded by the people, but it shakes the faith of the believers in representative government. The legislative action of the general court at this session involves more than the good faith of individual members. The merits of representative government in New Hampshire are on trial. When the will of the people is plainly manifested, if their legislative agents do not frame and enact fit laws to carry it into effect, representative government fails.[40]

Rublee warned that the "people of New Hampshire want the platform pledges redeemed" and cautioned that if the legislature fails to "execute their will, the people will feel a just indignation and resentment, of which the consequences cannot be foreseen." Rublee then proceeded to list the status of the bills that made up the 1910 campaign pledges, most of which were in danger of dying stillborn in the Senate.[41]

Rublee next turned to the battle over railroad rates. Although it was his least favorable outcome, he began by reiterating Bass' warning that if the legislature takes "no action it will be the plain and immediate duty of the attorney general to enforce the present legal rates." Rublee explained, however, that it had become clear that the special committee would not be able to reach a definitive finding on the question of rates before the end of the session because the railroad was dragging its feet and had not yet even "been able to state, upon the basis of the present volume of traffic, how much revenue it would lose if the unlawful rates were reduced to the legal limit." Nevertheless, Rublee asserted that "it does not follow that the public interest would be prompted by the immediate enforcement of these limitations without further investigation to ascertain the effect of such action upon the people's trade and commerce." Expressing a real commitment to ideas of efficiency and fairness, Rublee pointed out, "The people ought to have the best railroad service at the lowest cost, but the best service cannot be provided unless the rates allowed are sufficient, under efficient management, to pay a reasonable return upon the capital required for necessary improvement."[42] Admitting that the difficulty was that "nobody knows what an orderly examination of the remaining rates might disclose," Rublee turned to the proposed public service commission as a solution. Writing for Bass, he explained: "My suggestion, based on the advice of members of the committee and its counsel, is that, under proper safeguards, the present rates be continued for two years, that during this time the public service commission be instructed to investigate the illegal rates and make a report thereon before the next meeting of the general court."[43] Going on to explain the various stipulations built into the compromise, Rublee then concluded: "Such a plan in my judgement promises a just and satisfactory solution of this difficult problem. It preserves the present status until the general court can act advisedly. It protects the public and is absolutely fair to the railroad company. But, of course such a solution is impossible until a public service commission is enacted."[44] The Senate would therefore have to approve the bill creating the public service commission to implement the compromise.

As intended, Rublee's message created "a great rumpus" in the Senate.[45] The *Manchester Union* announced that "[i]t came unsuspected and unheralded" and reported that "it was not relished by a majority of the senators, as was doubtless expected."[46] Nevertheless, Rublee, Bass, and the progressive Republicans and Democrats were certain that Mellen would instruct his men in the Senate to accept the compromise. Joe Cotton, writing to Bass on 17 March, likewise expected that the railroad would accept the compromise, and he believed that the "surrender will have a very serious effect on the reactionaries in the Senate. It will have the same sort of effect as when a regiment goes over to the enemy just before a fight." Cotton was relieved that the "rate situation had been satisfactorily adjusted" because, as he admitted, "I do not believe you realize how bad the physical results to shippers would have been if you had not adjusted it."[47] The celebrations of victory, however, were premature. Rather than accepting the compromise, Mellen remained ambiguous until just before the close of the legislative session, when he at last made it clear that he would opt for a protracted court battle against the Bass administration, during which time he hoped a more accommodating administration would be elected.[48] Mellen's rebuff came as quite a shock to Bass and his supporters. It was late in the legislative session, and Bass had few options left. As the governor later recalled, the only hope he had to get his legislation passed was by "again taking the field and making speeches in the constituencies of all these senators...to see if [the people] would bring pressure to bear on their senators."[49]

Perhaps fearful that Bass would have to follow through with his threat to prosecute the B&M or perhaps because he felt responsible for the advice he had given, Rublee returned immediately to Concord in hope of finding some solution to the impasse. Rublee tracked down Edgar Rich, Mellen's chief counsel in Concord, and lambasted the railroad for refusing the generous compromise. Rublee told Rich that the decision to do battle "was a very a foolish thing for the railroad to do" because it would increase the public's hatred for the railroad and there was no telling what policies they might next advocate. Rich admitted that the bill "was fair to the railroad and ought to be accepted" but complained that "Mr. Mellen had made up his mind and [that] nobody could shake him." Rublee was willing to give it a try and proposed that if Rich would arrange a meeting, he would like to have the opportunity "to go and see [Mellen] and to try to convince him that he was making a mistake."[50] As it happened, the next day Mellen was scheduled to travel from Boston to Portland, Maine, to attend a meeting of his board of directors, and Rich thought that he might be able to arrange a meeting while Mellen was en route. Rublee next had to gain Bass' authorization for the unorthodox meeting. Although Bass was "very doubtful" that anything could be accomplished, he agreed to the meeting "as a last resort" before he began a swing around the state and before he began proceedings against the B&M.[51]

What became known as the "famous trip" occurred on 5 April when Rublee traveled to Portsmouth and joined Mellen in his private car traveling from Boston to Portland.[52] Several of Mellen's directors were traveling in the car as well, so the two went alone to a small room. Once situated, Mellen demanded "what it was that [George] had to say." Perceiving that Mellen likely expected that he had been sent to make some sort of bargain, Rublee explained from the outset that he "had no authority to make a deal" and that in the end the bill before the Senate on railroad rates would have to be accepted as it was, "without material change." Mellen argued that the bill was "not fair to the railroad," especially "the obligation imposed on the railroad to pay back this excess above rates subsequently found to be reasonable." Countering, Rublee "endeavored to show him that he had been wrongly advised about the temper of the people of the State." Rublee warned, "The responsibility for blocking the legislation which the people wanted would certainly be fixed upon the railroad, and the popular feeling against the railroad would be stronger than ever before." Rublee next brought up Mellen's testimony from the closed hearings before the rates committee and questioned him about his threats to injure New Hampshire's commerce to effect a change of administration. Rublee read some of his statements back to him and then asked, "How would this sound if you go before an investigation? What is this leading to?" Having conjured up the image of a dreadful public scourging at the hands of Louis Brandeis, Rublee next "flattered him and said, 'You're a man who can settle this thing. You have the absolute power to settle this thing. These [senators] will do what you tell them to do.'"[53]

When the train arrived in Portland, Mellen asked Rublee to wait while he attended his board meeting and suggested that the two would continue their conversation on the return trip to Boston. Evidently, Mellen wanted to determine how his directors would react to the idea of accepting the Bass administration's 9 March compromise. Upon his return, Mellen announced his acceptance of the compromise but asked that two adjustments be made to reduce the railroad's legal exposure. Rublee recalled that "they were unessential and merely face-saving" gestures and suggested that Bass and the progressives in the legislature would likely concede the points. Mellen then dictated a letter addressed to an "astonished" Rublee, saying that he gave up his opposition to the compromise bill pending in the Senate providing that the conditions for shippers' rights were changed. As he capitulated on the matter, Mellen cautioned, "[Y]ou people are having your way now, but it won't be forever. Money will tell in the end." Despite such barbs Rublee found Mellen "very agreeable and [continued] on to Boston with him." In Boston Mellen was met by one of his chief attorneys who had been active in Concord and who recognized Rublee. The man, as Rublee recalled, "looked at me in astonishment and said he really didn't understand how this could have happened."[54]

When Rublee returned to Concord that night he sought out Bass to report his success but found that the governor was away from the capital. While he waited, Rublee entered the hearing chambers, where "they were going at it hammer and tongs," and listened to Mellen's attorneys—who had no idea about the settlement—complain "that the bill as passed by the house was so drastic that the railroad could not live under it." The next day the attorneys, when they learned of the letter, "withdrew their objections and the senate [soon] passed the rate bill and all those other measures." As Cotton had surmised, with the railroad backing out, the old guard lost its nerve and collapsed, thereby giving Bass and progressives everywhere an invigorating victory.[55]

The Senate's sudden reversal caused a considerable stir among New Hampshire newspapers and for several days there was confusion as to how the issue had been settled. On 7 April, the *Manchester Union*'s headline read: "Something Must Have Happened: Rates Question Now Good as Settled."[56] The story of Mellen's letter soon began to circulate, and on 8 April the same paper's headline asked: "Who Got Letter from Railroad? Mystery as to Missive from Mr. Mellen."[57] Three days later, after the letter addressed to Rublee was released, the *Union*'s banner headline demanded: "Who Is George Rublee?"[58] As a paper aligned with conservative Republicans, the seemingly dumbfounded editors sought to cast doubt on Rublee's efforts: "The question that the people of New Hampshire want answered is this: By whose instigation does a stranger—an outsider—go to the president of the Boston and Maine railroad, talk over in a familiar and easy manner the great questions before the legislature, get a letter of a most important character, and presto—the next day something happens in the legislature that is a tremendous surprise to many people."[59] The *Union*'s assertions, however, were part of a hasty rearguard defense, as Rublee explained to Peabody: "The Manchester Union is hostile to Governor Bass' administration. They knew perfectly well who I was but hoped to make trouble because I was not known generally to New Hampshire people. By intimating that some kind of a deal had been made they hoped they might prevent action by the Legislature. They failed."[60] While the editors may have known who Rublee was, they were not the only ones skeptical of his activities. A number of progressive Democrats and Republicans were confused by the sudden conservative collapse and wanted an explanation for Rublee's clandestine meeting with Mellen. To allay the growing skepticism, Rublee and Raymond Stevens, now the leading Democrat in the General Court, traveled to Boston to meet with Brandeis to ascertain his opinion of the settlement. Brandeis, although likewise at first wary, found nothing untoward in the plan and approved it. Shortly after the meeting with Brandeis, the whole matter was resolved when the New Hampshire Senate passed all the pending bills in a single day.[61]

Rublee's remarkable intervention in New Hampshire and his intimate role in shaping the progressive message distinguished him among New England's leading progressives. The experience also sparked something deep inside him, rekindling a flame first fashioned and fanned by Horace Rublee and Endicott Peabody. George Rublee was suddenly acting out the role that for him had long represented the highest and most rewarding good. In making a contribution—as Horace Rublee once wrote—that seeks to "aid in determining and achieving what is really for the true welfare of the State," Rublee achieved a satisfying accomplishment that could stand the test of time. He was enthralled by his work in New Hampshire, and he wanted more of it. As Dean Acheson would later observe: "Now began, as in a symphony, the movement first indistinct and faltering, then repeated with growing clarity and insistence, which was to dominate George Rublee's life."[62]

NOTES

1. GR to Peabody, 15 January 1910, GSA; and Rublee, "Reminiscences," 56-57, 60.
2. Quoted in Lewis Paper, *Brandeis* (Englewood Cliffs, NJ: Prentice-Hall, 1983), 113.
3. Rublee, "Reminiscences," 57-59.
4. GR to Peabody, 3 March 1910, GSA; and Rublee, "Reminiscences," 63-64.
5. Rublee, "Reminiscences," 58-60; for a thorough discussion of the Ballinger-Pinchot controversy see George Mowry, *The Era of Theodore Roosevelt* (New York: Harper and Row, 1958), 250-259.
6. Paper, *Brandeis*,113-114; Rublee, "Reminiscences," 54-58; and Melvin Urofsky, "Brandeis, Louis D." in *The Readers Companion to American History*, Eric Foner and John A. Garraty, editors (Boston: Houghton Mifflin Company, 1991), 129.
7. Rublee, "Reminiscences," 60, 62; and GR to Peabody, 15 January 1910, GSA.
8. Melvin Urofsky and David W. Levy, *Letters of Louis D. Brandeis* (Albany: State University of New York Press, 1972), vol. 2, 323, note 5.
9. GR to Peabody, 3 March 1910, GSA.
10. Rublee, "Reminiscences," 63-64.
11. Ibid., 64.
12. GR to Peabody, 16 March 1910, GSA.
13. GR to Peabody, 24 May 1910, GSA.
14. Urofsky, "Brandeis, Louis D.," 129.

15. Louis Brandeis to Alfred Brandeis, 11 June 1910, Urofsky and Levy, *Letters of Louis D. Brandeis*, vol. 2, 344.

16. On Hearings Before the Joint Committee of Congress, Investigation of the Department of the Interior and of the Bureau of Forestry, Brief on Behalf of L.R. Glavis, signed Louis D. Brandeis, George Rublee, and Joseph P. Cotton, June 13, 1910, GRP.

17. Rublee, "Reminiscences," 61.

18. Melvin Urofsky and David W. Levy, editors , *"Half Brother, Half Son:" The Letters of Louis D. Brandeis to Felix Frankfurter*,(Norman: University of Oklahoma Press, 1991), 17.

19. Ibid., 65-66.

20. For Rublee's role in Churchill's 1906 campaign, see Winston Churchill to Edmund S. Cook, 18 April 1911, Robert P. Bass Papers, Baker Library Special Collections, Dartmouth College, Hannover, New Hampshire [hereafter RBP], box 31-5.

21. Jewel Bellush, "Reform in New Hampshire: Robert Bass Wins the Primary," *The New England Quarterly,* vol. 35 (December 1962), 469-472. See also Rublee, "Reminiscences," 69.

22. GR to Peabody, 5 August 1910, GSA.

23. Marc McClure, "Robert Perkins Bass," *American National Biography* (Cary, NC: Oxford University Press, 1998), vol. 2, 315-316; and George Mowry, *Theodore Roosevelt and the Progressive Movement* (Madison: University of Wisconsin Press, 1947), 129.

24. McClure, "Joseph Potter Cotton," *American National Biography* (Cary, NC: Oxford University Press, 1998), vol. 5, 567-569; and Daniel Rodgers, *Atlantic Crossings*, 248-250.

25. "Statement of Hon. Robert P. Bass, Republican Candidate for Governor at the Primaries, September 6, 1910," box 31-4:C, RBP; and Bellush, "Reform in New Hampshire," 483-484.

26. *Manchester Union,* 19 January 1911 and 25 January 1911 (microfilm), Library of Congress.

27. Testimony of Raymond Stevens, *Hearings Before a Subcommittee of the Committee on Interstate Commerce, United States Senate, Relating to the Fitness of the Members of the Federal Trade Commission, February 25 and 26, 1915* [hereafter *Hearings I*] (Washington: Government Printing Office, 1915), 18.

28. Rublee testimony, *Hearings I*, 29-30; Stevens testimony, *Hearings I*, 18; and Robert Bass testimony, *Hearings before a Subcommittee of the Committee on Interstate Commerce, United States Senate, Relating to the Fitness of the Members of the Federal Trade Commission, Part II, March 3, 1915* [hereafter *Hearings II*] (Washington: Government Printing Office, 1915), 59-60.

29. Rublee testimony, *Hearings I*, 29-30; Rublee, "Reminiscences," 70, 72; and Robert Perkins Bass testimony, *Hearings II*, 60-61.

30. Henry Hollis testimony, *Hearings I*, 14; and Rublee testimony, *Hearings I*, 30.

31. Joseph Cotton and GR to R. Bass, 27 February 1911, RBP, box 31-5.

32. Ibid.

33. Ibid.

34. Juliet Barrett Rublee [hereafter JBR] to Hand, 19 October 1910, HLS-Hand, box 107, folder 8.

35. Ibid.

36. Rublee testimony, *Hearings I*, 29-30.

37. Stevens testimony, *Hearings I*, 23.

38. GR to Peabody, 5 September 1911, GSA.
39. Rublee, "Reminiscences," 72.
40. *Manchester Union*, 10 March 1911 (microfilm).
41. Ibid.
42. Ibid.
43. Ibid.
44. Ibid.
45. Rublee, "Reminiscences," 71.
46. *Manchester Union*, 10 March 1911.
47. Cotton to R. Bass, 17 March 1911, RBP, box 31-5.
48. Rublee testimony, *Hearings I*, 30.
49. Bass testimony, *Hearings II*, 60.
50. Rublee testimony, *Hearings I*, 30-31.
51. Rublee testimony, *Hearings I*, 31; and Bass testimony, *Hearings II*, 61.
52. Hollis testimony, *Hearings I*, 14; and Rublee, "Reminiscences," 73.
53. Rublee testimony, *Hearings I*, 31; and Rublee, "Reminiscences," 73-74.
54. Rublee testimony, *Hearings I*, 31; and Rublee, "Reminiscences," 75-76.
55. Ibid.
56. *Manchester Union*, 7 April 1911.
57. Ibid., 8 April 1911.
58. Ibid., 11 April 1911.
59. Ibid.
60. GR to Peabody, 5 September 1911, GSA.
61. Rublee, "Reminiscences," 78.
62. Acheson, "George Rublee," *Groton School Quarterly* (Summer 1957), 3.

Horace Rublee

Katherine Hopkins Rublee

George Rublee in Geneva

George Rublee in 1879

1884, first year at Groton (Rublee second from right). Annotation: "Thanksgiving Day. Only boys who had no place to go."

1886, last year at Groton (Rublee in center, Peabody behind him to the left)

Second year at Harvard Law School, 1893-1894 (George Rublee third from left kneeling)

George Rublee, ca. 1898

Juliet Barrett, ca. 1898

"Crossways," Cornish, New Hampshire

Juliet Barrett Rublee, ca. 1910

George Rublee and Edward Burling

Left: George Rublee, 1913

Below: "Senatorial Courtesy"
Newark *Evening News*, 19 May 1916

At the March 1919 Spa Conference handling turnover of German merchant marine (Rublee fourth from left)

Norwegian arbitration, 1922 (Dean Acheson fourth from left, Edward Burling, fifth from left)

Likely on President Calles's December 1927 excursion (George Rublee seated second from right)

With Dwight and Bettie Morrow, likely on political campaign

George Rublee on train, possibly in Mexico

George Rublee, likely late 1930's

Returning to America on the Queen Mary, 1939

George Rublee, ca. 1940

5

"Garibaldi's Expedition" (1912)

George Rublee's work as an adviser to the Bass administration was stimulating and contributed to his interest in the growing progressive Republican insurgency. Although he continued his legal practice in New York, Rublee remained an active participant in the progressives' political struggles in New Hampshire. Throughout 1911 he continued to assist the Bass administration on problems related to the railroad settlement. As Bass confirmed in August 1911, Rublee was an important asset: "You certainly do get results and get them quick. I don't see how you do it."[1] However, as 1911 wore on without a healing of the schism within the Republican Party, the focus of Bass, Rublee, and other progressives began to shift to the national stage and the internecine contest that was certain to ensue in the coming campaign year. As that contest unfolded, Rublee would find opportunity, well beyond anything he might have expected, to give expression to his growing interest in making some public contribution.

Unlike other New England progressives who were reluctant to see Robert La Follette and western progressives lead the insurgency, Rublee had an attachment to La Follette, who had been a friend of Horace Rublee, and contemplated joining Louis Brandeis in support of the Wisconsin senator in the 1912 presidential race. Nevertheless, with Bass and a number of progressive friends, especially Herbert Croly and Learned Hand, encouraging Theodore Roosevelt to seek the nomination, Rublee found himself gravitating with his Cornish neighbors toward Roosevelt. TR's advocacy, however, of the recall of state judges whose conservative decisions tended to thwart the will of the people was a position that Rublee could not support and that prevented him and other moderate easterners from fully backing the former president.[2] Roosevelt began his attack on the conservative courts in May 1911, after the New York Supreme Court found New York's workers' compensation system unconstitutional in *Ives v South Buffalo Railway Company.* When a few weeks later the Arizona constitutional convention passed a provision allowing for the recall of elected state judges, Roosevelt praised the action and claimed that decisions such as *Ives* "would, in the end, render it necessary for the American people, at whatever cost, to insist upon having direct control over the courts." Although Rublee and many of his New England progressive friends—especially Joe Cotton, whose work the *Ives* decision overturned—were likewise angered by the conservative courts, they found judicial recall an appalling, constitution-threatening idea. Nevertheless, western progressives who championed direct democracy, and whom Roosevelt seemed to be courting were attracted to the idea.[3]

Rublee was not the only Cornish colonist who wanted to see Roosevelt alter his recall advocacy. Shortly after Roosevelt's initial attack on the *Ives* decision in May 1911, Learned Hand began a personal campaign to adjust Roosevelt's stand on the issue. Although Hand could not completely convert Roosevelt, toward the end of the year TR began to advocate a recall of judicial decisions rather than the actual judges. In a speech delivered at Carnegie Hall in October 1911 entitled "Conservation of Womanhood and Childhood," Roosevelt proposed, "The people should be enabled with reasonable speed and in effective fashion to determine by popular vote whether or not they will permit the judges' interpretation of the Constitution to stand."[4] Rather than assuaging his would-be New England supporters, Roosevelt's newest proposition, that of recalling the decisions rather than the judges, provoked a new round of criticism in the East. Responding in a letter to Roosevelt's speech, Hand allowed that although he agreed in principle with legislation limiting the number of hours women and children could work, he complained, "I cannot quite swallow the necessity of having public pressure put on a judge for any purpose, for it utterly perverts the assumption which is fundamental in his function."[5] To another, Hand privately described Roosevelt's proposal as "a stupid make-shift" idea.[6] Rublee, too, was frustrated with Roosevelt's speech because he had come to believe that Roosevelt was the only progressive capable of wrenching the Republican nomination from Taft. When on 22 February at the Ohio Constitutional Convention in Columbus Roosevelt again irritated eastern Republicans when he "spoke out plainly and courageously for the recall of state judicial decisions," Rublee began wrestling with the recall issue in hope of finding some way to make it less threatening.[7]

On 24 February, two days after the Columbus speech, Roosevelt replied to an open letter from six progressive Republican governors in which he was encouraged to seek the presidential nomination. In his nationally publicized reply, Roosevelt confirmed that he would "accept the nomination for President if it is tendered to me," thereby sounding the first official blast of his Bull Moose campaign. Two days later Roosevelt was scheduled to make a progressive policy speech before the Massachusetts legislature, which Robert Bass, the only New England governor to sign the letter inviting Roosevelt to run, planned to attend.[8] Evidently, in the two days following Roosevelt's Columbus speech, Rublee at last struck upon a way of rendering Roosevelt's judicial recall scheme less objectionable. Apparently feeling rather inspired, Rublee called Bass, who shared misgivings about Roosevelt's recall scheme, and explained his idea for improving upon what Judge Hand had begun. Bass thought Rublee's approach sound and agreed to arrange a short meeting with Roosevelt before his speech to the Massachusetts legislature, at which Rublee might explain his legal reasoning.[9]

Rublee's plan for rendering judicial recall a legally acceptable political device centered on Justice Oliver Wendell Holmes' then recent dissenting opinion in the Oklahoma bank case. In it Holmes had reasoned, "Police Power authorized the prevention of whatever is condemned by the prevailing morality."[10] Although Hand, according to his 20 November letter to Roosevelt, found Holmes' opinion in the case troubling, Rublee believed that Holmes had opened up an acceptable way to defend progressive legislation from conservative state judiciaries.[11] Rublee reasoned that if the majority of the people of New York determined that women should not work more than nine or ten hours a day, it could be made illegal on the basis of police power. Rublee believed that "[w]e could argue that a good way of determining morality is by a vote of the people."[12] If based on the notion of police power, judicial recall would be a legitimate device that, like the initiative and referendum, could be employed to promote and protect popular progressive legislation.

On the morning of 26 February Rublee and Bass traveled to Boston, where they were met at the train station by Arthur D. Hill, a prominent progressive Boston lawyer and a friend of both Rublee and Roosevelt. Rublee, who had asked Hill to attend the meeting, requested that he bring a copy of the Supreme Court reports that contained Holmes' opinion in the Oklahoma bank case. Although it is likely that Rublee had some contact with Roosevelt in recent years through his work with Bass, Rublee could have still been smarting from his embarrassing 1906 White House interview with Roosevelt and may have invited Hill to bolster his credibility.[13]

Rublee's audience with Roosevelt occurred at Judge Robert Grant's home, where Roosevelt attended a reception of notable Bostonians before he addressed the legislature. When Rublee, Bass, and Hill arrived, they found that Roosevelt was still engaged with guests and were required to wait until it was nearly time for Roosevelt to depart for the capitol before they could visit with him. When Roosevelt finally approached them, Rublee explained that they wished to "to talk to him about the recall of judicial decisions." Roosevelt agreed to listen, and, as Rublee recalled, they "all went into another room where [Roosevelt] took a pencil and a piece of paper and looked ready to use them." To Rublee's surprise Roosevelt "said gaily, 'Now, gentlemen, I'm ready to learn what I really think.'" While TR "took notes," Rublee quickly "outlined our idea and explained the Constitution and the legal parts of the matter, the theory which I had got out of Holmes' decision." Rublee recalled, "It was almost time to address the legislature but [Roosevelt] kept taking notes." As Roosevelt got up to leave, Rublee handed him a piece of paper containing a Guiseppe Mazzini quote and said, "You might find this useful in your speech." Roosevelt quickly scanned the quote and took it with him.[14]

Rublee, Bass, and Hill then "beat it down to the State house" and managed to find a place to stand in the back of the hall during Roosevelt's speech. To

Rublee's delight, Roosevelt worked the Mazzini quotation in early. The quotation was from one of George M. Trevelyan's books that Rublee had in Cornish and was one that he believed was "appropriate for the Progressive party and for what we and Roosevelt were fighting for."[15] Utilizing the passage, Roosevelt observed:

We of to-day, if we are worthy of endeavoring to lead the people aright, must be doing our part to secure social and industrial justice through genuine popular rule, and our object was set forth by the great Italian radical leader Mazzini, when he wrote: "No war of classes, no hostility to existing wealth, no wanton or unjust violation of the rights of property, but a constant disposition to ameliorate the condition of the classes least favored by fortune."[16]

This was to Rublee what it meant to be progressive, and apparently it meant that to Roosevelt as well. They wanted to see the plight of the working class and urban poor alleviated but wished to distinguish themselves from socialists and radicals who believed that revolutionary conflict and class warfare were the only paths left to them.

To Rublee's satisfaction, after his introduction, Roosevelt's entire speech focused on the judicial recall issue, and Rublee was pleased that the former president managed to present his police power theory rather well. As Rublee recalled, Roosevelt "had the whole thing very clearly in mind and got it all off."[17] Likely to the relief of most of New England, early in his speech Roosevelt announced: "I am not advocating the recall of Judges; I am advocating a measure which, if adopted, will prevent the necessity of the recall of Judges."[18] Nevertheless, Roosevelt's complaint was obviously with state judges, who he believed "underhandedly endeavor so to frame the Constitution and the laws that [they] trick [the people] out of their right of self-government." Rejecting the argument that he was attempting to "substitute the gusty passion of a mob for the decision of a court," Roosevelt stipulated that his "proposal applies only to the legislative acts which the courts declare unconstitutional" and that he was simply proposing a new political device that would ensure that the people were the state's sovereign rather than the courts and their judges. Roosevelt believed that if the people were indeed sovereign, then their will should not be frustrated by conservative courts that reflect only the narrow interests of a reactionary minority. He argued that "if the court has decided that the Legislature plus the Executive has exceeded the power granted by the people to them under the constitution," then the people should be asked to "pass final judgement." Following Rublee's advice, Roosevelt then turned to Holmes' opinion in the Oklahoma bank case to argue that the people did, in fact, have the right to establish social welfare laws. Quoting Holmes, Roosevelt observed: "It may be said in a general way that the police power extends to all the great public needs. It may be put forth in aid of what is sanctioned by usage or...by a strong and preponderant opinion to be greatly and immediately necessary to the public welfare." Roosevelt then argued, "All I advocate is giving the people of the several states the right to put that opinion into practical effect as part of the law of the State." This would be accomplished through a referendum put to people at "a regular election not less than six months distant after the appeal to the people is made." Roosevelt pointed out that the entire process, beginning with the initial framing of the laws, would take at least two years and that it was therefore "an obvious absurdity" to say that he was "proposing to submit such action to popular whim."

Although Roosevelt's speech did not quiet his conservative critics in the East, it did meet with much approval as a step in the right direction. The former president was pleased with the legislature's positive response and was happy with the advice he had received from the New Hampshire progressives. As Rublee later recalled, when Roosevelt left the building through a throng of enthusiastic supporters, he "leaned towards me and he said 'Rublee, I am profiting by your advice.'"[19] If Rublee orchestrated his contribution to the judicial recall issue and the Mazzini quote as a roundabout way of interviewing for a job as campaign adviser and speechwriter, it worked; he soon would be both.

Rublee seems to have merely needed an opening to become an insider in the Roosevelt camp, and he quickly exploited his window of opportunity. Writing to Bass the day after Roosevelt's speech, Rublee reported that his idea on the use of police power was meeting with approval: "Joe [Cotton] thinks my idea is sound. Judge Hand thinks it meets the situation perfectly [and] Judge Noyes of the U.S. Circuit Court, whom Taft considered for the Supreme Court, also thinks it adequate and workable."[20] Although Roosevelt had introduced the police power idea in his speech, Rublee realized that it was just a trial balloon and asked Bass, "How can we get the Colonel to adopt it?"[21] Evidently Rublee knew that Hand's approval was crucial and likely asked him to convey his support to Roosevelt. Writing to Roosevelt, Hand reported, "I have breakfasted and dined to-day with Rublee and I am so pleased with his idea that I want to write you of how perfectly I think it answers the situation." Hand added, "I can't see why Rublee's idea does not in much more thorough-going fashion than my suggestion go to the very heart of the difficulty." Evidently believing that Rublee both wanted to contribute and would be a positive influence, Hand fully endorsed Rublee as an adviser: "I hope you liked Rublee; I have mentioned him to you, but you never met him before to know him. He has more sagacity and clearness of mind than almost any man I know. He could and would help a good deal in such matters."[22] Roosevelt evidently liked the idea and met with both Rublee and Hand in New York the next day, 28 February, that meeting apparently establishing a unity of vision on a range of subjects. Roosevelt invited Rublee and Hand to join him at his estate at Oyster Bay two days later to discuss his budding campaign. Rublee, wanting to add another to their number, asked Roosevelt if he might bring Joe Cotton with him to Oyster Bay. Rublee was "very anxious" for Roosevelt to meet Cotton, whom he described as a successful Wall Street lawyer who yet "believes in the rule of the people and places human rights above property."[23] Roosevelt's friend Arthur D. Hill soon congratulated Roosevelt for his choice of new advisers: "I am awfully glad you have got George Rublee and Joe Cotton well aboard the lugger, for I think they are both first rate men."[24] In addition to Cotton, Rublee sought to add Brandeis to the Roosevelt camp. The Boston lawyer, however, declined, citing a preference for La Follette: "I should be glad indeed to go down to Oyster Bay with you to spend the evening talking social and industrial questions with Colonel Roosevelt.... I fear that should I hold a conference with Roosevelt, under the existing circumstances, La Follette might construe my so doing as a defection, and I want to avoid that possibility."[25] Although Brandeis could not bring himself to back Roosevelt, Rublee was becoming something of a enthusiast.

For the first month of Roosevelt's campaign, Rublee and Cotton were among his closest advisers. At first their task was overseeing what Roosevelt wrote regarding judicial recall. Moving Roosevelt on this issue, however, would be difficult owing to his deep resentment of the courts. Writing to Herbert Croly on 29 February, Roosevelt again defended his attack on the judiciary: "For the last thirty years there has been a riot of judicial action looking to the prevention of measures for social and industrial betterment which every other civilized nation takes as a matter of course, and in some way or other this riot must be stopped."[26] Believing that America "cannot permanently go on dancing in fetters," Roosevelt was committed to drastic action if need be.[27] Nevertheless, on 11 March in response to Arthur Hill's admonition that he have Rublee or Cotton approve "anything you use from a lawyer's point of view," Roosevelt agreed that he would allow "Cotton or Rublee to supervise possibly what I write on the courts."[28]

During March Rublee continued to work on the recall issue, and on 18 March he sent Bass a "memorandum on the recall of decisions" that provided the governor some talking points on the issue. Rublee noted that although Roosevelt considered the recall "a perfectly legitimate piece of machinery for the people to use where the judges are plainly not acting for the people," he stressed that Roosevelt advocated its use only as "a last resort."[29] George pointed out:

> The arguments against the recall of judges are rather absurd in the length to which they go, especially when one remembers that judges are elected for short terms almost everywhere. In Vermont the judges are elected for terms of only two years. A certain recall is always hanging over them, and in the case of the elective judges the recall may not be in the hands of the people, but in the hands of the political bosses who control the party nominating machinery.[30]

Although Rublee might have described some forms of progressive legislation when he first began advising progressives in 1910 as "emotional and crude," it seems clear that Rublee had warmed to novel methods of direct democracy and that he was earnest in his effort to curtail the influence of the dominant capital class for which he had long worked and been associated, if not, in fact, a part. Rublee's credentials as a progressive are brought into further relief when one considers that Roosevelt's recall scheme had been most threatening to eastern

Republicans of Rublee's class because, as George Mowry observed, having been "assailed for a half century by Greenbackers, Grangers, and Populists," industrialists and men of property had "found protection in the Republican party and the courts."[31] Roosevelt's campaign seemed likely to undermine both, but Rublee was willing to risk such an outcome.

Rublee's and Cotton's most important early contribution to Roosevelt's campaign was in helping him prepare his 20 March Carnegie Hall speech entitled "The Right of the People to Rule."[32] Although Learned Hand made some contribution to the speech, it appears that Rublee and Cotton worked most closely on it. Roosevelt sent his original text of the speech to Rublee, who made a copy for Cotton. Rublee recalled that "neither of us liked it" and that they took great liberties in changing it: "the last paragraph became the first paragraph, twelve pages were struck out entirely and twelve new pages were put in their place." While it was Cotton's version of the speech that Rublee, Cotton, and Hand finally agreed upon, it was Rublee, alone, who ended up taking the speech to Roosevelt at his home in Oyster Bay. Rublee recalled, "I was very much worried when I started [to explain the changes] because I thought he might be very much offended but he wasn't." Nevertheless, Roosevelt's acquiescence to the changes were not all easily won, and Rublee later recalled having to be rather firm with Roosevelt. Rublee found that his personal experiences with Roosevelt differed significantly from Roosevelt's public persona. Rublee concluded that "if you differed with him in public, he'd make a savage reply.... But if you could reach him in private, you'd find that he had an open mind and was not the conceited, dogmatic man that many people thought he was."[33]

Roosevelt delivered the speech at Carnegie Hall to an overflowing crowd on 20 March. The day before the speech Rublee wrote a note of encouragement: "Your meeting to-morrow night is going to be a tremendous success. The popular interest is so great that…I have so far been unable to get tickets for myself. That is bad for me, but I rejoice over the fact."[34] As Rublee predicted, the speech was well received, and Roosevelt's campaign, now centered around the Carnegie Hall speech, began to dominate national news.[35] Although the speech did help him get beyond the judicial recall issue and thereby allowed him to take up other issues in his New Nationalism program, it did not completely erase the doubts Roosevelt had raised among eastern Republicans in his 22 February Columbus speech. As George Mowry asserted, Roosevelt's attack on the judiciary in Columbus irrevocably "alienated the conservative wing of his party, which might have supported him for the sake of a possible victory."[36] The conservative vote, however, was clearly not what Roosevelt—or Rublee, for that matter—was seeking. As they proposed in the Carnegie Hall speech: "The great fundamental issue now before the Republican Party and before our people can be stated briefly. It is, Are the American people fit to govern themselves, to rule themselves, to control themselves? I believe they are. My opponents do not."[37] That conservatives were willing to risk a defeat with Taft rather than a victory with Roosevelt is not surprising.

Rublee was excited about Roosevelt's candidacy and about his own participation in the campaign. Writing on 15 March to Peabody to relate his political activities, Rublee reported: "I spent last night with Colonel Roosevelt at Oyster Bay helping in the reply to Taft which he will make at Carnegie Hall next Wednesday." Knowing that Peabody was concerned about the growing animosity between Roosevelt and Taft, both friends of Peabody, Rublee explained his decision to support Roosevelt. Rublee contended that Roosevelt was "fundamentally right in all his proposals—even the recall of judicial decisions," and suggested that Roosevelt represented Peabody's own "aims and principles." Rublee complained that Taft "stands for the worst side of the law" and argued that he "is not really interested in working out the most serious problems which confront us, the industrial and social problems." Rublee warned, prophetically, that if Taft "is nominated the party will split in two" and that, if elected, "the revolt would gain such momentum that four years from now there might be something like a real revolution—and leaders might be placed in power who would be dangerously radical and do things that TR would never permit."[38]

Although Peabody, in replying to Rublee's letter, admitted to having a "deep personal affection" for Roosevelt, he explained that he had "felt some disappointment in his course, both political and social, especially in his relations to Mr. Taft" since his return from Africa.[39] This complaint led Rublee to explain more fully his interest in Roosevelt. On 3 April he wrote:

> Whether he is right or wrong, I believe [Roosevelt's] action now is one of the bravest and most unselfish things he has done. He knew when he started that he had only a slight chance of succeeding against organized and entrenched opposition. He knew that if he stood quietly aside—how that his great prestige would be preserved—but he thought he ought to go out and lead the men who stand for the principles for which he has always worked.[40]

So fed up was Rublee with "the reactionary element of the party," led by such men as "Murray Crane, Gallinger [and] Guggenheim," that he observed: "One good thing [Roosevelt's] candidacy is likely to bring about...is the earlier formation of a new party—not that he has this view for he wants to save the Republican party—but that is likely to be the result. There is no longer any rational division between the parties, for political battles ought to be fought out between a conservative party on the one side and a liberal or progressive party on the other."[41] It is likely that Rublee's apparent support for the formation of a new party was influenced by the experiences of Horace Rublee, who in 1854 had helped found the Republican Party when it was clear that the Whig Party was disintegrating. The Republican Party also had a history of division between liberals, Mugwumps, and civil service reformers, on the one side, and so-called spoilsmen, stalwarts, and reactionaries, on the other. Rublee likely viewed the battle begun in 1910 as a sort of new round in the fight that had waxed and waned throughout the party's history.

Peabody's charge, however, that Roosevelt had "criticized [Taft] in a largely negative fashion" seems to have resonated with Rublee, who preferred dignified conduct in public forums.[42] In April the struggle between Roosevelt and Taft degenerated into name-calling, as Taft called Roosevelt a "dangerous egotist" and a "demagogue," and Roosevelt replied by referring to the president as "puzzlewit" and "fat head."[43] Rublee, apparently uncomfortable with the breakdown in civil discourse, wrote to Roosevelt at the beginning of May to encourage his leader to take the high road:

> You are the best judge of tactics and have doubtless decided upon the right course to take in Maryland; but possibly it may interest you to know that in our [his own, Hand's, and Cotton's] judgement it would be wise in Maryland, ...to say nothing or very little about the President personally, and to put the emphasis, as you did in earlier speeches, on the progressive principles, so that the course for which we are fighting may appear the salient thing.[44]

With only a month to go before the Republican Convention, however, neither Roosevelt nor Taft was prepared to back off, and their personal invective soon translated into actual brawling among some of their supporters.[45]

After having had significant influence on Roosevelt's campaign through their work on his 20 March Carnegie Hall speech, Rublee, Cotton, and Hand appeared to make little contribution to Roosevelt's campaign in April and May as the former president crisscrossed the nation. During April Learned Hand seems to have become rather disenchanted, or at least bored, with Roosevelt's and other progressives' enthusiasm. In a letter to Felix Frankfurter on 4 April he lashed out at progressives, complaining that he was "weary to death of the Rule of the People and a millennium created by constant elections and never ending suspicion of authority." Hand confessed that he was "sick of the whole lot, [because] either they are full of sound and fury and signify nothing, or they twist around a whirligig with prayers written on it...and think they can exorcize all the devils within the four seas."[46] Rublee, on the other hand, found the campaign inspiring and chided Hand for "standing outside and merely barking."[47] Writing to Roosevelt on 1 May, following what appeared to Rublee to be an "absolutely astonishing" show of strength in the Massachusetts primary, he congratulated Roosevelt for the triumph and observed, "It deserves comparison with Garibaldi's Sicilian expedition."[48] Rublee's use of the name of the mid-nineteenth-century Italian nationalist conjures a romantic view of the progressive insurgency that highlights an irony within the movement. While their fixation on science, rationalism, and efficiency seems a throwback to the Enlightenment, progressives' spiritual and often religious emphasis suggests an equally strong Romantic lineage.

Although Hand might have found his progressive comrades irksome, Roosevelt's success in Ohio, Taft's home state, and in the West in May suggested that Roosevelt might yet win the nomination at the Republican Convention and rekindled Hand's interest. Writing to Rublee on 23 May, Hand observed: "It looks now as though the Colonel would be nominated and if you are going to try for any strokes at the Platform, it is well to have something thought out and in hand sometime before the last moment arrives."[49] Hand proceeded to enclose a number of "purposely quite vague" ideas that he hoped Rublee "might be able to present to the Colonel in a way that would have some effect."[50]

As of late May, however, it seems that Rublee's influence in the Roosevelt camp was uncertain. As Roosevelt began to gather his supporters to travel to the Republican Convention in Chicago in the second week of June, it seems that Rublee was not on the roster, although he had prepared a platform draft for Roosevelt the week before and had recently traveled to Oyster Bay.[51] On 9 June, however, Roosevelt suddenly decided that he needed Rublee and, tracking him down at Groton School, asked him to come at the earliest possible moment to Chicago.[52] Having to decline a similar call for help from Winston Churchill in New Hampshire, Rublee related Roosevelt's call to arms in a letter written en route to Chicago: "I got your telegram and about the same time one came from the Colonel ordering me to Chicago. After vibrating a little I decided I must obey the big chief, and I'm now on the way to the ring side. Very sorry I can't be present at the hearing. I wish I could help you put something red hot into the railroad monster. May all the saints protect you."[53] Despite his suggestion of hesitancy, having had a hand in the progressive Republican insurgency since the Ballinger-Pinchot controversy in 1910, it must have been with great excitement that Rublee raced toward Chicago on the Twentieth Century Limited.

Once in Chicago, Rublee had two principal duties—to work on the platform committee and to fight for the right of Roosevelt supporters to claim their place as delegates to the convention.[54] Although it is unclear what success Rublee had in affecting the formation of the Republican platform, it seems that the bulk of his energy was spent attempting to secure voting seats for Roosevelt delegates. Roosevelt had long known that while he might win the support of Republicans nationwide, he still could lose the nomination at the convention because of Taft's control of the party apparatus—the Republican National Committee, elected in 1908 after Taft secured the nomination. As of 1912 only twelve states (none southern) had direct primaries that selected delegates to attend the national conventions. Of these Roosevelt won nine states, La Follette won two, and Taft only narrowly won one, Massachusetts. The delegates from the remaining states were chosen by various methods that allowed local party bosses rather than voters to select the delegates. This was especially true in the South, where Republican Party patronage controlled the selection of delegates for the convention. Thus, although Roosevelt had won 77 percent of the delegates from the direct primary states, Taft's control of the Republican National Committee enabled him to secure the remaining delegates.[55]

When Rublee arrived in Chicago, the situation was already looking bleak. Prior to the convention both Roosevelt and Taft laid claim to 254 delegates from nonprimary states, and it was up to the Republican National Committee to determine the contested seats. On 7 June the National Committee awarded Taft delegates 235 of the 254 contested seats, driving Roosevelt supporters nearly berserk.[56] Evidently, Roosevelt's call to Rublee on 9 June concerned the contested seats. Upon arriving in Chicago, Rublee was put to work with Arthur Hill documenting credentials and drafting briefs that demanded the seating of Roosevelt delegates. The effort seemed worthwhile because Roosevelt needed only fifty more of his delegates seated to prevent Taft's nomination. As one observer of the convention noted, "From the fall of the gavel, the Roosevelt forces fought with a vigor and determination for what they described as the 'purging of the roll' of those delegates whose names they declared had been placed upon it by fraud."[57] Nevertheless, with the sitting president in control of the convention, the Taft majority "remained intact, an impregnable defense against the Progressive attack." As Rublee recalled, "All the decisions were made against us and there wasn't anything we really could do about it. We were [then] voted down in the Convention and Taft was nominated."[58]

Roosevelt and his supporters had always known that Taft's nomination was a probable outcome. What remained uncertain was how progressive Republicans would respond to that eventuality. Progressives were especially irritated because Roosevelt had won "the great majority of the delegates from the States which are normally Republican and which must be relied upon at election time if a Republican President is to be chosen."[59] The conservatives' blatant disregard for the opinion of the bulk of Republican voters was too great an outrage to accept. Not surprisingly, throughout the frustrating, weeklong organizational period "the temper of the Roosevelt delegates had burned hotter and hotter."[60] Evidently, Rublee's temper was one of those inflamed, for he was ready to carry the insurrection to its next logical step. In his letter to Peabody in April, Rublee had warned of the creation of a new party if Taft was nominated and indicated that he would likely join it. What Rublee could, of course, not then know was that he would have a hand in the new party's formation. During the final days before the nomination a document was quietly circulated in an effort to warn conservatives of the consequences of their present course of action. The document stated that "in the event that the Republican National Convention…refuses to purge its roll," it was the intention of the signers of the document "to join in the organization of a new party" dedicated "to the progressive principles of genuine popular rule and social justice…under the leadership of Theodore Roosevelt." George Rublee's name appeared among the signers.[61] When Roosevelt delegates stormed out of the convention hall on 21 June and proclaimed the formation of a new party in Orchestra Hall following Taft's renomination, Rublee joined them.[62] Roosevelt, appearing before the insurgents, gave a stirring address that gave the meeting, as one observer noted, the "quality of religious exaltation."[63] Roosevelt charged his followers to return to their home states to build support and then to reconvene in Chicago in August for the first Progressive Party convention.

While much later in life Rublee downplayed his interest in the Progressive Party, during the heady days of the summer of 1912 his enthusiasm for the new party was great. Not all of Rublee's friends, however, were as sanguine. Learned

Hand, overcoming his former objection to religious fervor, did join the new party, but both Hapgood, a Roosevelt supporter, and Louis Brandeis, who had backed La Follette, switched their support to Wilson when he was nominated in July. Governor Bass, concerned about his political viability, at first believed that he ought to stay within the Republican fold. Rublee, however, convinced Bass that Roosevelt deserved his support since Bass was one of the original six governors who advocated Roosevelt's candidacy for president. Rublee later regretted pressuring Bass to support Roosevelt because it "ended his political career in New Hampshire" because the "Republicans never really forgave him."[64]

Rublee, who had no political career to lose, took a very active part in the Progressive Party both on the state and on the national level. He became a member of the state executive committee in New Hampshire and contributed $500 toward the founding of a Progressive Party newspaper in Manchester.[65] One of Rublee's most important actions on the state level, vis-á-vis his future political contests, was convincing the Progressive Party not to run a candidate against Democrat Raymond Stevens, who had decided to run for U.S. Congress. In addition to having become a friend, Stevens had so impressed him as a bipartisan progressive during the railroad fight that Rublee was sure the Progressive Party could not field a candidate as good as Stevens.[66]

Almost immediately after the Republican Convention Rublee, Hand, and Herbert Croly began crafting the social and industrial planks of a new platform. Rublee had hoped to win Brandeis for the Progressive Party, but "the People's Attorney" had no interest in Roosevelt. It seems that Brandeis mostly differed with Roosevelt—and Rublee—on questions of antitrust legislation. Brandeis had long deplored the growth of large corporations and hoped to see America return to a land of small producers. After the Democratic Party passed a platform in July calling for legislation that would "make it impossible for a private monopoly to exist in the United States," Brandeis joined the Wilson campaign, where he immediately became the chief adviser on antitrust policy. With the resolution of the trust question looming large in the coming campaign, Brandeis had the important role of providing Wilson with an intellectual framework to successfully fight the Progressive Party. Brandeis took the Democratic platform plank that called for the prevention of "the control of any one corporation of so large a proportion of any industry to make it a menace to competitive conditions" and created the New Freedom slogan "Regulation of Competition." Believing that big business had poisoned the American democratic system, Brandeis was intent on destroying the trusts.[67] Ironically, Brandeis was matched against a number of his close progressive friends from Cornish, New Hampshire. Writing to his brother, Alfred, Brandeis reported that "George Rublee, Croly, and Judge Hand are preparing with Pinchot the T.R. platform on social questions."[68]

Unlike Brandeis, Rublee, Hand, and Herbert Croly believed that big business could be beneficial to society if controlled by a strong federal government. In his 1909 work, *The Promise of American Life*, Croly offered a number of solutions to America's debilitating problems associated with industrialization and urbanization. Croly, who began working on the book around the time Rublee moved to Cornish, argued that large corporations were a result of a sort of economic evolution that made them more efficient than small businesses and thereby were beneficial to society and should be preserved. Rather than protecting small businessmen from large corporations, as Brandeis would later propose, Croly argued in 1909, "Whenever the small competitor of the large corporation is unable to keep his head above water with his own exertions, he should be allowed to drown."[69] Croly did not fear the total domination of the markets by large businesses because he believed that efficiencies of scale accrued only to certain high-input industries. Brandeis, on the other hand, was so opposed to big business that he would deny that economies of scale exist. On one occasion Brandeis wrote: "I am so firmly convinced that the large unit is not as efficient...as the smaller unit, that I believe that if it were possible to make the corporations act with what...should be the rules of trade no huge corporation would be created, or if created, would be successful."[70] Although Croly, too, believed that many corporations had become dominant through unscrupulous, anticompetitive practices that the government should forbid, he cautioned that "in restricting [the corporations] care should be taken not to destroy...the essential condition of the efficiency."[71] His solution to the trust problem, therefore, was to abolish the Sherman Anti-Trust Act and replace it with a federal public service commission that would regulate corporations operating in interstate trade. Such a commission would prosecute companies that sought monopolistic control through anticompetitive behavior but would permit those that captured markets through production and distribution efficiencies to continue their existence with minimal oversight.

Upon his return to the United States in 1910 from Africa, Roosevelt read *The Promise of American Life* and was converted on a number of issues, including Croly's approach to antitrust regulation.[72] When the Taft administration brought suit against U.S. Steel in October 1911—an obvious affront to Roosevelt, who had tacitly authorized the company's expansion in 1907—Roosevelt responded with an article entitled "The Trusts, the People and the Square Deal," in which he called for the substitution of the Sherman Act with a regulatory body. Although his administration had prosecuted several corporations under the Sherman Act, in 1911 Roosevelt described the destruction of trusts through the Sherman provision as "a return to the flintlocks of Washington's Continentals."[73] Roosevelt's article won him many supporters in the business world who, as one historian pointed out, were "exceedingly weary of the [Taft] administration's trust prosecutions."[74]

Although George Rublee in his 1906 article "Government Rate-making" had called into question commissions that had a "quasi-judicial function," by 1912 he, too, believed that the only solution to the antitrust question was the creation of a commission of experts authorized to determine the legitimacy of business practices. Interestingly, while Herbert Croly laid the intellectual foundation for Roosevelt's "New Nationalism" and likely had helped shape Rublee's views, he had little influence in Roosevelt's campaign until after the Republican Convention in June 1912. Learned Hand's biographer noted that "Croly, isolated in Cornish, had fallen out of touch with Roosevelt" and was "perhaps jealous of the attention that Hand, Rublee, and Cotton received."[75] It appears, however, that it was Rublee who helped bring Croly back among Roosevelt's council of advisers. Writing to Bass on 18 July about an upcoming Progressive meeting, Rublee informed him: "I will bring Herbert Croly with me because he is greatly interested in the new party and has good ideas. I think you know him—the author of the Promise of American Life—which has given the Colonel so many ideas and is the basis of the "New Nationalism."[76] Rublee had already been working on a platform with Hand, but he seemed to think that Croly's help was important. Although Rublee may have sought to involve Croly out of personal sympathy, he might have been most interested in gaining Croly's support for an internal contest over the drafting of the new Progressive platform. Writing to Hand on 27 June Rublee reported that he had seen the latest version of the platform and observed that the document "seems a reversion to the Garfield-Pinchot form—what we contributed before is eliminated." Reflecting the internal struggles surrounding the party platform, Rublee suggested: "[I]f we make any suggestions we had better make them over our joint signatures."[77] Croly's contribution, owing to his original influence on the New Nationalism, would, of course, add clout to Rublee's and Hand's proposals.

According to the records of the Progressive Party, it appears that there were three groups working on the platform in coordination with Roosevelt before the August convention: Gifford and Amos Pinchot; Arthur D. Hill and Chester Harvey Rowell; and Rublee, Croly, and Hand.[78] Although it appears that the Pinchot version became the basis for the platform negotiations, Rublee, Hand, and Croly managed to effect some changes to it before it was submitted to the convention platform committee in Chicago in August.[79] One effort in which Rublee, Croly, and Hand did not succeed was introducing a section in the business plank that specifically questioned the effectiveness of the Sherman Anti-Trust Act. Their rider to the plank suggested that the Sherman Act was an inefficient means of antitrust because "control cannot be successful which only operates after the event and by means of litigation." "Besides," they added, "it is a just complaint that capital cannot in advance know the limits of lawful cooperation and combination."[80] This clause was central to Rublee's and Croly's concern about antitrust legislation. As a Wall Street lawyer, Rublee empathized with corporate America's confusion regarding antitrust law, and he believed that businesses should be able to know in advance whether or not their practices were within the law. A trade commission of his and Croly's design would function chiefly to give advance advice on whether a business combination was in the public interest. Although the platform, when adopted, did not contain the Rublee-Croly-Hand clause, the closing sentence of the business plank of the final version did reflect their interest in clarifying antitrust law: "Under such a system of constructive regulation legitimate business, freed from confusion, uncertainty and fruitless litigation, will develop normally in response to the energy and enterprise of the American business man."[81]

In their revision of the platform, Rublee, Croly, and Hand attempted a number of other changes as well. They attached a rider to the preamble that was surprisingly radical. In it they pointed out that the two-thirds ratification requirement for a federal amendment to the U.S. Constitution was a measure initially designed to protect smaller states during the nation's infancy, a provision that they contended was no longer necessary. They argued that "the fundamental law should be made reasonably responsive to the demands of new conditions and changed political and economic convictions, so that a small minority of the people may not be able to defeat the will of the great majority."[82] Although this addition was not preserved in the preamble, it was ratified as an individual plank in the platform with somewhat different wording. To the "Social and Industrial Justice" plank the Cornish triumvirate added a portion that demanded a "minimum wage sufficient to enable workers to maintain their efficiency" and a social welfare program "to insure against pauperism those who are willing but unable to work."[83] The final platform, however, provided only a minimum wage for women, offering an indefinite "living scale" for all industrial occupations.[84] Another radical element of the Rublee-Croly-Hand platform was a provision that "[i]ndustry conducted in one state under laws designed to protect the standard of living of its workers should not be compelled to meet the competition of goods made elsewhere under a lower standard." As one reader of their platform pointed out: "Doesn't this mean the end of free trade between the states?" Although the question was crossed out in a dismissive fashion that might suggest that a reasonable explanation was offered, the platform committee did not adopt the provision.[85]

The Cornish pundits were also thwarted in their effort to undermine support for the tariff. The version of the platform that came to them proclaimed, "The Republican tariff policy has been of the greatest benefit to the country" because it had promoted domestic industry and had protected "our workmen against unfair competition with cheap labor abroad." The Rublee-Croly-Hand revision marked out that section, offering instead a criticism of the Republican tariff: "It is a perversion of the policy of protection to permit the tariff to foster monopoly and privilege or maintain inefficient industries at the expense of the consumer." Although the platform committee did not adopt such language, it did utilize a phrase that Rublee added in handwriting. His note read: "The benefit of the tariff should rightly show itself not only in reasonable profits, but in the pay envelope of the wage earner, the prosperity of the farmer, and the general standard of living."[86] Bringing together several Rublee-Croly-Hand ideas, the platform committee adopted the following lines: "Primarily the benefit of any tariff should be disclosed in the pay envelope of the laborer. We declare that no industry deserves protection which is unfair to labor or which is operating in violation of federal law. We believe that the presumption is always in favor of the consuming public."[87] Although they could not win a stronger stance against the tariff,

Rublee, Croly, and Hand did move the platform away from Hamiltonian notions of protectionism.

The final substantial alteration that the Cornish platform attempted regarded the plank on currency reform. In this case, rather than marking out sections and attaching riders, the complete plank was crossed out. In its place was a typed addendum on which Rublee wrote, "Offered in substitution for currency plank." The plank was evidently Rublee's work, for it essentially repeated Rublee's assertions in his 1906 article on currency reform in *Collier's*. It is likely, however, that Rublee consulted Victor Morawetz, whose ideas on currency reform Rublee championed and who, according to Hand, had made some contribution to the platform that Rublee and Cotton prepared for the Republican Convention in June.[88] Although Rublee's plank sought to educate the voter on the structural problems in the currency and banking system, it was too esoteric to be of much use in a platform. In the heart of the plank Rublee explained: "Excessive concentration of currency in the banks in the principal money centers and the resulting low interest rates on bank loans against stock exchange collateral, often encourage unwholesome speculation, while farmers and business men are cramped by inability to obtain legitimate credit at reasonable rates of interest."[89] It is, of course, interesting that Rublee and Morawetz, who had both made their fortunes in the stock market utilizing easy credit terms, sought to shine the progressive light on the system in which they prospered. Evidently understanding how the system allowed the rich to accumulate ever increasing wealth in the nation's capital centers—and fearful of the possible disastrous consequences of overspeculation—they were, as Rublee wrote in the currency plank, committed to "preventing the use of the credit of the banks, as a means of fostering speculation at the expense of honest business and enterprise." As Rublee pointed out, the only way to accomplish this goal was through "effective Federal regulation" that would "assure to the people of the United States through their government the control of the financial system of the country."[90] Although the platform committee did not come close to approaching Rublee's plank in the final version, it did reflect the gist of his and Morawetz's ideas. As one sentence in the brief plank proclaimed: "The control [of the currency system] should be lodged with the government and should be protected from domination or manipulation by Wall Street or any special interest."[91]

In their draft, Rublee, Croly, and Hand limited themselves to "social industrial justice" and economic policy. Other than the benefit that currency reform would offer the farmers, the only addition they made to policies regarding agriculture was a handwritten note that Rublee made in the section entitled "Country Life." In it he added a phrase that embraced farmers' long interest in a national subtreasury program.[92] Rublee called for the federal government to promote "more effective co-operation [among farmers] in the purchase of supplies, sale of products and procuring credit." Rublee, Croly, and Hand made no comment on the planks dealing with woman's suffrage, pure food, the Panama Canal, conservation, the Philippine Islands, and the size of the navy, which in the draft they worked on did not call for building two battleships per year.[93] Likely because of its divisive effect on sectional unity, they crossed out a single-sentence plank entitled "Pensions," which read: "We pledge ourselves to a wise and just policy of pensioning American soldiers and sailors and their widows and children." Under the crossed-out plank Rublee wrote in longhand, "We might feel like voting for Wilson if this plank is kept." Despite their protest, the platform committee adopted the plank verbatim. If any accommodation was made to Rublee's warning, it may have been the line that the platform committee added to the plank, stating: "And we approve the policy of the southern states in granting pensions to the ex-Confederate soldiers and sailors and their widows and children."[94]

Although Rublee did not get all that he wanted in the platform, he was enthusiastic about the new party. Writing to Endicott Peabody on 23 September, Rublee expressed his thoughts on the party and the coming campaign:

> I am greatly interested in the new Progressive Party—it seems to me the most promising political movement that has occurred in my life time. I think Mr. Roosevelt's part in its formation will be regarded sometime as his greatest service to the country—it is now so strong that I think it no longer depends on him—his individual importance is much less than it was. I think well of Wilson—but if he wins as seems likely, I do not think he can accomplish his purposes through the Democratic party—if that is so then next time we shall get all the progressives in our party and shall win—and we shall be ready to win then.[95]

Rublee evidently realized that for the Progressive Party to survive, it would have to transcend Roosevelt's leadership. He was also obviously realistic about the party's chances in November 1912. With the Republican vote divided between Taft and Roosevelt, the way was open for a Democratic victory, thereby making Woodrow Wilson only the second Democratic president in nearly sixty years. Nevertheless, Rublee seems to have concluded that a major realignment was taking place in American politics in which progressives in both the Democratic and Republican Parties would be driven together by the conservative element in each party. The key to Rublee's miscalculation seems to have been two unforeseen eventualities—the outbreak of war in Europe and Wilson's success in passing progressive legislation during his first term. Ironically, Rublee himself would play an important role in some of the Wilson administration's key legislative victories, thereby undermining his own prophecy that Wilson would fail to "accomplish his purposes." In September 1912, however, the idea that he might become a Wilson adviser and the progressive poster child for the Democratic Party must have been the furthest thought from George Rublee's mind.

NOTES

1. Robert Bass to GR, 17 August 1911, RBP, box 31-8.
2. Rublee, "Reminiscences," 79-80.

3. Gunther, *Learned Hand,* 212-213; and Mowry, *Theodore Roosevelt*, 215-217.
4. Quoted in Gunther, *Learned Hand*, 214.
5. Hand to Theodore Roosevelt, 20 November 1911, Theodore Roosevelt Presidential Papers, U.S. Library of Congress, microfilm [hereafter TRP-LoC], reel 117.
6. Quoted in Gunther, *Learned Hand*, 219.
7. Mowry, *Theodore Roosevelt,* 217; and Rublee, "Reminiscences," 81.
8. Bass to Roosevelt, 17 February and 22 February 1912, TRP-LoC, reel 130.
9. Rublee, "Reminiscences," 81-82.
10. Ibid., 81
11. Hand believed that "Holmes opinion…leaves so little of the Bill of Rights that it remains brutum fulmen for the most part." Hand to Roosevelt, 20 November 1911, TRP-LoC, reel 117.
12. Rublee, "Reminiscences," 81.
13. Ibid., 82.
14. Ibid., 83, 93.
15. Ibid., 82.
16. *The New York Times*, 27 February 1912.
17. Rublee, "Reminiscences," 83.
18. *The New York Times*, 27 February 1912.
19. Rublee, "Reminiscences," 84.
20. GR to Bass, 27 February 1912, RBP.
21. Ibid.
22. Hand to Roosevelt, 27 February 1912, TRP-LoC, reel 131.
23. GR to Roosevelt, 1 March 1912, TRP-LoC, reel 131.
24. Arthur Dehon Hill to Roosevelt, 18 March 1912, TRP-LoC, reel 134.
25. Brandeis to GR, 16 March 1912, Urofsky and Levy, *Letters of Louis D. Brandeis*, vol. 2, 568-569.
26. Roosevelt to Herbert Croly, 29 February 1912, TRP-LoC, reel 374.
27. Ibid.
28. Hill to Roosevelt, 9 March 1912, TRP-LoC, reel 133; and Roosevelt to Hill, 11 March 1912, TRP-LoC, reel 374.
29. GR to Bass, 18 March 1912, RBP, box 31-61.
30. Ibid.
31. Mowry, *Theodore Roosevelt*, 216.
32. Gunther, *Learned Hand*, 224.
33. Rublee, "Reminiscences," 88-90.
34. GR to Roosevelt 19 March 1912, TRP-LoC, reel 134.
35. Gunther, *Learned Hand*, 225; and Rublee, "Reminiscences," 93.
36. Mowry, *Theodore Roosevelt,* 217.
37. Quoted in John Allen Gable, *The Bull Moose Years: Theodore Roosevelt and the Progressive Party* (Port Washington, NY: National University Publications, 1978), 14.
38. GR to Peabody, 15 March 1912, GSA.
39. Peabody to GR, 18 March 1912, GSA.
40. GR to Peabody, 3 April 1912, GSA.
41. Ibid.
42. Peabody to GR, 6 April 1912, GSA.
43. Mowry, *Theodore Roosevelt*, 234.
44. GR to Roosevelt, 1 May 1912, TRP-LoC, reel 138.

45. Mowry, *Theodore Roosevelt*, 233-234.

46. Hand to Felix Frankfurter, 4 April 1912, quoted in Gunther, *Learned Hand*, 225.

47. Hand to Frankfurter, 11 April 1912, quoted in Gunther, *Learned Hand*, 225-226.

48. GR to Roosevelt, 1 May 1912, TR-LoC, reel 138. Roosevelt was expected to loose convincingly in Massachusetts.

49. Hand to GR, 23 May 1912, HLS-Hand, box 107, folder 2.

50. Ibid.

51. Hand to GR, 14 June 1912, HLS-Hand, box 107, folder 2; and Norman Hapgood to Roosevelt, 10 June 1912, TRP-LoC, reel 145.

52. GR to Roosevelt, 9 June 1912, TRP-LoC, reel 145.

53. GR to Winston Churchill, undated, located in RBP, ml 16-26:3-2.

54. Hand to Herbert Croly, 14 June 1912, HLS-Hand. Hand observed: "George left on Tuesday last on word from TR himself, who reached him at Groton, where George was then staying. He will stay there until the convention is over, and I understand is to be upon the platform committee."

55. Gable, *The Bull Moose Years*, 14; and Mowry, *Theodore Roosevelt*, 238-240.

56. Gable, *The Bull Moose Years*, 15.

57. Harold Howland, *Theodore Roosevelt and His Times: A Chronicle of the Progressive Movement* (New Haven: Yale University Press, 1921), 218.

58. Rublee, "Reminiscences," 94-95.

59. Howland, *Theodore Roosevelt*, 217.

60. Ibid., 218.

61. Ibid., 221.

62. Rublee testimony, *Hearings I*, 28.

63. Howland, *Theodore Roosevelt*, 223.

64. Rublee, "Reminiscences," 97.

65. Rublee testimony, *Hearings I*, 28; and GR to Bass, 1 October 1912, RBP.

66. Rublee, "Reminiscences," 100-101.

67. Democratic Party, *National Democratic Platform—Progress in Every Plank* (New York: Democratic National Committee, 1912), 2; and John Milton Cooper Jr., *The Warrior and the Priest: Woodrow Wilson and Theodore Roosevelt* (Cambridge: Belknap Press, 1983), 193-194.

68. Brandeis to his brother, Alfred, 29 July 1912, Urofsky and Levy, *Letters of Louis D. Brandeis*, vol. 2, 654.

69. Herbert Croly, *The Promise of American Life* (New York: Macmillan, 1909), 359.

70. Quoted in Danny Bring, "The Origins of the Federal Trade Commission Act: A Public Choice Approach," dissertation (George Mason University, 1993), 321.

71. Croly, *Promise*, 360.

72. Mowry, *Theodore Roosevelt*, 146.

73. Quoted in Mowry, *Theodore Roosevelt*, 192.

74. Mowry, *Theodore Roosevelt*, 192.

75. Gunther, *Learned Hand*, 227.

76. GR to Bass, 18 July 1912, RBP.

77. GR to Hand, 27 June 1912, HLS-Hand, box 107, folder 2.

78. Progressive Party Platform Drafts, 1912, Progressive Party Archives, Theodore Roosevelt Collection, Houghton Library Special Collections, Harvard University [hereafter HU-PPA].

79. Among the platform drafts is one that reads in Rublee's handwriting "Revised by Learned Hand, Herbert D. Croly, and George Rublee," Progressive Party Platform Drafts, 1912, HU-PPA, folder 6.

80. Progressive Party Platform Drafts, 1912, "Revised by Learned Hand, Herbert D. Croly, and George Rublee," HU-PPA, folder 6.

81. "A Contract with the People: Platform of the Progressive Party," Campaign Publications, HU-PPA, 7.

82. Progressive Party Platform Drafts, 1912, "Revised by Learned Hand, Herbert D. Croly, and George Rublee," HU-PPA, folder 6.

83. Ibid.

84. "A Contract with the People: Platform of the Progressive Party," Campaign Publications, HU-PPA, 5.

85. Progressive Party Platform Drafts, 1912, "Revised by Learned Hand, Herbert D. Croly, and George Rublee," HU-PPA, folder 6.

86. Ibid.

87. "A Contract with the People: Platform of the Progressive Party," Campaign Publications, HU-PPA, 8.

88. See Hand to Croly, 14 June 1912, HLS-Hand. In it Hand asked: "Have you seen the planks of the platform that George, Joe and Morawetz got up in part?"

89. Progressive Party Platform Drafts, 1912, "Revised by Learned Hand, Herbert D. Croly, and George Rublee," HU-PPA, folder 6.

90. Ibid.

91. "A Contract with the People: Platform of the Progressive Party," Campaign Publications, HU-PPA, 9.

92. See for instance Lawrence Goodwyn, *The Populist Movement: A Short History of the Agrarian Revolt in America* (New York: Oxford University Press, 1978), 109-112.

93. Progressive Party Platform Drafts, 1912, "Revised by Learned Hand, Herbert D. Croly, and George Rublee," HU-PPA, folder 6.

94. "A Contract With the People: Platform of the Progressive Party," Campaign Publications, HU-PPA, 15.

95. GR to Peabody, 23 September 1912, GSA.

6

"The Most Assiduous and Persistent and Tireless Lobbyist" (1913–1914)

The election of Woodrow Wilson as president in November 1912 came as no surprise to George Rublee. Although he and other Progressives hoped for a Bull Moose victory, Wilson's progressive credentials as governor of New Jersey prevented any significant loss of votes to Roosevelt among progressive Democrats. Fortunately, Rublee "thought well" of Wilson, and he could take comfort that the spirit of progressivism was ascendant and that reactionaries had suffered a sound defeat in the presidential election. If Rublee nevertheless believed that his opportunity to make a public contribution had been significantly curtailed, that would have been a reasonable assumption. Surprisingly, however, Rublee would come to have more opportunity to do really significant work with Wilson than he might have under Roosevelt. The key to Rublee's work in the Wilson administration centered on his friendship with Louis Brandeis, with whom he remained close despite the two men's profound differences in their approach to the regulation of big business. Also important to Rublee's unusual accomplishments during Wilson's first term would be Norman Hapgood and Raymond Stevens, whose successful bid for Congress sent the latter to Washington as a freshman congressman along with Wilson. In the end, however, although all three of these men were important to his work, it would be Rublee's tenacious, determined response to a sense of the historic moment that would allow him to make a major contribution to U.S. regulatory policy during the Wilson administration.

The winter of 1912 in Cornish, New Hampshire, was evidently a thoughtful one, as Rublee, Croly, Hand, Cotton, and their progressive friends reflected on the year's events. Croly, evidently energized by the fall campaign, turned his attention to the creation of a new national political journal that would continue the progressive voice. With the backing of financier Willard Straight, Croly organized *The New Republic* in the fall of 1913.[1] Although Rublee did not join the editorial staff, he did contribute to the journal's formation and soon became an important source on Washington politics.[2] Journalist Norman Hapgood, also making a fortuitous change, took over the editorship of *Harper's Weekly* in May 1913 and quickly aligned the magazine with the Wilson administration.[3]

Unlike the journalists, the Cornish lawyers had a more difficult time finding political expression after Roosevelt's defeat. While Judge Hand had ample work at his New York bench and Joe Cotton was always in high demand on Wall Street, Rublee seems to have been especially at a loss as to how to proceed given his growing interest in public policy. It seems likely that Rublee could have taken a place on the editorial staff of *The New Republic*, but he evidently had developed a preference for more active political work. Although he had often relied on his journalistic background in his work on the Ballinger-Pinchot controversy and in his political efforts for Bass and for Roosevelt, it seems that Rublee was most inspired by the excitement of clandestine, momentous projects that demanded energy and finesse. Evidently, Rublee required the excitement of active political battles to arouse the passion that could lead him to make heroic efforts. He clearly did not have the temperament of a journalist. He would never be a Hapgood, a Croly, or a Walter Lippmann. Instead, Rublee would become something of an independent crusader—according to some a "maverick"—who would enter the fray when circumstances, his ability, and his passion were all aligned.

Rublee's call to action after the 1912 defeat came from Brandeis in the fall of 1913. Rublee had returned to his work in Spooner's office, where he was a partner along with Cotton, but as Rublee later recalled, he "was really not interested in the practice" and did not think he "was much use in the firm."[4] Nevertheless, as Rublee testified before a Senate subcommittee in 1915, he had "an especially large experience in litigation under the Sherman Act in a considerable number of cases" between 1910 and 1913. As a result of this work, he had "became greatly interested in the Sherman Act, in its applications and meaning."[5] His experiences led him to believe that corporate managers were "confused about the Sherman law" and were in much need of clarifying guidance.[6]

Perhaps because his efforts before the courts were a constant reminder of the inadequacy of existing antitrust laws, Rublee evidently retained an interest in playing a role in shaping a new federal antitrust policy. Rublee had good reason to imagine that he might still influence national policy. Victor Morawetz, for instance, despite being identified with New York's so-called 'Money Trust,' was able early in 1913 to influence the development of the Federal Reserve System. Morawetz was able to contribute to banking reform because Wilson found the subject vexing and was willing to entertain ideas from several quarters.[7] Shortly after Wilson's election, Morawetz managed to have a friend persuade the new president to read a pamphlet that he had written on currency reform. Finding Morawetz's scheme for a federal banking system promising, Wilson invited him to the White House in January 1913 while Morawetz was in Washington to appear before a subcommittee of the House Banking and Currency Committee.[8] A friend of Morawetz's from the University of Chicago reported that after the interview Wilson had spoken to him "in terms of strong approval of the plan you had outlined." Morawetz's pamphlet was soon reprinted and "sent to…nearly all the members of the House and of the Senate." He then appeared before the Senate Committee on Banking and Currency in April, when the "Federal Reserve Bank bill was under consideration."[9] After the passage of the bill, Wilson reportedly remarked that Morawetz "ought to be satisfied with the bill as it was [his] plan."[10] Given the experiences of his former mentor, Rublee may have believed that he, too, might yet find the opportunity to shape federal policy if circumstances would allow.

It may have been the thought that he might still play a role that led Rublee to respond favorably to Brandeis' call to arms in the fall of 1913. How Rublee and Brandeis' friendship survived the passionate and bitter 1912 campaign remains a wonder. With each offering his own party ideas designed to prevail over the program of the other, it seems that their relationship must have been strained. That Brandeis again turned to Rublee for assistance in the fall of 1913 suggests that they had not allowed their political contest to become personal. Too, there was no one that Brandeis could rely upon who was better fitted for special assignments than Rublee. Unlike his New York friend, Brandeis was overwhelmed with work before the ICC in Boston and with requests from President Wilson, who wished him to initiate legislation that would fulfill the New Freedom pledge to destroy big business. Brandeis also had a number of pet projects that he wanted to see successfully legislated and needed someone to draft those bills as well. Coupled with articles he planned to write for *Harper's Weekly* exposing trusts, Brandeis was overwhelmed with work. Much in need of help, Brandeis turned to Rublee, who as usual was looking for more interesting work. Rublee soon traveled to Boston and lived with the Brandeis family for two weeks so that he and the "People's Attorney" could "talk things over, discuss them and plan what we were going to do."[11] Writing to Norman Hapgood in September 1913, Brandeis announced that Rublee had decided to join him: "George Rublee came over last Friday to tell me that he had severed his connection with Spooner and Cotton, and wanted to take hold in some of my public work. I was delighted to have him take up the Money Trust [articles]; and he has started to work with me today. This will be of very great value, not only in checking up and perfecting the articles, but in preparing the necessary legislation and the making of converts."[12] Rublee lived with the Brandeis family for two weeks in Boston, and then he and Juliet moved to Washington at the opening of Congress. Evidently, Rublee was at first just the sort of person Brandeis needed, for he quickly accomplished the disparate assignments that Brandeis gave him.[13] Writing to Endicott Peabody from Washington in December, Rublee described his efforts: "I am at work with Mr. Brandeis in the railroad advance rate case and also in the preparation of bills to stop what is called the money trust—bills to be introduced into Congress this session."[14] Although Brandeis' approach to antitrust was not his own, Rublee at this point seems to have accepted the idea that the New Freedom program would soon become the nation's new business policy.

Owing to Brandeis' work with Republican senator La Follette on antitrust measures dating to 1911 and his favored position in the Wilson administration, there was likely no single individual in so good a position to influence federal antitrust policy. In a series of articles that ran, with Hapgood's assistance, from November 1913 to February 1914 in *Harper's Weekly*, Brandeis initiated and sustained a relentless attack on large corporations and laid out a plan to destroy them.[15] Brandeis called for legislation to criminalize known monopolistic practices and proposed an act to enlarge the Bureau of Corporations to a three-man commission authorized to investigate corporations. In addition to assisting the Justice Department, the enlarged commission would seek to identify innovative business methods that allowed corporations to achieve monopolistic dominance. Upon identifying such practices, the enlarged commission would recommend new federal laws to eradicate those practices.[16]

In January 1914, Wilson delivered a State of the Union address during which he called for antitrust regulation that closely reflected that which Brandeis had put forth in his *Harper's Weekly* series. Brandeis believed that Wilson's message "paved the way for about all I have asked for" and reported that "some of the provisions specifically are what I got into his mind at my first interview."[17] In February Brandeis testified before the Committee on Interstate Commerce and the Committee of the Judiciary in the House, reiterating his "regulation of competition" approach. Based on his recommendations, the House Judiciary Committee drafted the Clayton Act, which prohibited about a dozen business tactics that led to monopolistic control of a market. Among the list of proscriptions were interlocking directorates, pricing agreements that restrained trade, and stock exchange among competitors. The bill also held company directors, officers, and their agents responsible for offenses and made them punishable by up to one year in prison and/or a fine up to $5,000. After Brandeis met with the Interstate Commerce Committee, it produced the Covington bill, a measure to enlarge the Bureau of Corporations and to rename it the Interstate Trade Commission. The enlarged bureau would be a sunshine commission that would investigate trusts but would have no authority to prosecute them, that power being reserved to the Justice Department. Finally, La Follette introduced bills in the Senate that complemented both the Clayton and Covington bills.[18] With these important committees now in line, Brandeis' long battle to stop the growth and domination of big business seemed on course for a successful conclusion.

With his antitrust program well established in Congress, Brandeis returned to Boston and left Rublee to watch over the bills in Congress, where committees continued to hold meetings and hearings. Brandeis also asked Rublee to develop what he termed a "price maintenance bill," the purpose of which was to protect small businesses—his preferred economic unit—from some of the proposed antitrust statutes in the Clayton bill.[19] Remarkably, it seems, Brandeis in effect asked Rublee to stay in Washington to oversee the final triumph of the 1912 New Freedom platform. Neither Brandeis nor Rublee seems to have understood the risk in giving him this task. Asking Rublee to monitor legislation that was inimical to his fundamental beliefs, however, was evidently too much to ask, and such a request, it is now clear, was a sort of tactical blunder on Brandeis' part in his long struggle against big business. Historian Thomas McCraw, critical of Brandeis for not "taking a major part in drafting and redrafting the bills until they were in exactly the right form," pointed out, "What might have been Brandeis' greatest role in forming national economic policy was played by a stand-in."[20]

Although it seems unlikely that Rublee meant to sabotage Brandeis' program from the beginning, not long after Brandeis returned to Boston, as he "listened to the testimony and hearings and thought about the matter," Rublee became increasingly convinced that Brandeis' program not only would be injurious to the nation's business but also would fail to successfully end legitimate complaints against big business.[21] Rublee was especially concerned that the Clayton Act, as reported, would prohibit the merger of corporations with a capital of more than $1 million and that the Covington bill would prohibit a number of marketing methods that he believed could be legitimate and beneficial under certain circumstances. As Rublee explained in an editorial later in 1914, "The provisions defining unfair competition [in the Clayton Act] if enacted would do much harm" to legitimate businesses. They "might prevent transactions against which there is no legitimate objection," and "they would occasion much litigation and introduce new uncertainties by reason of use of vague limiting adjectives which the courts have not defined."[22] Rublee had long believed that illegitimate business practices should be prohibited, but he agreed with Herbert Croly, who in *The Promise of American Life* pointed out: "[I]f the means taken to regulate [big businesses] impairs [their] efficiency, the government is merely adopting in a roundabout way a policy of destruction."[23] Reflecting upon the Progressive Party platform, it is easy to see how Rublee found the policy developing in 1914 a great mistake. The platform he helped write called for federal "regulation of the most efficient sort, which will preserve [big business'] good while eradicating and preventing its evils."[24] Another worry that Rublee and other progressive nationalists had was a concern that limiting the size of U.S. corporations arbitrarily might impair their ability to compete with large European combinations and cartels in foreign markets, especially Latin American and Asian markets.

Sometime in late February or early March, Rublee hit upon an idea of how legislation might be crafted that would end truly unscrupulous acts of businessmen while preserving methods whereby large corporations achieved market dominance through efficiency. As Rublee later explained, while he "listened to the testimony and hearings" before the committees, he was struck by the fact that

> in many cases in the courts under the Sherman Act, the final decrees prohibited sometimes seven or eight methods of unfair competition...and then added a last phrase reading, "and all other unfair methods of competition." ...It seemed to me that the best way to solve the problem of improving the anti-trust laws would be merely to prohibit

unfair methods of competition and to leave it to whomever was administering the law to determine whether a method in a particular case was unfair and harmful or not. It seemed to me you couldn't determine this in advance. In some cases a method of competition would be not dangerous to the public but in other cases it would be. This was not Congress' approach but this seemed to be the courts' approach.[25]

In the phrase "unfair methods of competition" Rublee had struck upon what he believed was a term of legal significance. He concluded that by simply outlawing "unfair methods of competition," Congress could do away with its list of proscriptions. Further, returning to his ideas in the 1912 campaign, Rublee believed that an independent commission made up of business and economic experts would be more qualified than the Justice Department to determine whether or not a corporation had acquired its market dominance through efficiency and economies of scale or through unfair methods of competition. Rublee believed that his approach would "stop monopoly at the threshold, and...do so with the least risk to legitimate business operations."[26]

Rublee now saw the way out of what he believed to be the mess that was taking shape in the House committees: simply substitute the term "unfair methods of competition" for the Clayton bill's proscriptive clauses and transform the sunshine commission in the Covington bill into a powerful regulatory body. As Rublee recalled:

I drew up a bill which created a trade commission—a Federal Trade Commission. ...My Bill increased the number of commissioners from three to five, and made the main change in Section V by putting in a general prohibition of "unfair methods of competition"—this being the phrase I got out of the court cases. It gave the Commission power to receive complaints, broadened its powers of investigation, gave it the power to hold hearings—first preliminary hearings of the complaint made and then if the Commission was impressed by the fact there was a real injury to the public, it could issue a formal complaint in its own name, then have hearings and finally come to a conclusion about whether the method was unfair or not. This Commission itself would not have the power to make a final decision but could appeal to a court in its own name.[27]

Rublee believed that with the right appointments, such a commission could protect legitimate businesses and hamstring those that attempted to gain monopolies through unscrupulous methods. Although he reasoned that a commission of business and economic experts could prevent the courts from injuring legitimate business methods, he also believed that a commission could act more quickly than the Justice Department to prevent unfair practices and thereby intercede on behalf of smaller companies before they were driven from the market.[28]

Rublee, of course, had a problem—he had no power to see such legislation passed. His base of influence in Washington was limited, at this point, to his relationship with Brandeis. And what Rublee proposed would undo the work for which Brandeis had for years been aiming. Rublee had only one other close associate in Washington, Democratic freshman congressman Raymond B.

Stevens of New Hampshire, but he was also close to Brandeis. In fact, Brandeis seems to have gotten Stevens on the Interstate Commerce Commission, where Stevens was working to pass Brandeis' price maintenance bill, the one Rublee had drafted in December. Although evidently a willing instrument of Brandeis' carefully orchestrated plan, Stevens was also a close friend of Rublee, and Rublee had no real option but to seek to convert him.[29] In his effort to win over Stevens, an advantage that Rublee had was the growing public opposition to the Clayton bill that suggested it might fail to win passage or that it might be dramatically altered before it could win passage in the Senate.[30]

Fortunately for Rublee, after Stevens heard the argument favoring a strong trade commission armed with a general prohibition against "unfair methods of competition," Stevens agreed that it was a better approach and promised to help introduce new legislation in the House. When Rublee completed his bill, Stevens tried to have it substituted in the Interstate Commerce Committee for the Covington bill. The committee, however, refused to act on Stevens' proposal and reported its original bill to the House. In the accompanying report to the House, Stevens affixed his "minority views," which listed his complaints against the Covington bill. Here Rublee had the opportunity to complain that the bill contained "no administrative power whatever" and that it made the new commission merely an aide to the Justice Department.[31] He argued that "an independent trade commission should have far greater purpose" and recommended the adoption of a bill that "declares unfair and oppressive competition to be unlawful and directs the commission to enforce the law."[32]

Hoping that the minority report had resonated, Stevens next attempted to substitute Rublee's bill for the Covington bill on the House floor in May, but, as Rublee recalled, "the House at once voted it down."[33] Following rejection by both the committee and the House, Rublee wavered a bit but then decided to seek support among Wilson's cabinet members. Although interior secretary Franklin Lane, a personal friend, was supportive, the more important Attorney General James McReynolds opposed Rublee's proposals. According to Rublee, McReynolds argued that "everything was decided" and suggested that he "give this up." At that point he very nearly did give it up, but, encouraged by Juliet, he decided to make a direct appeal to Woodrow Wilson.[34]

To get to Wilson, Rublee next converted his old friend Norman Hapgood, who as editor of *Harper's Weekly* had provided Brandeis a platform for his antibig business campaign. On 21 April, Hapgood sent a letter to Wilson in which he suggested a meeting with Rublee. Hapgood explained: "Mr. Brandeis has been so tied up with his railroad work that he has only given general thought to the trust situation as it has been developed in the bills now before congress.... The most important part of the really hard work done recently by the little group he represents has been carried out by George Rublee....[who has] one of the best minds for this kind of thinking that I ever knew."[35] Hapgood went on to explain the essence of Rublee's version of the trade commission bill: "Mr. Stevens has introduced the bill which was really drawn up by Mr. Rublee.... The Stevens Bill declares unfair competition to be unlawful, and empowers the Commission, whenever it has reason to believe that a corporation is using any unfair methods of competition, to hold a hearing, and if it is of the opinion that the method of competition in question is unfair to restrain the use thereof by injunction."[36] Hapgood concluded, "I cannot help feeling that in spite of the complication of burdens on you, a half hour with Mr. Rublee would not seem to you wasted."[37]

Wilson did not immediately agree to meet Rublee but instead sought the advice of a number of congressmen, including William Adamson, chairman of the Judiciary Committee. Adamson argued that the committee was satisfied with the bills as they were currently written and indicated that there was no point in visiting with Rublee. Wilson let the matter rest and gave Rublee no audience for the moment. It seems, however, that growing opposition to the Clayton bill likely convinced Wilson that there might be some merit to Rublee's approach, and he agreed to meet with him in late May.[38]

It was apparently not until after the appointment with Wilson was arranged that Rublee sought to involve Brandeis in his efforts. Realizing that Wilson would likely not act without Brandeis' consent, Rublee at last let Brandeis know what he had been up to for the past two months. It must have been awkward for Rublee to explain that, rather than working for Brandeis' program, he had in fact been working against it. As Rublee later recalled, "I knew this wasn't his approach to [antitrust] and I hadn't thought of him as going along with our plan—I was afraid he wouldn't go or would oppose it." Brandeis, however, seems to have taken the revelation graciously and agreed to attend the meeting with Wilson. He did not, however, endorse Rublee's proposals in advance and reserved the right to argue against them before Wilson.[39]

The White House meeting was held on the south lawn at the end of May and lasted well beyond its allotted half hour. Joining Rublee and Brandeis were Ray Stevens, New Hampshire senator Henry Hollis, Charles McCarthy (a Wisconsin progressive who had helped La Follette frame some of the laws that became known as the Wisconsin Plan), and a prominent progressive reformer from Kansas, possibly Victor Murdoch.[40] Following an opening statement by Stevens, who had made the appointment, Rublee explained his approach to antitrust regulation. He pointed out that the Clayton and the La Follette bills were flawed because "it was impossible to define these unfair practices" in a way acceptable to the courts. Rublee argued that it was better to simply prohibit unfair methods of competition and to create a strong trade commission that would determine whether or not a violation had occurred. He believed that a commission of experts would make a strong impression when it brought complaints before a court. He also pointed out that an added advantage of such a commission was that, if equipped with cease-and-desist powers, it could "nip restraint of trade in the bud." Rublee explained that in most cases, by the time the courts reached a decision that compelled a company to stop its unfair trading practices, the company usually would have already succeeded in driving its competitors from the market.[41]

As Rublee spoke, he could see that he was "making an impression on the President," who "listened very attentively and asked some questions." Evidently,

Brandeis was also impressed. When Rublee finished speaking, to his "great surprise, Brandeis entered the fray with great enthusiasm and backed [him] up strongly." Rublee recalled that Wilson "seemed much interested and quite stirred up" and that "it was clear to all of us that the President had accepted the idea." As they left the meeting, Brandeis confided to Rublee that it was "the most remarkable interview that [he had] ever been present at."[42]

Brandeis' conversion to Rublee's antitrust proposal is somewhat problematic for historians. Brandeis biographer Phillipa Strum argues that Brandeis "had not changed his principles" but instead had "become convinced that it was not possible to write a law covering all possible violations of antitrust policy."[43] This argument, however, seems misapplied since Brandeis' original intention was to have the enlarged Bureau of Corporations be an ongoing informational agency that would advise Congress on writing new legislation to cover malfeasant business innovations. Historian John Milton Cooper Jr. likewise attempts to argue that neither Brandeis nor Wilson made a substantive break with his New Freedom ideology in adopting the Progressive regulatory approach to antitrust. Because he apparently was unaware of Rublee's role both in drafting the 1912 Progressive Party platform and in converting Wilson, Cooper errs in dismissing the significance of the ideological shift. In his 1990 *Pivotal Decades* Cooper writes:

> Wilson had to overcome opposition from Bryanite Democrats and some Republican insurgents, who turned back on him his own campaign rhetoric against Roosevelt's support of regulation. They denounced the proposed agency as a covert servant of the trusts. There was poetic justice in the charge, but Wilson had really swung around to the regulatory approach for reasons that shared none of Roosevelt's fundamental approval of bigness. Instead he once again followed the advice of Brandeis, who argued that an expert regulatory commission could do a better job than the courts in curbing the trusts.[44]

Cooper is mistaken in identifying Brandeis as the source of the change. Brandeis was converted to the program at the same meeting with Rublee. Thomas McCraw, on the other hand, argues in his 1984 *Prophets of Regulation* that "Brandeis' support of the Stevens bill represented a dramatic turnabout from his longtime stance on the nature of a new trade commission."[45] McCraw goes on to point out that Wilson, upon "hearing Brandeis' endorsement" for Rublee's plan, "decided to shift his own position as well and go along with Rublee." An early source on Rublee's role in the formation of the Federal Trade Commission (FTC) that neither McCraw, Cooper, nor Strum seemed familiar with is Nelson Gaskill's 1936 *The Regulation of Competition*. Gaskill, an early member of the FTC, was the first to point to Rublee's central role in the creation of the commission. Noting the profound change in Wilson's approach to antitrust in the summer of 1914, Gaskill wrote: "Mr. George Rublee had been among the President's advisors in the preparation of the anti-trust program. He seems to have been at the very storm center when the reversal of the President's program took place. In fact, it would seem that he not only rode the storm but directed its course and procured the President's acquiescence in the change."[46] Certainly,

Rublee understood the significance of what was taking place. Writing to Learned Hand shortly after the White House interview, Rublee announced: "I am deep in the game now, doing much the same sort of thing I did in New Hampshire three years ago. We may succeed after all in putting over the Bull Moose idea of giving the Trade Commission power to prevent unfair competition—and if we do, we may kill the nonsense in the other bills."[47] Remarkably, while Brandeis laid the foundation for Wilson's antitrust program during the 1912 campaign and cultivated it throughout 1913 in his *Harper's Weekly* articles and early in 1914 through his appearances before congressional committees, it was Progressive George Rublee who stepped in and became the final architect of the project. From May until its final passage in September, Brandeis was only marginally connected to the legislation creating the FTC.[48] Rublee was the one who managed to see the legislation through both houses and through conference negotiations, surreptitiously taking on all challengers to his program.

While Wilson's support for Rublee's proposal would soon be complete, he was not entirely won over in the first meeting. In a 31 May letter to Learned Hand, Rublee reported that "the President listened very attentively when we talked with him and seemed to be really impressed." Rublee expected to have a second meeting with Wilson "pretty soon" to which he would bring "a new group of men." He also related his success in gaining support for his FTC bill in the Senate Committee on Foreign and Interstate Commerce and among several cabinet members, the only exception being "the Attorney General [McReynolds, who] will fight us to the finish." Given his growing successes, an optimistic Rublee believed that "the program will soon be settled one way or the other and I can then get away to Cornish."[49] The struggle that he had taken up, however, would dominate his time and energy and place him on a course that would render escapes to Cornish increasingly difficult.

Hand was happy to learn of Rublee's success because, as he explained in a letter on 9 June, he believed that "the court [had shown] itself incapable of any clear reasoning on the subject."[50] In his letter Hand complained that he had "before him a demurrer to a complaint under the Sherman Act which [was] troubling [him] a great deal." Hand believed that Rublee was "more familiar with the authorities" and hoped that he would do him the "great service" of explaining his "ideas on what kind of monopolies in restraint of trade the Supreme Court has prohibited under the Sherman Act in its latest cases." From his own study, Hand could only conclude that there was "no general rule that applies" and complained that one "can only try to steer about in the cases in a most haphazard and unscientific way." Such statements from an esteemed jurist could only confirm Rublee's belief that both businessmen and judges were greatly confused about antitrust law and that a new, clarifying policy was greatly needed.

Although Wilson was not persuaded in the first White House meeting, his conversion was not long in coming. A difficulty, however, was that Wilson's reversal came too late to stop the passage of the Clayton and Covington bills in the House. Evidently, Wilson believed that the two bills had required too great a show of strength to be radically changed just before their final votes, which might risk giving the opposition a footing to launch a counteroffensive that could scuttle the entire antitrust effort. Surprisingly, as Wisconsin Progressive Charles McCarthy revealed, Brandeis may, too, have regretted the Clayton Act's successful passage in the House. Writing to Hapgood on 3 June, McCarthy observed: "[I a]m sorry the Clayton bill is going so far, as I regard it as an entirely vicious bill. I think Mr. Brandeis is of the same opinion, as he expressed it to the President and to me." McCarthy hoped that "we can fix something up in the Senate."[51]

Wilson, too, believed that the Senate was the place to make the profound changes to the Covington and Clayton bills. On 10 June Wilson called Brandeis, Stevens, Hollis, and Rublee back to the White House to announce that he intended to have Rublee's provisions incorporated as section 5 of the Covington bill in the Senate.[52] Wilson planned to rely on Democratic senator Francis Newlands, chairman of the Committee on Interstate Commerce, to alter the Covington bill while in conference with House members. In addition to enlarging and renaming the Bureau of Corporations and arming it with cease-and-desist orders, section 5 of the proposed new Covington bill (renamed the Federal Trade Commission Act) would contain Rublee's prohibition against unfair methods of competition and thereby make the objectionable parts of the Clayton bill unnecessary.[53] As Rublee reported to Hand, he believed that with Wilson's help "the definition sections of the Clayton bill will be put to death."[54]

On 13 June New Hampshire senator Henry Hollis reported to Wilson on his success in rallying support in the Senate for Rublee's section 5. Hollis wrote: "We were able to get all the Democratic members of the Senate Interstate Commerce Committee in line on the Stevens amendment. The amendment was reported to the Senate this morning, and it seems likely that the Trade Commission Bill...may be put through the Senate without great delay."[55] Hollis, however, was overly confident. The incorporation of section 5 and other changes to the trade commission bill would meet strong resistance from conservatives in the Senate who feared that such a commission would have too much power. Interestingly, Rublee's moderate position fell between the positions of people like Brandeis who feared the growth of big business and those of conservatives who represented the capital class and who feared any government regulation of the economy.

When opposition from conservatives in both parties arose in the Senate during the summer, Rublee fought strenuously and successfully to defeat them. In a letter he wrote to Endicott Peabody at the end of the summer, Rublee related the extent to which he had struggled to see his version of the Federal Trade Commission created:

> You will be surprised to hear that I have been at work in Washington all summer. And I think it will interest you to know that I have been useful here. The Trade Commission Bill, which is the principal trust measure of the administration, is largely my work. Indeed the bill, as agreed to yesterday, by the conferees, is for the most part phrased by me. I suggested the central provision for the prevention of unfair competition. At first

everybody opposed it,—even including Mr. Brandeis—and I had gradually to convert them. The work of nourishing the debate by supplying materials, arguments, answers to objections etc. largely fell upon me. I have been in constant consultation with Committees, individual Senators and Congressmen, businessmen, and I have had several conferences with the President. The enclosed editorials from Harper's weekly, if you care to read them, will explain a little what it is all about. I must here confess that I wrote the editorials—and also Senator Hollis' speech which one of them so immodestly praises.[56]

In his fight to take control of federal antitrust policy, Rublee clearly pulled out all the stops and marshaled every bit of influence he had to win the contest.

Rublee's principal device to defend his provisions in the pending antitrust legislation was a twenty-two-page, unsigned pamphlet entitled *Memorandum concerning Section 5 of the Bill to Create a Federal Trade Commission.* Interior secretary Franklin Lane, who forwarded the memorandum to Wilson for his use in defending section 5, believed that the document "seems to contain the answers to most, if not all, of the objections that have been raised to this provision of the bill."[57] Rublee's memorandum is the most complete record of his conceptualization of the Federal Trade Commission. His primary purpose for the document was to help Wilson explain how section 5 would end unfair business methods and why it would complement, rather than threaten, the Sherman Act.

Rublee had no qualms in opening his defense with an unreconstructed Progressive Party definition of fair and unfair competition. In a passage that could have been lifted straight out of Croly's *Promise of American Life* or out of one of Roosevelt's campaign speeches, Rublee noted: "Fair competition is competition which is successful through superior efficiency. Competition is unfair when it resorts to methods which shut out competitors who, by reason of their efficiency, might otherwise be able to continue in business and prosper."[58] In defending section 5, Rublee stressed that it would offer greater protection for legitimate business than the Sherman Act, which allows "[c]ountless competitors [to] succumb before relief [is] finally obtained." Rublee argued that the current antitrust policy was flawed because "[t]he Department of Justice deals with monopoly as an accomplished fact." Pointing to the recent examples of Standard Oil and American Tobacco, Rublee pointed out that the Justice Department "did not attack the oil trust or the tobacco trust until after they had destroyed competition and obtained monopoly of markets." Rublee asserted, "The [Federal Trade] commission by reason of its knowledge of business affairs and the concentrated attention it will give thereto, its facilities for investigation, its rapid, summary procedure, will be able to protect business against unfair competition in much more effective and timely fashion than the Department of Justice can do."[59] Rublee added that an additional benefit would be that the Justice Department "will be relieved of a load of burdensome work which it is not well fitted to perform." Instead, Justice would "be able to give its main attention to the great task of prosecuting suits for the dissolution of monopolies" and leave to the FTC the "important service of policing competition so as to protect small business men, keep an open field for new enterprise, and prevent the development of trusts."[60]

Rublee's commission, to the extent that it was understood, was also being attacked as unconstitutional because it seemed to involve a delegation of legislative power to a "quasi-executive" body—a charge that Rublee himself had leveled against the Hepburn Act in 1906. In his defense of his trade commission, Rublee pointed to nine Supreme Court decisions in which the Court upheld the delegation of legislative capacities to administrative agencies, cases involving the ICC and the Treasury Department figuring prominently in his defense. Rublee also relied on a number of Supreme Court decisions to counter the argument that "'unfair competition' is too vague, that is has no certain meaning in the law." Rublee argued that, to the contrary, the term "has an unusually definite legal meaning" and defended his assertion, pointing to six federal decisions, four state laws, and six legal "text books on unfair competition in which the authorities are collected and analyzed." Rublee concluded his memorandum with a defense against Republican senator William Borah's assertion that section 5 of the trade commission bill would somehow both undermine the Sherman Act and also "put business in [a] straight jacket." Rublee countered, pointing out that [u]nfair competition is the most effective weapon of monopoly. Prevention of unfair competition, instead of putting business in a straight-jacket, will liberate business. Fair, free and open competition is the object of which the Sherman Act, no less than this bill seeks to promote. The two laws will be in perfect harmony."[61] Understanding that his arguments would become the basis of Wilson's statements on the proposed FTC bill, Rublee evidently sought to give a lofty tone to the defense of his bill.

In addition to his memorandum for Wilson, Rublee wrote various speeches for pro-administration senators. Rublee recalled that while listening to the debates in the visitor's gallery of the Senate, he could see the distinctive cover of one of his speeches lying on the tables of senators who were defending his proposals.[62] Rublee became completely absorbed with the fight in the Senate and devoted a great amount of time there. As he later recalled: "I was constantly going round to the Senate visitor's room in the Capitol and calling them out for consultation. I was there all of the time and didn't do anything else." Rublee was continuously "providing answers to opposing speeches, providing authorities and so on to reply to the Republicans who were attacking the bill." Rublee was proud of his intensive efforts because he thought that "it was perhaps the first time that anybody had done this without any pay, without any real interest in it except what he thought was right."[63]

Senators opposed to Rublee's efforts were well aware of his activities—it would have been difficult to miss a man of his unusual height and distinguished appearance dashing around the Capitol—and toward the end of the debates several of them attacked him as a lobbyist. The Republican attack on Rublee for lobbying was likely a poorly disguised effort to claim the moral high ground after Wilson's successful attack on Republican lobbyists in the 1913 tariff debate. Believing that his tariff reform effort was being undermined by private interests, in May 1913 Wilson claimed that an "insidious" lobby of corporate agents was paying large amounts in Congress to buy votes in support of the tariff.[64] With help from liberal Republican Robert La Follette an investigation was launched in the Senate to demonstrate the influence of lobbyists. Wilson's effective use of the lobbyist charge helped him win passage of the Underwood–Simmons Tariff, which lowered rates by about 25 percent. A year later Senate Republicans evidently still smarted from Wilson's use of the lobbying charge and sought to implicate Rublee in a Wilson lobbying effort. On 8 September the first of these attacks took place during a debate on the trade commission bill. Democratic senator James Reed, after having succeeded in getting Senator Francis Newlands to admit that the original version of the Covington bill did not contain the same section 5, suddenly turned his attention to Rublee's role in the bill's alteration and suggested that he was a lobbyist. When asked to clarify his statement, Reed explained: "I asked [Senator Newlands] if he does not know a man named Rublee, who has been weeks here in Washington, and has haunted the galleries and antechambers of the Senate. He has been very active in the advocacy of this bill, and I wanted to learn what the Senator knows about the activities of Mr. Rublee and whom Mr. Rublee represented, and who, if anybody, is paying Mr. Rublee."[65] Newlands replied that he did not believe Rublee to be "either employed or paid" by anyone in relation to the matter and stated that he believed that Rublee was "one of the few men who, without seeking place or reward of any kind, is desirous of dedicating himself to the public interest." Newlands asserted that "Mr. Rublee is a man of capacity, a lawyer by profession, interested in the Progressive movement, and he pursues such matters with a great deal of zeal and energy."[66]

After Senator Moses Clapp joined in the debate in support of Rublee, Senator Reed sought to qualify his statements: "Mr. President, I have not charged that Mr. Rublee is a lobbyist. I have charged that Mr. Rublee has been here lobbying and that he is about the most assiduous and persistent and tireless lobbyist I have seen around the Capitol at Washington."[67] Reed went on to point out the strong connection between Rublee and Stevens, who Reed had discovered was the author of a Senate price-maintenance bill (the one Rublee drafted for Brandeis the previous November), and he noted that it seemed to him that "to all intents and purposes they are hunting in pairs."[68]

Despite the efforts of Reed and other senators to undermine support for the bill through their attack on Rublee, the trade commission bill passed in the Senate on 5 August. Rublee was not yet, however, out of the woods, since the bill still had to meet certain adjustments in conference negotiations between the Senate and the House. Unwilling to allow the opposition a chance to regain ground, Rublee continued to pour all his effort into his crusade. On 1 September, in a letter to former governor Robert Bass, Rublee related some of his efforts during August:

I'm still in Washington, as you can see; and I can't leave until the Trade Commission bill comes safely out of conference. I hope that may be within a few days. There is no longer doubt that the provisions with regard to unfair competition will be enacted. The only matter in dispute is the power of the Court in reviewing the orders of the Commission. I have been having a long tussle with Senators Cummins and Newlands, and the Commissioner of Corporations, Davies, over that. It looks now as if my idea would prevail, as the President and the House conferees are on my side of the question.[69]

His view did indeed prevail. Although likely Rublee's work, on 20 August Joseph Davies, head of the Bureau of Corporations, submitted a brief that supported the constitutionality of section 5. The brief concluded that section 5 was legitimate as both a "quasi-judicial power" and a "quasi-legislative power" because it was "analogous to that exercised by the Interstate Commerce Commission."[70] Five days later Rublee submitted in his own name a brief that established the constitutionality of the court review function in the FTC bill.[71] These arguments, along with support from the Wilson administration and leading senators—who, of course, were working off Rublee's script—eventually overwhelmed the opposition. On 23 September 1914, the Act to Create the Federal Trade Commission became law.

Apropos of Rublee's tenacious efforts, Thomas McCraw, in his critique of Brandeis in *Prophets of Regulation*, complained that, given his fortuitous "circumstances, one would expect to find the Boston lawyer working night and day with congressional committees, shuttling back and forth between the White House and Capitol Hill, taking a major part in drafting and redrafting the bills until they were in exactly the right form."[72] That Rublee, an outsider, could garner the strength to alter the course of major legislation and see his own innovative and controversial design succeed was truly a remarkable feat. Evidently, the insight Rublee gained from his father, from his extensive reading in politics, and from his work with the Bass administration provided him with a sense of how to operate when he came to Washington—an idea of how to influence and direct the nation's most powerful institutions.

While likely no one was more surprised by Rublee's victory than Louis Brandeis, the Boston lawyer—though evidently largely out of the loop after the June White House visit—was supportive of the outcome. In a letter to Brandeis on 6 October Rublee thanked him for his "note about the Trade Commission bill" and observed: "If the bill is wrong I shall be much to blame. I drafted the conference report which was agreed to. Section 5 is exactly as I wanted it to be."[73] Replying 9 October, Brandeis observed: "I am delighted to know that the Trade Commission Bill is in a form satisfactory to you. Your season in Washington has been well worth while."[74] Impressively, with the exception of not succeeding in quashing the Clayton Act, Rublee had accomplished all of his objectives.

Although some historians have since made an effort to downplay it, there was quite a bit of buzz around the country concerning Wilson's abandonment of his 1912 New Freedom pledge to destroy big business rather than legitimatize it through regulation. Having the inside scoop on the political maneuvers that led to the passage of the FTC, the editors of *The New Republic* touted Wilson's conversion. Learned Hand, in an unsigned article entitled "An Unseen Reversal," paraded Wilson's capitulation to the New Nationalism platform. Hand argued that the act creating the FTC "may amount to historic political and constitutional reform" because in it "is contained the possibility of a radical reversal of many American notions about trust, legislative power, and legal procedure." Hand claimed to be most surprised because the act contains no guide for the limiting of the powers of the Commission and the courts but their general judgement of what is fair in the given case. "Do you think these practices serve the public interests or do you not? You must go over each case and look at the whole problem; there are no major premises for your guidance; yours is the responsibility for a right decision and yours the power; make your own rules for trade, but at your peril make them right." That in substance is the charter of these five Trade Commissioners, and the wonder is that so few have felt it to be a departure from American ideas.[75] Hand pointed out, "The Trade Commission act represents a totally different approach, a spirit strangely contradictory to the campaign theories of the President."

Although Rublee's Federal Trade Commission would soon suffer a series of setbacks and would be attacked from both the Left and the Right throughout the remainder of the century, his efforts were critical to the development of both corporate America and the regulatory state. The passage of his bill creating a strong commission to correct the abuses of big business rather than destroying it was both a personal victory and a triumph for centrist progressivism. The most vivid demonstration of Rublee's victory over the New Freedom Democratic platform lies outside the Federal Trade Commission building in Washington. Flanking the building's rotunda are twin monuments of a powerful horse being constrained by a large, muscular man.[76] The horse, representing big business, with its dynamic energy suggests that it could easily go on a rampage and leave a path of destruction behind it, oblivious to its own actions. The muscular man stripped to the waist standing beside the horse and gripping its reins symbolizes the federal government, which through intelligence and restraint forces the horse to submit its power to a useful purpose. This 1937 monument is an insightful interpretation of what George Rublee and the Progressive Party sought in an antitrust program. Had the New Freedom platform as originally proposed by Louis Brandeis succeeded, there would be no such monument—there would be no such horse.

NOTES

1. David W. Levy, *Herbert Croly of The New Republic: The Life and Thought of an American Progressive* (Princeton, NJ: Princeton University Press, 1985), 185-189.

2. Charles Forcey, *The Cross Roads of Liberalism: Croly, Weyl, Lippmann, and the Progressive Era, 1900-1925* (New York: Oxford University Press, 1961), 182. Rublee's long-time friend Phillip Littell, whom Rublee induced to take a house in Cornish in 1907, became a founding editor of *The New Republic*.

3. Norman Hapgood to Woodrow Wilson, 20 May 1913, Woodrow Wilson Presidential Papers, U.S. Library of Congress, Washington, D.C. [hereafter WWP-LoC], case file 510, reel 285.

4. Rublee, "Reminiscences," 101.

5. Rublee testimony, *Hearings I*, 32.

6. U.S. Government, *To Promote Export Trade, and for Other Purposes, Hearings before the Committee of the Judiciary, House of Representatives, Sixty-fourth Congress, First Session on H.R. 16707, Serial 46, July 18 and 20th, 1916* (Washington, D.C.: Government Printing Office, 1916), 25.

7. Cooper, *The Warrior and the Priest*, 233, and John Milton Cooper, Jr., *Pivotal Decades: The United States, 1900 - 1920* (New York: W.W. Norton, 1990), 196-197.

8. Morawetz to Edward M. House, 5 January 1927, Yale-House, box 82, folder 2769. Morawetz volunteered information on his role in the creation of the Federal Reserve because, as he explained: "I hear that a controversy has arisen as to the authorship of the Federal Reserve Bank plan and that Colonel Glass is about to publish in the Evening Post a series of articles controverting some statements in your recent book."

9. Morawetz to House, 6 January 1927, Yale-House, box 82, folder 2769.

10. Morawetz to House, 5 January 1927, Yale-House, box 82, folder 2769.

11. Rublee, *Reminiscences*, 101A (there are two pages identified as 101).

12. Brandeis to Hapgood, 30 September 1913, Urofsky and Levy, *Letters of Louis Brandeis*, vol. 3, 183-184.

13. A letter from Brandeis to Rublee on November 18 reflects the ease with which the two worked together: In the letter Brandeis asked: "May I add to your labors by suggesting that you consider carefully appropriate legislation to carry out the price maintenance principles advocated in my Harper's article of November 15th." Brandeis, having reiterated those points, explained: "There may be other provisions to be considered, and the above may not at all be sound. I am merely sending this . . . that you may be thinking over provisions of the bill" (Brandeis to GR, 18 November 1913, Louis Brandeis Papers, Brandeis Law Library Special Collections, University of Louisville, Louisville, Kentucky, microfilm [hereafter LBP], reel 32). Rublee had an initial draft of the bill completed by November 29.

14. GR to Peabody, 5 December 1913, GSA.

15. Brandeis reprinted the articles under the title *Other People's Money, and How the Bankers Use It* (New York: F.A. Stokes, 1914).

16. Louis Brandeis, "The Solution of the Trust Problem," *Harper's Weekly*, 8 November 1913, 18-19.

17. Brandeis to Alfred Brandeis in Lewis Paper, *Brandeis*, 190.

18. Paper, *Brandeis*, 189-191; and Thomas K. McCraw, *Prophets of Regulation* (Cambridge: Belknap Press of Harvard University Press, 1984), 119.

19. Brandeis to GR, 18 November 1913, LBP, reel 32. The bill that Rublee drafted was introduced by freshman Congressmen Raymond Stevens, who was a member of the House Interstate and Foreign Commerce Committee, possibly through Brandeis' influence (Gilbert H. Montague to Brandeis, 27 March 1914, LBP).

20. McCraw, *Prophets of Regulation*, 122. McCraw's description of Rublee as a "stand-in" fits a pattern among historians who, owing to a limited knowledge of his life and work, underestimate and—to a degree—denigrate him. McCraw, whose knowledge of Rublee's personal life seems to be limited to Rublee's oral memoir and his correspondence in the Brandeis papers, also errs in describing Rublee as a "self-styled

aristocrat." McCraw seems to have concluded that Rublee's description of his ease of lifestyle after 1900 was calculated to impress rather than to explain his ability to carry out pro bono work.

21. Rublee, "Reminiscences," 105.

22. Rublee editorial, *Harper's Weekly*, 13 June 1914, 4.

23. Croly, *The Promise of American Life*, 369.

24. S. J. Duncan-Clark, *The Progressive Movement: Its Principles and Its Programme* (Boston: Small, Maynard & Company, 1913), 214-218.

25. Rublee, "Reminiscences," 105-106.

26. Rublee editorial, *Harper's Weekly*, 8 August 1914, 121.

27. Rublee, "Reminiscences," 107.

28. Ibid., 106-107; and *Harper's Weekly*, 8 August 1914, 121.

29. Rublee, "Reminiscences," 106.

30. McCraw, *Prophets of Regulation*, 123. Although it not clear how McCraw reached this conclusion, he asserted that Rublee "accurately sens[ed] that the Clayton bill would be amended beyond recognition." It was, in fact, Rublee who most tried to scuttle the Clayton bill during the summer of 1914.

31. U.S. House of Representatives, 63rd Congress, 2nd Session, Committee on Interstate and Foreign Commerce, Report 533, Part Two: "Interstate Trade Commission, ...Minority Views" (Washington, D.C.: Government Printing Office, 1914). Copy in the FTC Library, Washington, D.C.

32. Ibid., 2. The Stevens minority report also complained that "Annual reports, unless based upon a sound and uniform system of accounting, convey little information and are of little value for the sake of comparisons." The report therefore insisted on "a uniform system of accounts" from corporations required to submit annual reports. Founding Federal Trade Commissioner Edward Hurley would champion accounting standards in 1915 and 1916.

33. Rublee, *Reminiscences,* 107-108.

34. Ibid., 108-110.

35. Hapgood to Woodrow Wilson, 21 April 1914, Arthur Link, et al. editors, *The Papers of Woodrow Wilson* (Princeton, N.J.: Princeton University Press, 1984), vol. 29, 481.

36. Ibid.

37. Ibid.

38. William Adamson to Wilson, 23 April 1914, *Papers of Woodrow Wilson*, vol. 29, 496.

39. Rublee, "Reminiscences," 112.

40. Wilson named Murdock to the FTC in 1917. Robert La Forte, *Leaders of Reform: Progressive Republicans in Kansas, 1900-1916* (Lawrence: University of Kansas Press, 1974), 246.

41. Ibid., 112-113.

42. Ibid., 113-114.

43. Philippa Strum, *Louis D. Brandeis: Justice for the People* (Cambridge: Harvard University Press, 1984), 215. Although Melvin Urofsky makes a similar argument in his work, *A Mind of One Piece: Brandeis and American Reform* (New York: Charles Scribner's Sons, 1971), 90-91, he describes Brandeis' support of Rublee's position as "almost involuntar[y]" in his article "Wilson, Brandeis and the Trust Issue, 1912-1914" in *Mid-America: An Historical Review* 49, no. 1 (January 1967), 26. Urofsky further suggests that Brandeis was converted to a new position when he observes: "But

Brandeis had gradually come to believe that it would be impossible to define statutorily all possible violations and that it was better to lay down legislative guidelines which could then be expanded by a regulatory agency" (27).

44. Cooper, *Pivotal Decades*, 200.

45. GR to Hand, 31 May 1914, HLS-Hand, box 107, folder 2.

46. Nelson Gaskill, *The Regulation of Competition* (New York: Harper & Brothers Publishers, 1936), 39.

47. GR to Hand, 31 May 1914, HLS-Hand, box 107, folder 2.

48. Strum, *Louis D. Brandeis*, 215; and Urofsky, *A Mind of One Piece: Brandeis and American Reform*, 91.

49. Ibid.

50. Hand to GR, 9 June 1914, HLS-Hand, box 107, folder 2.

51. Charles McCarthy to Hapgood, 3 June 1914, enclosure Hapgood to Wilson, 8 June 1914, WWP-LoC, reel 285.

52. Arthur Link, *Wilson: The New Freedom* (Princeton, NJ: Princeton University Press, 1956), 438; and GR to Hand, 8 June 1914, HLS-Hand, box 107, folder 2. The transcript of this letter (made for Gerald Gunther in preparation of his Hand biography) erroneously reads May 8 instead of June 8.

53. Rublee, "Reminiscences," 112-114; and Link, *The New Freedom*, 438.

54. GR to Hand, 8 June 1914, HLS-Hand, box 107, folder 2.

55. Henry Hollis to Wilson, 13 June 1914, Link et al., *Papers of Woodrow Wilson*, vol. 30, 181.

56. GR to Peabody, 4 September 1914, GSA.

57. Lane to Wilson, 10 July 1914, Link et al., *Papers of Woodrow Wilson*, vol. 30, 274.

58. George Rublee, "Memorandum Concerning Section 5 of the Bill to Create a Federal Trade Commission," WWP-LoC, case file 208, reel 60. While Link et al. give an extensive analysis of Rublee's "Memorandum" in vol. 30, 274, note 1 of the *Papers of Woodrow Wilson*, the document is only available in full on microfilm.

59. Ibid., 5.

60. Ibid., 5-6.

61. Ibid., 21.

62. Rublee, "Reminiscences," 117.

63. Ibid., 117-118.

64. Cooper, *Pivotal Decades*, 195.

65. United States, *Congressional Record*, 63rd Congress (Washington, D.C.: Government Printing Office, 1915), 14786-14787.

66. Ibid., 14787.

67. Ibid.

68. Ibid., 14787-14788.

69. GR to Bass, 1 September 1914, RBP, folder ML 31-12.

70. U.S. Senate, 63rd Congress, 2nd Session, "Brief by the Bureau of Corporations Relative to Section 5 of the Bill [H.R. 15613] to Create a Federal Trade Commission" (Washington, D.C.: Government Printing Office, 1914). Copy in the FTC Library.

71. U.S. Senate, 63rd Congress, 2nd Session, "Brief by George Rublee Relative to the Court Review in the Bill [H.R. 15613] to Create a Federal Trade Commission" (Washington, D.C.: Government Printing Office, 1914). Copy in the FTC Library.

72. McCraw, *Prophets of Regulation*, 124.

73. GR to Brandeis, 6 October 1914, LBP, reel 37.

74. Brandeis to GR, 9 October 1914, LBP, reel 31.

75. The New Republic, 20 (9 January 1915), 7-9. Hand's identity as the author of this article is established in Gunther, *Learned Hand*, 246.

76. Michael Lantz, the sculptor who before he won the competition for the FTC building worked for the Works Projects Administration, fittingly entitled the statues "Man Controlling Trade." See George Gurney, *Sculpture and the Federal Triangle* (Washington, D.C.: Smithsonian Institution Press, 1985), 391-392.

7

"An Ideal Public Servant" (1914–1916)

After struggling from April to September to see his version of a Federal Trade Commission created, George Rublee was in much need of a recess. With nothing remaining to do in Washington until early 1915, when Wilson would make appointments establishing the first FTC, in the autumn of 1914 Rublee returned to New Hampshire, where he soon began working with the Progressive Party to devise a strategy for the off-year election. While Rublee remained an important figure in the new party, his extended absence from the state seems to have cost him some influence. Throughout the summer Rublee petitioned without success to have the Progressive Party endorse Ray Stevens as candidate for Senate against archconservative Republican Jacob Gallinger. Writing to Robert Bass in July, Rublee asserted that he did not "know of anything more important to be done in politics this year than the replacement of a reactionary like Gallinger by a progressive with Stevens' ability and character."[1] Although Rublee was thinking of Gallinger's defeat as essential to ending conservative control of the Senate, within a year he would find that it was his own political future that was at stake in the contest. Coming off his stunning victory in Washington, however, Rublee evidently believed that Gallinger's defeat was within his and Stevens' reach. While they would both suffer setbacks at the hands of the "old reprobate," the shifting focus of American politics would eventually make their losses seem an advantage.[2]

Although Jacob Gallinger had been New Hampshire's senator for four terms and was nationally recognized as the "embodiment of 'stand-patism" owing to his conservative record, Rublee and Stevens seem to have believed that the seventy-seven-year-old senator could be beaten because he had never been popularly elected to the Senate.[3] The senior senator appeared vulnerable owing to the recent progressive ferment and the passage of the Seventeenth Amendment in 1912, which required Gallinger to submit himself for the first time to a popular vote to be returned to the Senate. Although Rublee and Stevens believed that Gallinger could be defeated, they realized that in a three-way race a Republican would likely be elected because the progressive vote would be split. In an attempt to overcome some Progressives' opposition to him as a Democrat, Stevens disowned the states' rights doctrine with a "speech on federalism" and performed some political favors for a leading New Hampshire Progressive.[4]

While Rublee was excited about Stevens' campaign and wanted to take an active and public part in it, he knew that he could do so only if the Progressive Party backed him. Rublee informed Bass, "If Stevens is nominated on our ticket I should like to give my time this fall to working for his election. I should like to go on the stump and to do any other work that might be assigned to me."[5] The party, however, was at a crossroads and was bitterly divided between zealots who would risk a Gallinger victory to preserve the party's identity and pragmatists like Rublee who believed that the Progressives should back whichever liberal candidate had the best chance of victory. When he learned that the diehards were successfully blocking support for Stevens, Rublee complained, "[t]hey don't seem to have a real grip of the progressive idea if they are willing to miss the chance of beating Gallinger with Stevens, because of past issues…which have no essential relation to the progressive movement."[6] Rublee was frustrated because without the nomination of the Progressives, Stevens would likely be unable to defeat Gallinger and Rublee would be limited in what he could do for Stevens' campaign. Despite his frustration with his fellow Progressives, he let Bass know that he would "be glad to help [the party] in any way I can after I get back to New Hampshire."[7]

Rublee, characteristically, did not give up easily and continued to seek the party's support for Stevens up to the New Hampshire Progressive Convention in the fall. Rublee, who was asked to write "an intelligent statement of the present position of the Progressive party" for the gubernatorial candidate, was a delegate to the convention and took that opportunity to make a speech endorsing Stevens as the Progressive candidate.[8] The speech reopened the rift between diehards and moderates and threatened the cohesion of the party. Bowing to pressure from the obdurate "never-say-die Progressive[s]," as novelist Winston Churchill called them, the convention nominated one of their own, Benjamin Greer, for Senate.[9]

Having failed to win Stevens' nomination, Rublee was in a quandary. He had little confidence that the Progressive Party would be successful in the election, and yet he could not align himself with either the Democratic or Republican Party owing to his personal convictions and an interest in his own future political viability. To help Stevens' campaign and yet proclaim himself a Progressive would be a difficult position to defend and might cost what influence he had left in the party. Having recently struggled against Gallinger and other conservatives in the Senate, however, a Stevens victory seemed more important than supporting a party that might be breathing its last breaths. Unable to abandon either path, Rublee decided to try to have it both ways; help Greer in his attack on Gallinger but encourage him not to criticize Stevens. Although Rublee could no longer be Stevens' campaign manager, he could advise the campaign privately and pull strings as best he could for his friend. Rublee understood that it was a precarious course but felt that it was his only option under the perplexing circumstances.

While Rublee and Stevens knew that they would be in for a tough campaign, they soon learned that Gallinger was up for the fight and that he was less unpopular than they had supposed. Writing to Louis Brandeis for help on 6 October Rublee explained that Stevens' campaign "is going to be a hard fight to win, because New Hampshire is normally a Republican state; and the people don't know much about their representatives in Washington."[10] Rublee reported that "Stevens is being misrepresented as an impractical, wild young man without experience who schemes dangerous, anarchistic things." Rublee complained, "What he has done at Washington is little known," and he pointed out that Brandeis could "help powerfully by making a speech for Stevens at Manchester." Apologizing for the inconvenience, he stressed how important it was "to keep out an old reprobate like Gallinger."[11] Indicative of Rublee's role in Stevens' campaign, Brandeis received a letter the next day from the chairman of the New Hampshire Democratic State Committee reiterating Rublee's request for help. The chairman, who also complained that Stevens was accused of advocating "anarchistic, socialistic doctrines," pointed out that "Mr. Rublee is here helping us."[12] Brandeis, however, did not immediately reply to Rublee's or Farrand's request for a date on which he could speak. Nevertheless, on 28 October Brandeis agreed to an urgent plea for a last-minute speech in Manchester despite having to reject a similar request from the Massachusetts Democratic Party chairman that he speak on behalf of its governor.[13]

Although Rublee attempted to stay in the background as best he could, in a letter to Brandeis on 18 October he announced his decision "to go on the stump this week" as he traveled around New Hampshire with the Progressive nominees. A momentous decision, Rublee, who evidently believed that Greer was ineffective against Gallinger, thought that Stevens "would win if the voters only could be made to understand the difference between him and Gallinger."[14] In an effort to be sensitive to both his position in the Progressive Party and the conventional rules of engagement, Rublee was careful not to support Stevens directly or to attack Gallinger on personal grounds but instead stressed Gallinger's "extremely conservative [voting] record."[15] Evidently, Rublee was not as circumspect as he hoped because on 29 October the conservative *Manchester Union* led with the headline: "Rublee Makes Warm Attack on Gallinger—Alleges Intimidation, Persecution, and Blackmail against 'Machine.'" Rublee's speech, however, does not seem to support the paper's allegation. Rublee's opening statement demonstrates his approach: "I am going to invite your attention to such portion of Senator Gallinger's record in the Senate on progressive measures as I shall have time for. It is perfectly fair to Senator Gallinger to judge him on that record. I am making no personal assault upon him. In voting and speaking as he has done I give him credit for expressing his honest convictions. What I want is to make known to you what his convictions are."[16] Rublee then proceeded to report Gallinger's voting record on progressive issues dating back to 1906, when Gallinger rejected La Follette's railway safety bill, which attempted to make it unlawful for any railroad employee to remain on duty more than sixteen consecutive hours or to go on duty without having had at least ten hours of rest.[17] Rublee continued pointing out that Gallinger voted against the popular election of U.S. senators, against a national presidential primary, against the regulation of railroads, against eight-hour and other labor laws, against the creation of the Children's Bureau, and against the FTC. Rublee noted in conclusion that "if you wished to sum up in one personality all the ideas in regard to government which the Progressive Party opposes, you could not improve upon Senator Gallinger. Such a chance to vote against the human embodiment of the policies against which we are contending seldom occurs. I hope you will make the most of it."[18]

In addition to criticizing Gallinger's conservative voting record, Rublee as best he could spoke in terms that would benefit Stevens' campaign. This Rublee achieved by stressing that "the most formidable obstacle in the way" of progress was the "political machines of the old parties." He pointed out that although Progressives could "not realize our hopes in full until we can work through our own representatives and executive officers," he allowed that the party could "always stimulate and arouse progressively minded men in the old parties." Rublee then asserted that Wilson's nomination and impressive record in the first two years resulted from Democratic fears that "a secession to the Progressive Party would take place which would put them out of office." Rublee argued that "President Wilson has served the country well" and that Progressives should be "grateful for those laws." Having earlier asserted that Gallinger was the "rankest standpatter in the land," Rublee concluded, contending: "There is but one true line of political division in this country now, and that is between Progressives and standpatters."[19]

Although Rublee believed that he had stayed within the acceptable bounds of criticism, he would soon learn that Gallinger vehemently disagreed. The election results confirmed Rublee's worst fears, with Gallinger drawing 42,113 votes against Stevens' 36,382 and Greer's 1,938. While a combined Democrat-Progressive vote would have lacked 3,800 votes to defeat Gallinger, Rublee could have argued that a fusion ticket from the beginning might have given the campaign added energy to get out the vote and to win the day. Instead, New Hampshire returned—as Theodore Roosevelt observed—"the very worst of its old leaders" to Washington.[20] More unfortunate for Rublee personally, Gallinger would soon have opportunity for revenge.

Although Stevens' loss to Gallinger meant that he would not be returning to his rather exciting work in Washington, Rublee still had a chance of returning to Washington through an appointment to the FTC.[21] It was briefly hoped that Stevens might also be appointed to the commission, but he was disqualified from serving owing to the constitutional provision that prohibits congressmen from holding high offices created during their term.[22] Throughout the months leading to Wilson's February announcement of the first commission, Rublee's nomination remained uncertain. With only five places available and many hopeful political applicants, Wilson was hard-pressed to find a place for Rublee on the commission. Writing to Hand on 30 January 1915, Rublee announced: "It is nearly certain that I shall not be appointed [but] that Record will be. Davies, with genuine grief, told me so this morning."[23] Rublee learned that "Colonel House and McAdoo had done their best to persuade the president" and that as a result he had "been on the list twice, but [was] off now." Instead, Wilson wanted "Record [who] had rendered such service in connection with the New Jersey anti-trust legislation that he wanted to do something for him." Complaining, Rublee added: "The Seven sisters! Think of that. All my work was aimed at removing from the National legislation all likeness to the sisters. The President approved. And now he wants to reward the parent of the sisters." Rublee confided, however: "I think the real reason is probably not stated. Record did render very valuable service in helping to elect W. W. Governor...and that election had important consequences." Although Rublee felt "the disappointment of one who has lost a game," he asserted, ironically, "Very likely I shall be happier than if I had won."

Nevertheless, when Wilson announced his appointments to the FTC on 22 February 1915, Rublee's name appeared on the list, and George Record's did not. Since Wilson's only limitation was that he appoint no more than three Democrats to the commission, he decided to appoint Rublee as a Progressive instead of two Republicans. The five staggered appointees were former Bureau of Corporations commissioner Joseph Davies (seven years), Edward Hurley (six years), William Harris (five years), William Parry (four years), and George Rublee (three years). Writing to Brandeis on 24 February, Rublee admitted that "the appointment came as a surprise."[24] Perhaps letters from Brandeis and Hapgood to Edward House in December helped secure Rublee's nomination. On 31 December Brandeis had pointed out prophetically to House that "the success or failure of the Commission will depend largely upon the quality of men selected," and three days earlier Hapgood warned that "commission government is in danger of cracking under the strain" and suggested that "nothing can save the idea except the enlistment of [well-qualified] men."[25]

Republicans were at once opposed to Wilson's list of appointments because they claimed that none of the appointees were "regular Republicans."[26] Although Rublee asserted that he was a member of the Progressive Party, the Republicans argued that the party held no official recognition. William Parry's nomination as a Republican was also questioned for similar reasons. The *New York Times* reported that Republicans believed that "Mr. Parry is an out-and-out Progressive, and seem to regard his selection with that of an acknowledged Bull Mooser like Mr. Rublee." With three Democrats, a Progressive, and a liberal Republican appointed to the commission, Republicans believed they had been cheated. Further, they believed that Wilson's appointment of Rublee and Parry was mostly aimed at winning the support of Bull Moosers in the 1916 campaign.[27]

In addition to the Republicans' general opposition to his proposed appointment, Jacob Gallinger immediately denounced Rublee's nomination. The *New York Times* reported on 27 February that Gallinger declared Rublee "personally offensive" owing to his role in Stevens' campaign and to the tactics he had employed to pass the FTC. The paper reported: "The greatest opposition is directed against George H. Rublee of New Hampshire, who was campaign manager for a Democrat against Senator Gallinger of that State, and was recently denounced on the floor of the Senate by Mr. Reed of Missouri for alleged lobbying against some of Mr. Reed's proposed amendments to the Anti-Trust act."[28] Although Senator La Follette came to Rublee's defense, stating, "It seems to me...that he has been doing some lobbying for the people—people who are not able to hire lobbyists," Gallinger's attack on Rublee meant that his appointment was in much doubt from the beginning.[29] Following his successful reelection, Gallinger returned as senior senator, caucus chairman, president pro tempore of the Senate, and leading champion of senatorial prerogatives.[30]

Rublee's close friends at *The New Republic*, Herbert Croly, Walter Lippmann, Philip Littell, and Walter Weyl (four of the six editors), soon came to his defense. On 27 February the journal reported: "Among the appointments to the new Trade Commission one man at least, Mr. George Rublee, possesses altogether exceptional qualifications for the office. It would be strange if he did not possess such an understanding, because he himself was most influential in obtaining for the Commission its enlarged powers."[31] Two weeks after the commission was named, a subcommittee of the Senate Interstate Commerce Committee was authorized to conduct hearings for Wilson's nominees. In addition to probing them on antitrust questions, the subcommittee called upon Rublee to answer various charges that Gallinger brought against him at the opening of the hearings.

Gallinger's indictment of Rublee was sweeping and at times sensational. At his first appearance before the committee Gallinger introduced a letter from a "correspondent" who charged that Rublee, after Bass' election as governor in 1910, "appeared and took possession, and was, to all intents and purposes, so far as public matters went, governor."[32] Gallinger also charged that Rublee was Stevens' "political manager of the [1914] campaign" and alleged that "it was a campaign of vilification." Although he believed that Rublee "went out of his way to belittle" him, under questioning Gallinger admitted: "I did not hear Mr. Rublee, but it was reported to me that his criticisms of me were offensive and in every way unbecoming." More sensational, however, were Gallinger's assertions that Rublee's successful mediation with Boston & Maine president Charles Mellen was improper and that Rublee had employed mercenary tactics on behalf of Louis Brandeis' price maintenance bill in 1914.[33]

One of Gallinger's statements concerning Rublee was, however, close to the truth. He described Rublee as "a political nondescript" and thought the "term of 'maverick'" fitted Rublee well, because "he is unmarked politically; he is a free lance [and] belongs to any party that suits his purpose best."[34] To Gallinger, this was an odious blot on Rublee's record. During the 1912 campaign the New Hampshire senator had grown to despise Theodore Roosevelt and supporters such as Rublee, whom he held responsible for Republican losses. Nevertheless, Gallinger's description bore some truth. Rublee was willing to work with the progressive element of either party so long as he was in agreement with the goals of reform. By 1915 Rublee had become truly independent, and he increasingly objected to the corrupting influence of political parties. As he observed in his November speech against Gallinger: "So long as the mass of party voters are enslaved by the party label, all that the bosses and the interests behind them have to do is to capture the party organization. Once in possession of the party organization, they select subservient men as candidates, rely on the blind party voter to elect them, and so acquire control of government."[35] Rublee was not alone in rejecting party politics; within a year Robert Bass would declare that he had become "in every sense an Independent."[36]

Rublee appeared before the committee the day after Gallinger and was called upon to answer the senator's various charges. In addition to explaining his role in the Bass administration and his negotiations with Mellen, Rublee was called upon to answer questions regarding the price maintenance bill that he had drafted for Brandeis.[37] At a second interview before the committee Rublee was called upon to answer Gallinger's assertions that he was responsible for various pieces of propaganda aimed at Gallinger over a ten-year period. Rublee denied all instances, evidently to the satisfaction of the committee. In addition to defending himself, Robert Bass, Ray Stevens, Senator Henry Hollis, and Winston Churchill testified on his behalf. Each dismissed Gallinger's charges against him, and each commented on Rublee's intellectual capacity for the position. Bass, for example, explaining both Rublee's lack of political alignment as well as his fitness for the position, observed:

> And it is that quality, [of having] a natural sympathy with liberal principles of government, combined with fairness of mind which prevents [Rublee] from going to extremes. Furthermore I, and other men of my acquaintance who have known Mr. Rublee for many years, consider that he had one of the best minds among the men of his acquaintance: one of the clearest intellects among the younger men who have been doing things in this country of late.[38]

Rublee's cause was also helped by Robert La Follette and Francis Newlands, who were both on the confirmation committee. Rublee's nomination was also championed by old friends at *The New Republic* and newer friends like Felix Frankfurter, then a professor at Harvard Law School. In an editorial in the *Boston Transcript*, Frankfurter outlined Rublee's legal career, lauded his "various public endeavors," and described him as "a man of breadth and scholarship, enriched by much travel and steeped in the humanities."[39] Frankfurter concluded: "I venture to say that his appointment is altogether ideal. As an advisor of business, as a student of affairs, as a citizen who has given his time and thought generously to working out our national problems of conservation and business, as a personality fine and vigorous, Mr. Rublee comes to the new work of the Trade Commission with unique qualifications."[40] Despite such recommendations and the subcommittee's favorable report of him, the Senate confirmed all the nominees except Rublee on 3 March 1915.

Rublee's confirmation failed because Gallinger, in calling Rublee "personally obnoxious," had invoked his right to so-called senatorial courtesy. A device designed to strengthen their control of political patronage, senatorial courtesy gave senators the final say over federal political appointments to offices in their home state. Gallinger's claim to this antediluvian prerogative in Rublee's case was something of a stretch because the appointment was to a national office. To make his point, Gallinger had to threaten a filibuster in a closed executive session at the close of the winter term to block Rublee's nomination.[41] Rublee soon learned, however, that Wilson was willing to face down senatorial courtesy and that he planned to give him a recess appointment within the week. Rublee confided to Brandeis that he was unsure that he should accept the appointment, but Brandeis encouraged him to take it, saying: "By all means accept. You will always be needed on the Commission, but most in getting it started."[42] Rublee agreed, accepting the recess appointment, and was sworn in with the other founding commissioners on 19 March.

Despite the uncertainty of his own position on the commission, Rublee was "shocked" by Wilson's nomination of Parry, Hurley, and Harris, who he thought were not well qualified. Although it was understood that Davies, who had been commissioner of the now dissolved Bureau of Corporations, would have a leading role on the new FTC, Rublee believed that the other men were appointed for political calculation rather than for expert knowledge of the issues. Rublee later observed that the nominations to the FTC "seemed to me totally inconsistent with what the President seemed to understand so well, when we were discussing the idea of the commission. But that was the Commission. It really had no chance to do its job with that kind of membership. It was hopeless, really. I didn't then quite know that it was hopeless but I was discouraged."[43] Although Rublee at the time found them "rather agreeable men," he confided to Bass that they all, including Davies, seemed "cautious and anxious to be peace makers."[44] He feared that "unless somebody furnishes motive power and positive ideas, they might do just nothing at all." While Rublee evidently never relied on his authorship of the commission to demand leadership, he seems to have decided early on that he would attempt to supply the "motive power" that the commission lacked.[45]

To Rublee's chagrin, the commission was plagued with confusion and various setbacks from the beginning. He soon found that the commission's appropriation bill had been mishandled in Congress and that there was a serious shortage of funds. Relating his frustration to Brandeis, Rublee complained: "I don't see how the Commission is going to get along with the funds available. It looks as if Davies was fast asleep while the appropriation bill was going through."[46] Rublee admitted to being "heavy hearted over the whole thing—including my own somewhat dubious status" but claimed to be determined "to go on and do my best on the job." Owing to its lack of funds, in early April commissioner Harris had to send the following humbling request to the White House on behalf of the new agency: "The Federal Trade Commission is without funds to purchase furniture and other supplies necessary for their work, and I have been requested by the Commission to take the matter up with the President and see if we can get some old furniture from The White House and also from the Commission on Industrial Relations when they have finished their work."[47] The commission was soon offered a variety of old desks and tables stored in the basement of the executive offices and given rooms in the Department of Commerce. Wilson also wrote to congressmen in search of funds for the commission so that "the first months of the action of the Trade Commission should not be disappointing."[48] The situation was saved, however, when Rublee managed to help the commission secure access to a large portion of the former Bureau of Corporations' unspent funds. He accomplished this by writing a brief supporting "a liberal construction of the appropriations acts" and visiting the judge in charge of the decision in the Department of Treasury.[49]

Although the lack of funds was somewhat disconcerting, the commission also suffered from a lack of cohesion and clear vision. Rublee, of course, had definite ideas about the work that the commission should take up, but his precarious position on the commission owing to Gallinger's challenge and Wilson's decision to give him the shortest term seems to have at first undermined his influence on the commission. Writing to Bass in March, he admitted that "the job will have some continuously unpleasant features," against which he "must cultivate a cool indifference."[50] Evidently, Rublee was reflecting on the difficulties that had arisen on the day the commission was installed. Following a swearing-in ceremony, Davies presented a resolution that established that he would remain chairman indefinitely. Although the other members agreed, Rublee demurred, arguing that "in the first place" it was improper and "in the second place, it was ineffective because we, at any time could repeal the resolution."[51] Rublee later recalled that his position "certainly didn't make a hit" and that the commission passed the resolution with his official dissent.[52]

Perhaps not surprisingly, throughout the two years that Rublee was on the commission he was often at odds with the majority of commissioners. Wanting the commission to have a strong start by taking on important cases, he was frustrated to find that Davies preferred to deal with what Rublee called the "little frauds." He later recalled: "I perhaps was wrong but I withstood the pressure to take up the little frauds that the courts could well handle and tried to get the commission to take up more important cases. The result was that the whole time that I was there [there] was no proceeding started.... I don't think I was altogether wise in this but I took an uncompromising position."[53] To Rublee, "little frauds" were squabbles between small producers that had little impact on the nation. In his effort to keep the commission from pursuing such matters, Rublee sought Brandeis' opinion. For instance, 18 August Rublee wrote:

Lit Brothers [department stores] have sent circulars to people in Delaware offering to sell B.V.D. underwear at 35 cents a garment only to persons who will open charge accounts. The regular price is 50 cents. It is alleged that the 35 cent price involves a loss. The [small] retailers cannot meet the price without losing money. Is this unfair competition and is the public interest so affected that the commission ought to issue a formal complaint against Lit Brothers? There is some difference of opinion among us. That is why I want your view.[54]

Had the circulars not crossed state lines, the FTC would, of course, not have had purview over this possible predatory pricing scheme involving B.V.D. underwear. Although Davies and other members thought this was a legitimate concern, Rublee, as he explained a few years later, "objected to extending the meaning of fraudulent practices" to small suits because it "would so increase the Commission's labors that with its limited appropriations and personnel it would not be able to give sufficient attention to the real task for which it was established."[55] Evidently, Brandeis agreed with Rublee, thereby helping him resist extending FTC jurisdiction over the "little frauds" while he remained on the commission.

Rublee also fought to keep the commission from offering advance advice to businessmen who wanted authorization for questionable business practices. This issue also arose in the first months of the commission's existence, first appearing during a lengthy excursion that Davies orchestrated. Davies succeeded in having the commission begin its work with a tour of the West in something of a publicity campaign, during which the commission held a series of public hearings. As Rublee explained a little later, "It appeared to be the common belief of business men that the chief function of the Commission was to give advice," so that "several hundred applications for advice" were laid before the commission during the tour.[56] Although Davies believed that the commission could give such advance advice, Rublee objected. He believed that it was "perfectly clear that nothing in the law authorized the giving of such advice and [that] the Congressional debates" at the time of the commission's creation "showed that Congress was strongly opposed to such action on the part of any government agency."[57] Rublee further reasoned that such advice "afforded no protection, since there was no assurance whatever that either the Department of Justice or the courts would pay any attention to it."

Rublee did not enjoy continually thwarting Davies' efforts, but as a lawyer and the commission's author, he believed that a sound beginning was crucial to the new agency's success. Unfortunately, pulling against Davies risked paralyzing the commission and earned him Davies' enmity. Of the wrenching and lengthy western excursion, which one reporter dubbed the "see-America-first-tour," Rublee complained to Bass: "I am having a rather arduous time traveling around with the Commission holding hearings, attending banquets etc."[58] Davies, however, who—although ostensibly a lawyer—was at heart a politician, may well have been departing from the commission's original aim at Wilson's suggestion. Fearing that his administration would be blamed for a recent economic downturn because of its vocal attacks on business, Wilson may have decided that the commission should take a less threatening approach. As one journalist pointed out, while on tour the commission seemed "anxious not to pester business, but to be helpful in a large constructive way."[59]

By the end of the summer of 1915 the FTC's unenthusiastic start was being reported. Gilson Gardner, a Washington correspondent with the Newspaper Enterprise Association, sent a copy of an article he wrote to Brandeis in which he called into question the FTC's work to date. Gardner, who in the enclosed article complained that "[u]p to date the commission has been merely a listening and a dining body," asked Brandeis in an accompanying letter: "How about it? This was a creature of your creating. Is this what you intended it to do?"[60] Replying, Brandeis admitted that the commission's recent activities "are not what I had contemplated would engage their attention" but added that "the fact that Rublee and Stevens are connected with the Commission leads me to believe that it will still prove a valuable governmental instrument."[61] Partially in an effort to counter Davies' limited vision, Rublee had managed to get Ray Stevens named FTC chief examiner and Joe Cotton named as an adviser.[62] Rublee also sought, with the help of Brandeis, to get his old friend and once and future partner Edward Burling named to the commission over a candidate whom Davies backed.[63]

The other commissioners did allow Rublee to pursue some of his goals. Among other work, Rublee wanted the FTC to present reports to Congress concerning the state of the U.S. economy, detailing "what was wrong, why, and so forth."[64] Rublee wanted the commission to assemble the most knowledgeable group of economists that it could afford and produce specific recommendations. Owing to the commission's meager funds, Rublee proposed that the commission seek "the very best young economists in the country, many of whom perhaps would welcome a period of work for the government."[65] Rublee recalled that the other commissioners did not object, so he wrote "to all the universities in the country and asked for their best economic students who were just graduating or had just graduated." Dean Edwin Gay of the Harvard Business School helped Rublee attract several economists. Nevertheless, Rublee recalled being somewhat frustrated with them because "they would fix their positions by what the Supreme Court had decided."[66] Rublee wanted them "to find out whether those decisions were right from an economic point of view" and ignore the courts. Only then could the FTC give advice to Congress that might benefit business.[67] As Rublee explained in 1926, he envisioned that the commission's power of investigation could be used to produce "really expert" reports that would affect "the judgment of Congress and the decisions of the courts," thereby "bringing our statutory and case law into harmony with economic law."[68]

Wilson reappointed Rublee early in 1916, and debates again erupted on the Senate floor over his nomination. Gallinger maintained his claim that Rublee was "personally obnoxious" and demanded the Senate reject his nomination. What began as a question of Rublee's fitness for the commission, however, soon blossomed into a nationwide debate over the use of senatorial courtesy to block nominations that affected the entire country. Rublee's friends at *The New Republic* immediately came to his defense and denounced senatorial courtesy. On 26 February 1916, the journal asserted:

The ordinary sane man is bewildered at this hocus-pocus which permits one Senator to do so much damage—for it is damage. Mr. Rublee is an extraordinary man, and his is one of the best appointments made by President Wilson. He understands [the FTC] as few others do, and his presence on the Commission may almost be called essential to give it a successful start. He is not a politician nor an office-seeker. He is an ideal public servant.... and if politics is ever to be lifted out of the rut of routine and little-mindedness, it will be because the government is composed of men like George Rublee.[69]

Since Gallinger maintained his previous charges, the Wilson administration knew that it would have to fight for Rublee's confirmation. Evidently, this was just the sort of contest that Wilson desired, and he called upon several senators seeking support for Rublee. On 12 May two days before Rublee's confirmation vote, Wilson wrote Senator Atlee Pomerene, Democratic leader in the Senate, to explain the importance he attached to Rublee's confirmation:

I know you will let me speak to you confidentially, and with the greatest freedom, about a matter which is troubling me a great deal. I mean the efforts that Senator Gallinger is making to defeat the appointment of Mr. Rublee to the Federal Trade Commission. It is a very serious matter to have a nomination of such importance defeated on the personal objection of a single Senator who cannot allege anything with regard to the record or qualifications of Mr. Rublee which shows unfitness for the position, and it would still be a more serious business to let the independent and progressive voters of the country get the impression that we on our side let those who are distinctly reactionary defeat appointments of this sort. Our whole fortune in the coming election depends upon whether we gain or do not gain the confidence of the independent voters, and I could not imagine anything that would be more likely to defeat us than the rejection of such nominations as [these of Rublee and Brandeis].[70]

Despite Wilson's efforts, Rublee's nomination was rejected by a vote of forty-two to thirty-six. Fourteen Democrats voted against Rublee, or in favor of retaining the senatorial privilege, and six Republicans, including La Follette, George Norris, and Miles Poindexter, voted in favor of Rublee.[71]

On 16 May *The New York Times* led the column that reported the outcome of the vote with the headline: "Gallinger Wins Fight On Rublee." The paper reported: "The Republican leader, Senator Gallinger, had opposed the nominee for fifteen months on the ground that he was 'personally obnoxious' to him, and the power of the Senatorial courtesy tradition was so great that Senator Gallinger won his point...in spite of a vigorous and insistent fight by the Administration for confirmation."[72] To Wilson's benefit, Rublee's rejection touched off a nationwide debate on senatorial courtesy. More then fifty papers in forty cities carried stories that denounced Gallinger's use of senatorial courtesy and the senators who backed him.[73] The *Indianapolis Star* charged, "It is a man of small caliber who will oppose a presidential appointment purely on personal grounds and the senators who sustain him put themselves in the same class." The *Biddeford* (Missouri) *Record* reported that "Gallinger and his colleagues of the straight goods element have put the knife in George Rublee" and noted that the act "shows how progressive the Republican Party has become since 1912."[74] The

Brooklyn Eagle interviewed Theodore Roosevelt on the matter, who said that he was "genuinely sorry" about the rejection and added: "There could have been no better man chosen. It is a real public loss that he is not able to serve."[75] *The New Republic*, as expected, denounced Rublee's defeat, describing it "as a deplorable breach of trust."[76] Walter Lippmann, who had become engrossed in the fight, informed Rublee privately that his defeat was "one of those outrages that leave a man spluttering impotently."[77]

The great irony in the debate over Gallinger's use of senatorial privilege is that by March Gallinger no longer actually thought George was "personally obnoxious." As Lippmann explained to Felix Frankfurter on 16 March "Old Gallinger no longer regards George as personally offensive, but having planted his bald-headed hulk at a certain post [he] cannot imagine a way of getting out of it without losing his dignity."[78] Gallinger evidently had his private change of heart following a meeting that Rublee requested in an effort to end the contest early in 1916. As Rublee recalled: "After we had gone over all his charges...and I had satisfied him that I had not been guilty of the mean things that he'd thought I'd done, [the] final outcome was that he seemed to rather like me and to rather wish that he could withdraw from his position but that he didn't see how he could. I said, 'I didn't either.'"[79] Although Rublee wished that Gallinger would publicly reverse his position, he was satisfied and "parted personally on friendly terms" with him.

Perhaps not surprisingly, while his nomination was being fought out in the Senate and on the public stage, Rublee disregarded his own fate and worked instead to see Louis Brandeis' appointment to the Supreme Court confirmed. Following Wilson's surprising nomination of Brandeis in January 1916, the Boston lawyer sustained a barrage of criticism that culminated in an open letter from seven former presidents of the American Bar Association claiming that he was "not a fit person to be a member of the Supreme Court of the United States."[80] As criticism of Brandeis increased, Rublee went into action. On 16 March Rublee reported on the state of his counteroffensive:

> Yesterday when I heard of the appearance of Taft on the scene I called up Gilson Gardner and got him to write something....which went out to all his papers. Kerby also promised me to see other newspaper men and try to get them to do something. I talked over the telephone with Walter Lippmann. There will be an article in the New Republic this week. I will do what I can to help Norman [Hapgood] wake up the newspaper men.[81]

Rublee consoled Brandeis, concluding: "I am entirely confident that you will be confirmed. You have lost no friends in Washington." Felix Frankfurter, another champion, was, however, not so sanguine. Of Brandeis' lack of support Frankfurter complained to Lippmann: "Perhaps the saddest feature of all is the impairment of independence—the fear of men who do know better."[82] Perhaps Rublee was especially motivated to help because he understood that on some level anti-Semitism was at play in the effort to keep Brandeis off the Court. The important role that Rublee played in Brandeis' confirmation battle is noted in

A. L. Todd's *Justice on Trial: The Case of Louis D. Brandeis*. In his work Todd found that "[t]he little group working on Brandeis' campaign were almost all friends of Rublee, and were spiritually with him in his months of trial."[83] As Brandeis authority Melvin Urofsky points out, Rublee had to conceal his efforts because Brandeis' confirmation could be a result only of "loyal Democratic Party strength."[84] Urofsky explains that "[t]his meant there could be only a backstage role for supporters like Rublee, La Follette, and Hapgood, and it also meant no obvious or concerted Jewish 'pressure.'" Brandeis' correspondence throughout the spring of 1916 confirms his reliance on Rublee to help answer charges against him in the press.[85]

Wilson's use of Rublee's failed nomination to attract independent progressive voters sustained Rublee as a prominent figure on the national stage. On 17 May a Wilson adviser observed: "You will probably have to make some short platform speeches on the way to North Carolina. Might it not be a good idea to discuss the evil of Senatorial courtesy? Rublee is a prominent progressive. The whole country is interested in this matter.... Gallinger typifies everything that constitutes 'standpatism'; Rublee, everything that appeals to the progressive heart of the country."[86] Wilson alluded to Rublee's failed confirmation in a speech he gave in Salisbury, North Carolina, on 20 May. Wilson charged that the Republicans "do not know the problems of the new day" and pointed out that "whenever I, for example, try to show my sympathies for the forward-looking men of their own party by nominating men of that sort they at once try to block progress."[87]

A final attempt was made on 23 May to secure Rublee's appointment. A motion to reconsider Rublee's nomination ended in a tie vote, but Vice President Thomas Marshall was somehow absent and thus unavailable to break the tie. Since the motion failed, the original decision stood.[88] On 24 May Hollis wrote Wilson to explain that "the Senate of the United States has not voted against George Rublee," but rather for "the Senatorial courtesy rule."[89] Hollis encouraged Wilson to give Rublee another recess appointment to "show so plainly your sympathy with the Progressive element in the Republican Party."[90] Hollis was not alone in recommending Wilson's continued support. Joseph Teal, an Oregon lawyer and Democrat, wrote on 27 May in favor of continuing the nomination fight. Teal, who may have known Rublee from the Ballinger–Pinchot controversy, believed that "[t]he country has been deprived (I hope but temporarily) of the services of a truly public-spirited citizen, one who has the confidence of every one who knows him or his work."[91] Teal believed that whether or not he won the fight, "whether as a private citizen or as a public official, Mr. Rublee will always be found doing his level best for the right as he sees it."

Rublee's work with the FTC was, in fact, not yet over. With support pouring in for him and with progressive votes on the line in the fall, Wilson asked Rublee to stay on and gave him a second recess appointment. As Rublee stated in a letter of resignation several months later, he agreed to continue on the FTC "until certain work in which my help was needed should be finished."[92] The work that

Rublee hoped to accomplish included an attempt to stabilize the FTC, which seemed in danger of collapsing because of a personal feud between chairman Davies and vice-chairman Ed Hurley. The fight evidently dated to the commission's 1915 summer tour, when during the course of the trip Hurley and Harris became frustrated because Davies "always made all the speeches and he was the whole thing everywhere."[93] By spring 1916, Hurley and Harris found Davies unbearable.

On May 27 Norman Hapgood wrote Wilson's cabinet secretary, Joseph Tumulty, to request a meeting with Wilson so that he could explain the origins of a power struggle raging in the commission. Hapgood explained: "Harris, Rublee and several others think I am the person to tell the President the truth about recent events. It is not a pleasant job, but I can't well dodge it. It ought to be done, for the future good of the Commission."[94] In the *Papers of Woodrow Wilson* Arthur Link, the president's principal biographer, notes that "a bitter personal struggle" had been going on for several months between Davies and Hurley. Davies charged that Hurley was actually a "reactionary" who wanted to make the commission "a friend to big business and one that failed to protect small competitors."[95] Wilson was evidently aware of the struggle, but, because Davies was Wilson's close friend, Hapgood and Harris believed that the president might be misinformed. Hapgood secured a meeting with Wilson for 31 May to present the other side of the story.

Rublee's role in the struggle between Davies and Hurley proved decisive and somewhat personal. The commission had divided into two camps: Davies and Parry versus Hurley and Harris. Rublee, who largely stayed out of the struggle in previous months, learned from Senator Hollis that Davies played a role in Rublee's failed confirmation. Hollis learned after the tie vote on 23 May that Davies persuaded Senator Willard Saulsbury, who was an FTC supporter, not to vote for Rublee's confirmation. Rublee, who already thought that Davies was unfit for his post, was further displeased with the man for taking an active role against his confirmation.[96] A letter from Learned Hand to Felix Frankfurter in January 1916 sheds much light on both the contest with Davies and important attributes of Rublee's personality. Of his friend's 1916 nomination Hand observed:

George's chances are slim, per Henry Hollis through Winston Churchill. Newlands and some of the old supporters have deserted; Gallinger has got his second-wind and hates George, and things are worse than they were. I cannot drive it out of my head that Davies and Hurley are really at the bottom of it. George must be a thorn in the side of each. It may sound strange to you, but I can even understand how they feel. There is at the bottom of George a kind of imperiousness which often at times grows insupportable. I love him as I do few other men, but I should not want to have to cooperate with him in matters about which he felt strongly. I should be submerged by a stronger will, and a kind of concentration of purpose, which I have never experienced in another. These two second-rate, unintelligent fakers may well have felt that George's mere presence was a protest against them. I find I keep recurring to this in my mind, almost without meaning to. Davies, the shoddy little pup, is one of the most liked of that selected few who are welcome chez Wilson, and a little indication that George was a spoil-sport, an impractical academician, a meticulous lawyer, ...might be enough to take the edge off the President's support, and then "good night."[97]

Whether or not he communicated his suspicion of Davies to George, Hand's intuition was evidently prescient. Sadly for Rublee's hard-fought commission, the innovative body had succumbed to internecine backstabbing.

Davies' untoward efforts, however, soon caught up with him. According to Rublee, toward the end of May Hurley and Harris came to him and asked that he draft a resolution repealing Davies' perpetual chairmanship. Not surprisingly, Rublee thought their plan a good idea, and he suggested that the resolution provide for a revolving chairmanship similar to that of the Interstate Commerce Commission, this being Rublee's preference from the beginning. Hurley and Harris agreed, and Rublee drafted a resolution to that effect. During a meeting of the FTC on 31 May, the same day that Hapgood met with Wilson about the growing feud, Harris moved that the chairmanship of the commission rotate. The motion passed three to two, Rublee siding with Hurley and Harris. Hurley was then elected chairman.[98] Although blindsided by the coup, Davies had the presence to request that the announcement be withheld from the press until after his wife, who was soon expected to deliver, had given birth. Following the 2 June birth, Davies asked that the announcement of Hurley's election as chairman be postponed another six days. Hurley and apparently Rublee, who was traveling with him in Chicago at the time, evidently guessed correctly that Davies was seeking Wilson's intervention and preempted the effort by releasing the announcement regarding the chairmanship change to the Associated Press on 7 June.[99] While Rublee's role in the ensuing contest is not conspicuous, it seems reasonable to assume that his was one of the hands that pulled the carpet from under Davies. Given that his own place on the commission would shortly be terminated, it is unlikely that Rublee was willing to leave the body with Davies at the helm.

Former chairman Davies met with Wilson on 8 June and asked the president to encourage Harris to reverse his vote and to help him be reinstated as chairman. Likely owing to Hapgood's 31 May visit, however, Wilson hesitated to give Davies a hearing. Feeling himself shut out, Davies wrote to Edward House on 9 June warning that the problems of the commission "may become so bad that [it may become] my duty to the President and to the country to make public what differences are in the Commission."[100] Without subtlety Davies noted that his statement "will feed the opposition with satisfaction, and [offer] ammunition to attack one of the agencies of this administration" in the coming election. Nevertheless, this would be his duty if "the situation is permitted to obtain."[101] On 10 June Davies sent a letter to Wilson reiterating his request that the president intercede, stating: "And again, I would appreciate it for myself & for my country...if you could add the weight of your personal appeal to Harris."[102]

A letter from Hapgood to House on 18 June indicates that Davies at last succeeded in securing Wilson's support: "Probably there is nothing that you can do about it, but Davies has been to the President and caused him to send such a message to Hurley that Hurley and Harris will probably both resign this week. Davies simply told the President a mass of lies. The President asked to have a recent vote of the Commission rescinded (which it will not do)."[103] The next day, 19 June, House wrote Wilson relating what he had learned from Hapgood: "I am sorry to hear of the trouble in the Trades Commission. I sympathize with Davies and yet from what [Attorney General Thomas] Gregory, Hapgood and others tell me, there is another side to it. I hope you will be able to reconcile their differences in a way that will prevent public exposure. I understand that Hurley and Harris are about to resign and may do it before this reaches you."[104] On 21 June Hapgood again met with Wilson to discuss the crisis. Although there is no record of the conversation, Wilson apparently decided to abandon Davies and agreed to withdraw his request to have the vote rescinded. A 1 July letter indicates that House induced Davies to remain on the commission and to withhold his public statement "exposing" Hurley.[105]

While Hurley and Harris had Davies penned down, Rublee took the opportunity to turn his attention to an important matter that he wanted to accomplish before Gallinger forced him off the commission. Working with several senators, Rublee drafted and advanced a bill that would allow American companies to enter combinations for export trade that would otherwise be illegal under the Sherman Act.[106] Rublee believed with other nationalists that American companies needed to be allowed to combine in order to compete with European—especially German—cartels in Latin American and Asian markets. Although he had evidently attempted without success to secure authorization for export combinations in 1914, Rublee managed to lay a foundation for the FTC taking up the issue in section 3 of the commission's organic act, which read: "The commission is hereby directed to investigate…trade conditions in foreign countries where associations, combinations, or practices of buyers, dealers, or traders may injuriously affect the export trade of the United States."[107] Wilson had been troubled by this provision but eventually allowed the foothold. As the president explained in a letter in August 1914: "This is a question on which my mind has changed sides several times, but while I think it would perhaps now be safe to authorize the commission to allow domestic combinations to meet foreign competition I think it might at least be very wise to authorize the commission to investigate these matters…and report to Congress."[108] The commission's investigation during 1915 and 1916 of export trade combinations was its one successful undertaking during Rublee's term. Accompanying the commission's two-volume report on its investigation was a summary that concluded that "other nations enjoy marked advantages in foreign trade from superior facilities and more effective organizations."[109] The commission also found that U.S. businesses refrained from effective combinations for the export trade owing to "doubt and fear as to legal restrictions" that might exist under the Sherman law.[110]

Following the FTC coup displacing Davies, Hurley and Rublee appeared alone before the Committee of the Judiciary in the House on 18 July to explain the FTC's export report findings and to support a bill that would specifically authorize corporate combinations for export trade, the Webb-Pomerene bill. In his testimony, Rublee attempted to convince the committee that "it is the misunderstanding or doubt as to what the law is that creates the very bad situation that exists in a time like this, when there is an opportunity to develop our export trade."[111] Rublee, of course, was referring to the opportunity that war in Europe, beginning in 1914, had afforded American businessmen to make inroads into markets that European cartels formerly dominated. Rublee pointed to testimony in the FTC report that showed that American businessmen "are confused about the Sherman law, and [that] they are rather in doubt about going into the export business anyway."[112] Although Rublee, of course, did not volunteer the information, he had drafted the Webb-Pomerene bill, which his and Hurley's testimony as well as the FTC report supported.[113] Norman Hapgood identified Rublee as the author of the bill in a letter to Wilson on 5 July in which he advocated another recess appointment for Rublee. Hapgood explained: "There has been introduced into Congress a bill taking foreign trade out of the operation of the Sherman Act. This bill was introduced by Mr. Webb. It was drawn by George Rublee and revised by Louis Brandeis."[114] With administration support, the Webb-Pomerene Act passed Congress in 1918.[115]

Rublee's testimony before the Committee of the Judiciary seems to have been his last prominent appearance as an FTC commissioner. Evidently, Rublee was uncomfortable with continuing in his post, having twice been rejected, especially since Wilson's support seemed to be waning. In Hapgood's 5 July letter to Wilson he stressed Rublee's importance to the commission and asked Wilson to reappoint him. Hapgood explained:

> Mr. Rublee has not felt comfortable remaining on the Commission. He thought it would be easier for you if he retired at once, but Hurley, Harris, Senator Hollis, Mr. McAdoo and myself thought differently. Mr. Rublee does not feel, however, that without subjecting himself to the general suspicion of holding on to an office, he could stay more than a couple of weeks longer. Whether it is possible to get in the United States another man as well equipped as Rublee, is not for me to say. Hurley and Harris do not think it is, nor, I [believe], does Brandeis.[116]

Hapgood noted that Rublee's reappointment would be helpful "just now when we are all playing for what we can get of the Bull Moose vote."[117] On 7 July, however, Wilson wrote: "I think [Rublee's] rejection was one of the worst pieces of business the Senate has engaged in our time, but my present feeling is that I ought to find somebody else."[118] Evidently, Wilson did not ask Rublee to step down, so he continued with the commission through the July committee hearings on export trade. On 25 July, however, Edward House wrote to Wilson suggesting that Rublee be asked to stay on the commission until after the election. House explained that Rublee had agreed to continue if Wilson would "send him a note in reply to his resignation, which will go to you this week, saying that you would appreciate it if he would continue for the present."[119] Rublee sent his resignation to Wilson on 1 August 1916. In the letter, Rublee expressed his appreciation for Wilson's confidence and support but believed that having been twice rejected by the Senate and because he had finished "certain work," it would be appropriate for him to resign.[120] Wilson, who evidently decided to take Hapgood's and House's advice, asked Rublee to withhold his resignation "for the present."[121] Supporters such as Walter Lippmann were eager for Wilson to send Rublee's name back to the Senate. Writing to Hapgood on 23 August, Lippmann complained: "I wish the President would announce some time before the campaign is over that he is going to reappoint George so that I can really do a hallelujah."[122] Hapgood, however, had already written to Wilson suggesting Rublee's reappointment on 14 August. Replying, Wilson maintained his hesitance, confessing: "The Rublee matter has so many sides to it that I find myself walking around it without going in any particular direction."[123]

In late August Gallinger introduced a resolution in the Senate that inquired why Rublee was allowed to continue to be a member of the commission despite his failed confirmation.[124] *The New Republic* called the resolution the work of a "spiteful old man."[125] In early September, Wilson was at last converted and announced that he intended to put Rublee's name before the Senate yet again at the beginning of the next session of Congress—that is, providing he was reelected. Likely in an effort to win progressive voters, on 5 October Wilson also appointed Rublee to the Eight-Hour Commission, recently created to deal with railroad labor conditions.[126]

There is no indication that Rublee felt any uneasiness about being a featured instrument in Wilson's campaign. With the party he had helped create four years before now defunct, perhaps Rublee believed that Wilson had been so converted to Progressive Party principles that there was no reason to abandon him for the somewhat progressive Charles Evans Hughes, the Republican nominee. As one editor observed:

> [In the coming campaign] it is likely that the Progressives will remember the appointment of Brandeis, the insistence upon George Rublee as member of the federal trades commission. The Progressives may even remember the passage of the law creating that commission, and may think of the tariff commission, and the rural credit measure, which are fundamentally not Democratic demands, but Progressive measures, and then the drift may be back to Wilson, if not to the Democratic party.[127]

Being finished with party affiliation, however, Rublee would not join the Democrats upon Wilson's reelection victory but, as Gallinger once noted, would continue to work with whichever party suited "his purpose best."[128]

On 6 January 1917, Hurley surprised the commission when he tendered his resignation to Wilson effective 1 February. Perhaps impressed by business opportunities abounding in the international market, Hurley based his need to resign "on account of certain large plant improvements" that he wanted to carry out in his washing machine company.[129] Hurley's resignation caused Rublee to reconsider his continued work on the FTC. Writing to House on 26 January 1917, Rublee explained that while he "deeply" appreciated Wilson's offer to reappoint him, "Hurley's resignation has weakened the commission so much that its reorganization ought not be delayed by re-opening the controversy about me."[130] Rublee's resignation amounted to a farewell address that admitted real concern for the foundling commission that he had worked hard to establish and nurture. Rublee acknowledged: "The condition of the Commission is very serious and I am greatly concerned about its future. The truth is that the Commission has not yet made a record to justify its existence and to fulfill the expectations of those who hoped it might become an agency of great benefit to the public."[131] Rublee feared that "If the Trade Commission were discredited the effect would be not only to jeopardize a very promising experiment in the regulation of big business, but the whole idea of regulation by commission in other fields as well would suffer. The danger is that the public might condemn the idea as impracticable, losing sight of the fact that the failure was due to the incapacity of those who were charged with the duty of carrying it out."[132] Rublee believed that there was "still a chance for [the FTC] to make good" but believed that only two exceptionally well qualified men could save the commission. Rublee pointed out that "the weakness of the Commission is most apparent on its legal side," and he complained that the body had "done little in the way of clarifying or using its power to prevent unfair methods of competition." For that reason, he urged that the president appoint two "throughly qualified" lawyers "rather than one lawyer and one business man."[133]

Although Rublee was aware that there was "a prejudice against lawyers" in the administration, he argued that "only lawyers of rather extraordinary flexibility of mind, soundness of judgement and large experience in business affairs can" supply the qualities necessary to save the FTC. Rublee listed the attainments and attitudes that would best serve the commission. These included an avoidance of the "useless invasion of the province of the courts by undertaking" fraudulent cases of a provincial character, "avoid[ing] clashing with the Department of Justice" and the ability to "make up [the commission's] records, findings and reports [so] that they will bear scrutiny by the court" and to be able to "devise and apply a new method of procedure so as to exercise its quasi-judicial functions with the greatest promptness and certainty." Rublee believed that "the commission has to map out and chart a new field and then lay out its course," and he argued that such work could "only be done by a creative, imaginative lawyer versed in affairs." Rublee thought that "Mr. Justice Brandeis is an eminent example of the type of man to be sought."[134]

Wilson may have smarted a little from Rublee's letter because it showed so clearly that he had tragically miscalculated with his first appointments. Nevertheless, Wilson could not bring himself to share Rublee's confidence in lawyers. Shortly after Rublee sent his letter, Judge J. Harry Covington visited Wilson apparently at Rublee's suggestion. Writing to Rublee on 1 February, Covington reported that he was "not very hopeful that [Wilson] will select two lawyers for the now vacant places on the commission."[135] Covington reported that when he argued that "the delicate legal problems" facing the FTC "require lawyers of broad conception and wide experience," he found that Wilson "simply did not agree with me." Covington added: "When I told him that I was firm in my belief that the Commission ought to be composed at all times of three lawyers, he said he had a fear that that would bind it to a narrow rule of procedure which would entirely nullify the objects [for which Wilson thought it was created]."[136] Although Wilson would not overcome his prejudice against lawyers, subsequent appointments to the FTC through 1969 rendered it the commission with the greatest percentage of lawyers, the average being 82 percent.[137]

Rublee's concern for the commission he helped create was well founded. The agency's clumsy beginning set it on a confused and impotent course. While Rublee clearly hoped that the commission would improve with time, a 1920 Supreme Court decision soon dashed his hopes. The conservative Court's ruling in *F.T.C. v Gratz* struck at the heart of the commission when it found that "[t]he words 'unfair methods of competition' are not defined by statue and their meaning is in dispute."[138] Exercising judicial review, the Court determined that "[i]t is for the courts, not the Commission, ultimately to determine as matter of law, what [methods] they include."

In 1926, Rublee took the opportunity to shed some light on the development of the FTC by delivering a paper entitled "The Original Plan and Early History of the Federal Trade Commission" before the American Academy of Political and Social Sciences.[139] Although in his address Rublee seems to have intimated disapproval of the FTC's relaxed acceptance of "the rules laid down by the courts," he reserved his criticism for the commission's decision to assume "jurisdiction over every sort of fraudulent and immoral business practice" in the land. Rublee believed that the commission should have instead relied upon its remaining power of investigation to influence "public opinion and [affect] the judgement of Congress and the decisions of the courts." Rublee complained: "In so extending its jurisdiction the Commission has spread its effort over so wide a field that it has perhaps not been able to do the particular job for which it was established as well as it otherwise might have."[140] While not directed at the history of the FTC, James Kloppenberg's observation in *Uncertain Victory* regarding the general failure of progressive legislation seems apropos: "The different levels of political power, the competition among existing groups with vested interests, the preference of government officials who ended up implementing programs planned by others—all of these factors complicate political life. That the final product seldom resembles the model ostensibly followed should occasion little surprise."[141] In 1926 Rublee could only complain: "In its investigations [the FTC] has appeared to be rather more concerned with exposing abuses than with discovering the answer to disturbing business problems."[142] Unfortunately, what Rublee once thought was "a very promising experiment in the regulation of big business" instead proved a disheartening failure. Economic historian Thomas McCraw, in his award-winning study of the history of regulation, charges that Rublee was "woefully naive in thinking that the phrase 'unfair methods of competition in commerce' meant something clear and coherent."[143] Such a conclusion seems facile at best, considering that the history of the Court indicates the influence of shifting political winds on its decisions. The postwar Court's attack on a liberal regulatory commission does not render its author's reasoning "woefully naive" prima facie. The Court's decision certainly could have been more accommodating had the FTC had a more adroit start and had not progressivism been generally vanquished during the war. Describing Rublee's approach as naive also seems in error upon consideration of his prime objectives in 1914. Given Rublee's hostility to the Democratic effort to destroy big business, it seems clear that he would have preferred to risk an eventual reversal by the Court rather than see American business, and thereby the nation, seriously injured.

If blame must be fixed, it seems that the ultimate responsibility for the FTC's early failure rests with Woodrow Wilson, who, with the exception of Rublee and possibly Hurley, appointed inept commissioners to set the course for an agency that embodied a "method for the control of [business] such as was never before conceived."[144] With the mounting pressures of war in Europe and the various complications of domestic politics, Wilson might be excused for not having had the wherewithal to restore the commission's vitality before it collapsed in confusion. A more critical view would be that Wilson never understood the complexities of antitrust regulation either as governor or as president and that he was out of his depth on the subject in both offices.[145] Having allowed Rublee to convert him to the New Nationalism program in 1914, Wilson should have turned the thing over to him, or, if he had no intention of earnestly following the course, he should have kept Rublee far away from it and let mediocre political hacks take their cues from his administration as political necessities dictated without Rublee in a position to object. In expecting Rublee—who converted two of three branches of government to his own position—to submit to Davies' partisan leadership of the FTC, Wilson seems to have been the one who was "woefully naive."

NOTES

1. GR to Bass, 23 July 1914, RBP, folder ML-31-12.

2. Rublee described Gallinger thus in GR to Brandeis, 6 October 1914, LBP, reel 37.

3. Gallinger is described as the "embodiment of 'stand-patism'" in the *Concise Dictionary of American Biography* (New York: Charles Scribner's Sons, 1964), 325.

4. James Wright, *The Progressive Yankees: Republican Reformers in New Hampshire, 1906-1916* (Hannover: University Press of New England, 1987), 148, 234, note 20; and GR to Bass, 21 and 23 July 1914, RBP, folder ML 31-12. Stevens helped devise a way by which Henry Allison, a New Hampshire progressive, could temporarily resign his post as assistant postmaster general so that he could run for governor of New

Hampshire without risking his lucrative appointment in Washington should he lose the election.

5. GR to Bass, 23 July 1914, RBP, folder ML 31-12.

6. GR to Bass, 31 July 1914, RBP, folder ML 31-12.

7. Ibid.

8. Wright, *Progressive Yankees*, 150.

9. Ibid., 149-150.

10. GR to Brandeis, 6 October 1914, LBP, reel 37.

11. Ibid.

12. George E. Farrand to Brandeis, 7 October 1914, LBP, reel 37.

13. Brandeis to George E. Farrand, 28 October 1914, LBP, reel 37; Michael O'Leary to Brandeis, 31 October 1914; and Brandeis to O'Leary, 31 October 1912, LBP, reel 37.

14. GR to Brandeis, 18 October 1914, LBP, reel 37.

15. Rublee's information on Gallinger's voting record was compiled by the staff of *Collier's*, likely at Hapgood's direction. The record was forwarded to Robert Bass who then made it available to Stevens and Rublee. See M. Farmer to Bass, 9 September 1914, RBP, folder ML 31-12.

16. Clipping from *Manchester Union* submitted by Senator Henry Hollis at Rublee's confirmation hearing, *Hearings, II*, 55-56.

17. Ibid., 56.

18. Ibid., 57.

19. Ibid., 55.

20. Quoted in Wright, *Progressive Yankees*, 152-153.

21. See Juliet Barrett Rublee to Learned Hand, 17 November 1914, HLS-Hand, box 107, folder 8.

22. Henry Hollis to Brandeis, 5 November 1914, LBP, reel 37.

23. GR to Hand, 30 January 1915, HLS-Hand, box 107, folder 2. For George Record's influence in New Jersey progressive politics, see Ransom E. Noble, *New Jersey Progressivism before Wilson* (Princeton, NJ: Princeton University Press, 1946). Incidentally, Record's name is misspelled "Recard" in the transcript of this letter in the Hand papers.

24. GR to Brandeis, 24 February 1915, LBP, reel 35.

25. Brandeis to Edward House, 31 December 1914, LBP, reel 35; and Norman Hapgood to Edward House, 28 December 1914, Yale-House, box 55, folder 1722. Hapgood, evidently at Rublee's direction, was writing to nominate Joseph Cotton to the commission. In addition to a lack of political clout, Cotton also seems to have been excluded because of his close ties to Wall Street interests.

26. *New York Times*, 23 February 1915.

27. Ibid.

28. Ibid., 27 February 1915. This seems to be the only instance where Rublee listed a middle initial. As it likely stands for Horace, Rublee may have employed it as a tribute to his father.

29. Ibid.

30. Leon Schlup, "Jacob Harold Gallinger," *American National Biography* (Cary, NC: Oxford University Press, 1998), vol. 8, 653; see also Leon Schlup, "Consistent Conservative: Jacob Gallinger and the Presidential Campaign of 1912 in New Hampshire," *International Review of History and Political Science*, 21 (1984), 49-57.

31. *The New Republic*, 17 (27 February 1915): 83.
32. Gallinger testimony, *Hearings I*, 6, 9.
33. Ibid., 8-11; and *Hearings II*, 68-72.
34. Gallinger testimony, *Hearings II*, 66.
35. Clipping from *Manchester Union* submitted by Senator Henry Hollis in support for Rublee. *Hearings II*, 55.
36. Quoted in Wright, *Progressive Yankees*, 155.
37. Rublee testimony, *Hearings I*, 36. Regarding the price maintenance bill, Rublee explained: "I think that under the industrial system every man has a right, or should have the right, to do as well as he can with his own property, and this is a question merely whether we shall enable people to have a national distribution for their products. Unless they can fix their prices through agents...they will not be able to obtain a national market. A very powerful capitalist, like Ford, can perfectly well afford to have his own agents everywhere, so that the title does not pass until the consumer purchases the article he manufactures, but a man with limited capital can not do that. He must sell his product to the distributers and part with the title in order to get his money to put back in his business." It seems that Brandeis, for whom Rublee drafted the bill, proposed legalizing price fixing for smaller producers because it would prohibit volume discounts and thereby allow "the small dealer [to] be on exact equality with the large department store or mail-order house."
38. Bass testimony, *Hearings II*, 63.
39. Felix Frankfurter, editorial in the Boston *Transcript*, 1 March 1915, Rublee file, HUA, HVD 290.505, box 350.
40. Ibid.
41. GR to Peabody, 6 March 1915, GSA; and "Statement of the Rublee Case" (perhaps a Lippmann article), undated, Walter Lippmann Papers, Sterling Library, Special Collections, Yale University, [hereafter Yale-Lippmann], box 31, folder 1156.
42. GR to Brandeis, 4 March 1915, and Brandeis to GR, 6 March 1915, LBP, reel 35.
43. Rublee, "Reminiscences," 125.
44. GR to Bass, 19 March 1915, RBP, folder ML 31-13:R.
45. Based on letters from Juliet Barrett Rublee to Learned Hand, it seems that Rublee was so surreptitious in his work on Capitol Hill that no one—including Wilson—understood the extent to which he controlled the outcome. Notoriously reticent, Rublee seems to have relied on anonymity to accomplish his aims. See JRB to Hand, 17 and 18 November 1914, HLS-Hand, box 107, folder 8.
46. GR to Brandeis, 4 March 1915, LBP, reel 35.
47. William Harris to Joseph Tumulty, 3 April 1915, WWP-LoC, subject file 1105a, reel 308.
48. Wilson to Senator Thomas Martin, 1 March 1915, WWP-LoC, subject file 1105, reel 307.
49. GR to Wilson, 5 April 1915, WWP-LoC, subject file 1105b, reel 308. Rublee also had a personal incentive in seeing the FTC properly funded. He had recently confided to Peabody that "During the last two years I have not been earning anything and have barely made both ends meet, particularly as I have a number of financial outgoings which may be regarded as public or charitable." GR to Peabody, 28 February 1915, GSA.
50. GR to Bass, 19 March 1915, RBP, folder ML 31-13:R.
51. Rublee, "Reminiscences," 126.

52. Ibid.
53. Ibid., 130.
54. GR to Brandeis, 18 August 1915, LBP, reel 36.
55. George Rublee, "The Original Plan and Early History of the Federal Trade Commission," *Proceedings of the American Academy of Political and Social Sciences*, 11 (January 1926), 114-120, 118.
56. Ibid., 119.
57. Ibid.
58. GR to Bass, 10 August 1915, RBP, folder ML 31-13:R; and *Memphis Press*, 20 August 1915, enclosure in Gilson Gardner to Brandeis, 23 August 1915, LBP, reel 36.
59. Memphis Press, 20 August 1915, enclosure in Gilson Gardner to Brandeis, 23 August 1915, LBP, reel 36.
60. Gilson Gardner to Brandeis, 23 August 1915, LBP, reel 36. Although it is not clear whether or not Rublee knew Gardner in 1915, in 1916 he relied on him to write political articles in a subsequent but not wholly unrelated contest, the confirmation of Louis Brandeis (See GR to Brandeis, 16 March 1916, LBP, reel 41). If Rublee in fact used Gardner in 1915 to put pressure on Davies' program, it would not at all be surprising.
61. Brandeis to Gilson Gardner, 7 September 1915, LBP, reel 36.
62. GR to Brandeis, 6 March and 22 March 1915, LBP, reel 35.
63. GR to Brandeis, 1 October 1915, LBP, reel 35; Brandeis to Charles Crane, 9 October 1915, LBP, reel 36; and Edward Burling to Learned Hand, 31 May 1917, HLS-Hand, box 100, folder 5. Of Rublee's efforts to secure him on the FTC and Hand to a federal court, Burling wrote: "I bet George succeeds in making you Circuit Judge, but I am sure he won't succeed in landing a job for me.... He is the only man who knows of my great reputation as a Chicago lawyer. If he could stop all communications with Chicago, he might succeed."
64. Rublee, "Reminiscences," 127.
65. Ibid., 128.
66. Ibid., 131; and GR to Brandeis, 3 April 1915, LBP, reel 36.
67. Rublee, "Reminiscences," 128, 131.
68. Rublee, "The Original Plan," 120.
69. *The New Republic*, 69 (26 February 1916), 90.
70. Wilson to Pomerene, 12 May 1916, Link et al., *Papers of Woodrow Wilson*, vol 37, 25. Rublee's confirmation for the FTC and Brandeis's confirmation for the Supreme Court were grouped in several articles during May 1916. See, for example, the New York City *Press*, 24 May 1916, and *The Christian Science Monitor*, 22 May 1916.
71. *The New York Times*, 16 May 1916.
72. Ibid.
73. Clippings from the following newspapers and journals referring to Gallinger's defeat of Rublee's confirmation were found in a bound volume in Rublee's home in Cornish, New Hampshire: *The Kansas City Post*, 3 March 1916; *La Follette's Magazine*, May 1916; *Herald*, Lexington, KY, May 1916; *Republican*, Fresno, CA, 26 May 1916; *New*, Dallas, TX, 9 May 1916; *Star*, Indianapolis, ID, 13 May 1916; *Evening Record*, Boston, MA, 15 May 1916; *Evening News*, Newark, NJ, "between 15th and 25th" May 1916; *Evening News*, Baltimore, MD, 16 May 1916; *Eagle*, Brooklyn, NY, 16 May 1916; *Standard Union*, Brooklyn, NY, 16 May 1916; *Christian Science Monitor*, Boston, MA, 16 May 1916; *Enquirer*, Buffalo, NY, 16 May 1916; *Tribune*, Des Moines, IA, 16 May

1916; *Star*, Kansas City, MO, 16 May 1916; *New York Evening Post,* NYC, 16 May 1916; *Bulletin*, Philadelphia, PA, 16 May 1916; *Evening Telegram,* Philadelphia, PA, 16 May 1916; *Press*, Pittsburgh, 16 May 1916; *Dispatch*, St. Paul, MN, 16 May 1916; *Times*, Washington, DC, 16 May 1916; *Journal*, Albuquerque, NM, 17 May, 1916; *Evening Post*, Chicago, IL, 17 May 1916; *Journal*, Lincoln, NB, 17 May 1916; *Dispatch*, Lock Haven, PA, 17 May 1916; *Telegraph*, Macon, GA,17 May 1916; *Times-Picayune*, New Orleans, LA,17 May 1916; *Journal of Commerce*, *Evening Mail*, *Evening Sun*, and *New York World*, NYC,17 May 1916; *Virginia Pilot*, Norfolk, VA,17 May 1916; *Public Ledger*, Philadelphia, PA,17 May 1916; *Journal*, Portland, OR,17 May 1916; *Union* and *News*, Springfield, MA,17 May 1916; *Herald*, Vicksburg, MS, 17 May 1916; *Every Evening* and *News*, Wilmington, DW, 17 May 1916; *Courier*, Evansville, ID,18 May 1916; *Record*, Ft. Worth, TX, 18 May 1916; *Evening Bulletin*, Providence, RI, 18 May 1916; *Post*, Hartford, CT, 19 May 1916; *Enquirer-Sun*, Columbus, GA,19 May 1916; *Gazette*, Charleston, WV, 20 May 1916; *Leader*, Gutherie, OK, 20 May 1916; *Republic*, St. Louis, MO, 20 May 1916; *Tribune*, Oakland, CA, 21 May 1916; *Advocate*, Newark, OH, 22 May 1916, *Enterprise*, Beaumont, TX, 24 May 1916; *Banner*, Nashville, TN, 24 May 1916; *News*, Charlotte, NC, 25 May 1916; and *Journal*, Louisville, KY, 28 May 1916.

74. *Record*, Biddeford, MO, 15 May 1915.

75. *Eagle*, Brooklyn, NY, 17 May 1916.

76. *The New Republic*, 81 (20 May 1916), 49.

77. Lippmann to GR, 24 May 1916, Yale-Lippmann, box 29, folder 1076.

78. Lippmann to Frankfurter, 16 March 1916, Yale-Lippmann, box 10, folder 419.

79. Rublee, "Reminiscences," 141-142.

80. Quoted in McCraw, *Prophets of Regulation*, 135.

81. GR to Brandeis, 16 March 1916, LBP, reel 41. Another telling, though more subtle, example of the extent to which Rublee worked on behalf of Brandeis is a letter from Hapgood to a source typed on Federal Trade Commission stationary (see Hapgood to Edward McClennan, 21 March 1916, LBP, reel 41).

82. Frankfurter to Lippmann, undated (though apparently March 1916), Yale-Lippmann, box 10, folder 119.

83. A. L. Todd, *Justice on Trial: The Case of Louis D. Brandeis* (New York: McGraw-Hill, 1964), 227.

84. Urofsky and Levy, *Letters of Louis D. Brandeis*, vol. 4, 43, note 2.

85. Ibid., vol. 4, 27, 118, 127, 140, 176

86. Joseph Tumulty to Wilson, 17 May 1916, Link et al., *Papers of Woodrow Wilson*, vol. 37, 67.

87. Washington *Evening Star*, 20 May 1916. This quotation comes from a copy of the article sent to Rublee from Josephus Daniels on 16 December 1936. In the accompanying letter, Daniels wrote: "I am enclosing an article from the Washington Star of May 20, 1916, which contains a reference to you. I thought it might interest you.... (Rublee Papers, Covington & Burling law firm, Washington, DC)."

88. Editorial note, Link et al., *Papers of Woodrow Wilson*, vol. 37, 102, note 1.

89. Hollis to Wilson, 24 May 1916, Link et al., *Papers of Woodrow Wilson*, vol. 30, 101.

90. Ibid.

91. Joseph Teal to Joseph Tumulty (Wilson's cabinet secretary), 27 May 1916, WWP-LoC, reel 308.

92. GR to Wilson, 1 August 1916, Link et al., *Papers of Woodrow Wilson*, vol. 37, 512.

93. Ibid., 132.

94. Hapgood to Tumulty, 27 May 1916, Link et al., *Papers of Woodrow Wilson*, vol. 37, 117.

95. Editorial note, Link et al., *Papers of Woodrow Wilson*, vol. 37, 117, note 1.

96. Rublee, "Reminiscences," 144.

97. Hand to Frankfurter, 10 January 1916, HLS-Hand, box 104, folder 5. Hand seems to have suffered throughout their friendship from Rublee's blatant honesty and piercing criticism. In the 10 January letter he noted: "Glad you like the Marienelli decision; most have told me they hadn't any idea what it meant. George so discouraged me about it that I didn't publish it for over a year."

98. Ibid., 132, 136.

99. Editorial note, Link et al., *Papers of Woodrow Wilson*, vol. 37, 205, note 2; and Davies to Edward House, 9 June 1916, Yale-House, box 36, folder 1116.

100. Davies to House, 9 June 1916, Yale-House, box 36, folder 1116.

101. Ibid.

102. Davies to Wilson, 10 June 1916, Link et al., *Papers of Woodrow Wilson*, vol. 37, 204.

103. Editorial note, Link et al., *Papers of Woodrow Wilson*, vol. 37, 205, note 3.

104. House to Wilson, 19 June 1916, Link et al., *Papers of Woodrow Wilson*, vol. 37, 268.

105. Editorial note, Link et al., *Papers of Woodrow Wilson*, vol. 37: 205, n3.

106. Brandeis to GR, 13 April 1916 (with enclosures containing Rublee's corrections to the export bill), LBP, reel, 36; and Rublee, "Reminiscences," 133-134.

107. H.R. 15613, "An Act to Create a Federal Trade Commission," National Archives, Record Group 49, series 63A-C3, box 79, folder 17.

108. Wilson to Congressman Covington, 27 August 1914, WWP-LoC, reel 307.

109. Federal Trade Commission, *Report on Cooperation in American Export Trade, Part One, Summary and Report* (Washington, D.C.: Government Printing Office, 1916), 3.

110. Ibid.

111. Rublee testimony, *To Promote Export Trade, and for Other Purposes, Hearings before the Committee of the Judiciary, House of Representatives, Sixty-Fourth Congress, First Session on H.R. 16707* (Washington, D.C.: Government Printing Office, 1916), 24.

112. Ibid., 25.

113. Rublee, "Reminiscences," 134.

114. Hapgood to Wilson, 5 July 1916, Link et al., *Papers of Woodrow Wilson*, vol. 37, 363.

115. Walter LaFeber, *The American Age: United States Foreign Policy at Home and Abroad*, volume II (New York: W.W. Norton & Company, 1994), 292.

116. Hapgood to Wilson, 5 July 1916, Link et al., *Papers of Woodrow Wilson*, vol. 37, 363.

117. Ibid.

118. Wilson to Hapgood, 25 July 1916, Link et al., *Papers of Woodrow Wilson*, vol. 37, 374-375.

119. House to Wilson, 25 July 1916, Link et al., *Papers of Woodrow Wilson*, vol. 37, 475.

120. GR to Wilson, 1 August 1916, Link et al., *Papers of Woodrow Wilson*, vol. 37, 513.

121. Wilson to GR, 3 August 1916, Link et al., *Papers of Woodrow Wilson*, vol. 37, 517.

122. Lippmann to Hapgood, 23 August 1916, Yale-Lippmann, box 12, folder 504.

123. Hapgood to Wilson, 14 August 1916, WWP-LoC, reel 285; and Wilson to Hapgood, 17 August, 1916, WWP-LoC, reel 285.

124. Resolution ("In the Senate of the United State, August 21, 1916"), enclosure in GR to Lippmann, 21 August 1916, Yale-Lippmann, box 29, folder 1076.

125. *The New Republic*, 96 (2 September 1916), 102.

126. GR to Joseph Tumlty, 3 October 1916, LoC-WWP, reel 308; Rublee, "Reminiscences," 147-149; and *New York Times*, 6 October 1916. See also Louis Brandeis to Felix Frankfurter, 19 November 1916, Urofsky and Levy, *Letters of Louis D. Brandeis*, vol. 4, 266.

127. Article from an unidentified Kansas newspaper in July 1916, an enclosure in William Harris to Joseph Tumulty, 6 July 1916, WWP-LoC, reel 308.

128. Gallinger testimony, *Hearings II*, 66.

129. Hurley to Wilson, 6 January 1917, Link et al., *Papers of Woodrow Wilson*, vol. 40, 419.

130. GR to House, 26 January 1917, enclosure in GR to Lippmann, 31 January 1917, Yale-Lippmann, box 29, folder 1076. Rublee's letter began: "At your request I am putting in writing the substance of my talk with you about the situation in the Trade Commission."

131. Ibid.

132. Ibid.

133. Ibid.

134. Ibid.

135. J. Harry Covington to GR, 1 February 1917, GRP.

136. Ibid.

137. From table in McCraw, *Prophets of Regulation*, 136,

138. Quoted in Ibid., 125.

139. Rublee, "The Original Plan," 114-120.

140. Ibid., 120.

141. James Kloppenberg, *Uncertain Victory: Social Democracy and Progressivism in European and American Thought, 1870-1920* (New York: Oxford University Press, 1986), 354.

142. Rublee, "The Original Plan," 120.

143. McCraw, *Prophets of Regulation*, 125.

144. Senator Reed before the Senate, 8 September 1914, United States, *Congressional Record*, 63rd Congress, 14790. Reed intended this statement to be derogatory. Louis Brandeis reached the conclusion that the FTC's failure was a result of Wilson's inadequate appointments. Urofsky and Levy, *Letters of Louis Brandeis*, vol. 3, 394, note 1.

145. Arthur Link and Richard McCormick seem to likewise suggest that Wilson was not very well equipped to take the lead on such issues. In their work *Progressivism* (New York: Harlan Davidson, 1983), Link and McCormick note that Wilson's political

experience was limited and that his "ideological metamorphosis had been relatively quick . . . and Wilson only slowly deepened his understanding of progressivism" (44). Link and McCormick also argue that Wilson erred in his "tendency to trust his own judgement and that of a small coterie of advisers" (45). John Milton Cooper Jr., on the other hand, argues that Wilson benefited from "Not having technical knowledge or settled preferences" on business and banking, and praised him for his "willingness to take advice and change his mind." See Cooper, *The Warrior and the Priest*, 236.

8

"A Vision as Mystical and Inspired as That of the Holy Grail" (1917–1919)

When George Rublee sent Wilson his FTC resignation on 26 January 1917, he noted that there was as little point in trying to resurrect his nomination because, in part, "[t]here are so many great matters engaging the attention of the country and of Congress" that either his nomination "would again fail" or "no action would be taken."[1] Although it would seem that Gallinger had at last won the contest, it appears that Rublee's interest in the FTC peaked in 1916, when it became clear that the agency was unlikely to become the innovative regulatory body that he had envisioned. Moreover, it appears that Rublee, like Congress, had become more interested in the "great matters engaging the attention of the country"—that being war in Europe. Long interested in foreign affairs, Rublee early on became concerned about the war and its likely impact on Europe and on international relations.[2] Given his interest in the European war and an apparent expectation that America would soon become a belligerent, Rublee's resignation may well in part have stemmed from a desire to free himself for important war work rather than continue struggling with Gallinger and members of the FTC. When America did become a belligerent, Rublee's independence allowed him to quickly move into a position to contribute to the war effort. Characteristically, Rublee was most interested in questions of efficiency and the mobilization of the economy for war. As another lawyer engaged in the war effort would conclude in 1918, "[T]his War is a gigantic business enterprise, consisting of business problems of great perplexity," and the successful prosecution of it "calls for the best business and professional talent that can be obtained."[3] George Rublee was one of the first of such men to step forward to offer his services. Although his work would not be the sort that grabbed headlines, Rublee would contribute to what chronicler Ernest Fayle described in 1927 as "one of the most important, and perhaps least appreciated [aspects] of the war," that is, the work of the Allied Maritime Transport Council.[4] In representing the U.S. on this enigmatic intergovernmental body, which continues to elude historians, Rublee would have the opportunity to experience innovative international cooperation firsthand and would become a zealot for the development of an international community of states. At war's end he would carry on a personal campaign to see America maintain international cooperation and would strive for control of U.S. policy against forces intent on ending America participation in wartime organizations. These experiences would be a watershed event for him and would set his course as an internationalist throughout the remainder of his life.[5]

Rublee's contribution to the international struggle began shortly before America's declaration of war in April 1917. With Germany gambling that unrestricted submarine warfare could force Great Britain and France to sue for peace before America could bring its power to bear in the conflict, the United States was called upon to meet the daunting challenge of supporting the European war effort while also training, outfitting, and transporting a two million man army to Europe. On the civilian side, the two greatest challenges to such an effort were the creation of an organization to facilitate the economy's conversion to a war footing and the construction of ships to replace the hundreds of thousands of tons of shipping that Germany was sending monthly to the ocean floor. Rublee would soon work with boards dealing with both issues.

Sometime in late March, Rublee was contacted by Chicago industrialist Arch Shaw, who believed that the U.S. government would need to take an active and early role in organizing the economy when war came. As Rublee recalled, Shaw wanted to organize a board that would "save men and material for the war by cutting out unnecessary doings in industry."[6] Rublee, whose work with the Eight-Hour Commission was coming to a conclusion, was interested in contributing to the war effort and found Shaw's idea appealing. He soon arranged for a luncheon with Shaw and cabinet members Franklin Lane and Davis Houston, secretaries of interior and agriculture, who were also members of the president's "provisional war defense board."[7] Lane and Houston were likewise impressed with Shaw's ideas and helped Shaw and Rublee organize the Commercial Economy Board in April 1917. Shaw was named chairman, and economist Edwin Gay of Harvard and noted progressive Henry Dennison, both leaders of the national Chamber of Commerce, served as commissioners. Rublee and Wallace Simmons, a leading hardware distributor, were named to the board on 11 May.[8]

Rublee learned some early and important lessons on the Commercial Economy Board. Lacking coercive power, the board had to rely on patriotism and cooperative leaders of national manufacturing associations to accomplish its aim of reducing "the number of styles, patterns, models, or grades" of product lines in various industries.[9] For instance, the board was successful only when it could get organizations such as the shoe manufacturers' association to implement rules that bound the entire industry. The less organized a trade, Rublee and the board found, the more difficult it was to secure compliance. One of the board's earliest and least successful aims was to end the wasteful practice of retailers returning unsold, stale bread to bakers. Owing to the unorganized and competitive nature of the baking industry, the Commercial Economy Board (CEB) was unable to win compliance from either retailers or bakers. Another lesson that Rublee learned on the CEB was that international competition could complicate national economizing schemes. For instance, when U.S. garment makers were asked to reduce the number of styles and length of women’s skirts, they complained that they would suffer in the international market because competitors in Paris were under no such restrictions. Although the Parisian and American skirt makers would come to an agreement owing to the cooperation of the French ambassador Jean Jules Jusserand, the CEB soon realized that only much stronger national and international boards could force businessmen in free market economies to submit their individual interests to the collective imperative.[10] As Rublee would learn in 1918, however, the creation of such an international organization would meet stiff political opposition in both the United States and Europe.

Not long after he began work with the CEB, Rublee was also asked to join the Emergency Fleet Corporation, a subdivision of the U.S. Shipping Board. The Emergency Fleet Corporation was organized for the purpose of increasing America’s inadequate merchant marine fleet, which would ultimately be responsible for transporting and maintaining American troops in Europe. Following America’s entry into the war, Congress gave Wilson broad powers to create a sizable merchant marine through the Emergency Shipping Fund Act of June 1917. Wilson used the act to increase the authority of the U.S. Shipping Board, created in 1916, and also to establish the Emergency Fleet Corporation.[11] Wilson named Panama Canal builder General George Goethals head of the Emergency Fleet Corporation (EFC) and authorized $50 million to build, buy, or seize 3,000 ships.[12] Shortly after taking control, Goethals called upon Rublee, with whom he worked on the Eight-Hour Commission, to help him get the EFC up and running. As Rublee recalled, at the time he was increasingly concerned about “the confusion that existed with regard to getting our troops over to Europe and supplying them,” so he shifted his focus from the CEB to the EFC, where he organized a team of lawyers to handle the new organization’s legal work. Not surprisingly, he turned to Edward Burling, Charles Norton, with whom he and Burling once lived in Chicago, Joe Cotton, and George Franklin, whom Cotton had brought to Spooner & Cotton—all highly talented corporate lawyers. In addition to helping Goethals on the EFC, the five lawyers advised Herbert Hoover, whom Cotton and Burling knew, when he was named Food Administrator in June 1917. Writing to Robert Bass in July about the legal team’s work, Rublee observed: “We are to advise Goethals on ship building matters and Hoover on food administration. How this will work out remains to be seen, but the [law] board is all right.”[13] Indicating the extent to which his interests had shifted, Rublee, commenting on a rumor he had heard that Wilson was considering him for the ICC, observed: “I wish the President would appoint either Benton or Niles.... I don’t want to be on the Interstate Com[merce] Commission.”[14]

Rublee’s uncertainty over “[h]ow this will work out” may have been something of a warning. It was nearly mid-July, and the country seemed to be making little progress toward preparing for war or for replacing the ships that Germany continued to sink. Although Rublee was hoping that the new war boards would pick up the pace, he knew that Washington was plagued with confusion, and he admitted to Bass that he "was depressed about the war" and was "not very happy" with the progress.[15] Unfortunately, things would get much worse before they improved.

With an appropriation of $50 million the Emergency Fleet Corporation and U.S. Shipping Board set about planning to build ships. Almost immediately, however, a struggle ensued between Goethals and Shipping Board chairman William Denman over the best method and materials to be employed in ship construction, Denman calling for wooden ships, whereas Goethals insisted on steel. With the two organizations relying on the same shipyards, including the colossal construction at Hog Island near Philadelphia, and time being a crucial factor, unity was essential. The dispute between Denman and Goethals soon became public, the two were called to testify before Congress and during the hearings relations between the two men deteriorated rapidly.[16]

On 21 July Rublee wrote private secretary Joseph Tumulty requesting an audience with Wilson, at which he hoped to give insight into "the circumstances surrounding the existing deplorable state of things" between Goethals and Denman.[17] Rublee explained: "I have no interest in the personal aspect of the situation. I am concerned only in its national aspect—in the tremendous importance to the country of building ships without delay." Although Wilson chose not to see him on the matter, Rublee did manage to get across his view of the situation to Tumulty.[18] Rublee and the legal team next suggested that Goethals offer his resignation to force the situation to a swift conclusion. Writing the resignation letter in a manner they hoped would win Wilson's support, the lawyers were surprised when Wilson accepted it and then asked for Denman's resignation as well.[19] The reorganization of the EFC and the appointment of a new director, Rublee recalled, "broke up the party of five lawyers that we'd had." Cotton and Norton returned temporarily to New York, and Burling became chief counselor for the Shipping Board. Burling's move was facilitated by the naming of former FTC chairman Edward Hurley to replace Denman as shipping commissioner and Ray Stevens as assistant chairman, both of whom knew Burling through Rublee.[20] Rublee, on the other hand, found work in the Treasury Department, where he "assumed the work of drafting the war savings stamp."[21] With autumn approaching and no significant improvement in the shipping and economic situation in sight, Rublee began to worry that the German government had been correct, that America was so ill prepared for war that it could make no serious contribution to it before the Allies were defeated. In Washington Rublee began "to hear constantly about the demoralization in the actual movement of ships carrying supplies to Europe" and decided that he would do all he could "to find some cure or correction" for the situation. Toward that end Rublee convinced Hurley to hire Edwin Gay, who had returned to Harvard, to develop a department of statistics that "would study the matter of supplies, where they were, and how they should be allocated."[22] As Rublee recalled, Hurley, "in a quite irregular way, turned [the proposed department] over to me to organize and gave me authority to employ people and fix salaries."[23] After Rublee organized the department to Gay's liking, he managed to have himself named U.S. Shipping Board representative to the

Priorities Committee of the new War Industries Board, where he thought he might make a contribution.[24] It was from that position that Rublee would soon launch into the international arena.

While Rublee was searching for a solution to the shipping crisis in the United States, across the Atlantic, two young Europeans of internationalist mindset, James Arthur Salter of England and Jean Monnet of France, believed that they had found the solution—although a highly controversial and complicated one. Salter, a young bureaucrat promoted to director of ship requisitioning early in the war, and Monnet, former cognac salesman given command of the London Mission of the French Ministry of Commerce and Maritime Transport, struggled throughout 1916 and 1917 to secure modest cooperation between their governments on shipping and import programs. Although both had to overcome opposition from British and French business leaders who struggled against centralization and the suspension of free market principles, the destruction of Allied and neutral shipping at last forced the governments to cooperate at unprecedented levels. At the close of 1916 Monnet and Salter won support for the creation of a so-called wheat executive authorized to purchase grain in the international market for England, France, and Italy, to share those purchases, and to coordinate efficient shipping. Although the Western Allies did not then go so far as to pool their shipping (a very contentious issue), the new body was approved for its supposed ability to make more efficient use of shipping and to reduce the cost of grain for the Allies by ending inflationary competition.[25]

Whereas Salter and Monnet had been required to campaign strenuously for the increased cooperation in 1916, a new round of crises in 1917 eased their work by convincing Allied governments that only complete coordination could preserve them. The destruction of Allied and neutral shipping in the wake of renewed and expanded German submarine warfare created a critical shipping shortage on a global scale by the fall of 1917. Compounding the tonnage shortage was an unexpected failure of the French and Italian harvests, placing even greater demand on the remaining tonnage. The level of destruction and increased need of marine transport became so extensive that European economizing schemes could no longer salvage the situation. On 31 October 1917, Prime Minister David Lloyd George stated in a cabinet meeting that the time had come to "impress on the Americans the grave situation as regards shipping" and to convince them "that it was no use their devoting themselves to [training and sending] troops if the European supplies were such that the Allies were unable to carry on the war."[26] In a subsequent meeting, Foreign Secretary A. J. Balfour, commenting on Germany's effective "method of strangulation," argued that "the question of tonnage is the military question, compared with which other questions had diminished in importance."[27]

The crisis the British cabinet faced resulted from the devastatingly effective German submarine campaign of 1917. Whereas 4 million tons of shipping had been sunk between August 1914 and December 1916, 6 million tons were sunk in 1917 alone, an amount neither the British nor American shipbuilding programs could replace under existing schedules.[28] The impact of these sinkings was reflected in a British report that found that 8 million tons of cargo would have to be cut from the nation's import program in 1918. The total Allied tonnage shortage, including the ships necessary to compensate for the failure of French and Italian harvests, was calculated at 10 million tons.[29] This figure, however, did not take into consideration the growing transport needs of the American army. Regardless, these losses rendered the Allied import programs for 1918 alone simply unworkable—drastic reductions had to be made. The only question remaining was to what extent the Allies would share the austerity measures that the situation demanded.

Fortunately for the Allied cause, Monnet and Salter were nearing completion on a design for a new international organization that they believed might salvage the shipping crisis. They believed that a powerful intergovernmental board could mitigate the shipping crisis by eliminating imports in all countries that it deemed unessential to the war effort and by rationalizing shipping. In a postwar explanation of the work of the Allied Maritime Transport Council, Rublee described the rationalization it hoped to accomplish: "For example, a ship loaded with wheat from India to England would pass in the Mediterranean a ship carrying wheat from America to Italy. If the Indian wheat had gone to Italy and the American wheat to England the voyage of each ship would have been shorter, and both would have avoided the exceedingly serious submarine peril of the western Mediterranean."[30] Salter and Monnet realized that the only way to make rational reductions in the import programs was to establish an inter-Allied body that could adjust each nation's import program to conform to available shipping and military priority. As Salter later explained, however, there "was no precedent for any such system, nor anywhere the knowledge and experience required to construct it."[31] Governments, Salter complained, had no idea "what were the total demands of the world or of any particular county, how these compared with...available shipping, still less what was the intrinsic importance of the different supplies...if measured in terms not of money but the public interest." Explaining the daunting work ahead of them, Salter observed:

> The delicate and intricate machine by which [international] supply and demand had been balanced and adjusted was smashed [by the war]. The constructive brain had to build something that would take its place; to survey needs and resources as a whole; to measure the relative importance of food beyond a certain amount, and of munitions beyond a certain amount, and so on. Thus, one by one, the necessities of life must be controlled, their purchases curtailed, their transport allotted, their prices fixed, their consumption rationed. For this new task, the skill had to be developed, the organization improvised.[32]

Worse still, the work had to be done immediately, and the political will for such invasive measures was lacking, especially in America, where free enterprise traditions were nearly insuperable. For those with left-leaning sentiments, these wartime measures were an exciting opportunity to demonstrate that a government might organize the economy equally as well as the free market. Businessmen on both sides of the Atlantic seemed to have understood the potential ramifications of such experiments and appear to have agreed to them with a great deal of trepidation.

As Rublee worked in Washington trying to coordinate greater cooperation among American businesses in the fall of 1917, Monnet and Salter accomplished something of a coup when they successfully convinced their governments to create the new inter-Allied body charged with adjusting import programs and controlling all available tonnage. The final obstacle to the agreement concerned the commitment of British ships to carry out the French import program. The British were reluctant to take on the responsibility of supplying France without a promise of U.S. support. Nevertheless, the British at last agreed, with or without the help of America, to pool proportionally to their respective means " all necessary tonnage" to carry out the Allied war effort.[33]

In many respects the creation of the Allied Maritime Transport Council primarily concerned Anglo-French relations. Nevertheless, the new commitment to France and the crisis driving that development dramatically increased Britain's desire to secure much greater U.S. participation in the Allied war effort. Toward that end, the British began focusing their efforts on obtaining maximum American involvement on Salter's and Monnet's innovative international board so that the burdens and costs of the war might be more evenly borne (and likely so that the postwar trade situation would be closer to the status quo ante). However, owing to the strained relations between the two countries in 1915 and 1916 over neutral trading rights and the blockade of Germany, there would be significant resistance in Washington to working closely with Britain on economic matters. Additionally, as Monnet pointed out, "It had taken two years of persistent effort, and the deadly threat of unlimited submarine warfare, before [France and Britain] could combine…resources and pool…shipping."[34] That the United States would never reach a similar level of cooperation seems understandable. Nevertheless, the lack of cooperation was a source of frustration for the British as well as American internationalists, such as Rublee, and would not bode well for Anglo-American relations in the postwar period.

The British recognized that the November 1917 Supreme War Conference in Paris offered the best opportunity to secure greater U.S. involvement in solving the Allied shipping crisis. In a diplomatic maneuver aimed at making the United States less an associate—as Wilson continued to stipulate—and more an ally, the British introduced a document entitled "The Need for American Assistance and Allied Co-operation" in the economic section of the Paris conference. The British hoped that the document (drafted by Salter and Monnet) would convey to Colonel Edward House and his small delegation the full extent of the impending crisis in Europe and induce the Americans to support U.S. participation on the new inter-Allied shipping and economic council.[35] The British were successful in that effort. The document's introduction announced that "the losses of British, Allied and Neutral ships and the serious failure of the French and Italian harvest this year have created a tonnage situation of great gravity." To meet the crisis, the Europeans proposed the establishment of a permanent council, the Allied Maritime Transport Council, consisting of representatives from France, Italy, Britain, and America, which would exchange information concerning the Allied shipping and supply situation on an ongoing basis. This council would control an adequate supply of pooled Allied shipping and would allocate those ships based on the recommendations of the council's executive, that body basing its decisions on economic data supplied by each government. The memorandum also requested that the United States increase its shipbuilding program by one-third (from 6 to 9 million tons dead weight per year), that it take "every possible step" to bring neutral vessels lying dormant in its docks into war service, and that it "drastically" reduce its own import programs.[36]

The Special Committee for Maritime Transport and General Imports of the Paris War Conference, upon which U.S. envoys and Allied representatives sat, unanimously resolved that each country would send "one or two ministers—the United States one or two special delegates" who would meet in London to represent their governments on the new Allied Maritime Transport Council (AMTC).[37] The two resolutions establishing the power of the AMTC were historic for the cooperation and integration they provided between recent economic competitors. The first authorized the council to "allot [pooled] Allied tonnage as between the different needs of the Allies in such a way as to add most to the general war effort." The second authorized the council to make recommendations to "adjust the programmes of [import] requirements of the different Allies in such a way as to bring them within the scope of the possible carrying power of the tonnage available."[38] Although each country would retain final authority over its programs and therefore could resist cooperation on some level, Salter and Monnet envisioned each country sending ministers who had the authority to bring their nation's import program into line with the decisions reached by the council.

Although the American representatives in Paris supported the resolutions establishing the AMTC, it was unclear from the beginning to what extent the United States would participate in the new council. Somewhat surprisingly, upon the House delegation's return in early December, the greatest initial obstacle to American involvement was President Wilson, who had strong reservations about submitting American import programs to an international body. It seems that Wilson continued to distrust the European Allies and still thought it possible to prosecute the war with them without becoming too entangled politically or economically.[39] Additionally, according to U.S. Shipping Board member Bainbridge Colby, who attended the Paris conference, Wilson was opposed to maintaining representatives in Europe on permanent councils because "he felt that it was only a matter of time until the American member…would be influenced by the atmosphere in which he was working and become European in his views."[40] Nevertheless, Wilson was in something of a quandary because House, Colby, and other members of the delegation had supported the creation of the AMTC and had committed America to sending at least delegates (as opposed to high-ranking cabinet secretaries) to represent the United States on the council. Perhaps as a compromise between wanting to appear cooperative yet still distrusting the Europeans, Wilson agreed to send an official from the U.S. Shipping Board and a small delegation of technical advisers to London to represent the United States on the AMTC.[41] There the American delegate would join an impressive group of European ministers on the council: Britain's Lord Robert Cecil, minister of the blockade, and Sir Joseph Maclay, minister of shipping; France's Étienne Clémentel, minister of commerce, and Louis Loucheur, minister of munitions, the latter having earlier staunchly opposed the creation of the AMTC; and Italy's Salvatore Orlando and Silvio Crespi, minister of supply.[42] Despite the obvious disparity between the rank of the European and American members, the Europeans appear to have been relieved that the American government was willing to participate.

Although Wilson was wary of the AMTC and American role on it, internationalists in Washington welcomed the development. No one was more enthusiastic about the new council than George Rublee, who learned about the organization from Louis McBride and Nelson Perkins, both members of the House delegation to Paris.[43] While it remains unclear how it was accomplished, Ray Stevens, vice-chairman of the U.S. Shipping Board, was named delegate to the AMTC, and Rublee was named delegate to the Allied Maritime Transport Executive, which would control the day-to-day operations of the AMTC. Although he could not know it, Rublee was about to have a life-changing experience and develop lasting friendships with many progressive-minded Europeans, chiefly James Arthur Salter and Jean Monnet, who not surprisingly controlled the AMTC Executive.

Rublee, Stevens, and a number of technical advisers traveled to England in convoy on 31 January 1918. Allowed to have extensive input over the selection of the delegation, Rublee and Stevens gathered a number of economists with Edwin Gay's help and enlisted several corporation and finance lawyers to work on the AMTC subcommittees.[44] Rublee's most important recruit for the delegation was international financier Dwight Morrow, who traveled with Rublee and the American delegation to London, where he was to perform a temporary mission for J. P. Morgan & Company. Stevens managed to have Wilson appoint Morrow to the American delegation, even though the president balked at sending a Morgan man.[45] While in Europe, Morrow, who later served as ambassador to Mexico, became absorbed with the work of the AMTC and joined the board full-time with Rublee's help. Morrow's decision to join the delegation altered the course of his life, creating close friendships with internationalists that led him evermore deeply into a liberal internationalist mind-set.[46]

In London, Stevens joined the European ministers on the AMTC, and Rublee served as the U.S. delegate on the Allied Maritime Transport (AMT) Executive with Monnet, Salter, and Bernardo Attolico of Italy. According to Monnet's and Salter's scheme, the Executive, with the assistance of supporting program committees, would have the "necessary but ungrateful role" of reducing the individual Allied import programs to the available Allied tonnage.[47] Once the Executive adjusted the Allied programs, it would pass on its recommendations to the ministers of the AMTC, who would authorize the programs and see to it that their home governments implemented the

Executive's economizing import programs. As Salter later explained, the Executive, which met both formally and informally, was "the instrument through which liaison between the Governments was secured on all shipping questions."[48] Describing the difficulty of the Executive's work, Salter observed: "To the national departments the member of the Executive always represented the Allied point of view; he was always urging his own country to abate its demands or increase its assistance. To his Allied colleagues, on the other hand, he was always representing his own country's point of view, urging its needs and trying to influence the other countries' action in the direction of its policy."[49] Salter found that such delicate work was "only possible at all under conditions of personal confidence and long personal association."[50] While the work was difficult, Salter and Monnet evidently wanted the import schedules and shipping assignments to be taken out of the hands of ministers, who were under heavy political pressure, and instead placed in the hands of technical experts such as themselves. To their satisfaction the AMTC met on only four occasions prior to the armistice and in each case authorized the AMT Executive's programs.[51]

Although it is unclear how it was decided that Rublee would work with Salter, Monnet, and Attolico on the Executive, Rublee's knowledge of French and Italian and his familiarity with European civilization likely played a role. Stevens, on the other hand, had never traveled abroad and was at the time still somewhat provincial.[52] It may have been that House made the decision before the delegation left. A letter from Norman Hapgood to House on 27 January suggests that the two anticipated Rublee's meeting informally with notable British lords to understand the war situation from a European perspective.[53] Rublee's ease in European society, his ability to speak European languages, and his background on various commissions and war boards likely made him the obvious choice for the AMT Executive. Still, when Rublee arrived in London, it is unclear how well he understood Monnet's and Salter's designs. Rublee had heard about Monnet from McBride, who described him as "quite a remarkable man," so he arranged to meet the Frenchman soon after arriving. Rublee quickly realized that "Monnet was a key person and established good relations with him."[54] Following a number of informal meetings with London officials to become acquainted with England's economic and shipping controls, Rublee, Stevens, and Morrow accompanied Monnet to Paris, where they studied the French system. The three then traveled on to Chaumont, France, where American general John Pershing had his headquarters. Having envisioned discussing the army's import programs with a view to eradicating inefficiencies, the three technocrats were surprised to find that Pershing "didn't understand" the serious shipping crisis confronting the Allies. What they told Pershing "frightened" him, and he designated a colonel to return with them to London so that he could keep in touch with them on the shipping situation. Pershing also requested that Dwight Morrow return to Chaumont to create a schedule to forecast the amount of shipping he would need.[55] Morrow agreed to return to perform the important work if he could win the approval of his Morgan manager, Thomas Lamont.[56] Toward this end both Rublee and Paul Cravath, another New York lawyer associated with the AMTC, wrote to Lamont at the Morgan House in New York to secure Morrow's continued work in Europe.[57] Morrow soon returned to assist Pershing and produced what Edward Hurley would call "one of the most valuable pieces of statistical work of the war."[58]

Although the inaugural meeting of the AMTC was not held in London until 11 March, Rublee was soon called to sit with the Executive to consider issues that the council would have to act on at its first meeting. The gravest immediate problem was a coal crisis in Italy. Owing to the destruction of shipping, Italy had been forced to deplete its reserves to dangerously low levels. The Executive faced the difficulty of finding ships to provide an emergency shipment of coal to Italy without risking those vessels to submarines in the Mediterranean. With representatives from Britain, France, and Italy in the same room the Executive soon produced an easy answer; the French would ship coal from strategic reserves by rail to Italy, and Britain would resupply France using smaller vessels crossing the Channel. Although an obvious solution, it was possible to implement such an arrangement only through the new international apparatus. During the first meeting of the AMTC, the council took up the Executive's scheme and hammered out a way to make it work.[59]

During its meeting the AMTC also examined the Executive's preliminary balance sheet relating import programs to available tonnage. The report showed that with the schedules that were currently known, there was a 10 million-ton deficit in shipping available for the British and French programs alone. The AMTC charged the Executive with either reducing national import programs or reallocating tonnage.[60] A difficulty for Rublee and the other members of the U.S. delegation was that, unlike France, Great Britain, and Italy, the U.S. government did not provide them with statistical information for its various industrial and agricultural programs. The Executive, therefore, could only recommend reductions in the European programs. As Dwight Morrow complained to Assistant Secretary of War Edward Stettinius, the American government and some European leaders did not seem to understand that "there is *one* tonnage problem—not *four* tonnage problems" and that "one nation's shortage is the shortage of all nations."[61] Morrow argued that the "belief that there is *somewhere* some tonnage that at the last minute can be drawn upon...leads to a very uneconomical use of the [available] tonnage." Rublee, too, complained that the "relations between the [AMTC] and the various groups in Washington...were not very good," there being "no very direct communications with anybody but the Shipping Board," which had no control over American programs. Rublee believed that "[t]hey were making the mistake in Washington of trying to run the war from Washington, whereas the war had to be run from London really."[62] Shipping Board chairman Edward Hurley later admitted that "Stevens and Rublee were handicapped" in London and that "America did not at first see eye to eye with the Allied Maritime Transport Council."[63] Most surprising, however, was the U.S. State Department's lack of knowledge of the AMTC. On 9 April, more than two months after the U.S. delegation sailed, the State Department sent a cable to the London Embassy requesting the names of the British, French, and Italian representatives on the

AMTC and a "statement of its functions and the character of the questions it considers."[64] Rublee would make it his personal mission to increase U.S. awareness of, and cooperation with, the AMTC throughout the remainder of the war.

To adjust Allied import programs, the Executive needed more precise and more timely information from the national governments. In an effort to secure that information and also to encourage greater U.S. participation, the Executive recommended the creation of twenty program committees, which would be headed by "actual officials who [exercise] direct executive authority in their own national departments."[65] As Rublee explained shortly after the war, the statistical data required were extensive:

> (1) Normal pre-war imports. (2) Normal pre-war production. (3) Last year's imports. (4) Last year's home production. (5) The estimates of current year's home production. (6) The ration allowed and the numerical strength of the armed forces. (7) The fixed ratio or reasonable scale of production per head of the civilian population. (8) The normal quantity of each food-stuff consumed per head, taking into account national idiosyncrasies. (9) The description and quality of food normally consumed by the country. (10) The amount of tonnage and finance which the particular Ally can command and devote to the purchase of each article. (11) The existing stocks in the country. (12) The relative urgency of needs.[66]

Such information was necessary, Rublee explained, to forecast shipping programs and to provide for "equality of sacrifice" among the Allies in reducing import programs.

A passage in a letter from Morrow to Stettinius also offers insight into the pressing need to take import programs out of the hands of politicians. Relating the incompetence he had witnessed in France, Morrow observed:

> When I was in Paris last week I got a vivid picture of the situation from one of the Ministers. He says a very large part of the Prime Minister's time is spent in listening to the several ministers explaining the terrible calamity that will befall if this, that or the other thing is not forthcoming at once. [Thus, the prime minister] is required to guess at the intensity and seriousness of the particular panic, compared to other panics that are pressing. The result is that, to an amazing degree, the fateful decisions of the War are made not by intelligence—not even by pretended intelligence—but by panic or, what is even worse, *competitive* panic.[67]

Morrow noted, "The intelligent and patriotic men in each Nation want to get together," but "[t]he difficulty is to get the machinery started which will carry out the will to cooperate."[68] The AMTC Executive hoped that the program committees would supply the machinery necessary to alleviate the debilitating inefficiencies.

Shortly after the Executive settled down to work on reducing the import programs in March 1918, the early successes of the German spring offensive rendered the Allied position dramatically worse. Among other difficulties, the German offensive "deprived France of coal from the Pas-de-Calais," through which Britain planned to make up for the emergency shipments of French coal to Italy.[69] As Monnet recalled, the Executive was "forced to produce [further] cuts in civil and even military supplies—a necessary but ungrateful role." With foreshadowing, Monnet pointed out, "Some people thought that we were exceeding our authority."[70] More difficult for the Executive to deal with than the strategic losses in northern France, however, was handling the new priority placed on transporting U.S. troops to Europe after the German offensive. Although the November 1917 Supreme War Conference in Paris established that the United States would deploy fifty divisions to Western Europe by late summer 1918, in the wake of the German spring offensive the United States agreed to the Allied request to supply eighty divisions by the same target date. Incredibly, given the shipping crisis, the military leaders demanded that American troop strength in Europe increase from 350,000 in March to 2 million by early autumn. This increase could be accomplished only through further reductions in civilian import programs.[71]

To carry out the requisite cuts in already austere programs, in its second full meeting 23–25 April in Paris, the AMTC called for the previously proposed program committees to "be constituted immediately."[72] The council specifically called for U.S. participation on the new commodity committees, noting that: "it is desirable that there be an American representative on each of these [committees] who would be a full member in the same sense as the representatives of the three European Allies." Although Rublee and Stevens fully supported these steps personally, Shipping Board chairman Hurley instructed them by cable just prior to the conference to "avoid any commitment or action until your report [of the proceedings] is received and instructions can be formulated on your report as basis."[73] Lacking plenipotentiary authority, Stevens abstained from voting on the resolutions that touched upon increased American participation.[74]

Despite the handicap he and Stevens faced, Rublee was excited about his work on the AMTC. Writing to Learned Hand on 4 May upon his return from the Paris council meeting, Rublee reported: "Most interesting experience and real headway made at the Council's meeting. We are beginning to have considerable influence. I mean our American crowd in shaping the work, and we may yet accomplish something."[75] Nevertheless, Rublee complained that the Wilson administration "in their ponderous slowness remind me a little of glaciers" and related his concern that Washington might continue to ignore the American delegation.

Apparently having concluded that Hurley was not giving adequate attention to the work of the AMTC, Rublee and Stevens reported the results of the second AMTC meeting directly to President Wilson. Their report explained that the "recommendations of the Council are of such importance" that it is a "duty to report them directly to you."[76] The program committees, they explained, would "be constituted for the purpose of agreeing upon the quantities of imports to be brought into Great Britain, France, Italy and the United States." Aware of the Wilson administration's reluctance to allow its programs to be scrutinized by an international body, they pointed out that the program committees were created in accordance with the resolutions of the Paris War Conference, "in which Colonel

House participated." Stevens and Rublee agreed "that in order to deal effectively with [an] extremely serious deficit of tonnage it is necessary...that the associated Governments should consider together through technically competent representatives, their several import requirements, commodity by commodity, with a view of agreeing upon joint programs."[77] They stressed the importance of appointing American representatives—if the plan were approved—"as speedily as possible" so that the critical work facing the program committees could commence.

Despite the American representatives' expression of urgency and the council's explicit request that the program committees be "constituted immediately," there was no response to the proposal from anyone in the Wilson administration for nearly two months. The situation was frustrating for Rublee who complained to Thomas Lamont on 4 May that the AMTC "is still but imperfectly comprehended by many branches of the different governments" and argued that "there is no time to lose in bringing it home to them."[78]

Although Rublee realized that the AMTC was "as yet a rather tender plant, with inadequate powers and prestige," he believed that "it is the only organ" for sustaining "the vital needs of the allied nations." With still no response from Washington, on 18 May Rublee complained to Dwight Morrow: "We have not made very much progress in the work since you left. We get few answers to our cablegrams to America. No response has yet come from the President, or from anybody representing him, in regard to the proposal to establish Executives and Program Committees."[79] The lack of responsiveness from the Wilson administration is difficult to judge. Although the silence may, in fact, have been stonewalling, it may also have simply resulted from a combination of Edward Hurley's slow reaction to the request and indecision on the part of Wilson. For example, it was not until three weeks after the council met, 17 May, that Hurley wrote Wilson to give his approval of American participation on the proposed program committees.[80] After another week passed, Wilson wrote back to Hurley asking if he had any "further particulars from Stevens" or had Hurley "been able to give any thought to the best persons whom we could assign to take part in the new plan?"[81] Whatever the cause, Hurley and Wilson somehow did not grasp that the situation was urgent.

America's reluctance to cooperate with the AMTC was a source of irritation for British leadership, as the minutes of a 24 May cabinet meeting demonstrate. On that occasion Lord Robert Cecil, minister of blockade and AMTC chairman, was noted as having observed

> that as regards America, there was a fundamental difference between that country and the other co-belligerents. The Washington Government was apparently not prepared to trust, or concede any real authority to, their representatives. This, he said, was conspicuously the case as regards their shipping delegates and he cited other instances of the reluctance of the United States to allow their representatives freedom of action.[82]

Lord Cecil noted that there had been no response yet from the Wilson administration to the 23 April AMTC request that the United States send representatives to London to join the Executive's program committees.

Sometime late in May, Rublee and Stevens decided that Rublee should return to Washington and attempt to personally convince Wilson to appoint American representatives to the various program committees. Rublee arrived in Washington in early June and, characteristically, began working to build support among the leaders of the war agencies before he approached Wilson. Morrow, who returned to America for a short visit a few weeks after Rublee arrived, helped Rublee convince Hurley and Bernard M. Baruch, head of the War Industries Board, of the importance of American representation on the program committees. Rublee recalled that, of those who were approached, the "greatest difficulty was with [food administrator] Herbert Hoover, who didn't like the idea—he wanted to keep control from start to finish in Washington but he finally consented also."[83]

After convincing Hurley, Baruch and Hoover, to a degree, Rublee made an appeal to Wilson in a letter on 20 June. He began by explaining that Hurley had told him that Wilson was "about to consider the papers relating to the participation of the United States in the proposed Allied Program Committees."[84] Rublee pointed out that, having dealt with "this matter for a long time with Mr. Stevens and with the leading French, British and Italian officials," he might be of help to Wilson in explaining "just how it is conceived by the other governments." Rublee believed that it was "urgent" that America should appoint representatives to the program committees and "leave any question of conferring executive powers of any kind" until "after the committees have organized and have started their fundamental work of investigation and planning."[85] Wilson replied to Rublee on 21 June, announcing that he believed that "the advisory committees ought to be worked out on the lines that you indicate," and asserted that he would contact Rublee if he got "confused in drawing up the memorandum which I now have in mind."[86] Wilson's memo went out soon thereafter instructing various war boards to send representatives to London. On 10 July Wilson sent a message to the Allied governments that began: "The Government of the United States recognizes that in addition to military and naval action a careful coordination is necessary...in Finance, Shipping, Export and Import relations, Food Stuffs, Raw materials and manufactured or partly manufactured products."[87] A victory for Rublee and the American delegation in London, the document promised American representation on the new Executive priority committees and provided for consultation among heads of state in the event that "it is impossible to secure a unanimous acceptance of a programme by the various Ministers."

Having secured Wilson's approval for U.S. participation on the program committees, Rublee returned to London in July 1918 with most of the experts he had sought. Reporting to Morrow his success in Washington, Rublee observed: "I did everything in Washington that I could. I think it was well for me to leave. Else I might have outstayed my welcome and run the risk of boring people and being too officious. I went rather far on that road as it was."[88] Rublee managed to secure internationally minded men for the London committees, among them Joe Cotton, who was appointed as Hoover's representative for the Food Administration. Rublee later recalled that the trip to Washington was a success because the American "representatives for the different commodities were all able men. Once in England they understood the situation and all worked harmoniously" with the European members.[89] Rublee also believed his mission to be a success because U.S. participation fostered better relations between the Allies. Writing shortly after the war, Rublee observed: "Each Government knew what the total resources were, and what were to be the shares of each country, with the reasons which justified them. Assurance of a fair distribution powerfully strengthened willingness to endure privations in the common cause."[90] Likely owing to his de facto leadership of the American mission, following his return to London, Wilson appointed Rublee as the second American delegate on the Allied Maritime Transport Council, so that he sat on both the Council of Ministers and the Executive. A telegram to U.S. ambassadors in London, Paris, and Rome on 27 July announced Rublee's promotion.[91] Rublee's friends in Washington and New England seem to have been impressed with the way George managed to move ever closer to the center of power once his passion was engaged. Writing to a common friend, Learned Hand observed that Rublee's new appointment "gives him equal authority with Stevens and therefore changes his status a good deal. To be of equal authority with Stevens is to be absolutely the leader, for as he was before he was that."[92]

Curiously, at about the same time that the United States was entering a phase pointing toward closer cooperation with the AMTC, attitudes in France toward the council took an opposite course. Although Jean Monnet had gained French support for extensive Allied economic integration, the reshuffling of cabinets in Paris undermined his program and removed a veil of protection from around him. Louis Loucheur, French delegate on the AMTC and minister of munitions, who had earlier failed in his effort to block Monnet's and Salter's integration plan, took advantage of French political turmoil to strike at Monnet and the AMTC. When Rublee returned to London in July 1918, he was surprised to find that Monnet had been drafted into the French army as a soldier. Rublee soon learned that Loucheur and accomplices in the French government had arranged for Monnet to be conscripted because they felt he was "much too international" and believed that he was not promoting France's best (e.g., business) interests.[93] In his *Memoirs*, Monnet explained that because he had "ignored hierarchical channels," he made "a number of enemies," of whom the "most powerful was undoubtedly Louis Loucheur."[94] Rublee, who had befriended Monnet and considered him too important to the AMTC to be lost to the French army, traveled to Paris in an effort to have him returned to London. After consulting with Monnet and learning about Loucheur's machinations, Rublee secured the backing of assistant secretary of war Edward Stettinius, who was at the time in Paris, and addressed a letter to the French government asking that Monnet be reinstated on the AMTC. Rublee recalled that his letter was "circulated throughout the departments of the French government and the result was that the French government withdrew [Monnet] from the army and let him go on with his work in London."[95] Of the ordeal, Monnet recalled: "A week later, the Prime Minister called me back. He handed me a piece of paper. On it read: 'Lieutenant Monnet is to return at once to his post in London.' It was a decree that he had just had approved by the cabinet. Among the signatures was Loucheur."[96] Charles Howland, a member of the new delegation representing the United States, noted American involvement in extracting Monnet from the French army:

All the nations represented [on the AMTC] have great respect for our power as well as for our purposes: upon the urgency of our representatives the French retained on the Council one of their representatives, a most valuable man, whom they had intended for their own political reasons to withdraw but whom they retained as a result of vigorous protest by our representatives in Paris.[97]

Considering Monnet's later contribution to international affairs, including his role in the creation of the European Economic Union, Rublee's intervention had lasting significance.

The decision in early summer 1918 to increase American troop strength in Europe to eighty divisions presented a great challenge to the AMTC Executive. Whereas it had been hoped that the U.S. shipbuilding program would offer some relief to the European transportation crisis, instead, Britain was called upon to allocate more ships to transport and feed the American army. Doing so meant that the Executive had to cut an additional 8 million tons of cargo for the cereal year (September to August) 1918–1919 from an already austere import program.[98] The most pressing issue before the Executive was the need to devise a plan that would supply the raw materials required for the European munitions industry while maintaining civilian food requirements. The Inter-Allied Food Council, a program committee established in July following Rublee's trip to Washington, came into sharp conflict with the Executive over the allotment of food.[99] During the winter of 1917–1918 shortages of food existed everywhere in Europe, and in some areas conditions "had approached local starvation."[100] As a result, the members of the Food Council were determined to fight for as much tonnage as possible to provide food for civilians. Laying counterclaim to the scarce tonnage were such enthusiasts as Winston Churchill, minister of munitions.

Lacking tonnage to meet both military and civilian requirements, the Executive devised a bold plan to meet the necessities of the grave situation. To provide for the requirements of the munitions industry, the Executive suggested that the European Allies substantially forgo food imports during the winter of 1918–1919. Although Salter, Monnet, Rublee, Attolico, and their staffs realized that depleting European food reserves would be dangerous, they reasoned that the deficit could be made up by U.S. shipping in the spring and summer of 1919, when it was supposed that the American shipbuilding program would have at last lived up to its potential.[101] Realizing that the Executive's proposal would place the Europeans in grave jeopardy, during September 1918 Rublee, Stevens, and other U.S. representatives in London repeatedly expressed the need for America to cooperate more fully with the AMTC. Despite having sent representatives to London, it seems that U.S. agencies continued to be far from cooperative.[102]

Not surprisingly, before accepting the Executive's "munitions in winter—food afterward" plan, the British demanded that the U.S. government demonstrate a substantially increased commitment to cooperate and share the commercial burdens of war.[103] On 2 September Wilson forwarded a communiqué to secretary of state Robert Lansing from Lord Reading that concerned America's request for British ships to facilitate the deployment of eighty troop divisions to Europe. In his message Reading pointed to the privations that the European Allies would experience in allotting British ships to transport American troops, and he related the desire among the Allied governments for an assurance "that the sacrifices are…made in pursuance of a common policy followed by the four Governments." Reading explained that to guarantee an equality of sacrifice, the British and Allied Governments would earnestly request that those responsible for the allocation of American tonnage and limitation of American imports should come to London as soon as possible. "We will arrange for the Ministers of Great Britain, France and Italy to meet them in London and determine the final action. It is in proof the promptest and most effective way of arriving at a decision."[104] In an accompanying letter to Lansing, who well may not have been informed about the AMTC's workings, Wilson explained, "These are the very questions Baker has gone over to settle.... I have authorized him to assemble all programmes that we have had any part in formulating and discuss all the elements."[105] Short-lived though it proved to be, Wilson's policy change would seem to be the reversal for which Rublee and the American internationalists in London had been hoping.

In addition to American delegates Stevens and Rublee, Newton D. Baker and Edward Stettinius, secretary and assistant secretary of war, attended the fourth and final meeting of the Allied Maritime Transport Council, prior to the armistice, held in London 30 September through 2 October.[106] First-time persons in attendance also included Britain's Winston Churchill and Rear Admiral Hugh Tothill, Fourth Sea Lord, and Italy's General Armando Mola. The main work before the council was consideration of the Executive's "munitions in winter—food afterwards" plan. Following an introductory statement concerning the general situation, AMTC chairman Lord Robert Cecil asked "for an assurance that the United States Government was prepared to participate in the fullest sense in the work of the Council."[107]

In response to Cecil's pointed query, Secretary Baker made a lengthy speech confirming America's commitment to participate in, and cooperate with, the AMTC. In the course of his speech, Baker attempted to explain America's previous reluctance to full cooperation: "The difficulties [faced by the AMTC] …heretofore I know very little about. I suspect that the width of the Atlantic is in part responsible for much of the hesitancy and uncertainty which has seemed to attend the getting of statistics and the getting of programmes from the United States."[108] Although Baker's excuses likely did little to build confidence in the American leadership, the new level of commitment must nevertheless have been a welcome change. For Rublee, sitting in the room full of European and American statesmen and military leaders, the meeting was the climactic moment of his war work. Voting with Stevens and the six European ministers of the

AMTC, Rublee helped pass a resolution that would truly integrate the Allied economic war effort. It provided "[t]hat America should, with the European Allies, table her programmes of imports for joint consideration by the Allied Program Committees, and her tonnage for similar joint consideration by the Allied Maritime Transport Council, and enable her representatives on these bodies to consider adjustments in the programmes of her imports and the allocation of her tonnage."[109] The meeting was a great success for those in the room, like Rublee, Monnet, and Salter, who believed that robust international cooperation during the war could lay a foundation for the much anticipated postwar new world order that Wilson had projected in his January Fourteen Points declaration.

The council's decision to accept the Executive's "munitions in winter—food afterwards" plan reflected great determination and faith on the part of European Allies. Rublee later recalled that in order to carry out the plan, "it would be necessary for the British to kill *all* their herds of cattle and sheep that winter to provide food for their people—the situation was *so* tight." He considered the decision "a wonderfully courageous undertaking by the British."[110] As a result of the armistice on 11 November, however, the British were never called upon to take such drastic steps. Neither, it should be pointed out, was America called upon to demonstrate its commitment to full cooperation with the Allies. On this point Salter later wrote: "The real and crucial test [of America's commitment] would have come, if the war had continued, in the spring of 1919."[111] Correspondence between Rublee and Stevens and U.S. war agencies indicates, however, that there continued to be great reluctance among American war boards to comply with the decisions reached at the fourth meeting of the AMTC. Writing to Baker on 31 October, three weeks after his assurances of U.S. participation, Rublee and Stevens expressed their concern over the continued lack of cooperation: "With these conditions [of hardship] existing among the European Allies, it is essential that we on our part should cut off the import of non-essentials and limit the import of essentials to the programs agreed upon.... We have hitherto assumed that this was in fact being done and that American shipping was being used solely for essential imports. [Edwin] Gay's report, if correct, clearly shows that this is not the case."[112] Evidently, greater pressure would have to have been brought to bear on the various wartime organizations to induce them to carry out Baker's vow of American cooperation.

America's steps at the October AMTC meeting were the climax of international cooperation, excepting the military arrangements reached by the Supreme War Council. Following the signing of the armistice, however, this cooperation quickly evaporated. Writing a few years later, Salter commented on what he believed to have been a lost opportunity: "The Allied Maritime Transport Council and its Executive reached the climax of their authority and their utility in the autumn of 1918. From the Armistice onwards their power diminished to a mere shadow of its former self.... [T]o trace the course of this decline from power...is a somewhat painful duty for any one who was associated with the Allied organization in the period of the war."[113] Rublee and other Americans on the AMTC organization would likewise be disheartened when the cooperation between governments came to an abrupt end with the armistice. All of these men had experienced international cooperation on an unprecedented level. Keenly aware of the influence of Great Power brinkmanship and diplomatic intrigue on the origins of the war in 1914, the American and European internationalists believed that the AMTC provided a basis for intergovernmental cooperation that might usher in a period of lasting international peace. As Dean Acheson later explained, "Gradually a vision as mystical and inspired as that of the Holy Grail began to come to this brilliant and devoted group. It seemed to them that here in this body of disciplined men, a technical staff, might lie the secret of subordinating national interests in the creation of a new world order. Reason and knowledge could be, they thought, so powerful as to overwhelm prejudice and narrow interest."[114] Not surprisingly, no American would fight harder than George Rublee to preserve that which the AMTC had gained for international understanding during the war. What is surprising, however, is that Rublee's struggle to preserve this vision of a new world order was waged against his own government, against the American president who had a messianic vision of international cooperation and yet failed to realize that his greatest chance to accomplish his world historic aim rested with his representatives in London and the organization in which they worked. Ironically, Wilson would instead rely on the guidance of none other than Herbert Hoover, a man then and later devoted to shielding America from what he called "entangling" Europan alliances. Under Hoover's influence, Wilson would discount the Americans in London and agree to destroy what Dean Acheson would later call "that great innovation in international organization," the AMTC.[115]

The struggle for control of postwar international relations began in the last weeks of October 1918. Concerned about the critical shortage of food in Germany and Austria and believing that the AMTC had a vital and legitimate role to play following the war, on 28 October Rublee joined his European colleagues in the Executive in passing a resolution that would give the council control over postwar relief operations in Central and Eastern Europe. Perceiving that shipping and food supplies would continue to be in a state of a chaos, the AMT Executive also reasoned that it should be authorized to continue allocating food, raw materials, and transportation between the nations until the free market mechanisms of supply and demand could be restored. Four days prior to Rublee's vote, however, Herbert Hoover, who evidently got wind of the effort from Joe Cotton and other Food Administration representatives, sent a preemptive letter to Wilson warning that "some members of the Allied Food Council are putting forward suggestions for international control of world distribution of food after peace."[116] Although, like the Executive, Hoover believed that there would be "an international shortage in several vital commodities if consumption is to be restored to normal" levels, he argued that his "own instinct is entirely against any such agreements or entanglements" because they would allow Europeans to control "distribution of our supplies." Hoover not only wanted to control food but suggested that Wilson also resist international control of raw materials. Alluding to the possibility of friction with the European Allies, Hoover argued, "[I]f we maintain control of our supplies of food and raw material we will be in position to make such arrangements as will insure our own interests." Invoking a touchstone of American foreign policy, Hoover concluded, "[I]f you hold the view that we shall enter no entanglements whatever I shall take steps at once to maintain such a stand."[117] Historian George Nash, however, points out that Hoover's opposition to the AMTC plan was more than ideological. He explains that having worked hard to fill U.S. granaries with wheat and slaughter yards with pigs, Hoover feared that the AMTC proposal "imperiled his ability to dispose of his soaring stocks of wheat and pork."[118]

Although perhaps knowledgeable of Hoover's sentiments and concerns, Joe Cotton nevertheless communicated his support for the Executive's resolution in early November. Cotton pointed out that it would be unwise to dismantle the existing inter-Allied bodies in favor of new ones upon which "the Allies might have weaker and certainly would have no better representatives."[119] Hoover voiced his opposition in no uncertain terms on 8 November, a little more than a month after Secretary Baker's speech promising American cooperation. Evidently believing he had won Wilson over, the future Republican president observed: "This Government will not agree to any programme that even looks like inter-Allied control of our economic resources after peace. After peace over one-half of the whole export food supplies of the world will come from the United States and for the buyers of these supplies to sit in majority in dictation to us as to prices and distribution is wholly inconceivable. The same applies to raw materials."[120] With the conclusion of the armistice three days later, the contest taking shape between internationalists in London and independent nationalists in Washington ensued in earnest.

In a letter to Louis Brandeis on 14 November Rublee, possibly seeking support in Washington, related his concern about postwar relations. Rublee began by noting that his "joy" that the war had ended was "necessarily mixed with anxiety in regard to the use which the nations are going to make of the extraordinary opportunity which is presented."[121] As opposed to Hoover, Rublee believed that "at least until world conditions become more nearly normal, the national controls over shipping and commodities should be continued...through the existing allied organizations." Rublee also believed that "[f]or a considerable time to come food, raw materials and shipping ought to be apportioned according to need rather than according to the ability to pay." Rublee admitted that his main concern was the "attitude of America," which he believed would prove "conclusive": "If America decides to act independently, it will be impossible for Great Britain to resist the exceedingly strong pressure of private interests to remove governmental controls which is already being exerted. The result, it seems to me, would be a state of economic chaos producing grave international friction, not to speak of serious harm to the weaker nations who are less well supplied with food materials and ships."[122] Rublee noted that his "chief reason for concern is what I hear of the attitude of Hoover and Hurley who are to arrive here next week, presumably with the authority of the President." Rublee had learned that they planned to "wind up all allied organizations so that

America, having as they believe, the dominant economic power, may be free to act as she thinks best." Rublee believed that such a policy would be "disastrous" not only for the weaker nations but also because Hurley and Hoover "greatly underestimate the economic power and resources of Great Britain."[123]

Rublee's concern that Hoover would attempt to end international cooperation and that such an attitude would lead to "grave international friction" proved correct. When Hoover arrived in Europe, he was confronted with a formal proposal from the British government advocating the continuation of inter-Allied cooperation through the creation of a General Economic Council, which would absorb the AMTC, as set out in the Executive's 28 October resolution. Hoover, in his work *Famine in Forty-Five Nations*, later explained his reluctance to allow the AMTC to continue its role as the pivot of inter-Allied economic cooperation:

> Because of our knowledge that the Allies—all of them—were dependent on the United States for food and credits during the Armistice, we became convinced that behind this whole pool idea and this council organization there was something else troubling the Allied minds. We were fully aware of the reluctance of the Allies to accept the President's "Fourteen Points and subsequent addresses" as the basis for peace. It was obvious to us that they were groping for some plan which would prevent the President from exercising his power to use supplies and credit for imposing his political ideas.[124]

The Allies, however, were not so much concerned about Wilson's political machinations as they were about American suppliers capturing Central and Eastern European markets in the wake of the war. Having spent over a $100 billion dollars in the four-year war, the British, who had also financed their Allies' war effort, could not risk losing traditional markets to Americans. As Edward Hurley, whom Rublee had somewhat converted, would explain to Wilson on 12 December:

> In all the conferences I have had on this side, I have been impressed with the fact that it is not the League of Nations, nor an International Court, nor even the Freedom of the Seas that is feared by Lloyd-George, Clemenceau, Orlando or their associates. What they are thinking about, as you are probably already aware, is the increased power of our shipping, commerce and finance. In every conversation the commercial question has come to the front. France fears that she will not be able to get the raw materials she needs at the same price as other nations; Great Britain fears that we will have a bigger merchant marine than she will be able to build, and that our government will operate it regardless of cost, so that we can capture the best markets in the world.[125]

Concluding, Hurley reiterated that the British were afraid that "the United States, with its present wealth and commercial power, may get the jump on the markets of the world."[126]

Despite Hurley's warning, Wilson, at Hoover's suggestion, rejected the proposal to retain the AMTC as the General Economic Council and suggested instead that the Europeans join America in creating a completely new body organized under a director-general of relief, "whose field of activities [would] cover not only enemy populations, but also the whole of the populations liberated from the enemy yoke and the neutrals contiguous to these territories."[127] Because America would be the principal supplier of food and credit, Wilson proposed that Hoover be made director-general over the new body, which they proposed to call the Supreme Council of Supply and Relief. Pointing to approaching famine conditions in Europe, Wilson requested that the British blockade of the North Sea be relaxed at the earliest possible moment. Not surprisingly, the British and French countered Wilson's plan, seeking something of a compromise. On 12 December they agreed to "associate themselves…with the organization and general policy of supply which the United States Government has proposed" and agreed that Hoover could be director-general.[128] The Europeans were not prepared, however, to dismantle the blockade, their only security against rapidly inflating U.S. power. Instead, pointing to the shipping shortage, they stipulated that American relief destined for enemy and contiguous neutral nations be coordinated with the AMTC. Upon that body's recommendation, the blockade council would provide access to Central and Eastern European markets.[129] Perhaps not surprisingly, the British and Americans were fast regressing to the strained relations of 1915 and 1916, owing to Britain's continued control of access to European markets to which Americans demanded entrance. With the United States now controlling the world's surplus food and credits and the British controlling the blockade, each had a provocative check on the other.

The Allied compromise was unacceptable to Hoover and therefore, it seems, to Wilson. Hoover later explained his and Wilson's response:

> When I met the President on December 15, I reported to him that only he could break through the London fog of power politics. I voiced my belief that the Allied pool proposals stemmed partly from fears of his use of pressure on their food supplies and partly from the wish to control food in the rest of Europe for political purposes. …The President emphatically declared that he would insist on the American plan. I recommended that he ignore the "document" and allow Colonel House to undertake the negotiations with the Allied Ministers over the heads of the bureaucrats [i.e., Rublee, Salter, and Monnet].[130]

The impasse between the Allies and the United States abated briefly between Wilson's arrival on 14 December and the end of the month. Although the British and French continued to seek a plan closer to their 12 December proposal, they agreed to the creation of the Supreme Council of Supply and Relief based on Wilson's original plan. Hoover, whose appointment as director-general would be announced in early January, attributed America's victory in the contest to Wilson's popularity among the civilian populations in Europe: "To them, he was a second Messiah. …No Prime Minister could refuse the President his wishes on so secondary a question as the method of organization of relief and reconstruction."[131]

Rublee was highly discouraged by Wilson's decision to follow Hoover's advice and vented his frustrations to Brandeis in early January:

The period since the armistice has been most discouraging. When the armistice was signed America was in the most favorable position possible to carry out the aims of the President. The other nations were ready to respond and follow our lead. All that was needed was a clear policy and ordinary tact in the necessary negotiations. The President's chief advisors, however, arrived in a spirit of distrust and suspicion. They did not understand the situation here, and did not seem to care to get information from those who were able to give it. They did not discriminate between the persons in the governments who were our friends and those who were not well disposed, but regarded all as hostile. The result is that we have made little progress and there is irritation and perplexity among those with whom we must work.[132]

"The great disappointment," Rublee explained, was Hoover: "He seems incapable of working with other people. He lacks entirely the gift of diplomacy." Rublee added, "To borrow the words of the Psalmist, he raises up his own horn and speaks with a stiff neck." Although Rublee believed that Hoover "would do his work effectively" if he "could only get to [it]," he had unfortunately "lost his time in wrangling over the powers he should have and in ascribing bad motives to the wicked British."[133]

In late December Rublee and Stevens made a final attempt to persuade Wilson not to abandon the AMTC as the central body for postwar international cooperation. They met with Wilson for "about an hour" and sought to impress upon him the need to maintain the inter-Allied bodies and to retain American representation on them. In a letter to Brandeis, Rublee reported that although Wilson "was very gracious and willing to listen to us," they soon "found that he had not understood the true function of the allied organizations."[134] In a follow-up letter to their meeting, Rublee and Stevens made a final plea to Wilson for continued cooperation:

Through the Allied organizations, the nations have been learning to work together in harmony and friendliness. It would be a loss to do away with this spirit of cooperation during the Peace Conference. ...It would be an advantage to have full and frank interchange of information so that each nation may know exactly what the others are doing and why, at each step in the return to normal conditions of trade, instead of getting information through newspaper reports and by false rumor. In this way much harmful suspicion and bad feeling may be avoided.[135]

Despite their passionate and progressive plea, for some reason Wilson chose to trust Hoover over the advice of Rublee, Stevens, and other internationalists in London. Rublee recalled being frustrated that Wilson discounted them: "All of the Americans who worked [with the AMTC and its program committees] were internationally minded and the men in these organizations were the ones most likely to stand for what the President wanted to achieve. ...House didn't understand that, and I don't think the President did. His idea was that he was through with all these economic people and had better send them all home."[136] No longer wanted after the armistice, the American internationalists returned home en masse. Rublee reported dejectedly on 6 January: "We have lost a good many valuable men. Morrow has gone home. Joe Cotton sailed yesterday. He went because he felt he could no longer work with Hoover. Most of the

American representatives on the program committees have gone. Ray Stevens sails next week."[137]

The friction between the United States and the European Allies concerning relief to Central and Eastern Europe and thus the supposed control of those markets soon resumed and reached a climactic and dramatic moment on 31 December, when the British sent an unmistakable warning to the United States. Having concluded that the Wilson administration was intent on using America's dominant economic position to influence the postwar settlement, the British boldly called that economic power into question by canceling "all outstanding Allied contracts with American processors for beef, pork, and dairy products and with the Grain Corporation for grain, cottonseed, beans, and other ground crops."[138] Because they financed French and Italian purchases, the British moved to have those countries' food orders with U.S. producers likewise canceled.[139]

The British maneuver was nothing less than a shot across the bow and sent Wilson and Hoover scrambling to mitigate its effect on American markets. Hoover complained to Wilson on 9 January that American manufacturers had produced "particular types of manufacture required by each of these governments and have enormous stocks of these materials in hand ready for delivery." The "most acute situation," however, was "in pork products which are perishable and must be exported." Hoover warned: "If there should be no remedy to this situation we shall have a debacle in the American markets, and with the advances of several hundred million dollars now outstanding from the banks to the pork products industry we shall not only be precipitated into a financial crisis but shall betray the American farmer who has engaged himself to these ends. The surplus is so large there can be no absorption of it in the United States and it, being perishable, will go to waste."[140] Hoover added, "I cannot impress upon you too strongly the reaction that will arise in the United States if this situation falls to the ground." Hoover enclosed a proposed memorandum for Wilson that, if delivered, would have amounted to an ultimatum demanding that the British, French, and Italians uphold their orders with American producers. While Wilson deliberated Hoover's memo, the president quickly cabled Newton Baker instructing him to consider making "the necessary purchases to protect the American situation and ship the material to Europe for distribution under their direction as a military measure."[141] This quick reaction would both save Wilson from the scrutiny of a hostile Congress and get American products through the blockade at least as far as France.

The U.S. and British governments continued to grapple over the blockade and relief until February 1919, during which time famine ripped through Central, Eastern and Southern Europe.[142] Although it is unclear how an accommodation was reached, it appears that the Americans blinked first after the British indicated that they could endure vast suffering and upheaval in Europe longer than Americans could. Having sent hundreds of thousands of their own young men to their deaths in Flanders' fields apparently steeled the British leadership for such brinkmanship. The disastrous rift between the world's leading economic powers came to an end in February with the replacement of the Supreme Council of Supply and Relief with the Supreme Economic Council, created along the lines that the AMT Executive proposed in late October. James Arthur Salter, in an unusually critical, yet typically understated, passage, noted the role that the growing Anglo-American rivalry played in European famine:

During December prolonged discussion took place between the Food Controllers and other members of the Allied and Associated Governments as to the principles upon which a new body to be concerned with the re-victualing of Allied, neutral, and enemy countries should be formed. Agreement on a document was arrived at on December 12 and the resulting Council, the Allied Supreme Council of Supply and Relief was established in January 1919. This Council, ...without the assistance of a staff accustomed to work together and without the driving force of the war..., proved ineffective. In February 1919 it was merged in and replaced by the Supreme Economic Council, which was in personnel, in functions, and in general principles of organization, almost exactly the same as the body into which the Transport Executive had proposed to transform the Transport Council at the beginning of the previous November.[143]

Salter pointed out that "three invaluable months had in the meantime been lost" and expressed the belief that if the Executive's proposals "before the armistice had been adopted the economic position in the spring of 1919 and possibly afterwards would have been substantially better." If those plans had been adopted, Salter argued, "German ships would have been at work in December instead of March, and food would have gone into Germany as from January instead of April." Salter implied that the results of such adoption, though "not easy now to measure exactly," would have likely diminished "the consequent difficulties of the earlier peace negotiations."[144] From a longer view, the consequent results include the radicalization of politics in Central and Eastern Europe, including a foundation for the rise of fascism in Germany.

Perhaps not surprisingly, Hoover's description of the creation of the Supreme Economic Council makes no mention of the prearmistice AMTC proposals: "When Lord Robert Cecil joined the British economic activities in Paris, I suggested to him that we do away with the whole Supreme Council of Supply and Relief apparatus and substitute a new organization, to be called the 'Supreme Economic Council,' with a preamble and an authority, the text of which I had drafted. Cecil fully approved and agreed to support its adoption by the Big Four."[145] It is little wonder, however, that Lord Cecil, who had been associated with economic considerations throughout the war, approved of a plan that he had supported since the 28 October AMTC meeting.

Rublee, who witnessed this series of travesties, became increasingly depressed about the prospects for a lasting peace in Europe. Even before the Anglo-American debacle, Rublee had been concerned that a just peace might not be fashioned. Writing to Louis Brandeis in December, Rublee had observed:

There has been a lot of wild and foolish talk about making Germany pay impossible indemnities contrary to the terms we offered at the time of the armistice. The election in England did harm. Punishing the Kaiser and making Germany pay were easy and popular election issues. In reality, I do not find that responsible men in the British and French Governments believe in this talk. Much depends on economic arrangements and the sort of league of nations that is created. Take France as an example. What France wants is first a world in which she may reasonably feel that she is safe.... If France can be assured of these things she will give up her imperialistic claims and her extreme demands for indemnities. But if she lacks this assurance she will grab all she can and in self-defense try to keep Germany down.[146]

Because he cared about the final peace and could not leave Europe without attempting to influence the peacemakers, Rublee did not return with Morrow, Cotton, Stevens, and the other AMTC internationalists in December but decided to remain in Europe. To Brandeis he explained: "If I find I can be of no use in Paris I shall go home too before long, but I will try again first."[147]

While Rublee would fail in his effort to influence a just and lasting peace, he did manage to remain in the sphere where the decisions were made. Although Hoover and Hurley brought a California banker to replace Rublee on the Shipping Board, Rublee still managed to be appointed to the staff of the American Commission to Negotiate Peace and was a U.S. representative at the Spa Conference, which arranged for the transfer of Germany's merchant marine in March to the AMTC in return for limited assurances for their use in feeding Germany.[148] Rublee also retained his position in the AMTC and the Executive until the end of the Spa Conference in late March 1919. At the AMTC's February meeting Rublee had some success in securing a resolution granting the United States a share of German passenger liners for the repatriation of American troops.[149] When the AMTC was absorbed by the Supreme Economic Council on 7 April 1919, however, Rublee was not named a member of the body.[150] Strikingly, Salter and Monnet, men with whom Rublee shared a new world vision, both served on the Supreme Economic Council and became members of the League of Nations Secretariat, Monnet serving as interim general secretary. Although Wilson would not live to know it, two of the staunchest advocates for the League of Nations were within his reach in November and December 1918, but he was unable to recognize their attributes.

While Salter and Monnet moved on, Rublee performed ad hoc work in France during the latter part of March and early April until he suffered a life-threatening appendicitis. The most significant aspect of his work involved the organization of the International Red Cross. Rublee spent several weeks in Cannes, France, with Henry Davison, head of the American Red Cross, whom he helped "plan the organization of the new league of Red Cross Societies which is to be active in peace in the work of improving health and preventing disease throughout the world."[151] Once the concept of the organization was established, Rublee returned to Paris, where he worked to get a statement regarding the new International Red Cross adopted into the League of Nations charter. Knowing a number of American lawyers on the covenant-drafting committee, Rublee succeeded in having Article 25 added to the league document identifying the work of the Red Cross.[152] This was Rublee's last association with the peace conference. On 3 April, after telegraphing to Davison "that what he wanted had been accomplished," Rublee suffered an appendicitis attack and spent the next six weeks in the American Hospital of Paris.[153]

Writing to Brandeis on 14 May from the Hotel Ritz in Paris, Rublee related both his serious illness and his disappointment with the outcome of the Paris Peace Conference. Concerning the draft of the peace treaty, Rublee observed philosophically: "I'm unhappy over the peace. It does not seem to give joy to anybody. It's a terribly difficult thing to make peace after such a war. The peace is a kind of resultant of forces which it may be nearly impossible to control. I'm not sure. What I don't like is the feeling towards the Germans now [that] they are beaten. It is natural, but not admirable. Success is rarely good for the soul. But we must take the world as it is, be patient, and not lose hope."[154] Approaching the prophetic, Rublee concluded, warning: "The fear that is so apparent tends to create the thing that is feared. In making peace with the Germans I have thought that we ought to be just and hard. We are hard, but are we just? And have we kept our word? There is no joy among the people in Paris. I think they feel that something is wrong."[155] Rublee was not alone in his disappointment with the peace. Herbert Croly, writing to Brandeis on 13 May to notify him that *The New Republic* had decided to voice its objection to the peace treaty, reported: "After much searching of heart and prolonged discussion we felt obliged in the New Republic this week to write ourselves out from under the Treaty. It is a bitter decision to make because it is practically a confession of failure, so far as our work during the last few years is concerned, but it was unanimous and we shall have to take whatever loss follows from adopting it. I agree with you that Germany will probably have to sign."[156] On 24 May, the progressive journal pronounced that the "Treaty of Versailles is impossible of execution and will defeat itself."[157]

Although irritated with Wilson for his lack of regard for the American internationalists in London and dissatisfied with the form of the Versailles Treaty, unlike Hoover, who broke with the president, ironically Rublee returned to America as an ardent supporter of the League of Nations and the treaty that would create it.[158] Taking a position against his friends at *The New Republic*, Rublee wrote an editorial in the journal in which he defended Wilson's position on the highly controversial Article X of the league covenant. In his article Rublee argued that Article X "has far less importance in its practical bearing than has been supposed, and that in the actual working of the League it will seldom be invoked."[159] Rublee was not the only returning internationalist who supported U.S. ratification of the Versailles Treaty. Morrow, upon his return to America, wrote a series of articles appearing in *The New York Evening Post* in February and March 1919 and reprinted as *The Society of Free States*.[160] While advocating membership in the league, Morrow also took the opportunity to highlight the work of the AMTC, virtually unknown in America, pointing out that the wartime organization had become the new model for international relations.[161] In June Joe Cotton joined Morrow in writing an exposition of the work of the AMTC in "International Cooperation during the War" in *Atlantic Monthly,* and Rublee followed with "Inter-Allied Machinery in War-Time," a chapter in *The League of Nations Starts: An Outline by Its Organizers*.[162] None of these publications were overtly critical, but each suggested that an opportunity had been missed.

Owing to his various efforts during the war and the peace negotiations, Rublee would become a leading figure in America’s internationalist community and would work throughout the interwar period to stabilize international relations in the wake of the tragically flawed Versailles settlement. Like Rublee, a number of other members of the AMTC organization would become Eastern Establishment internationalists. Given the lasting commitment of Rublee and other like-minded Americans in London to liberal internationalism, it seems clear that Wilson made a tragic error in discounting these men during the armistice period and peace conference. As one internationalist would poignantly observe upon the conclusion of the Versailles Treaty: “Had our policy been in the hands of sagacious, far-seeing men—cool and imperturbable, with knowledge of political history and strong schemes for settling the future—this peace might have been a great thing. We had such men, and their service to the nation and to the world would have been of inestimable value.”[163]

NOTES

1. GR to Edward House, 26 January 1917, enclosure in GR to Walter Lippmann, 31 January 1917, Yale-Lippmann, box 29, folder 1076.

2. For example, in 1915 Robert Bass, knowing Rublee’s interest in the subjects, sent him *Problems of Readjustment after the War* (New York: D. Appleton and Company, 1915) and Frederic Howe’s *Socialized Germany* (New York: C. Scribner’s Sons, 1915). See GR to Bass, 20 December 1915, RBP, folder ML 31-13R.

3. Paul D. Cravath to Guy E. Trip, Herbert Hoover Presidential Papers, Pre-Commerce Correspondence, Herbert Hoover Presidential Library, West Branch, Iowa [hereafter HHPL-Pre-Com], box 3.

4. Ernest Fayle, *The War and the Shipping Industry*, vol. 18, Carnegie Endowment for International Peace, Economic and Social History of the World War, British Series (New Haven, CT: Yale University Press, 1927), 403.

5. Rublee’s experiences in the war are in keeping with those of other Eastern Establishment types as described in Priscilla Roberts, “The Anglo-American Theme: American Visions of an Atlantic Alliance, 1914-1933," *Diplomatic History* 21, no. 3 (Summer 1998), 333-364. Roberts found that “it was the experiences of World War I and its immediate aftermath that acted as a catalyst in creating and defining their foreign policy tradition (333).”

6. Rublee, “Reminiscences,” 150.

7. Ibid.

8. Herbert Heaton, *A Scholar in Action: Edwin F. Gay* (Cambridge: Harvard University Press, 1952), 98; and *New York Times*, 12 May 1917.

9. Heaton, *Scholar in Action*, 99.

10. Ibid., 99-101. When the United States decided to strengthen its war boards later in 1917, the CEB was renamed the Conservative Division of the War Industries Board (Rublee, “Reminiscences,” 152).

11. Edward Hurley, *A Bridge to France* (Philadelphia: J.B. Lippincott, 1927), 24-25.

12. Heaton, *Scholar in Action*, 104-105.

13. GR to Bass, 8 July 1917, RBP. Noting his other commitments, Rublee also reported, "In addition I have been passing round on the Commercial Economy Board and the Eight-Hour Commission."

14. Ibid.

15. Ibid.

16. Hurley, *Bridge to France*, 17, 27; and Heaton, *Scholar in Action*, 104.

17. GR to Joseph Tumulty, 21 July 1917, WWP-LoC, reel 89.

18. Rublee, "Reminiscences," 156. Curiously, in a note to Tumulty, Wilson asked: "Have you the least idea what Rublee has in mind? I think interviews of this matter are likely to be very unprofitable just now." Note attached to GR to Tumulty, 21 July 1917, WWP-LoC reel 89.

19. Rublee, "Reminiscences," 156. Following an interim appointment, Charles Schwab ultimately succeeded Goethals.

20. Ibid., 159.

21. Ibid., 152.

22. Ibid., 160-161; and Heaton, *Scholar in Action*, 102.

23. Rublee, "Reminiscences," 161.

24. Ibid., 159-160. The War Industries Board, under the leadership of Barnard Baruch, absorbed the Commercial Economy Board in the later part of 1917.

25. Jean Monnet, *Memoirs*, translated by Richard Mayne (Garden City, NY: Doubleday & Company, 1978), 54-58; and James Arthur Salter, *Memoirs of a Public Servant* (London: Faber and Faber, 1961), 72-75. Some French ministers believed that the pooling of ships was a British scheme "to establish permanent economic superiority over her allies" and some British feared the curtailments in British trade that would result from taking responsibility for French trade.

26. Great Britain, Public Record Office, London, War Cabinet 261, 31 October 1917, CAB 23/261 (microfilm).

27. Ibid., 6 November 1917, CAB 23/266 (microfilm).

28. Monnet, *Memoirs*, 60.

29. James Arthur Salter, *Allied Shipping Control: An Experiment in International Administration*, Carnegie Endowment for International Peace, Economic and Social History of the War, British Series (New Haven, CT: Yale University Press, 1921), 155.

30. George Rublee, "Inter-Allied Machinery in War-Time," in *The League of Nations Starts: An Outline By Its Organizers* (London: Macmillan and Company, 1920), 33.

31. Salter, *Memoirs*, 100.

32. Ibid., 101-102.

33. Ibid., 68.

34. Monnet, *Memoirs*, 18.

35. Salter, *Allied Shipping Control*, 151, 285. Accompanying House were Admiral W.S. Benson, General Tasker Bliss, Oscar Crosby, Vance McCormick, Bainbridge Colby, Dr. Alonzo Taylor, Thomas Perkins, and Gordon Auchincloss. For documents relating to the conference see *FRUS*, 1917, supplement 2, 334-445.

36. Salter, *Allied Shipping Control*, 285, 293-294.

37. Ibid., 154.

38. Ibid., 153.

39. Rublee, *Reminiscences,* 162.

40. Quoted in Jeffrey Safford, *Wilsonian Maritime Diplomacy, 1913-1921* (New Brunswick, NJ: Rutgers University Press, 1978), 149.

41. Hurley, *Bridge to France*, 199.

42. Salter, *Allied Shipping Control*, 298; and Monnet, *Memoirs*, 57.

43. Rublee, "Reminiscences," 160.

44. Ibid.; and Ray Stevens to Wilson, 28 January 1918, WWP-LoC, reel 277.

45. Rublee, "Reminiscences," 165-166. Wilson was reluctant to confirm Morrow because of his association with the international banking house. Rublee recalled that "the President consented but said something like, 'We mustn't have any more of those men.'"

46. Harold Nicolson, *Dwight Morrow* (New York: Harcourt, Brace and Company, 1935), 205.

47. Monnet, *Memoirs*, 69.

48. Salter, *Allied Shipping Control*, 177.

49. Ibid., 178.

50. Ibid., 180. Rublee recalled that he, Salter, and Monnet regularly gathered at Morrow's suites in the Berkeley Hotel (Rublee, "Reminiscences," 169).

51. Salter, *Allied Shipping Control*, 298.

52. Relating the story of Stevens rejecting a French minister's offer of cognac on their first trip to Paris, Rublee observed: "Stevens had never been in Europe and Clémentel in great astonishment threw up his hands and cried, "Cent ans (a hundred years old) and you decline!" (Rublee, "Reminiscences," 172). However, evidently finding his foreign experiences stimulating, Stevens would serve as an advisor to the King of Siam for about ten years during the interwar period.

53. Hapgood to House, 27 January 1918, Yale-House, box 55, folder 1730. Hapgood wrote: "I am arranging for [Rublee] to see certain people. I thought perhaps you might be inclined to have him meet informally with Lord Milner and Lord Lansdowne and anyone else who will put Rublee's somewhat too rigid ideas on the general situation into a more fluid state." It is not currently clear what Hapgood meant in this characterization.

54. Rublee, "Reminiscences," 172.

55. Dwight Morrow to Edward Stettinius, 5 April 1918, DMP, series 7, reel 1.

56. GR to Learned Hand, 4 May 1918, HLS-Hand, box 107, folder 3.

57. GR to Thomas Lamont, Thomas Lamont Papers and Diaries, Baker Library Special Collections, Harvard Business School, Boston, Massachusetts [hereafter HBS-Lamont], box 113, folder 13; and Nicolson, *Dwight Morrow*, 219.

58. Hurley, *Bridge to France*, 205.

59. Salter, *Allied Shipping Control*, 160-162.

60. Ibid., 163.

61. Morrow to Edward Stettinius, 5 April 1918, DMP, reel 1. Emphasis in the original.

62. Rublee, "Reminiscences," 173-174.

63. Hurley, *The Bridge to France*, 207.

64. U.S. State Department, Record Group 59, Decimal File 763.2/9499a, National Archives II, College Park, Maryland.

65. Salter, *Allied Shipping*, 181. The twenty committees were: (1) wool, (2) cotton, (3) flax, hemp and Jute, (4) hides and leather, (5) tobacco, (6) paper, (7) timber, (8) petroleum, (9) coal and coke, (10) cereals, (11) oil seeds, (12) sugar, (13) meats and fats, (14) nitrates, (15) aircraft, (16) chemicals, (17) explosives, (18) non-ferrous metals, (19) mechanical transport, and (20) steel (Salter, *Allied Shipping Control*, 183).

66. Rublee, "Inter-Allied Machinery," 39.

67. Morrow to Edward Stettinius, 21 May 1918, DMP, reel 1. Emphasis in the original.

68. Ibid.

69. Monnet, *Memoirs*, 69.
70. Ibid.
71. Ibid.
72. Great Britain, *The Allied Maritime Transport Council* (London: H.M. Stationary Office, 1919), vol. 1, 71.
73. *FRUS*, 1918, vol. 1, supplement 1, 511.
74. *Allied Maritime Transport Council*, vol. 1, 71.
75. GR to Hand, 4 May 1918, HLS-Hand, box 107, folder 3.
76. *FRUS*, 1918, vol. 1, supplement 1, 517.
77. Ray Stevens to Wilson, 6 May 1918, WWP-LoC, reel 96.
78. GR to Lamont, HBS-Lamont, box 113, folder 13.
79. GR to Morrow, 18 May 1918, DMP, reel 1. At the time Morrow was in France working with General Pershing.
80. Edward Hurley to Wilson, 17 May 1918, WWP-LoC, reel 277.
81. Wilson to Hurley, 24 May 1918, WWP-LoC, reel 277.
82. Great Britain, Public Record Office, London, War Cabinet 417, 24 May 1918, microfilm CAB 23/417.
83. Rublee, "Reminiscences," 176.
84. GR to Wilson, 20 June 1918, WWP-LoC, reel 277.
85. Ibid.
86. Wilson to GR, 21 June 1918, WWP-LoC, reel 277.
87. State Department to American Embassy London, 10 July 1918, State Department, Record Group 59, Decimal file 800.88/142, National Archives II, College Park, MD.
88. Quoted in Nicolson, *Dwight Morrow*, 216. While Rublee was in Washington he also visited with Italian embassy officials who had no idea about the work of the AMTC. Following his visit, the Italian officials requested that Rome submit all requests for supplies from America to the AMTC Executive in London rather than to them in Washington (Rublee to Stevens, 22 June 1918, U.S. State Department, Record Group 59, Decimal file 7.W.800.88/157a, National Archives II.
89. Rublee, "Reminiscences," 177.
90. Rublee, "Inter-Allied Machinery," 44.
91. *FRUS,* 1918, vol. 1, supplement 1, 518. On June 28, Stevens wrote to Wilson requesting that Rublee be named as the second delegate to the AMTC. Stevens asserted that "The experience Rublee has already had over here, his knowledge of the situation at home, and his personal relations with Hurley, Gay, and other important men in your administration, all would combine to make him valuable as a member of the transport council" (Stevens to Wilson, 28 June 1918, State Department, Record Group 59, Decimal file 800.88/159, National Archives II).
92. Hand to Edward Burling, 12 July 1918, HLS-Hand, box 100, folder 5.
93. Rublee, "Reminiscences," 178, 179.
94. Monnet, *Memoirs*, 70.
95. Rublee, "Reminiscences," 177-179.
96. Monnet, *Memoirs*, 71.
97. Charles P. Howland, "Memorandum on the Advisability of Giving Voting Power to our Representatives on the Allied Maritime Transport Council," [no date], DMP, reel 62. It is unclear how or if this memorandum was circulated.
98. Salter, *Allied Shipping Control*, 211. By mid-summer 1918, America had built nearly 1.5 million more tons (dead weight) worth of ships than were sunk during that

period. However, all of these and more were needed to transport and maintain U.S. troops in Europe.

99. Ibid., 198, 304-310.

100. Ibid., 197.

101. Ibid., 204-210.

102. *FRUS*, 1918, vol. 1, supplement 1, 524, 594-595, 606-607.

103. Ibid., 524.

104. Lord Reading to Robert Lansing, 30 August 1918, Link et al., *Papers of Woodrow Wilson*, vol. 49, 419.

105. Wilson to Lansing, 2 September 1918, ibid., vol. 49, 417.

106. Rublee and Stevens prepared Baker, who knew little about the AMTC, for the meeting by providing him with a nine-page document that explained the council's background. Rublee and Raymond Stevens to Newton D. Baker, 26 September 1918, DMP, reel 62.

107. Minutes of the Fourth Session of the AMTC in *Allied Maritime Transport Council*, vol. 1, 185-186.

108. Ibid., 203. Baker's full speech printed in Appendix 48, 202-204.

109. Ibid., 186.

110. Rublee, "Reminiscences," 181-182. Rublee noted in his chapter that one reason or the necessary slaughtering of the majority of Britain's livestock was that there would not be enough grain to maintain them (Rublee, "Inter-Allied Machinery," 43-44). Emphasis in the original.

111. Salter, *Allied Shipping Control*, 176.

112. *FRUS*, 1918, vol. 1, supplement 1, 532-533. Gay's report showed that America had employed 2.28 million tons of shipping (U.S. and Neutral) "in excess of an amount ...required to carry out the essential import program of the United States."

113. Salter, *Allied Shipping Control*, 216.

114. Acheson, "George Rublee," 4.

115. Ibid.

116. Hoover to Wilson, 24 October 1918, HHPL-Pre-Com, box 19 (copied from Wilson Papers in the Library of Congress).

117. Ibid.

118. George Nash, *The Life of Herbert Hoover*, vol. 3: *Master of Emergencies, 1917-1918* (New York: W.W. Norton, 1996), 355-356.

119. *FRUS*, 1918, vol. 1, supplement 1, 616.

120. Ibid., 616-617.

121. GR to Brandeis, 14 November 1918, LBP.

122. Ibid.

123. Ibid.

124. Herbert Hoover, *Famine in Forty-Five Nations: Organization Behind the Front, 1914-1923*, vol. 2 of *An American Epic* (Chicago: Henry Regnery Company, 1960), 267.

125. Hurley to Wilson, 12 December 1918, WWP-LoC, reel 385.

126. Ibid.

127. Wilson to J. A. Balfour via Edward House, 1 December 1918, quoted in Hoover, *Famine in Forty-Five Nations*, 269-272.

128. British Memorandum, "For Mr. Hoover with Lord Reading's compliments," 12 December 1918, WWP-LoC, reel 385.

129. Ibid.

130. Hoover, *Famine in Forty-Five Nations*, 284-285.

131. Ibid., 285.
132. GR to Brandeis, 6 January 1919, LBP, reel 62.
133. Ibid.
134. Ibid.
135. GR and Stevens to Wilson, 30 December 1918, GRP. (Also in Wilson papers).
136. Rublee, "Reminiscences," 184-185.
137. GR to Brandeis, 6 January 1919, LBP, reel 62.
138. Hoover, *Famine in Forty-Five Nations*, 305.
139. Hoover to Wilson quoted in Wilson to Newton Baker, 9 January 1919, HHPL-Pre-Com, box 19.
140. Ibid.
141. Ibid.
142. A report from an AMTC representative in Austria sent the following report: "The situation in Vienna is extremely bad. Flour ration is five ounces per day, fat ration is two ounces per week, meat ration is three ounces per week. People living mostly on cabbages and turnips." Quoted in Hoover to Food Administration, 9 January 1919, WWP-LoC, reel 389.
143. Salter, *Allied Shipping Control*, 221-222.
144. Ibid., 222.
145. Hoover, *Famine in Forty-Five Nations*, 295.
146. GR to Brandeis,14 November 1918, LBP.
147. Ibid.
148. Rublee, "Reminiscences," 186-187; and Salter, *Allied Shipping Control*, 341. On the matter of his replacement, Rublee recalled that Hurley "brought over a man who was head of one of the big banks in Los Angeles, whom he intended to have supersede me completely. It became rather impractical for some reason for him to do that and so he had him there, and it was always a little embarrassing for me because he was Hurley's favorite and I was not."
149. *Allied Maritime Transport Council*, vol. 2, 116.
150. Salter, *Allied Shipping Control*, 227, 229. See also *FRUS*, 1919, "The Paris Peace Conference," vol. 10, 1-2, 717-718.
151. GR to Endicott Peabody, 19 April 1919, GSA.
152. Rublee, "Reminiscences," 187. Rublee's negotiations regarding inclusion of the passage is briefly described in David Miller's *The Drafting of the Covenant*, (New York: G.P. Putnam's Sons, 1928), vol. 1:400-402, 407. Article 25 of the covenant reads: "The Members of the League agree to encourage and promote the establishment and co-operation of duly authorized voluntary national Red Cross organizations having as purposes the improvement of health, the prevention of disease, and the mitigation of suffering throughout the world."
153. Rublee, "Reminiscences," 188; GR to Peabody, 19 April 1919, GSA; and David Hunter Miller, *My Diary at the Conference of Paris, with documents* (New York: Printed for the author by the Appeal Printing Co., 1924), microfilm, reel 1, 220, 223.
154. GR to Brandeis, 14 May 1919, LBP, reel 60.
155. Ibid.
156. Croly to Brandeis, 13 May 1919, LBP, reel 60.
157. *The New Republic*, 24 May 1919.
158. Hoover broke with the president over Article X and became an outspoken critic. See Walter LaFeber, *The American Age: United States Policy at Home and Abroad* (New York: W.W. Norton, 1994), vol. 2, 336.

159. George Rublee, editorial, "President Wilson and Article X," *The New Republic* (17 September 1919). In his editorial Rublee responded to an assertion in *The New Republic* (dated 3 September) that Article X actually offered no protection to smaller countries from aggression. Prophetically, the 3 September writer used the example of a future Japanese invasion of China and argued that Article X would, as Wilson had explained it, actually not demand League intervention so long as the territorial integrity was not transgressed. Although Rublee agreed that under the League charter international intervention on behalf of China was not necessarily obligatory, he thought that there was too much focus on Article X, which he believed "has far less importance in its practical bearing than has been supposed, and that in the actual working of the League it will seldom be invoked."

160. Dwight W. Morrow, *The Society of Free States* (New York: Harper and Brothers Publishers, 1919); and Morrow to Lippmann, 17 April 1919, Yale-Lippmann, box 21, folder 842.

161. Morrow, *Society of Free States*, chapters six and eight. Morrow pointed out to Lippmann that "the fundamental principles of this peace covenant seem to me to be drawn largely from the inter-allied war organizations" (Morrow to Lippmann, 17 April 1919, Yale-Lippmann, box 21, folder 842). The Institute of International Affairs, *A History of the Peace Conference of Paris*, edited by H.W.V. Termperley (London: Oxford University Press and Hodder & Stoughton, 1920), also noted that the Versailles Conference Secretariat and League of Nations Secretariat were based on the model of the AMTC organization (250).

162. Joseph Cotton and Dwight Morrow, "International Cooperation During the War," *Atlantic Monthly* (June 1919), 804-810; Rublee, "Inter-Allied Machinery in War-Time."

163. Buckmaster to Paul Cravath, enclosure in Cravath to Morrow, 24 June 1919, Cravath Papers, HHPL, box 4.

9

"A Man of Mystery… with No Definite Work" (1919–1929)

When in March 1920 the last fight for the League of Nations was over—and with it the great hope of internationalists that something worthwhile would come out of the war—George Rublee's passionate ten-year run ground to a halt. In the torrent of progressivism Rublee was in the leading skiff when the deluge ended. A decade before at age forty-two, in answering a nagging urge that he make some sort of public contribution, Rublee had attended a few meetings with Norman Hapgood and Louis Brandeis over charges Louis Glavis made against secretary of agriculture Richard Ballinger, and then suddenly he was in and part of the progressive torrent sweeping through the nation. With the energy and opportunity that that movement provided, Rublee had removed obstacles to progressive legislation in New Hampshire; helped shape TR's Bull Moose campaign; joined in the formation of, and helped define, a new party; took control of, and shaped, the nation's antitrust policy; became the national embodiment of what it meant to be progressive in his fight with Gallinger; strove to make the FTC a viable antidote to anticompetitive monopolies; and then joined with international progressives in Europe in an effort to both win the war and create a new international association of states to usher in a period of lasting peace. Transcending nationalism in London, Rublee, Salter, Monnet, Morrow, Cotton, and others aimed for a new world order, the outline of which they just perceived as the progressive waters began to recede. When the historic vessel carrying them came to an abrupt halt, Rublee and his internationalist comrades were far from whence they had come. While a depressing outcome for each of them, this vanguard would not forget their vision and they would not surrender the future. As Dwight Morrow observed prophetically to Jean Monnet in 1919: "You and I cannot afford to wait more than fifty or sixty years, but perhaps the world can. Your League of Nations may not get started, or it may get started and it may fail, but men will come back to the work that you did in London during the war and will turn over the precedents that you made, and some of them will be used in the real concert that will last."[1] Resolving to maintain a union between them before quitting the stage, these men and a number of their countrymen would make it a mission in the interwar period to keep hope in liberal internationalism alive. Informally at first, in small groups such as Rublee's "true blue inter-allied club" or the more organized Institute of International Affairs in New York, the Americans would soon create the Council on Foreign Relations and its journal, *Foreign Affairs*, in an effort to sustain generations of progressive internationalists.[2] When, as they expected, the teetering Versailles system eventually collapsed, these men would have an institution that could contend for a leading role in the development of U.S. foreign policy.

Like many internationalists, the 1920s for Rublee was mostly a period of waiting. While when he returned to America in the summer of 1919 he had little idea what he would do, leading Morgan partner Thomas Lamont soon asked him to act as a director of the *New York Evening Post*, which Lamont had purchased from Oswald Villard. While Lamont, who backed the League of Nations, asked Edwin Gay to be editor, the Wall Street financier wanted Rublee to act as an adviser. Although it was not necessary for Lamont to request it, Gay and Rublee devoted the paper to the defense of the Versailles Treaty through the fall 1920 presidential campaign. During his yearlong stint with the *Evening Post* Rublee met with the board of editors every day and occasionally wrote editorials. With the defeat of Democratic presidential nominee James Cox in November, however, the treaty was finally declared irrevocably dead, and Rublee's interest in the newspaper waned. Evidently, Lamont's interest in keeping the expensive paper alive was also spent, and he sold it within the year.[3]

With his investments performing poorly as a result of the 1921 depression and having not made a sufficient income to keep up with his and Juliet's lifestyle in the past decade, at age fifty-three Rublee was in the uncomfortable position of needing to find work. Rublee had thought when he left New York in 1913 to join Brandeis in Washington that he would never practice law again.[4] There was, however, little government work that appealed to him, and government pay then was generally modest at best. According to Juliet, only "some International work—or work abroad somewhere" appealed to him.[5] An offer to work with the U.S. Shipping Board was flatly rejected because Rublee, again according to Juliet, "hated the idea of being connected, or having anything to do with" the board because "the men there were the kind he particularly disliked & couldn't get on with" and because he believed that "they would not like or understand him."[6] After considering work with a number of firms, Rublee decided to join good friends Edward Burling and Judge Harry Covington, two men he brought together during the war, who had established Covington and Burling in Washington in 1919. While Rublee kept a home in New York City and always maintained Crossways in Cornish, in 1922 he began a twenty-year practice of renting houses in Washington to work with Covington and Burling, where he immediately became a partner. Although Rublee did not feel that he maintained a "technical competence" in law, he recalled that "with sufficient help, I was a desirable person to have as an associate."[7] Key to his desirability, it seems, were his influential connections in New York, Washington, Chicago, Boston, London, and Paris.

While Rublee had taken an interest in Edward Burling's career since they had worked together in Chicago in 1897, Rublee was likely drawn to the Washington law firm because its first major case dealt with an international arbitration between the United States and Norway. The arbitration, agreed to in June 1921, concerned the value of contracts in American shipyards that the U.S. government through its Emergency Fleet Corporation had expropriated from Norwegian shipping lines in 1917.[8] Not surprisingly, Burling, who was representing Norway against the United States, thought that Rublee "could be of particular assistance to him in [the case]."[9] Having worked alongside Burling and Joe Cotton on the Emergency Fleet Corporation and having increased his influence in Europe during the war, it is no wonder that Burling thought Rublee valuable to the case.

Although Judge Covington brought the case to the firm, the brief and its defense at The Hague fell on Covington, Rublee, Manly O. Hudson (brought in on assignment from Harvard Law School), and Dean Acheson, then twenty-eight and having just come to the firm from Justice Louis Brandeis, for whom he served as secretary for two years after graduating from Harvard Law School.[10] The firm sent its brief on behalf of Norway to The Hague Tribunal in February 1922, eight months after the arbitration agreement was signed, asserting that Norway was owed nearly $16 million. The firm charged that Norway was owed the 1917 market value of the contracts because the U.S. government seized and then enforced the contracts upon the shipyards; therefore, the contracts were not null and void as the U.S. State Department maintained. Balking at the heavy claim, the United States asserted that at most the contracts were worth $2.5 million, the peacetime market value of the ships.[11] Further, State Department officials insisted that the seizures were sanctioned under U.S. laws that they believed also governed foreign interests operating in America.[12] With no agreement in sight, Rublee, Covington, Hudson, and Acheson departed for The Hague in June to represent Norway. The U.S. defense team included William Dennis and former senator George Sutherland. Upon dividing up the case, Rublee was assigned sections dealing with "principles of law and equity," U.S. obligations under international law, and an explanation of the indirect expenses in the claims.[13]

The arguments at The Hague lasted six weeks, and in the end the decision was for Norway, which was awarded nearly $12 million. To Rublee's and Covington's advantage much of the case against the United States centered on the work of the Emergency Fleet Corporation and U.S. Shipping Board. Pointing to policies formulated by close friends Joe Cotton and Ray Stevens, with whom they in 1917 worked and acted as co-counsel, Rublee and Covington were able to show that the U.S. government had accepted the principle that ship contract holders should be compensated, the only outstanding issue being agreement on the value.[14] The decision was an impressive first victory for Covington and Burling law firm and energized young Dean Acheson. Acheson was particularly impressed with the habitually reserved Rublee, who on the last day of the trial gave a commanding closing argument. Acheson later described Rublee's summation at The Hague: "As he mounted the pulpit-like advocate's stand in the

Peace Palace, he was a man I had never seen. Confident, even arrogant in his assertive power, he dominated the room. His usually quiet voice rang with authority. He pushed his notes aside and told that tribunal exactly what it was called upon to do."[15] While Rublee had begun as a tradition for Acheson (a 1911 graduate of Groton School), the young, gifted lawyer now seemed to view him as something of a mentor. The admiration was well met, for Rublee, according to an Acheson biographer, soon thought of the young lawyer as "a kind of adored 'son'" and described him as "the shiniest fish that ever came out of the sea," borrowing a phrase that William James once used to laud George Santayana.[16]

Dean Acheson was not at first sure how to take George Rublee, who to him was a "restless figure whose presence was captivating."[17] Writing to Endicott Peabody in 1923, Acheson reported that "Mr. Rublee"—as he addressed him always—"doesn't really find much interest in the practice of law" but thought that he "could be of great service to the government and [be] really happy, I think, in some difficult administrative post."[18] With no interesting public work available, however, Rublee simply carried on with what legal work came his way, keeping an eye, as always, on national and international political developments. Despite Rublee's political inactivity, Acheson evidently realized that he could learn much from Rublee. In another letter to Peabody, he observed: "I am hoping that Mr. Rublee will be seized with political fervor in 1924 and launch into the McAdoo Campaign so that I may hang on to his coat tails."[19] Although Rublee evidently did not take an active role in the 1924 election, through their close relationship, which continued the remainder of Rublee's life, Acheson would have the opportunity to glean much knowledge from Rublee's insight into politics and international affairs.

For Rublee, the 1922 trip to Europe was emotionally mixed. Writing to Learned Hand from Geneva at the end of the summer, Rublee observed: "I am constantly meeting old friends who are all most cordial and I have an illusion of being almost at home."[20] In Geneva he found the "Secretariat Building... humming with hustle and [thought that] appearances would indicate that the League is very, very busy." There, too, he found his internationalist European friends representing their countries. Rublee reported that he stayed two nights with Jean Monnet and James Salter, who was also visiting Monnet, and the three "sat up late talking as we used to do." The second night Monnet held a dinner at which, Rublee reported, the "whole lot of our old Transport Council Executive were present—Monnet, Salter, Attolico and I—and besides we had Lord Robert Cecil, Sir Eric Drummond (the Secretary General of the League), Comert, the head of the Publicity Section, and Mantous[,] who is now head of the Political Section."[21]Interested in the workings of the league, Rublee attended a "meeting of the Council where they were discussing Danzig."

While, in Geneva, Rublee had found his old friends continuing in their struggle to bring peace to Europe through international cooperation, at home in Washington there was nothing of interest for him to do. Whereas London had its Salter and Paris its Monnet, Washington had Herbert Hoover, who after the war had parlayed his work as food administrator into a cabinet post in the Harding administration. Accepting the position of secretary of commerce after Harding agreed that he would be allowed to have influence "in key diplomatic decisions," Hoover worked with Secretary of State Charles Evans Hughes to establish what became known as "independent internationalism" or "American individualism" in world affairs.[22] Hoover's postwar policy was the same as his 1918 vision: keep "American hands as free as possible to build a world order in which Americans could prosper."[23] Hoover's formula for U.S. foreign policy was to demand repayment of Allied loans at their wartime value, compete aggressively with Europeans for foreign markets, maintain protectionist policies at home, and prevent U.S. banks from financing projects in countries that resisted American leadership. According to progressive or liberal internationalists such as Rublee, Morrow, and Paul Cravath, Hoover's vision was a recipe for disaster. According to biographer Harold Nicolson, Morrow was "irritated by those who regarded post-war stabilization in terms of immediate financial advantage," and he decried "the whole pound of flesh treatment of debts and reparation and was especially incensed by the 'holier than thou' attitude adopted by some American politicians."[24]

Owing to their wholly divergent view on American foreign relations and the postwar settlement, Morrow and Hoover would have a number of clashes during the interwar period, the first of which occurred in 1921, when Morrow called upon Cuban president Alfredo Zayas to discuss a new loan for the semiautonomous island republic. After having won Zayas' confidence "by treating him as if he were an honest man" (when they both knew better), the Cuban president presented Morrow with a cable he had received that morning from the U.S. State Department asserting that Cuba was producing "far too much sugar" and should immediately destroy one-third of its crop.[25] When asked how to respond, guessing correctly that although the document bore Hughes' signature, it actually originated with Hoover, Morrow suggested that Zayas reply to Hughes by quoting a provocative section from the text of the letter, assert that sugar production was of domestic concern only—thereby out of the purview of the U.S. government as stipulated in the Platt amendment—and note his intention to publicize the letter. While Hughes complained to Morrow when next he saw him that the "impertinent note was not drafted by Zayas," Morrow replied that he was "equally certain that the note to which it was a reply was not drafted by Charles Evans Hughes." Hoover, when he heard of Morrow's intervention, "was much displeased."[26]

During the interwar period Dwight Morrow was one of America's leading progressive internationalists, and George Rublee was his closest adviser and assistant. Together, they represented an American Jean Monnet or Arthur Salter, working as they did to undermine Hoover's myopic "American Individualism" in foreign affairs. Curiously, if Hoover was ever aware of the extent to which they worked against his purposes, his awareness is nowhere evident; it does not appear that he ever realized that they viewed him as something of a nemesis. Getting into a position where they could have the chance to seriously undermine Hoover's policies, however, took some time and appears to have been a result of historic opportunity rather than of careful planning. The first step along that route occurred in September 1927, when President Calvin Coolidge, after four years of toying with the idea of giving his old college friend and supporter an important government post, turned to Morrow to head off a dangerous rift growing between the United States and Mexico.[27]

Morrow's ambassadorship to Mexico remains one of the most celebrated in U.S. history. Going into what was thought to be an impossible situation, Morrow was able to completely dispel an escalating crisis that threatened war between the two countries and managed to help bring some stability to revolutionary Mexico.[28] Although the principal issues dogging relations between the two countries were arbitrary Mexican encroachments on U.S.-owned oil concessions dating to the Porfirio Diaz era and the confiscation of large tracts of American-owned land, the bloody strife between the Mexican government and the Mexican Catholic Church added to the chorus of voices in the United States calling for armed intervention. Noting the level of hostility that existed between the two countries, one Mexican paper, for instance, observed, "After Morrow come the Marines."[29]

Morrow's success, when it came, seemed fantastic because the United States and Mexico had been on volatile terms since 1910, when the revolution against a landed aristocracy and foreign exploitation began in Mexico. After seventeen years of bristling on either side it seemed incredible that Morrow could simply arrive in Mexico City and convert the revolutionaries overnight. So dramatic was the change that it became, as one historian observes, the stuff of legend: "According to this myth, the diminutive envoy [Morrow] captivated Calles and his followers with his disarming charm, persuaded them to alter their evil radical ways and gently moved them into line behind the United States on major issues—including the oil question, the church-state conflict, and the agrarian reform."[30] Although revisionist historians of Latin America tend to demonstrate that Morrow's success derived in part from Mexican president Plutarco Calles' interest in stabilizing his government and dramatically slowing the revolution, it is nevertheless admitted that Morrow established the "genius of the new diplomacy" that was the "prototype of the Good Neighbor Policy."[31]

An important actor in Morrow's delicate negotiations leading to the profound changes in the Mexican system was, of course, George Rublee. While Morrow defied many of the conventional restraints on ambassadors, he still required the services of Rublee, who shuttled between Washington, New York, and Mexico City helping facilitate Morrow's diplomatic coup. Rublee's interest in the growing U.S.–Mexican crisis actually predated Morrow's appointment as ambassador in September 1927. Eight months earlier, in January, Rublee apparently became agitated and alarmed with the growing belligerent attitude that Secretary of State Frank Kellogg was adopting toward Mexico's new oil and land policies. The oil controversy dated to December 1925, when Calles signed Mexico's new Petroleum Law, which required foreign oil companies to reapply for drilling concessions. The law limited new leases to fifty years, thereby ending the perpetual rights that had earlier been conceded to foreign producers. A further stipulation required that actual production take place in the near term; concessions were no longer being granted for indefinite future use. The 1917 Mexican constitution, upon which the Petroleum Law was based, proclaimed that the government owned all subsoil minerals. The revolutionary constitution, however, in another section contained a provision that prohibited the retroactive application of laws. In 1923 President Alvaro Obregon had attempted a similar petroleum confiscation but soon backed down when it was made clear to him that Mexico would be cut off from future international lending. Calles' 1925 Petroleum Law appeared to be an effort to fulfill the intentions of the 1917 constitution and to demonstrate Mexican political, financial, and economic independence. American oil companies and the U.S. State Department on their behalf argued that the 1925 Petroleum Law was unconstitutional based on the Mexican constitution and a violation of international conventions. The oil companies refused to apply for the new fifty-year leases, arguing that the arbitrary encroachment would allow the Mexican government to soon supplant the fifty-year lease with one of any duration it wished. According to the new law, however, in not reapplying for their drilling concessions the oil companies' previous contracts were rendered null and void. Having failed to reapply, the oil companies were stripped of their landholdings on 1 January 1927. The companies, however, immediately began to fight the Petroleum Law in Mexican courts. They also called upon the State Department to pressure Calles and began intriguing with enemies of the revolution.

Having attempted without success to induce Mexican president Calles to suspend his expropriation of U.S.-owned properties, Kellogg began to step up pressure on Calles early in 1927, when he rejected the effort of peace advocates to agree to an international arbitration. Concerned with the deteriorating situation, George Rublee wrote to Walter Lippmann in hopes of feeding the journalist ideas to counter Kellogg's arguments against arbitration. Writing to Lippmann in January, Rublee explained that he was "too much out of the world to write letters to the papers" and hoped that Lippmann might be able to make use of his insights into the U.S.–Mexican contest. Rublee complained that he was "puzzled by repeated statements by high authorities that arbitration with Mexico is impossible because it would be incompatible with sovereignty to submit the constitution or laws of a nation to arbitration."[32] Rublee believed it was certainly a valid contest to bring before an international court, and he argued that the United States had a good case and believed it would prevail in demanding "just compensation" for U.S. citizens and businesses whose property had been confiscated for public use in Mexico. As an internationalist who believed that wars might be avoided through civilized discourse and submission to an international legal system, Rublee complained, "If our position is that any nation may exercise the right to nullify international law by domestic legislation then we might as well stop talking about settling disputes between nations by the Hague Tribunal or the World Court."[33]

Walter Lippmann was exceedingly happy that Rublee had taken an interest in the case. Replying to Rublee on 1 February Lippmann wrote: "I can't tell you how glad I am that you're willing to go into these things, because I haven't the equipment to master them, and I can't find anybody who has given, or is willing to give, serious effort to finding a way out of the whole mess."[34] Lippmann believed that he knew "pretty well how to carry on an agitation against the

[United States'] use of violent methods," but he was troubled because the "various associations that are raising their voices [for peace] haven't any plan" to avoid war. Having found no "professors of international law" to devise a plan and believing that his newspaper, the *World*, "now has the attention of a sufficient number of important people to make what it says of some consequence," Lippmann declared that he would "be everlastingly grateful if we could feel that you would guide us."[35] Toward that end, he sent Rublee a "complete set of the correspondence between the two governments" so that Rublee might "disentangle the issues for a solution."[36] Believing that Coolidge "wants Mexico to back down and that he's not ready to accept a judicial settlement," Lippmann pointed out, "Our job, as I see it—by that I mean all the people who are opposed to a break in the diplomatic relations—is to show how a possible settlement could be made."[37]

Rublee spent the month of February reading the diplomatic correspondence between the United States and Mexico and on 28 February sent Lippmann a document that he hoped would shed light on both the oil controversy and the Mexican government's insistence that foreign landowners sell their holdings in Mexico over a number of years. After two weeks of trying to "see a way of making" Rublee's insights "plain to the readers," Lippmann wrote back asking for suggestions.[38] Lippmann admitted: "I realize that this is hardly the kind of thing I ought to put up to you, but you have such a genius for lucid exposition that I am sending along the request for help." Lippmann therefore asked: "Suppose you had to sit down with a moderately intelligent person and could make only one or two fairly simple points, what would you seize upon in all this complex business as the thing which ought to be driven home?" Replying three days later, Rublee explained that first he would "make it clear that Mexico, like any other state, is entitled to take private property for public use if it pays the owner what the property is worth. So I should tell him, if Mexico has enacted laws taking American property for public use without providing for compensation, the remedy is to sue for compensation and not to complain of the laws."[39] Next he would explain that the "United States courts are full of cases in which property owners assert that the Government took their property and must pay for it" and the "government on the other hand denies that it took the property or denies that it is liable for as much as the plaintiff demands." Pointing out that the court decisions on such cases in the United States were "not at all consistent with one another," Rublee suggested: "This being the state of things at home it would seem that the Mexican Government, like our own Government, is entitled to its day in court before anybody starts a war." Rublee soliloquized the concluding point he would make:

"But if that is all there is to it," my listener may ask "why is it that the State Department does not say a word about compensation, but talks as if the Mexican statutes in themselves were an offence against international law?" "Because," I should reply, "the State Department represents American oil companies which do not want compensation, but want to keep their oil. Compensation, even if fairly estimated, would be a bad risk. Nobody knows how much oil there is."[40]

Thanking Rublee for his letter, Lippmann observed, "It's just what I wanted." Lippmann soon completed his article on the subject, and it was carried in *The New York World*, where he was a columnist, and around the country through syndication.[41]

Although Lippmann's articles in newspapers and *Foreign Affairs* contributed to the peace effort in providing a countervailing argument against armed intervention in Mexico, the cause of peace was secured only when Dwight Morrow was named ambassador in September 1927, thereby allowing a liberal internationalist to take command of the situation. Rublee, of course, was immediately interested in Morrow's mission. Soon after hearing that Coolidge had nominated Morrow to represent the United States. in Mexico, Rublee arranged a meeting with him at the beginning of October, at which he offered his services.[42] Rublee's friends also thought that he was just the person to assist Morrow. Writing to Walter Lippmann on 22 September, Learned Hand observed that Morrow's appointment "brings up the possibility of his using George in his work down there."[43] Believing that Lippmann appreciated "the value that George might have to him and to the country, if he could be employed on this work," Hand hoped that the journalist would "broach the matter" with Morrow. Like many progressive internationalists, Hand hoped that Morrow's appointment was "the beginning of the dawn" in U.S. foreign relations, adding, "At any rate it was dark enough before it to justify us in some hope."[44]

Perhaps not understanding Rublee's interest and understanding of the issues in Mexico, Morrow, however, at first had other work in mind for Rublee. Since 1923 Morrow had maintained an active interest in German reparations, and it appears that he would have been named the first agent general for reparation, created out of the Dawes Conference, except for the as yet unexplained intervention of a high-ranking American official.[45] Despite being passed over, Morrow remained interested in the work of the reparations commission and kept up communication with Gilbert Parker, who was named the first agent general in his place. As 1927 came to a close, Parker's three-year term expired, and Morrow, still interested in European developments, wanted Rublee to succeed Parker as the next agent general. Morrow had been rather dissatisfied with the Dawes settlement, which he believed set reparation payments too high, and evidently wanted Rublee to take the position and work to ease the financial pressure on what he believed was yet a fragile German republic. Writing to Morrow on 8 October, however, Rublee explained that although he believed he could succeed as agent general if he "had the chance," he would "*enjoy* more being in Mexico" if Morrow could use him. Rublee added: "When you get there if you want me and think I could help you send a telegram and I'll come. Don't bother about compensation as that would be difficult to arrange and I'll gladly come as a volunteer. The fun of working with you and the interest of this particular work would be enough for me."[46] While the reparations work would have taken him back to Europe, Rublee was highly concerned with the U.S.–Mexican crisis and wished to have a chance to work toward an accommodation. Too, Rublee may have wanted the freedom of action that the work of a confidential adviser would allow. Regardless, after waiting five years he was clearly eager to leave Washington for more interesting work.

Prior to leaving for Mexico Morrow arranged a final meeting with Rublee and Walter Lippmann on 16 October "to have good talk" about his mission.[47] Evidently, Morrow envisioned Rublee and Lippmann looking after his nomination before the Senate and continuing to exert their influence in publishing circles to counter the pressure of publicists calling for armed intervention, including William Randolph Hearst, who as one of the three largest U.S. landholders in Mexico objected to the revolutionary government's land expropriations.[48] While Rublee worked in Washington on Morrow's behalf, Morrow would settle into the embassy in Mexico and seek an arrangement whereby Rublee might assist him in an unofficial capacity.

Once Morrow departed, Rublee made a trip to Washington, where he sounded out senators on the prospects for Morrow's confirmation. Rublee found that the only opposition organizing against Morrow were progressives such as Senator Gerald Nye, who opposed Morgan men and would soon dub them "Merchants of Death" for their influence in bring the United States into World War I. Rublee managed to arrange a meeting with Nye, during which he convinced the senator that Morrow was also a progressive and secured Nye's support. Rublee also met with Louis Brandeis and a number of progressive journalists, including Norman Hapgood, whom he asked to work to secure the backing of other progressive senators. In addition to working on Morrow's confirmation, Rublee had "a long talk with Frank Tannenbaum and with Chester Wright of the American Federation of Labor" so he could come up to speed on labor questions in Mexico.[49]

By the time Rublee arrived in Mexico on 16 November Morrow was already a great success and his work seemed half-finished with regard to ending talk of war. Taking great pains to distance himself from the overtly "belligerent," outgoing ambassador James Sheffield, Morrow against the embassy staff's advice took no interpreter with him to meet Calles, instead relying on the Mexican president's own staff.[50] Within two days Calles invited Morrow to his ranch outside Mexico City, where the two on friendly terms took up the contentious issues threatening war between their countries.[51] Not long after arriving Rublee would report to Learned Hand "that they are all eating out of [Morrow's] hands."[52] Evidently, by treating the Mexican leadership with respect and expressing a sympathetic understanding of Mexico's situation, Morrow was able to arrange the basis for a settlement on the oil question after only a few meetings with Calles. The oil companies had won their first victory in a Mexican state court in the summer of 1927, when the Texas Oil Company was able to show that the Petroleum Law and the corresponding power given to the Department of Commerce were unconstitutional. The case was pending before the Mexican Supreme Court when Morrow arrived in Mexico City in late October 1927.[53]

Morrow, of course, realized that President Calles was the key to the settlement despite the ostensibly independent Mexican court system. Writing to Dean Acheson, Rublee explained the unusual circumstances in Mexico.

Admitting that the situation was "quite different from what [he had] expected," Rublee explained that in Mexico

> [p]ersonal feelings count tremendously. The key to everything is the President. He controls everything, the courts, the legislature, the army and about everything else. And he impresses me as a very decent, simple, earnest and hardworking man. Morrow has already accomplished three quarters of his job. He has won the President's confidence and friendship. He will get the settlement he wants.[54]

Rublee later reported that, during one of their early conversations, Morrow had explained to Calles how the oil expropriations would ultimately injure Mexico's economy and would lead to a demand for U.S. intervention. Morrow also argued that the situation could be improved if the Mexican government would commit itself to an orderly process of expropriation. Morrow, who asked Rublee to produce something of an aide memoir shortly after his 8 November interview with Calles, explained: "I agreed [with Calles] that the oil companies had not behaved well, but I added that there was a principle for which they were contending which was right and which the United States Government was bound to support. This was the principle of stability of property, so that men might depend on getting the fruits of what they had sown."[55] Morrow, stressing the importance of compensation, asked Calles "how he would feel if, after he had planted his alfalfa crop and it had ripened, someone came along and took it without paying for it." Morrow then turned to the state court decision and "made a long and full explanation" of the arguments against the government. To Morrow's surprise, Calles declared, "Nobody has talked with me like this before" and asked, "Would it help us to reach a solution if the Supreme Court affirmed the Texas Cases?" Upon Morrow's acknowledgment that it would, Calles declared "with an emphatic gesture: 'It is decided.'"[56] Although Morrow and Rublee were evidently amused that Calles could have something of an epiphany regarding the sanctity of property but fail to appreciate the importance of an independent judiciary, they were nevertheless pleased when a week later the Mexican Supreme Court handed down the decision that Calles had promised.

In his letter to Acheson regarding the importance of "personal feelings," Rublee explained, "In the future, [Morrow] will have no difficulty with Mexico, because they want a settlement and are sure that their face will be saved and because [Morrow] will ask for nothing unreasonable."[57] Morrow's friendly attitude and candid advice coupled with Calles' desire for a reconciliation were the basis for Morrow's successful mission. As one historian explains, although yet full of bombastic revolutionary rhetoric, Calles was "eager to control the revolutionary forces that had played havoc with Mexico's political, economic, and social stability for nearly two decades."[58] The difficulty for Calles was that each time he was prepared to check the revolution, a reactionary challenge emerged, sending the country back into violent conflict. In order to rally peasants and laborers to take the field against reactionaries, Calles was forced to further radicalize the revolution, promising more confiscations and land redistribution. What Morrow and Rublee soon learned was that Calles needed help in stabilizing the situation. He needed protection from the reactionary Right in Mexico and the United States so that he could control the radical Left. Calles believed that if the enemies of the revolution were held at bay, he could bring Mexico closer to a political center.

Fortunately for Calles and all interested parties, Morrow was an expert troubleshooter who, according to James Arthur Salter, employed an enlightened approach to problem solving that would have allowed him to understand Calles' predicament where others had failed. Salter described Morrow's three-step approach to negotiating in his 1948 work *Personality in Politics*: "First find the facts—all the important facts that are relevant—before you let yourself even begin to form a policy; second, try to penetrate the real mind of the person you are negotiating with, to see the problem as he sees it, to understand what it is that is really important to him; third, try to evolve out of this a solution which will really be to the common interest."[59] While, when Calles offered his dramatic overture rescinding the offending oil laws, Morrow had not even begun his trademark negotiations, the banker's friendly and disarming manner allowed the harrowed Mexican president to make a leap of faith.

Although Dwight Morrow quickly set the stage for resolving the contentious oil dispute that had threatened war, the Morrow mission became as much about improving Mexico for Mexicans as it had been for improving diplomatic relations. Toward that end, Morrow desired to resolve Mexico's external debt crisis, see its land reform policy become more moderate and productive, and achieve a peaceful resolution to a bloody conflict between the Catholic Church and the Mexican government. To help solve these contentious issues, Morrow needed to begin his fact-finding stage in earnest. Although it was unclear how Rublee might exactly answer Morrow's needs, the ambassador wanted Rublee to surreptitiously scope out the situation and learn what he could. As George explained to Juliet, because Morrow worried about the U.S. Embassy staff's response to his unofficial presence and potential influence on matters of state, Morrow "gives out that I am here to study Mexico and to prepare an article for *Foreign Affairs*."[60]

After taking two days to acclimate himself to his new environment, George reported to Juliet that he would "soon move about and see people" and added that he found "it all very interesting."[61] After a week of prodding here and there and meeting with various government officials and American businessmen, Rublee reported, "I am gradually getting information and these interviews may open the way to getting a good deal more."[62] By 25 November Rublee had worked his way up to Calles' cabinet officials, meeting that day with both Puig Casauranc, minister of education, and Luis Morones, minister of commerce and a leading labor figure. Rublee evidently made quite an impression on Casauranc, who gave him a "handsome volume" on his rural schools project, "through which [he] hoped to raise the condition of the Indians," and he sent another seventeen books to him the next day.[63] Rublee reported that Morones was "not a Bolshevist or anything like one" and found that what "he said to me about labor matters was a good deal like what Louis Brandeis says on this subject."[64] A few days later he met with a "sensible" and "well informed" Methodist bishop "to talk about the Catholic question" and also with "an Englishman, who is head of...the biggest business in the city" to talk "about the labor laws and labor questions."[65]

Rublee's success with government officials was likely in part a result of his own positive response to Mexicans and Mexico. All of his letters coming out of Mexico in November and December 1927 indicate that he had an earnest interest in Mexico and its people. His letters almost seem an independent writing campaign to change U.S. public opinion, one influential person at a time. To Learned Hand, for instance, Rublee observed that Mexico City "is a handsome city—more like Paris than any other I can think of—but of course not much like it—extremely clean and well kept—with high mountains looking down at you at the end of every street. Flowers everywhere—and the best climate for me I have ever found—warm summer, brilliant blue sky and exhilarating air."[66] He added, "I like the Indians very much—and most of the people seem to be Indians." While Rublee had gotten to know something of Mexican culture on local excursions with Morrow, he also ventured out with a small group on a Sunday to visit "an Indian village out in the country."[67] Writing to Juliet, George related that he had "attended the service which the Indians held in their church—saw how they lived and did their farming—and then had lunch in one of their adobe houses—just one room with an earth floor." During lunch he used " tortillas—a kind of corn pancake used instead of bread—so as to make scoops to pick up the food," which he thought "wasn't at all bad." George concluded: "I liked the Indians—they were clean, good looking and polite without any servility." To Dean Acheson he described Mexicans as a "[p]leasant, attractive people," and to Endicott Peabody he observed: "The country is one of the loveliest and most interesting I have ever seen and I like the Mexican people. I didn't expect to, but I like them very much. I believe they have great latent capacities and at least they deserve a chance to make something of their country."[68]

Incidentally, Rublee's decision to take up work in Mexico had lasting personal significance to his life. Finding Mexico very appealing, he convinced Juliet to join him, thinking that she would also enjoy life there. Like George, Juliet had led an active life throughout her adulthood. Her most important efforts involved her support of Margaret Sanger, of whom she became an intimate friend and important supporter around 1912. While George served on the Federal Trade Commission, Juliet and Margaret were jailed in New York City for disseminating information on birth control. Flamboyant and courageous, Juliet proved an important figure in Sanger's birth control movement.[69] When George traveled to London to work on the AMTC in January 1918, Juliet traveled with him and joined the Red Cross, for which she worked as a nurse in an army hospital in France until the end of the war. Although Juliet continued her support of Sanger's birth control movement throughout the 1920s, including an effort to get the League of Nations to support the cause, by 1928 Juliet was evidently looking for a new project.[70] Joining George and Dwight Morrow in Mexico, she, too, became interested in improving U.S.–Mexican relations and decided to make a film showing the beauty of Mexico and the attractiveness of its common people, as well as their exploitation by wealthy landowners. Juliet spent the next three years of her life and the remainder of her fortune making *The Flame of Mexico*. Although the movie failed in the box office and caused the Rublees great financial loss, Juliet was committed to the project for its importance in showing Americans a more attractive Mexico. Speaking at a special screening at Washington's prestigious Rialto Theater in June 1932, Juliet asserted, "Many people still think of Mexico as a land of bandits and dry cactus." She explained that, instead, "[i]t is really the wonderland of the South and to have such a beautiful and fascinating country as our next-door neighbor and not know it better seemed to me a great pity."[71] Breaking with tradition and at great cost, the movie was shot in Mexico using a Mexican cast and a leading film crew from Hollywood under the direction of David Kirkland. The decision to use a Mexican cast, however progressive, was ruinous to the project, for by the time the movie was released, sound motion pictures were the standard, and it proved impossible to add spoken dialogue to the film. As one reviewer explained it, "The reversion to the use of printed titles has a further effect of stamping 'Flame of Mexico' as a product of an earlier and almost forgotten era."[72] Although its opening in Washington brought "an incessant barrage [of] leaders of Washington's official, diplomatic, social and professional sets," it was not picked up for national release and soon made a home in a closet at the Rublees' residence in Cornish, New Hampshire.[73]

While George Rublee was quickly impressed with Mexico shortly after arriving in 1927, his fascination with the country seems to have become complete after a six-day train trip around the northern part of the country in early December. President Calles organized and hosted the extravagant excursion so that while feting Morrow, he could also show off new dams and a model agricultural college and land bank that his administration had recently established. Morrow contributed to the journey's merriment by inviting satirist Will Rogers to join the entourage. A few days after the party's return to Mexico City, Charles Lindbergh, Morrow's future son-in-law, added a final touch of goodwill when he made the first nonstop flight from Washington to Mexico City on 14 December.[74] Owing to these acts of friendship, many in Mexico and the United States could no longer contemplate the thought of war between their countries. Morrow's actions had thereby significantly and swiftly undermined the work of U.S. interventionists who had been hoping for a diplomatic break. As Rublee later recalled, Morrow's approach "was regarded as a brilliant diplomatic success and it was. Here was a country which was almost at war with us and suddenly turns around and becomes friendly. It was wonderful diplomacy."[75]

Rublee was thrilled that Morrow's mission was succeeding, and he believed that Calles deserved a share in the credit. As he grew to know him, Rublee was increasingly impressed with the Mexican president. On 7 December he reported to Juliet: "Last night I had a private talk with President Calles in which he spoke with a good deal of feeling about what he is trying to do for his country and expressed his liking for and trust in Morrow. He said that when I returned to my country he wanted me to think of him as my friend. He is a strong, simple man and I liked all that I saw in him during the trip."[76] Calles' candor and warmth toward Rublee were well placed; for the next ten years the Washington lawyer would, in turn, demonstrate himself to be a friend of Mexico.

By early December Rublee was convinced that he wanted to remain and help Morrow, but he was growing uncomfortable with his unofficial capacity. Only a little more than a week after arriving an article identifying him and raising questions about his role appeared in the prominent Mexican newspaper *Excelsior*.[77] Rublee hoped that after returning to New York at the end of December he might be able to return on "some definite basis—as counsel or something like that—and not as a man of mystery as I am now with no definite work."[78] With Morrow a little over five feet and Rublee perhaps six feet five inches, it is not difficult to imagine that Rublee had difficulty blending into the crowd on Morrow's outings. Evidently, it was the mystery surrounding his work in Mexico that led Will Rogers to dub Rublee "the Colonel House of the Republicans."[79]

Despite Rublee's interest in remaining in Mexico, Morrow was not yet prepared to release him from the reparations work in Europe. On 9 December Morrow wrote to Morgan partner Russell Leffingwell advocating Rublee's nomination to the reparation commission. Morrow observed: "If I were in Gilbert's place I should prefer Rublee to Norman Davis. He is a quiet, hardworking fellow, without any thought of 'blue ribbons.' Moreover, particularly because of his retiring and studious disposition he can exert considerable influence. If any such thing as a revision of the Dawes Plan should come about in the next year, Rublee has not a little influence among a certain type of progressive or radical in Washington."[80] Despite Morrow's effort he was unsuccessful in securing Rublee for the post.[81] Learning on 12 December that he was not selected, George wrote to Juliet to inform her that "Dwight was very much surprised and sorry" and added: "Apparently he did not have as much influence as he thought or did not exert it promptly enough."[82] Although the rationale for Rublee's return to New York in December was rendered void, he determined to leave Mexico so that Morrow could "make up his mind whether he does want me." If Morrow wished him to return, George thought he would attempt to convince Secretary Kellogg to expedite his appointment as embassy counsel during the upcoming January PanAmerican Conference in Havana.[83]

In the meantime, there were a number of ways that Rublee could assist Morrow's mission back in the United States. Both the external debt crisis and the conflict between the Mexican Catholic Church and the government were issues in which Morrow could not directly involve himself. Rublee, however, acting in an unofficial capacity, could begin maneuvering on Morrow's behalf. Too, Rublee could give Lippmann and other influential publicists an informed, sympathetic view of the Mexican situation. With several clandestine duties to discharge, Rublee departed Mexico City on 19 December, arriving in New York on 24 December. Taking advantage of the long trip to improve his knowledge of Latin American issues, Rublee read Bryce Wood's *South America*.[84]

Rublee returned from his five-week visit to Mexico inspired to do something for the country that had invigorated and captivated him. Having had a dearth of meaningful activity during the past six years, Rublee's passion was rekindled in

Mexico. Characteristically, with his passion stirred, Rublee launched into activity. On 27 December he paid a visit to the senior partners at J. P. Morgan to prepare the way for the foreign debt settlement that Morrow wanted. With Thomas Lamont acting as the manager for European claims against Mexico as well as for a large number of U.S. investors, Morrow knew that Lamont had to join the consortium agreement he had in mind in order for it to succeed. Toward that end, Rublee sounded out Lamont and other partners on the issue.

Rublee found the Morgan partners greatly interested in Morrow's work and very pleased with his accomplishments. He reported to Morrow that Tom Cochran, who participated in the attempt to nominate Coolidge in 1920, "is terribly interested in your success and is planning your political future. Nothing less than the presidency for you will satisfy him."[85] Despite an interest in Morrow's success, the Morgan partner retained a dim view of Mexicans. For instance, Rublee reported that Cochran "maintained a passionately unsympathetic attitude towards Mexico and all Mexicans. It was amusing to hear him repeat with conviction, 'They are all sons of bitches. I know for I've dealt with them for years.' I didn't attempt to argue the question."[86] Worse than Cochran's personal cynicism was Lamont's unyielding belief that Mexico's finances could not be put in order even with Morrow on hand to exert pressure. Rublee explained that in a "little hurried talk" to sound him out, he found that Lamont "had decided to stand pat and not get his bonds mixed up with the claims indebtedness." Nevertheless, the next day Lamont asked Leffingwell to meet with Rublee over lunch to go into Morrow's ideas on a Mexican debt settlement in further detail. In addition to Leffingwell, Vernon Munroe and Arthur Anderson joined them, and toward the end of the meeting Lamont himself showed up.

Although Rublee maintained during the luncheon that Morrow "had not consulted me about the Mexican debt and that I knew very little about it," he nevertheless explained the gist of Morrow's approach. Writing to Morrow after the meeting, Rublee explained that he had related to the Morgan partners that he "had gathered that [Morrow] thought the essential thing was for the bondholders to survey the situation as a whole and to take such action as would tend to bring Mexico back to a condition of prosperity as soon as possible without giving undue weight to the amount of money that it might be possible to collect immediately. Until that time came the bonds would never be worth very much."[87] Rublee added that Morrow also believed that "the bondholders ought to get more knowledge of the entire problem and ought to have better conduct with the Mexican Government than they now have." Lamont, however, informed Rublee that for the moment he opposed the idea of entering into any new general agreement but "would just rock along and collect something, [maybe] thirty million pesos this year." Lamont allowed that "if skies grew clearer, they might cooperate in some general plan for dealing with the situation."[88] Despite his early proclamations, Lamont proved less intransigent than he originally indicated.

With his visit to 23 Wall Street Rublee prepared the way for Morrow to carry on a sensitive negotiation with his former partners. Replying to Rublee's letter, Morrow observed, "On the financial question I think what you said to Lamont was just right." Since the Mexican government would not be "able to complete its 1927 schedule," however, Morrow "was amused by [Lamont's] statement...that he was going to be satisfied with $30,000,000.00 pesos for the bondholders in 1928."[89] Despite Rublee's assistance, Morrow was in a complicated situation. Writing to Rublee in February 1928, Morrow explained how interwoven his relations had become:

President [Calles] sent for me at the end of the year and laid the financial problem before me. I was pleased to have him tell me that although I had been firmly on the bondholders' side, he knew that I would advise Mexico in her own interests. The curious result followed that in the negotiations between [Treasury Secretary] Montes de Oca and Lamont, I was in the strange position of having the President send Montes de Oca to me for advice as to how to answer [Lamont's] telegrams. The result that has been reached is very satisfactory. In fact, the thing has come off exactly as you and I discussed when you were down here.[90]

Owing to Rublee's influential soundings at J. P. Morgan and Morrow's guidance to de Oca in Mexico, Morrow was able to convert Lamont to his plan to devise an international committee of bankers representing all of Mexico's indebtedness. On 16 January, Lamont wrote to Jack Morgan (J. P. Jr) to let him know of his changed perspective: "The whole situation hangs together. The Committee cannot work out its problems for the long future without a decent prosperous Mexico and a revival of the oil business; Dwight cannot work out his settlement of the oil and land questions, unless there is a chance that the external debt question can be handled, too. This is the best chance we have had yet."[91] Despite Lamont's conversion in January 1928, to Morrow's disgust, shortly before the international bankers' meeting two years later, Lamont pulled his bonds out of the deal, and the conference proved meaningless.[92] In Lamont's defense, however, the U.S. stock market crash and the collapse of the world economy in the intervening period changed the situation dramatically.

When Rublee returned to Mexico in March 1928, Morrow set him to work on the two remaining crises undermining U.S.–Mexican relations: the Mexican effort to force Americans to liquidate their landholdings in Mexico and the tenacious and sometimes bloody rift between the Catholic Church in Mexico and the government, the latter leading some Catholics in America to favor U.S. intervention. Morrow's and Rublee's position on Calles' land confiscation was that it was not currently useful. As Rublee later recalled, they were opposed to Calles' "indiscriminately taking properties that were being well managed...and giving them to people who would not develop them well." They found that the ongoing seizure of large landholders' property was not benefiting Mexico because the uneducated farmers were not yet able to sustain productivity, so that food production continued to drop. Morrow "wanted this reform to go on in an orderly but slower way than the ardent reformers who didn't understand the consequences."[93] Morrow and Rublee were able to convince Calles to take a hiatus from land seizures and to make sure that property owners were fairly compensated.

The church–state conflict in Mexico proved much more difficult for Morrow and Rublee to solve. It dated to the 1910 revolution, when the church opposed the revolt against Porfirio Diaz, who had ignored the restrictions placed on the church in the 1857 constitution and restored it to a place of preeminence and authority in Mexican life. The socialistic 1917 constitution greatly reduced the authority and role of the Catholic Church, but little was done to enforce these provisions until 1925, when a number of liberal state legislatures began enacting anticlerical legislation. In January 1926, the church leadership in Mexico published a statement against these acts that struck at the "sacred rights of the Catholic Church" and disavowed the constitution and anticlerical legislation. In response, Calles implemented the original provisions allowed in the constitution, closing religious primary schools and ordering priests to register with local government officials. Calles also nationalized church property, deported foreign priests, and forbade clergy from serving as teachers in any school and forbade the teaching of religious subjects in all schools. In August 1926, the Mexican bishops with the approval of the Papacy suspended public worship in the churches of Mexico and also called for an economic boycott that requested Catholics buy only items of absolute necessity. Soon after, a militant "Cristeros," or Church Party, was formed and prepared to take up arms in southern Mexico against the federal government.[94] When government-appointed teachers began to show up in the state of Jalisco, many were attacked, and some were killed. The government responded with equally vicious attacks, and the rebellion soon took on an organized form with the armed Catholic units periodically attacking government installations. When Rublee arrived in the autumn of 1927, he found "a state of war going on in some parts of the country."[95]

Neither Morrow nor Rublee was an expert on the church–state controversy, so they began to send for materials to bring them up to speed. They particularly wanted to know how the French Third Republic had solved its religious controversy toward the close of the nineteenth century and what accommodations had been reached between fascist Italy and the Papacy a few years before. Rublee sent for a summary from noted political scientist Harold Laski of the London School of Economics and one from professor Othon Guerlac, a political scientist at Cornell. Rublee also asked his friend Louis Dow, professor of French at Dartmouth, to send him a number of books on the history of the struggle between socialism and Catholicism in France.[96] Morrow asked his former partner, Arthur Springer, to send J. Bodley's *The Church in France* and Nielson's *The History of the Papacy in the Nineteenth Century* and "any books of Lord Acton's which are available in New York."[97] Morrow and Rublee also relied on Walter Lippmann for sources and for suggestions on how to end the deadlock between the Catholic Church and the Mexican government. From their study Rublee and Morrow realized that the Mexican revolution mirrored the general nineteenth-century European effort to undermine landed aristocracy. Sympathizing with the cause of revolution in Mexico, Rublee later recalled: "It was true that there had been very great injustice in Mexico. The peons had been very unjustly treated. There was a real reason for the revolution in their treatment. They'd been almost in a condition of semi-slavery and had not had any opportunity for education and improvement. In order to become good citizens there was need for reforms in Mexico, which Morrow saw."[98] Rublee believed, too, that the "Catholic Church had a very bad record in Mexico" and admitted that he thought there "were strong reasons for disliking it." He pointed out that "at one time almost all the property in the country was under the control of the Church which was very rich."[99] Nevertheless, although Morrow and Rublee understood the anger and aspirations of the revolutionaries, they were pragmatic and circumspect enough to understand that acting on unbridled passion could make the situation even worse for the common Mexicans. They also believed that the church could yet play a positive role in Mexico if liberal theologians could take control of the Church and make an accommodation with the revolutionary government.

While the State Department expected Dwight Morrow to remain an impartial spectator to the church–state crisis, Morrow immediately realized that it would be impossible to permanently improve conditions in Mexico until the Mexican church as an institution was no longer an enemy of the revolution.[100] Given his conviction, for the next year and a half Morrow, with the help of Rublee and others, carried out a high-stakes clandestine diplomatic operation without the knowledge or approval of the U.S. State Department. When Morrow at last acknowledged his role in the settlement that ended the crisis, he observed that although "I never officially took any position with respect to the religious controversy...I did what I could in an unofficial capacity to bring about a better modus vivendi."[101] An expert problem solver, Morrow early on concluded that the religious conflict in Mexico could be "terminated [only] by a modus vivendi, in which neither the Government nor the Church would surrender its fundamental position, but which would enable the Church to resume its spiritual functions, leaving the fundamental questions to be settled at a later time in an atmosphere of good will."[102] To get to such a point, however, involved delicate negotiations, which many times nearly collapsed.

Rublee, of course, enjoyed secretive operations that aimed to solve profound problems. Writing in April 1928 to Endicott Peabody to let him know of his work with Morrow, Rublee explained, "Unluckily all the interesting things are so secret that I can't write about them."[103] What Rublee likely had in mind was a secret meeting that Morrow had arranged on 4 April between President Calles and liberal theologian Father John Burke, general secretary of the National Catholic Welfare Conference in the United States. After the meeting the two exchanged letters, Burke's being drafted by Morrow, likely with Rublee's assistance. Burke's letter proposed the resumption of religious worship if Calles would "make a declaration that it was not the purpose of the Constitution and laws, nor his purpose, to destroy the identity of the Church."[104] Burke's letter also stipulated that "in order to avoid unreasonable applications of the laws the Government would be willing to confer from time to time with the authorized head of the Church in Mexico." Calles' letter contained the "desired" declarations. Morrow and Rublee were hopeful that the conflict could soon be ended. A series of setbacks, however, arose and prevented the accommodation they sought for more than a year. The delay initiated with the Papacy, which was not satisfied with the terms of Calles' letter, preferring, as Morrow observed, "to wait until a settlement more favorable to the Church could be made." As Morrow noted, "A considerable part of the Mexican hierarchy, as well as leading Mexican Catholic laymen who were hostile to the existing Mexican Government, were opposed to the proposed adjustment. They had access to the Holy See and much influence there."[105] All hopes for a compromise disappeared when President-Elect Alvaro Obregon was assassinated by a Catholic fanatic in July 1928 and a general Cristeros rebellion broke out in March 1929. The Cristeros forces numbered nearly 10,000 and by May more than a 1,000 men on each side had been killed, and acts of violence and terror were being committed against noncombatants on both sides. Morrow and Rublee were opposed to the conservative Cristeros rebellion and abhorred the violence taking place on both sides. To forestall the bloody rebellion, they worked quickly to convince the new Hoover administration to condemn the uprising and to get Catholic prelates in America to speak against it as well. When it finally became clear that the Cristeros rebellion would be put down, Morrow successfully approached Mexico's new president, Portes Gil, to reopen negotiations with the Papacy. To facilitate Gil's cooperation, Morrow apparently arranged for a number of moderate Mexican prelates to issue "public statements condemning violence, and urging peace and order, respect for the constitutional authorities and devotion to the reconstruction of the common Fatherland." Morrow believed that "these statements were influential in counteracting the propaganda of" militant Catholic conservatives "and in preparing the mind of the country for peace."[106]

During May and June 1929 Morrow orchestrated a series of public statements that led to the successful conclusion of a religious settlement in Mexico. The use of the press in these negotiations suggests that Rublee was highly involved in the strategic planning. Following the statement of the moderate Mexican prelates, Morrow arranged for Gil to make a statement in New York papers denying that he persecuted Catholics and maintaining that "the Catholic Church as an institution was not involved in the military uprising" in Mexico. To demonstrate that fact, he pointed to the statements of "certain representatives of Catholicism [who] had advised respect for the law and order"—these statements, of course, having been arranged by Morrow. Under Morrow's guidance, the exiled Mexican archbishop Ruiz y Flores then made a statement in Washington declaring that "the religious conflict in Mexico was not motivated by any cause that might not be corrected by men of sincere good will." Morrow then "drafted and submitted" a statement for Gil to deliver "in the form of an interview with the press." Gil's statement stipulated that although the Mexican government could have no "official relations with the Church," it was possible for the government to conduct "conversations with dignitaries of the Church as to the scope and interpretation of the laws applicable to the clergy." Gil also agreed to grant amnesty for those involved in the Cristeros rebellion. These acts won the support of the Papacy, which soon appointed Archbishop Ruiz as apostolic delegate to Mexico, who traveled to Mexico City on 8 June to meet with Gil. Morrow and Rublee were keenly aware that the delicate negotiation could break down at any time owing to fundamental differences between the parties and the active sabotage of Catholic prelates and conservatives associated with the Cristeros Party. As Morrow explained, to prevent a rupture, "During the negotiations that followed, I was in constant touch with both sides." With growing fear that the negotiation would fail, Morrow at last "felt it advisable to intervene more actively as an adviser" and "drafted statements to be publicly and simultaneously made by the president and Archbishop Ruiz." On 20 June, the papacy gave its approval to the settlement, and on 21 June Catholic priests returned to their churches.[107]

The effort to solve the church-state crisis was the most difficult of Morrow's mission, and George Rublee was evidently involved in each stage of the sixteen-month negotiation. As George explained in a letter to Juliet, his work amounted to "a lot of research…and consultation and negotiation."[108] In his memoirs, however, Rublee refrains from giving any detail about his contribution. Instead, he simply explained: "I was with Mr. Morrow, while he was in Mexico, as his assistant, helping him and I had a good deal to do with these matters. But this is really not my story but Mr. Morrow's story."[109] Although Rublee's role was limited to that of adviser, analyst and expert information gatherer, his experiences in Mexico rendered him an authority on Latin American affairs and prepared him to carry out independent missions in the region throughout the 1930s. As Rublee related to Senator George Norris, his work with Morrow had been a "most interesting and informing experience."[110] Equally important, Mexico provided the spark that Rublee needed to rekindle his interest and involvement in international affairs and public work. Joining Morrow in 1927 initiated a final twelve-year episode in which he contributed to significant world events.

It is interesting to note that as the 1920s came to a close, a number of progressive internationalists began to emerge from Wall Street to reenter the public arena to contribute to the development of reasoned public policy. Although Morrow and Rublee took up public work again in 1927 under Coolidge, ironically, Herbert Hoover was responsible for the return of Henry Stimson and Joseph Cotton, who as secretary and under secretary of state, respectively, would both prove much stronger internationalists than Hoover likely anticipated. Perhaps the most unusual work went to Ray Stevens, the onetime provincial New Hampshire farmer, who ended up becoming a political adviser to the king of Siam (Thailand) for about eight years beginning in 1928. A newcomer to the progressive internationalist club was Reuben Clark, whom Morrow brought to Mexico to assist him on Mexico's debt reconstruction. Clark later served as undersecretary of state in the Hoover administration and was author of the Clark memorandum that repudiated Theodore Roosevelt's Corollary to the Monroe Doctrine and thereby ushered in what became known as the Good Neighbor Policy.[111]

While Felix Frankfurter was responsible for suggesting that Joe Cotton be sought out for a position as undersecretary, George Rublee took an active part in his seeing his nomination approved in the Senate in May and June 1929. Rublee's involvement began when he learned that Cotton's nomination was being in challenged by liberal Republicans who believed that Cotton was a conservative Wall Street lawyer interested only in enriching U.S. business interests in Latin America. Although stationed in Mexico City, Rublee began an active campaign to win over these Republicans for Cotton's appointment. Writing to Dean Acheson, for instance, he explained that "some opposition has developed to confirmation of Joe Cotton," and "[i]t appears to come from progressives like Norris, La Follette etc.," who "think that Joe may be an imperialist dollar diplomat who will be intervening all over the place for oil."[112] Rublee believed that "this is nonsense" and argued that "Joe would be the best possible protection against such policies." Believing Cotton's nomination to be critical to improved U.S. foreign policy, Rublee asked Acheson to seek out "progressive friends, newspaper men, etc. to help us."

Rublee himself proceeded to write to George Norris asking for the senator's support. Although the letter describes Cotton's attitude toward foreign policy, in describing his friend's views, Rublee relates his own. In his letter Rublee explained that Cotton "has long taken great interest in foreign relations. He is opposed to intervention and strong-armed methods. He wants peace and favors conciliatory and constructive methods. With what is known as 'dollar diplomacy' he has no sympathy whatever."[113] Rublee also made Norris aware of some subtle deceptions that he believed conservative Republicans were employing. Noting that conservatives were erroneously connecting Cotton to oil interests in New York, Rublee explained: "Indeed I am positive that while the oil companies might not take the attitude openly, their real desire would be to have his confirmation defeated. He is altogether opposed to their views of the function of the State Department in the matter of the protection of their interests in foreign countries and they would prefer to have someone not be experienced and alert as he to deal with in the State Department."[114] Rublee concluded by arguing that Cotton was essential to "the promotion of enlightened policies in the whole international field." Cotton was confirmed, and he proceeded to make an important contribution to U.S. foreign relations until his premature death in 1931. During his three years in office Cotton reorganized the department to put more experienced and more liberal lawyers in key Latin American posts and also worked to end lingering slave trade in Liberia.[115]

While Rublee's support for Cotton was evidently well founded, his somewhat desperate effort on behalf of his friend's nomination evidently stemmed from his deep mistrust of Hoover. Writing to Dean Acheson in September 1928 as the presidential campaign neared its end, Rublee made plain his concerns about a Hoover presidency. Rublee confided: "Somehow I distrust Hoover. He is able and efficient in planning and doing any particular job. But I doubt his capacity to decide what jobs should be done. He seems to me to have a kind of belief in his infallibility, being a bit like Wilson in that respect; and I think he might develop weaknesses similar to those of Wilson. I regard him not as a wise or cool man, but rather as a headstrong, passionate one who is unable to recognize what may be sound in the position of those who differ with him."[116] Rublee hoped to see Al Smith win the contest, believing that he could "get a fairer hearing from him and receive a more understandable answer" from him than Hoover. Although a Republican, Dwight Morrow also preferred Smith.

According to Rublee, Morrow "believes that Hoover would not do very well as President and that in his heart he hopes that Smith will win."[117] While Herbert Hoover would prevail in the contest, neither Rublee nor Morrow ever developed any loyalty for him. In fact, in the first year of his presidency they would have opportunity to challenge his foreign relations policy at the London Naval Conference, and with the election of Morrow as senator in November 1930 they would begin to lay the foundation for a challenge to Hoover's control of the White House and the Republican Party.

NOTES

1. Quoted in Nicolson, *Dwight Morrow*, 241.

2. GR to Paul Cravath, 27 June 1919, Cravath Papers, HHPL, box 4. Rublee observed: "We must later carry out the resolve we made at our last lunch with you in Paris at Henry's to form a little true blue inter-allied club." Also see Heaton, *A Scholar in Action* (206), for a sixteen-member group, including Rublee and Gay, that met to discuss international issues; and Robert D. Schulzinger, *American Diplomacy in the Twentieth Century* (New York: Oxford University Press, 1994), 132.

3. Rublee, "Reminiscences," 190-191; Heaton, *Scholar in Action*, 141-142; and Edward M. Lamont, *The Ambassador from Wall Street: the Story of Thomas W. Lamont, J. P. Morgan's Chief Executive* (Lanham, MD: Madison Books, 1994), 141-142, 181.

4. Rublee, "Reminiscences," 192.

5. Juliet Barrett Rublee to Learned Hand, 14 July 1921, HLS-Hand, box 107, folder 8.

6. Ibid.

7. Rublee, "Reminiscences," 193; and James Chace, *Acheson: The Secretary of State Who Created the American World* (New York: Simon & Schuster, 1998), 52. After Rublee joined the firm it was renamed Covington, Burling & Rublee. The firm went through a variety of name changes during Rublee's lifetime and eventually decided upon simply Covington and Burling, which it retains to this day. For simplicity sake, the firm will be referred to as Covington and Burling in this study. The other members of the firm when Rublee joined were Spencer Gordon, Oscar W. Underwood, Jr., and Paul E. Shorb. Dean Acheson and Newell Ellison were then clerking at the firm.

8. *FRUS*, 1921, vol. 2, 596-599.

9. Rublee, "Reminiscences," 194.

10. Ibid.; Dean Acheson to Manly O. Hudson, 3 May 1922, Manly O. Hudson Papers, Harvard Law Library Special Collections, [hereafter HLS-Hudson], box 35, folder 5; and Chace, *Acheson*, 53-54. Rublee seems to have come to know Hudson during the Versailles Treaty period when Hudson served with Rublee on the staff of the American Commission to Negotiate Peace.

11. Chace, *Acheson*, 53.

12. Rublee, "Reminiscences," 196; and GR to Lippmann, 28 January 1927, Yale-Lippmann, box 29, folder 1076. In the letter Rublee explained the State Departments rational in 1921 as it seemed to relate to U.S.-Mexico accords in 1927.

13. Rublee, *Reminiscences* 197; and "Outline of topics to be considered in the agreement," 13 May 1922, HLS-Hudson, box 35, folder 5.

14. Chace, *Acheson*, 53-54; [Covington & Burling], *Permanent Court of the Arbitration at the Hague: United States-Norway Arbitration, The Argument of Norway*, 22 June 1922 [no publication data], 51; and United States, *Permanent Court of the*

Arbitration at the Hague: United States-Norway Arbitration, Appendix to the Counter-Case of the United States of America: Documentary Evidence (Washington, D.C.: Government Printing Office, 1922), 1-4, and 19-20. Rublee retained a three-volume set of the Norway and U.S. cases in his Cornish library.

15. Acheson, "George Rublee," 5.

16. Walter Isaacson and Evan Thomas, *The Wise Men: Six Friends and the World They Made: Acheson, Bohlen, Harriman, Kennan, Lovett, McCloy* (New York: Simon and Schuster, 1986), 131.

17. Chace, *Acheson*, 56.

18. Acheson to Peabody, 26 April 1924, GSA.

19. Acheson to Peabody, 14 April 1923, GSA.

20. GR to Hand, 22 September 1922, HLS-Hand, box 107, folder 4.

21. Ibid.

22. LaFeber, *The American Age*, vol. 2, 335-336.

23. Ibid., 336.

24. Nicolson, *Dwight Morrow*, 242.

25. Ibid., 262-263.

26. Ibid.

27. Ibid., 267-269, 309; and Rublee, "Reminiscences," 201-202.

28. Richard Melzer, "The Ambassador *Simpatico*: Dwight Morrow in Mexico, 1927-1930," *Ambassadors in Foreign Policy: The Influence of Individuals on U.S.-Latin American Policy*, C. Neale Ronning and Albert P. Vannucci, editors, (New York: Praeger Publishers, 1987), 18.

29. Nicolson, *Dwight Morrow*, 309.

30. Melzer, "The Ambassador *Simpatico*," 18.

31. Ibid., 20.

32. GR to Lippmann, January 1927, Yale-Lippmann, box 29, folder 1076.

33. Ibid.

34. Lippmann to GR, 1 February 1927, Yale-Lippmann.

35. Ibid.

36. Lippmann to GR, 26 January 1927, Yale-Lippmann.

37. Lippmann to GR, 1 February 1927, Yale-Lippmann.

38. Lippmann to GR, 14 March 1927, Yale-Lippmann.

39. GR to Lippmann, 17 March 1928, Yale-Lippmann.

40. Ibid.

41. Lippmann to GR, 18 March 1927 and 5 April 1928, Yale-Lippmann.

42. GR to Morrow, 27 September 1927, DMP.

43. Hand to Lippmann, 22 September 1927, Yale-Lippmann, box 12, folder 499.

44. Ibid.

45. Nicolson, *Dwight Morrow*, 273-274.

46. GR to Morrow, 8 October 1927, DMP.

47. Morrow to GR, 15 October 1927, DMP.

48. Information on Hearst is from Melzer, "The Ambassador *Simpatico*," 2 and note 7.

49. GR to Morrow, 3 November 1927, DMP.

50. Rublee, "Reminiscences," 202-203.

51. Melzer, "The Ambassador *Simpatico*," 7-8.

52. GR to Hand, 30 November 1927, HLS-Hand, box 107, folder 5.

53. Nicolson, *Dwight Morrow*, 326-327, 329.

54. GR to Acheson, 12 December 1927, Dean Acheson Papers, Sterling Library Special Collections [hereafter Yale-Acheson], box 27, folder 340.

55. "Report by George Rublee from Notes Taken at the Time (November, 1927) of the Account Given him by Ambassador Morrow. . . ," DMP.

56. Ibid.

57. GR to Acheson, 12 December 1927, Yale-Acheson, box 27, folder 340.

58. Melzer, "The Ambassador *Simpatico*," 3.

59. James Arthur Salter, *Personality in Politics: Studies of Contemporary Statesmen* (London: Faber and Faber, 1948), 161.

60. GR to JBR, 16 November 1927, GRP.

61. GR to JBR, 18 November 1927, GRP.

62. GR to JBR, 23 November 1927, GRP.

63. GR to JBR, 28 November 1927, GRP.

64. Ibid. Of Morones, Rublee observed: "My mind is still open about Morones. He is strong and very intelligent and able. His manners are good and he speaks clearly."

65. GR to JBR, 30 November 1927, GRP.

66. GR to Hand, 30 November 1927, HLS-Hand, box 107, folder 5.

67. GR to JBR, 28 November 1927, GRP.

68. GR to Acheson, 12 December 1927, Yale-Acheson, box 27, folder 340; and GR to Peabody, 23 December 1927, GSA.

69. For Juliet's important role in the birth control movement see Ellen Chesler, *Woman of Valor: Margaret Sanger and the Birth Control Movement in America* (New York: Doubleday, 1993). For the first study of Juliet Barrett Rublee see Jane E. Bowers, "'Oceans of Love': An Introduction to and Excerpts from Juliet Barrett Rublee's Letters to Margaret Sanger," University of Texas at Austin, 1994.

70. On her effort with the League see John M. Keynes to JBR, 30 August 1922, Juliet Rublee Papers (from Crossways, Cornish, New Hampshire) [hereafter JRP]. Replying to her effort to get him to use his influence with the League, Keynes observed: "I should not think that there is the faintest chance in the world of the League of Nations taking up the question of Birth Control. Of course they ought to do so. But I am sure that it is far too controversial and terrifying a subject for them to dream of touching it."

71. *Washington Post*, 4 June 1932.

72. Ibid.

73. George Rublee, II donated the film to the Library of Congress in 1997.

74. Rublee, "Reminiscences," 206-208; and Nicolson, *Dwight Morrow*, 317-318. Rublee enjoyed Rogers and described him at length to Juliet: "Rogers is rather crude and rough, but he is very full of life and very amusing. He has a warm and friendly way with him that is genuine, is sensitive I think, serious and thoughtful too underneath, intelligent and not conceited. I like being with him." GR to JBR, 7 December 1927, GRP.

75. Rublee, "Reminiscences," 205.

76. GR to JBR, 7 December 1927, GRP.

77. GR to JBR, 28 November 1927, GRP. Rublee explained: "Dwight said one of the American newspaper men here had recognized me. So the facts probably came from him and the rest was made up."

78. GR to JBR, 10 December 1927, GRP.

79. George Rublee Papers. At the bottom of a photograph of himself, Rogers wrote: "George Rublee, The Colonel House of the Republicans. With much friendliness —Will Rogers, Amateur Democrat."

80. Morrow to Russell Leffingwell, 9 December 1927, Russell Leffingwell Papers, Sterling Library Special Collections, Yale University [hereafter Yale-Leffingwell], box 6, folder 130.

81. See Leffingwell to Morrow, 16 December 1927, Yale-Leffingwell, box 6, folder 130.

82. GR to JBR, 12 December 1927, GRP.

83. Ibid.; and GR to JBR, 10 December 1927, GRP.

84. GR to Morrow, 22 December 1927, DMP.

85. GR to Morrow, 31 December 1927, DMP. On Cochran at the 1920 Republican Convention see Nicolson, *Dwight Morrow*, 229.

86. GR to Morrow, 31 December 1927, DMP.

87. Ibid.

88. Ibid.

89. Morrow to GR, 2 February 1928, DMP.

90. Ibid.

91. Thomas Lamont to J.P. Morgan, 16 January 1928, quoted in Linda B. Hall, *Oil, Banks, and Politics: The United States and Postrevolutionary Mexico, 1917-1924* (Austin: University of Texas Press, 1995), 102-103.

92. Rublee, "Reminiscences," 215.

93. Ibid., 213.

94. Langsam, *The World Since 1914*, 269-270; and Walter Lippmann, "Church and State in Mexico: The American Mediation," *Foreign Affairs* (January 1930), 187-192.

95. Rublee, "Reminiscences," 213.

96. GR to Morrow, 5 February 1928, DMP.

97. Morrow to Arthur H. Springer, 2 February 1928, DMP.

98. Rublee, "Reminiscences," 212.

99. Ibid., 213, 218.

100. Morrow "draft" memoir, 1, DMP.

101. Ibid.

102. Ibid.

103. GR to Peabody, 5 April 1928, GSA.

104. Morrow "draft" memoire, 3, DMP.

105. Ibid., 5.

106. Ibid., 4-6.

107. Ibid., 7-9.

108. GR to JBR, 3 April 1928, GRP.

109. Rublee, "Reminiscences," 200.

110. GR to George Norris, 31 May 1929, enclosure in GR to Acheson, 31 May 1929, Yale-Acheson.

111. For information on the Clark Memorandum, see Ferrell, *American Diplomacy*, 767-768.

112. GR to Acheson, 31 May 1929, Yale-Acheson.

113. GR to George Norris, 31 May 1929, enclosure in GR to Acheson, 31 May 1929, Yale-Acheson.

114. Ibid.

115. McClure, "Joseph Potter Cotton," 569.

116. GR to Acheson, 16 September 1928, Yale-Acheson.

117. GR to Hand, 16 July 1928, HLS-Hand.

10

"Dwight Morrow's Colonel House" (1930)

Although George Rublee remained in a sort of political exile during the 1920s, as the decade of instability dawned, he found himself back in Europe and in a unique position to attempt a repeal of America's withdrawal from Europe. Through an ironic twist of fate, Rublee traveled to London in January 1930 with an American delegation that President Herbert Hoover selected to negotiate a new naval treaty between the United States, Great Britain, France, Italy, and Japan. During the midst of a crisis in the London conference that focused the attention of the world on the diplomatic negotiations, Rublee was able to force the Hoover administration to take a more positive stance toward Europe's security system. So adroit was his exploitation of the situation, however, that only a select group of internationalists and a few journalists ever learned that Rublee was responsible for the diplomatic move that saved the conference from total failure.

By the time the London Naval Conference convened in late January 1930 it was clear that something was dramatically wrong with the new world order established at Versailles. Although it was not yet clear that the world was sliding back into the abyss, the stock market crash a few months before, growing unemployment in Europe, the incessant rise of fascism, and the teetering of the international banking system provided ominous signs for any who were watching. The fact that a disarmament conference was even necessary was disconcerting enough, for it reminded the public that the promises of Versailles had not been realized. Worse yet, the conference was necessary to preserve peace among the victors of the world war—Great Britain, France, Italy, Japan, and the United States—which had grown increasingly distant and competitive since the war's end. Great Britain and the United States were antagonistic and distrustful; France and Italy were openly menacing; and the United States and Japan had reached a new level of acrimony in the wake of the 1924 U.S. immigration bill that explicitly excluded Japanese immigration. The promises of Versailles and the hope of a safer, happier new world order were nowhere evident.

The postwar period had opened with some hope. At the Washington Naval Conference in 1921, Great Britain, the United States, Japan, France, and Italy agreed to a 5-5-3-1.67-1.67 ratio agreement, respectively, covering battleships and aircraft carriers to end what was believed to be an incipient naval race between the first three powers. Equally important, the United States managed to bring to an end the Anglo-Japanese alliance of 1901 by devising a four-power treaty making the United States, Britain, France, and Japan jointly responsible for preserving the status quo in East Asia. This pact provided that in the event that hostilities broke out among any of the four powers, a conference would be called to deal with the dispute. The treaty also provided that if the Pacific interests of any of the four powers were threatened by a nonsignatory state, the remaining members agreed in advance to meet in consultation. This agreement was labeled a "consultative pact." It appears that although the United States was unwilling to enter pacts tying it to the European security system, leaders in Washington had less strict reservations when it came to securing interests in Asia. Among others, one disconcerting aspect of the conference was that despite strong pressure from Britain and America that the treaty outlaw the use of submarines, France would not agree to any such resolution.[1]

Despite the agreements reached in 1921, a naval race ensued almost immediately thereafter between Britain and Japan in cruisers and submarines, categories of warships not limited by the treaty. Italy and France soon followed suit. Between 1922 and 1927 Great Britain laid down fourteen cruisers, Japan ten, France four, Italy two, and the United States two. Through 1929 Great Britain laid down twenty-two destroyers, Japan forty-seven, France fifty, Italy thirty-seven, and the United States none. Additionally, despite the widespread condemnation of submarine warfare during the world war, Great Britain laid down nineteen submarines, Japan thirty-five, France sixty-seven, Italy thirty-two, and the United States three through 1929.[2] While the United States stayed out of the naval arms race for five years, by 1927 it was clear that America must either dissuade Britain and Japan from building or join the race. Toward that end, in 1927 President Calvin Coolidge called for a new round of negotiations in an attempt to end the burgeoning naval race by extending the ratio and parities of the 1922 agreement to the smaller classes. In that way the United States could put a halt to the arms race, in which it was falling increasingly behind, and then build up to parity strength over time. Since French and Italian antipathy was such that a conference could not accommodate their joint presence, Britain, America, and Japan struggled alone for seven weeks in Geneva to reach a new agreement that would cover cruiser and submarine parity. The conference, however, broke down over the inability of Great Britain and the United States to come to an agreement on the relative strength of small and large cruisers; the Americans, owing to a lack of bases, preferred a small number of large cruisers, while the British preferred a large number of small cruisers to protect their far flung empire. Behind the naval parity issue, however, was a now little-remembered Anglo-American rivalry that dominated the first decade of the interwar period. As historian Stephen Roskill points out, "serious differences of opinion" and a "rivalry in many fields" raised the prospect of America's replacing Germany as

Great Britain's major international competitor following the world war.[3] Owing to a lack of understanding between the Americans and British, the 1927 Geneva conference broke down in failure, and Coolidge was charged in some European quarters with "insufficient preparation," which diplomatic historian Robert Ferrell explains "was equal to saying that Coolidge was an ignoramus in international affairs."[4] Piqued by the Geneva "fiasco," the U.S. Congress, demonstrating its capacity to compete, passed an appropriation for fifteen large cruisers and an aircraft carrier early in 1929.[5] This shot across the British bow in the form of a real naval race made possible the London Naval Conference of 1930.

Although armed with an appropriation bill to start a serious naval competition, Herbert Hoover thought armaments a wasteful public expenditure and preferred to attempt another round of negotiations. Shortly after his inauguration in March 1929, Hoover made an overture to the signatories of the 1922 Washington Naval Treaty to reconvene to extend the life and scope of that compact. Ambassador Hugh Gibson conveyed Hoover's message at the League of Nations in Geneva on 22 April 1929, when he suggested that differences between the United States and Great Britain might be amicably settled, thereby clearing the way for a general naval agreement. So as not to be accused of insufficient preparation, Hoover appointed Charles Dawes as ambassador to England, where he soon took up negotiations on the competing naval programs. The Labor Party's narrow victory and the election of Ramsay MacDonald as prime minister in 1929 gave new life to the negotiations, and by early autumn a preliminary understanding between the United States and Britain was reached regarding cruiser parity. Following MacDonald's well-publicized visit to America in early October, the British and American leaders invited Japan, France, and Italy to meet in London beginning in January 1930 to reach a new naval agreement. Despite the New York Stock Exchange crash a few weeks after MacDonald's visit, Hoover could at least look back on his first year in office with some satisfaction on the diplomatic front and looked forward with confidence to a successful naval limitations conference early in the new year.[6]

Although Hoover and MacDonald thought that the conference would amount to fairly smooth sailing because of the Anglo-American accord, they soon learned that they had made a tactical error in ignoring the French during the preconference negotiations. As George Rublee later pointed out, the Hoover–MacDonald consultation "awakened the suspicion and hurt the pride of France."[7] What was especially troubling to the French was their fear that an Anglo-American agreement might signal a British withdrawal from the European security system established at Versailles. Throughout the 1920s the French had been fixated on improving their security against Germany and possibly Italy, and the British were central to their security scheme. As Walter Lippmann asserted in a 1930 article, "French foreign policy since the war has been haunted by a sense of insecurity arising out of the historical accident that France attained the temporary hegemony of Europe."[8] Because France "inherited from her allies, Britain and America, a political estate which she has not the resources to maintain," Lippmann argued that the French had "sought for ten years to make her position secure by supplementing her own resources with pledges of assistance from other powers." A central aim of French diplomacy in this period was securing an unconditional British pledge to support sanctions against an aggressor state (i.e., Germany or Italy). Although Great Britain had become a league member, the British resisted the adoption of a French-sponsored protocol in Geneva and other overtures aimed at locking in British action. With British public opinion hardening against France after the 1925 Locarno agreements, the French perceived in the 1929 Anglo-American rapprochement a possible British effort to withdraw from obligations to continental Europe. Having spent the past decade trying to lock Britain into a defense of the European status quo, the French protested any Anglo-American understanding that did not offer new guarantees to French security.[9]

From October to December 1929 the French sought to insert themselves in the Anglo-American naval parley and attempted to strengthen French–American relations by adding new features to the 1928 Kellogg-Briand Pact, a compact that the French had proposed in an effort to draw America into the European security system but that the United States adroitly recast as a meaningless worldwide declaration outlawing offensive war.[10] Beginning in October 1929, the French sounded out the new secretary of state Henry Stimson on adding strengthening features to the Kellogg-Briand Pact of Paris. On 10 October French ambassador Paul Claudel called on Stimson to discuss the pact and found a surprisingly warm reception. In an aide-mémoire of the conversation, Stimson asserted that what Claudel proposed "presented just the line of thought which I had been following, particularly the suggestion of the extension of the Pacific Treaty of the four powers to other parts of the world."[11] What the French had in mind was extending to the Mediterranean the four-power Pacific treaty established at the 1922 Washington Naval Conference, whereby Great Britain, Japan, France, and the United States agreed to meet in consultation in the event of conflict in Asia. The 1922 agreement was an American coup because it supplanted the 1901 Anglo-Japanese alliance with a four-power agreement to respect each other's territorial possessions and to meet in conference in the event of controversy between them and "an agreement for consultation in event a non-signatory should threaten the rights" of any of the four powers.[12] The French wanted to apply the same treaty obligations to the Mediterranean, where they felt threatened by the nationalistic aspirations of fascist Italy.

In what was a significant departure from the actions of his predecessor, Stimson agreed with Claudel that "in the Kellogg-Briand pact, unlike the League of Nations, we had no sanction except the public opinion of the world," and he agreed that the extension of the provisions of the Pacific treaty to other parts of the world was warranted.[13] Evidently surprised, Claudel asked "whether [Stimson] thought that such a treaty would not meet opposition in the Senate." Stimson replied that he "could not go so far as to say that [it would not], but [he added that] it would be less likely to meet opposition than any other treaty because the MacDonald visit had stimulated great interest" among the American public. Not surprisingly, Claudel asked Stimson to "give him an aide-mémoire" of their conversation.[14]

Claudel's dismay at Stimson's accommodating attitude likely stemmed from the strikingly different tone he had heard in Hoover's speech earlier in October, when the president announced America's intention to participate in the upcoming naval conference. In his speech, Hoover pointed out that although his administration was seeking "the promotion of world peace" through naval limitations, he made it clear that the United States "will never consent to become entangled in European diplomacy."[15] Evidently, Hoover did not realize that his new secretary of state, Henry Stimson, was a closet internationalist and that Stimson would seek during his tenure in office to strengthen America's participation in international security schemes. In 1935 journalist Drew Pearson, in his study *The American Diplomatic Game*, would assert that Stimson had approached his office with the belief that America should "be weaned from the Harding–Coolidge policy of 'power without responsibility' and finally take its seat among the council of nations."[16] It seems surprising that Hoover could have selected as secretary of state a man who opposed the very policy that he had helped shape as secretary of commerce in the Harding and Coolidge administrations.

In addition to Stimson, Hoover was responsible for approving three more internationalists to positions where they could subvert his vision of America's place in the world. At Felix Frankfurter's suggestion Joe Cotton was sought out for the post of undersecretary of state to Stimson.[17] Although Stimson was surprised that Cotton would take the position, Cotton, as Rublee explained, "had become very rich" on Wall Street in the 1920s, "had lost interest in the practice of law and was wanting to find some other interesting occupation."[18] In addition to Cotton and Stimson, Hoover also decided to reappoint Dwight Morrow as ambassador to Mexico and selected Morrow as a delegate to the London Naval Conference in November 1929. Morrow was chosen because of his notoriety as an expert negotiator and because of his influence in European circles. The internationalist cadre was complete when Rublee was appointed as one of two civilian advisers to the U.S. delegation traveling to the London Naval Conference. It is profoundly curious how Herbert Hoover could approve these three men, who bitterly opposed his methods and leadership during the 1918 armistice period, to positions of influence in the development of U.S. foreign policy in 1930. Whatever the reason for his decision to send Morrow and Rublee to London, if he ever learned the extent to which they worked against him, he would likely have opportunity to regret their appointment.

Likely at Hoover's direction, the promising exchanges between Stimson and Claudel and other American and French officials on the subject of strengthening the Pact of Paris came to an abrupt end in December. On 27 December the French leveled an attack on the upcoming conference, stating that, as the Pact of Paris was an insufficient basis on which to disarm, the London conference could be considered only a non-binding prelude to a general disarmament conference under league auspices. The French stipulated, however, that the establishment of a Mediterranean Pact along the lines of the 1922 four-power Pacific treaty would provide a basis for some armament reductions. Having spent the past decade trying to lock Britain into a defense of the European status quo as arranged by the Versailles Treaty, the French apparently feared any Anglo-American understanding that did not offer new guarantees of French security. Although Henry Stimson and other State Department officials' were willing to give France some reassurance, evidently on Hoover's insistence the U.S. delegation joined the British in calling the French position an extreme demand, and both governments accepted that it was unlikely that the French would be a signatory to a London treaty. It seems that since the naval race mostly concerned Britain, America, and Japan, French opposition was not viewed as a deterrent to a successful conference.[19] The French would make it their aim in London to disabuse the British and Americans of that view.

Rublee and Morrow arrived in Washington in early December 1929 to join the rest of the delegation in preparation for the upcoming conference. The other delegates were Secretary of State Stimson, Secretary of Navy Charles Francis Adams, Republican senator David Reed, Democratic senator Joseph Robinson, Ambassador Charles Dawes, and Ambassador Hugh Gibson.[20] Rublee was one of five official advisers to the delegation. At an organizational meeting on 11 December, Rublee and Morrow were briefed along with the other delegation members on the major issues that would confront them in London. Reflective of France's marginal position, a thirty-seven-page background study supplied to the delegation made no mention of French security aims, and an introductory memorandum observed only in passing that "France wants result contingent on general disarmament."[21] On 20 December Rublee received a letter from Walter Lippmann in which the journalist complained: "Pretty soon I hope somebody in authority will take the trouble to give editors in a key position some real background on the naval conference."[22] Lippmann pointed out, "At present we are all in the dark and there is growing mass of speculation and rumor coming in here from London, Paris and Tokyo in which it's very easy to lose one's way." Rublee replied that he, too, "knew very little about this business" of naval tonnage and parities when he and Morrow were selected and that he was simply "trying to catch up."[23] The French broadside a week later may have been the first that any of them heard regarding a rupture between the United States, Great Britain, and France. That conflict would soon come to dominate Rublee's and Morrow's work in London. As Rublee later recalled, Hoover did not give "much consideration to France and Italy" because he was solely concerned about an "agreement with Great Britain and Japan." With understatement Rublee observed, "Difficulties with Mr. Hoover's point of view developed after the conference got started."[24]

Although the United States largely resigned itself to the fact that France would likely not be a signatory to the London naval treaty, Stimson assigned Morrow and Rublee to handle the French, perhaps hoping that if they could not get the French on board, they could at least prevent them from sabotaging the conference. Apparently owing to Rublee's long familiarity with editors and journalists, Stimson also appointed him to quietly handle press relations at the conference. Rublee was supposed to maintain contact with influential members of the press corps because, as he recalled, "it was important to have the correct news sent to the United States."[25] Rublee worked especially with Paul Scott

Mowrer of the *Chicago Daily News* and *Foreign Affairs*, William T. Stone of the Foreign Policy Association, and Drew Pearson of the *Baltimore Sun*, later noted for his influential journalism during the Lyndon Johnson administration. Rublee would get along well with liberal members of the press, both American and British. After the conference, for example, Drew Pearson would describe Rublee as "one of those rare characters who can be a successful corporation lawyer and yet retain the liberal leanings of his youth."[26] Rublee's clandestine relationship with these journalists would allow him to shape information coming out of London to suit his and Morrow's purpose at a critical juncture of the conference. Finally, Stimson set Rublee to work on winning support for a provision outlawing the use of submarines against merchant marine and passenger liners.[27]

The American delegation arrived in London on 16 January 1930. The first week was marked by pageantry, dignified speeches, and sumptuous dinners. Although Rublee did not take a room at the Ritz with the rest of the delegation, as an official member he attended all the celebrations. Rublee may, in fact, have preferred not to be in the Ritz to preserve a certain freedom of movement. While various ministers and delegates made speeches and attended banquets, Rublee began to reestablish old relations and form new ones. In the first week he met Philip Baker, a British official "in the Foreign Office" who was "very close to" Ramsay MacDonald. He then interviewed with Morrow the French ambassador Louis Aubert, who was a friend of Monnet, and met with James Salter "to get from him more accurate accounts of the British situation." He also met with Drew Pearson and a journalist from *The New York World*, and "established friendly relations with most the admirals in our party," whom he found "able and interesting men."[28] After ten days George would report to Juliet: "I am making friends slowly but am very much in the background and so far have had but little to do. It is hard to find out just what is going on as I do not attend the meetings of the delegates. I breakfast with Dwight every morning and see a good deal of him during the day. I think I get most of the news from him—at least all he knows—and we are working out certain ideas together."[29] As the conference progressed, however, where Rublee at first seemed far removed from the decision making, he would soon be at the heart of the negotiations, which had by then removed to the shadowy world where he operated. As journalist William Stone pointed out after the conference ended, because the delegations were dealing with "delicate and unresolved difficulties," the "dangerous issues were avoided, or reserved for the intimate contacts to be afforded by the method of private negotiation."[30] Stone further explained: "And for this reason the record of the London Naval Conference is not to be found in the minutes of the plenary sessions, nor in the proceedings of the committee and subcommittees. The historian sifting the documentary residue of the formal sessions will find little to reward him for his search."[31] Stone was prescient. Because the real story—Rublee's intervention—was the stuff of stealth tactics, the naval conference appears dry and has become one of the least remembered events of the interwar period. In their authoritative surveys of diplomatic history, for example, Robert Ferrell and Robert Schulzinger give scant attention to the conference, each offering but a few lines. Ferrell notes that "with the London Naval Conference the question of disarmament virtually ceased to have meaning for European and American diplomacy," and he dismisses the efforts of the entire period in a sentence: "The grand campaign for peace through disarmament, begun in 1921 with much hope and some minor achievement, disappeared in another naval race which terminated in war in 1939-1941."[32] Ferrell also asserted that at the London Naval Conference "[t]here were no political questions on the agenda, such as had figured so prominently in Washington."[33] Political questions if not on the official agenda—nevertheless dominated and threatened the success of the conference and the waning cohesion of the Western democracies.

From the conference's opening on 21 January until the fall of the French government on 17 February, Rublee's and Morrow's principal work was to keep the French delegation in line. This was no easy mission. As Drew Pearson later explained, the two "most ingenious negotiators in France," Andre Tardieu and Aristide Briand, adopted a course that had Tardieu "discussing tonnage and gun calibers," while "Briand's 'cello voice was booming consultation and Mediterranean Pacts." Pearson observed that "the combination was so effective that… MacDonald and Stimson assigned Dwight Morrow to camp on the trail of the Frenchmen while they themselves went ahead" with their promising tonnage negotiations. Pearson pointed out, "Adroit sabotage was the French watchword, and Dwight Morrow, realizing it, divided his time between nursing the French and trying to convince [Stimson of] the danger lurking in the French frame of mind."[34]

Despite a feeling of optimism between the English-speaking countries at the outset of the conference, a series of small squabbles generated by navy leagues in Britain and America ensued, and a tentative agreement was not reached between the United States and Britain until mid-February. When it was at last clear that the Anglo-American agreement was taking a final form, the French, it seems, were finally in a position to demand consideration of their interests. About the time that the British and the Americans were reaching their agreement, Tardieu let it be known that, owing to the development of "pocket-battleships" in Germany and growing tensions with Italy, France was required to build more cruisers than originally planned. Because Italy was demanding parity with France out of nationalistic pride, any new French building would induce the Italians to respond in kind or a least declare their intentions to do so. Owing to Britain's sacrosanct two-power standard requiring Britain to have a navy equal to the next two strongest European navies, the British programs would have to be revised upward, thereby rendering the Anglo-American agreement unworkable. Following strong protests in the British press against the French, news circulated that Tardieu would reduce his demands by 10 percent if a pact were established providing for consultation in the event of war and 20 percent if an agreement was reached by which signatories to the treaty would promise not to supply an aggressor with munitions and supplies in war. The French maneuver evidently aimed at blocking any Anglo-American agreement that did not take into account French security. A few days after the French broadside, the government suffered a vote of no confidence as a protest to British intransigence and fell on 17 February leaving the conference in limbo.[35]

In the wake of the French bombshell, rumors started to emerge in Washington and London, some stating that the conference was soon to collapse, others suggesting that the United States was willing to consider a consultative pact to save the conference. On 3 March Hoover sent Stimson a telegram in which he observed: "[I]t is repeatedly asserted here that you are personally in favor of expanding the Kellogg Pact by a Presidential declaration."[36] Hoover also had heard reports that the "delegation is divided" on the idea of political guarantees and that Senator Robinson definitely "disapproves." Letting Stimson know his feelings on the matter, Hoover asserted, "We do not believe, however, either of these reports," and he attributed them to the "agitation...of the Foreign Policy Association."[37] Hoover asserted that "the entanglement of political guarantees in these negotiations, though they may be indirect, is more dangerous than anything else to the whole American acceptance" of a treaty originating out of the conference. Hoover was certain that the French would use even an agreement to consult "as a tangible justification" to demand U.S. assistance in the event of a crisis involving league sanctions. For that reason, Hoover insisted, Stimson must not be tempted to placate the French.

Following the reorganization of the French government, a slightly revised French delegation returned to London on 6 March and immediately took up the theme of linking naval reductions to security agreements. How exactly Stimson viewed the idea of a consultative pact at this point in the conference is difficult to tell. Based on subsequent events, it seems that he maintained an interest in expanding the Kellogg-Briand Pact but that he abided by Hoover's clear instructions to refrain from entering into any political agreements. On 10 March Stimson let the British and French leadership know that "any blending of a successful naval treaty and the Kellogg pact now would be disastrous to both."[38] Interestingly, because it relates to a divergence in Rublee's and Morrow's thinking, in reporting the substance of a conversation to Hoover, Stimson observed: "Morrow concurs with me in thinking that a consultative pact purely would not help in reducing France's figures, unless the French people would falsely conceive them to imply that we would be willing to protest against an aggressor; and that what France really wants is a security pact of mutual military [aid]."[39] Stimson added that he and Morrow were "convinced, in other words, that American newspapers which have been attacking [Hoover] for not favoring a purely consultative pact" were "wrong in their belief that France would be satisfied with such a pact." It is striking that Morrow took this view as well after his numerous conversations with the French leadership.

Unlike Morrow and Stimson, Rublee was beginning to take the French at their word and was beginning to see how a U.S. commitment merely to consult in the face of a European conflict could save the conference and bring an added measure of stability to Europe. On 1 March, for instance, Rublee explained to Lippmann that a successful conclusion to the conference "depends on what we can do with France when the French Delegation returns."[40] Rublee argued, "A new line of negotiation will have to be taken in order to secure a change in France's program," and he insisted that "something must be given to France." While Rublee did not "want to go into the question of management and tactics now," he admitted that "Dwight has tried hard but we haven't been able to function effectively." Although Rublee believed that "the present outlook is discouraging," he hinted that "the atmosphere might change. One can never tell."

Despite Rublee's hope that the French demands would be accommodated to some degree, the conference began to disintegrate after 11 March when Henry Stimson made a public declaration indicating that the United States would not agree to a political arrangement guaranteeing to consult in the event of a European war.[41] Stimson called together a select group of American journalists, including Drew Pearson, and explained that the idea of America entering a consultative pact was dead. He explained that if the French reduced their naval strength based upon such an agreement, they might feel America owed them a moral debt and might "claim reimbursement in kind in an emergency."[42] To France's further irritation, two days before Stimson's statements to the press, British prime minister Ramsay MacDonald made a public pronouncement indicating that Great Britain would provide no further guarantees to the European status quo. In a letter to Hoover following his press conference, Stimson related that he and MacDonald intended to "proceed with the drafting of a two-power treaty."[43]

Sometime after the French delegation's return to London and the American proclamation that it would not enter any political agreements touching upon European security, Rublee decided upon a high-stakes course to save the conference and bring America closer to an understanding with its former European partners. By mid-March Rublee knew that the conference was collapsing, that the French delegation planned to pull out, and that Hoover was unconcerned about such an outcome. Communicating through Joe Cotton, Hoover let Stimson know that he approved of his standing pat and suggested: "It might be greatly helpful to public opinion here if the information leaked out that what the French want is a Security Pact of mutual military action against an aggressor and that a purely Consultative Pact would not help in reducing her figures. Of course we cannot do that here. The newspaper reporters…writing for the American papers give just the opposite impression."[44] If Stimson thought Rublee would plant such a story on behalf of the Hoover administration, he was mistaken. Instead, Rublee had become the source for those American papers' giving "just the opposite impression." Although Hoover believed that France was selfishly attempting to draw the United States into a defense of the European status quo, during the conference Rublee came to understand that America's withdrawal from Europe after the world war put the European defenders of the Versailles Treaty system in a precarious position owing to America's traditional insistence on neutral trading rights during European wars.

While Rublee later hinted in his oral memoir at the diplomatic gambit he launched at the London Naval Conference, the complete picture takes shape only in the papers and manuscripts of his contemporaries.[45] The best of these sources are the papers of journalist Drew Pearson, one of Rublee's chief oracles in his campaign against the Hoover administration's individualist stance in international relations. In his 1935 *The American Diplomatic Game (*and unpublished portions of his original manuscript), Pearson outlined Rublee's reasoning on a

Anglo-American consultative pact and his role in securing American support for establishing one. According to Pearson, "as the Conference neared its crisis," Rublee, after days of "quiet talks" with "his friends in French and British liberal circles," became "convinced that the only key which could possibly unlock the Conference deadlock was the old and rejected proposal of a consultative pact."[46] Rublee realized that although an American agreement to consult "would not itself appease the French," he argued that it might "induce the British to appease the French." Rublee explained to Pearson:

> The key to the peace machinery of Europe lies in Article XVI of the Covenant of the League of Nations providing for sanctions against an aggressor nation. The most powerful factor in such sanctions would, of course, be a blockade of the recalcitrant nation by the British fleet. But now Britain, in agreeing to grant parity to the United States, has robbed itself of the power to enforce a blockade without risk of serious challenge from a fleet just as powerful as its own. And since the United States traditionally had insisted upon the right of trade with blockaded nations, and since the United States is not bound by the Covenant of the League of Nations, Article XVI of the Covenant is seriously weakened by British unwillingness to enforce it.[47]

Rublee argued that "should the United States agree to consult in case of European war clouds, and should Great Britain know that the United States would at least listen to reason before using her fleet to break a blockade, then in this case, Britain might well consider giving greater security to France under Article XVI."[48] Pearson reported that "Rublee turned this idea over in his mind" and then approached Morrow on the subject. Rublee stipulated that "it being specifically understood...that consultation in time of emergency does not obligate the United States to follow through with armed force," then "consultation is a perfectly praiseworthy principle against which no one can object."[49]

Agreeing that Rublee had recast the old consultative theme in such a way that the American delegation might offer a simple commitment to consult with league representatives in the face of European war, Morrow hurriedly sought out Stimson at his estate outside London on 22 March to convert him before the French delegation pulled out of the conference. Although, according to Pearson, it "took some time to get the idea into Mr. Stimson's cautious cranium," Morrow eventually converted Stimson, who authorized him to return to London and present the idea to the other five delegates.[50] Meanwhile, to disprove Hoover's assertions that the French were aiming only for a military alliance and that a purely consultative agreement was worthless, Rublee secured an eight-page, handwritten statement from French ambassador Aubert to the opposite effect.[51] The document may have been used to help persuade the U.S. delegation that a consultative pact was apropos.

Once in London, Morrow quickly converted the other delegates, apparently including Senator Robinson, and wrote—certainly with Rublee's help—a lengthy cable to Hoover over Stimson's name in which it was announced that the consultative pact might yet be revived.[52] The Morrow cable let Hoover know that Stimson had left the door open to the consultative pact when the secretary had explained to Briand and Tardieu "that there was nothing inherently objectionable to America in a consultative pact...[but] that our objection was to a pact given under circumstances which would make it a quid pro quo for a French reduction in military armament and thus lay the foundation for a future demand for military assistance on the basis of the pact."[53] The cable explained that Tardieu "fully appreciated that we could not give any pact that could possibly be construed to be an implied promise of military assistance." Instead, Tardieu sought an "amplification or clarification of Britain's existing obligations" because he feared that Britain "apparently wishes to back away from the European commitments which she already has made."[54] Hoover was warned that France's effort to "force Britain's participation in European sanctions," while "understandable," was "very alarming to British public opinion and gives us serious anxiety about the future of European politics."[55] Prepping Hoover, the Morrow and Rublee cable explained on Stimson's behalf that the delegation members "feel that in case negotiations are resumed between Great Britain and France a situation may possibly arise in which a promise of some consultation on our part may be appropriate and safe and I lay it before you for your consideration."[56] Clarifying for Hoover the value of such an American statement, they explained: "It might be of moment to both France and Great Britain if they had an assurance that we could be consulted when an emergency arose with respect to our method of exerting our peaceful influence toward maintaining the world's peace."[57] To counter what they expected to be Hoover's objections, Morrow and Rublee asserted that the delegation members "feel that a consultative arrangement of this sort would have to be safeguarded (1) by a separate security pact between France and Great Britain, and (2) by specific clauses which would clearly and expressly deny any promise of [American] military assistance."[58] The letter concluded, "Confirmation of my views as to the effect of France's position...has been gotten as a result of a conference Saturday with our delegation."[59]

Although Stimson was moved enough by the circumstances to allow Morrow and Rublee to draft the cable to Hoover on Sunday, he evidently lacked the courage to have the delegation strike out on its own and instead awaited Hoover's reply. Throughout the day on Monday and Tuesday Stimson held back the delegation as best he could and continued to give Hoover time to answer. On Monday Stimson met with the British and French leadership, following which he let Hoover know by cable that he had explained to them that if "other nations would take care of the question of mutual assistance in such a way as to secure a substantial reduction of armament," he thought America might "consider with an open mind the question of a provision for consultation [providing it contained an] explicit denial of military action."[60] The communiqué was evidently designed as a second request for Hoover's endorsement. Not only did Hoover not give his approval, but to the delegation's irritation (especially to Rublee's and Morrow's) he made no reply at all. Pearson asserts that "Hoover was exceedingly wroth with his delegation" for reviving the consultative pact and that he could not "cool off enough to put his views in the form of a cablegram" before control of the situation passed out of his hands.[61]

Rublee and Morrow did not give Hoover much time to think, partially because they had little time left to save the conference. On Monday, 24 March, as the French delegation began packing to leave, Rublee began leaking information through William Stone and Drew Pearson that the delegation was prepared to offer a consultative pact but that Hoover was holding them back. Rublee may have planted the same information as early as Saturday, when Morrow went to see Stimson. On that day Laura Puffer Morgan, a representative of the National Council for Prevention of War, wired the following from London: "Have learned from authoritative American source that revival consultative pact would enable MacDonald to negotiate reduction French figures[.] Move must come from Hoover who has given delegation no help at once[.] Concentrate on him...conference cannot survive week without concession from United States."[62] In addition to Morgan's telegram stirring up her organization to pressure Hoover, for some reason a secretary in her Washington office forwarded the letter to Secretary of the Interior Ray Wilbur, who then sent it on to the White House. While Laura Morgan's telegram made its way around Washington, Drew Pearson's article under the headline "U.S. Reopens Idea of Joining Political Pact" claimed the front page of the *Baltimore Sun* on Tuesday morning, 25 March.[63] Pearson's article observed that although "it was on definite advice from President Hoover that Stimson [had rejected] even an innocuous consultation pact" on 11 March, nevertheless "the question of American willingness to consult...is now being rediscussed within the American delegation." Appropriately, Pearson pointed out, "Whether the American delegation now reverses [Hoover's position] depends chiefly on its courage and its desire to bring home a five-power treaty."

Owing to such articles and maneuvers, the White House and State Department experienced a deluge of inquiries and protests on Tuesday, 25 March. At the end of the day, Hoover sent two cables to Stimson via Cotton relating his day of affliction and blasting Stimson's lack of control over the situation. The first dispatch referred to the activity of "[p]eace societies" that had that day asserted that "everything would be settled if the President would take action in offering a consultative pact."[64] Hoover complained, "These reports are persistent and, obviously, annoying and the subject is given much space in the press." He concluded by asking, "Are you not able to reassure us as to the position of the delegates? It would be helpful under the circumstances if you could do so."

In the second cable, an hour later, Hoover informed Stimson, "Persons connected with the Foreign Policy Association have received cable advices from E.T. Stone" (evidently William T. Stone) saying "that he learns from important members of your staff that the delegation is dissatisfied, that they receive no constructive support from the President," and that the conference could be saved with an American consultative pact. Owing to Stone's cable, "the Foreign Policy Association [has] proposed to call a general meeting in New York in protest at the action of the President and the Administration." Hoover had managed, however, to put a stop to "this action for the present."

Reflecting the complex web of individuals involved in the unfolding events, Hoover learned of the planned demonstration from internationalist Thomas Lamont only by a stroke of fortune. During a call to Lamont on Tuesday, 25 March, Hoover learned of the Foreign Policy Association's plans and managed to forestall the protest. Although Lamont spoiled the maneuver, he was prudent enough not to let Hoover know that the ploy originated with Rublee. A letter from Lamont to Dwight Morrow on 26 March documents Rublee's central role in inspiring an internationalists' effort to wrench American foreign policy free from the grasp of Hoover's "power without responsibility" approach. It was an effort that Hoover would resent. Lamont reported:

A curious...episode took place yesterday. President Hoover, with whom I have been in occasional contact on the business situation, called me up before breakfast yesterday morning. He and Harry Robinson were at the White House together and explained that they had heard that McDonald's Foreign Policy Association was about to get out another broadside urging the country to root for a Consultative Pact. He said the situation was bettering at London, and he thought it would mess it up to have more publicity about the pact. He asked me if I had any contacts that I could utilize. So I called up McDonald and one or two others and found they were agreed about holding renewed conferences on this subject, having been spurred on to do this by reason of a cable which they had received from their man, E. T. Stone, in London, only Monday. They showed me a copy of the cable which in effect stated that the American Delegation was depressed and felt that they were getting no help at all from Mr. Hoover,—they needed help. Therefore these worthy citizens at this end of the line decided to help them with some further public demonstration. McDonald mentioned that Stone had gotten his dope from George Rublee.[65]

Lamont then convinced the Foreign Policy Association leadership to "hold their horses for the time being." He did so because "the President had been quite emphatic on the matter of a Consultative Pact, feeling that if one were entered into it would mean that France would be able to call our American boys to France to fight for her." Lamont observed, "This view McDonald and his friends did not share." The next day after Lamont learned that "the American Delegation was considering seriously a possible Consultative Pact," he called "Joe Cotton [and] asked him how he reconciled the President's statement to me yesterday and this news statement from London." Cotton replied that "in fact they were a little hard to reconcile." Upon Cotton's asking "what had stirred up the Foreign Policy and other groups over here," Lamont " told him that their observer in London had cabled them the gist of a talk that he claimed to have had with a staff member of the American delegation." Lamont added, "Of course, I didn't mention George's name."[66]

Rublee's effort to rally support in America was evidently necessitated by Stimson's unwillingness to lead the delegation in open revolt against Hoover. Lamont's ill-considered intervention undermined Rublee's gambit and gave Hoover a bit of breathing room to put up a defense. On 25 March, prior to cabling Stimson about Stone's role in the transatlantic putsch, Hoover held a press conference at which he "stated that no consultative pact had been proposed" to the U.S. "by any of the governments represented at the conference" and that he was certain that a consultative pact "would not secure any reduction of tonnage."[67] Rallying, Hoover made it clear in his second cable to Stimson later that day that he was against a consultative pact, and he asserted that "the whole...idea has originated by these New York groups who have been...in some contact with the French delegates [and are] endeavoring to secure its advancement in London through propaganda" in America. Hoover asserted: "It seems to us that outside agencies undertaking to propound ideas to set up activities with other governments are treading on dangerous ground both in the interest of the United States and the work of our delegation in London."[68] In a subsequent cable at 9 P.M., Cotton wrote Stimson saying, "The matter is assuming considerable seriousness over here, and the President is bothered."[69] Cotton added that he was "amazed at the cable advices of which Stone is the source." Unfortunately, Rublee seems to have been unable to communicate his new interpretation of the consultative pact to Cotton.[70]

Although Lamont's intervention had worked against Rublee, the five-hour time difference from Washington to London saved the situation. While Hoover was still drafting his cables to Stimson between 7 and 8 P.M., Rublee's second line of attack came into play and forced Stimson's hand. The second attack was a leak in the British press that Drew Pearson in 1935 called "a 'plant' to force Mr. Stimson into the open."[71] As *The London Herald* (considered the Labor Party's official source) went to press on the night of 25 March, it contained an article that reported that the conference was being saved by the American delegation's decision to back a consultative pact. At about 11 P.M. American journalists pounded on Stimson's door demanding "to know if the report was true."[72] The "plant," as Pearson called it, obviously came from Rublee, who had access to *The London Herald* through, among others, Philip Baker, MacDonald's parliamentary secretary.

Whether or not he put them up to it, Rublee was fortunate that members of the press sought out Stimson immediately. Had they waited until the next day, Stimson might have lost his nerve upon reading Hoover's cables. Instead, the journalists' inquiries forced Stimson into action. Pearson, writing in the *Sun* a few days later, stated: "Undoubtedly had there been no leak that night the American delegation never would have authorized the midnight statement and the move which has now put vitality in the conference might never have been made."[73] Recording the night's events in his diary, Stimson observed that he had learned that

> *The London Herald* was printing a story for the following morning to the effect that the American delegation had changed its position on consultative pacts and as a result of that Briand was coming back from Paris. I at once telephoned the Prime Minister that such a story was on the way and that I should have to make a public statement [immediately] . With the aid of [Arthur] Page and Morrow I drew up our so-called midnight statement which was given to the press that night.[74]

Significantly, Stimson had still not received a reply from Washington when he gave his statement advising the press of America's acceptance with reservations of a consultative pact.

Although in his midnight statement Stimson sought to stress that, in fact, no real change of U.S. policy had occurred, his concluding sentences reflected Rublee's approach to the issue and were a significant departure from previous statements. Stimson explained: "If, however, this demand for security could be satisfied in some other way, then the danger of misunderstanding a consultative pact would be eliminated and in such case the question would be approached from an entirely different standpoint. In such a case the American delegation would consider the matter with an entirely open mind."[75] Despite Stimson's effort to demonstrate continuity in policy and solidarity in the American camp, headlines in the United States would soon join the *Sun* in reading: "Naval Envoys Push Pact Idea despite Hoover's Disapproval."[76] Pearson wrote on 28 March, "What the American delegation did, in effect, was to cut loose from Washington and gamble on its ability to bring home a five-power pact." Pearson added, "This declaration of independence—some people here even call it revolt—...is generally recognized as one of the most daring diplomatic moves Europe has seen in years." In his oral memoir Rublee did not claim responsibility for the story in the *Herald*, observing only that "something got out about" a change of American attitude in London and that "in the middle of the night Mr. Stimson gave out a statement that the United States had agreed to a consultative pact."[77] Rublee pointed out, however, that "if [all] this hadn't been done so very quickly the President might have vetoed it because he didn't want" a consultive pact; "yet it was an absolute condition of any naval agreement at all."

Rublee, however, was aiming at more than just a naval agreement. As Pearson observed in the *Baltimore Sun* on 28 March, the American agreement to consult "in case of war or blockade is the most definite move for cooperation in European affairs since the Senate overthrew Woodrow Wilson's League of Nations."[78] It seems that Rublee saw in the 1930 naval conference an opportunity to replay the events of the armistice period and reverse the course that Hoover had managed to establish for U.S. foreign policy beginning in November 1918. Perhaps it was a feeling that the contest was somewhat personal or a belief that the stakes were of the first order that enabled Rublee to act so audaciously against an American president. To his benefit, so adept was he by age sixty-two at clandestine operations that few ever learned of his daring gambit. One who did know was Pearson, who all but identified Rublee with the *London Herald* "plant" in *The American Diplomatic Game.* Pearson wrote (somewhat erroneously) that Rublee "held no official position at London, but lurked in the shadowy background working long hours of the day and night to help [Morrow] and the cause of disarmament."[79] Pearson noted that "Rublee was variously known in Conference circles as 'Morrow's shadow,' 'the mystery man,' and Dwight Morrow's 'Colonel House.'"

Despite Pearson's 1935 account of the conference, it seems that Hoover never learned that Rublee was the source of his tribulation. In his memoir Hoover blamed the consultative putsch on "our usual New York associations on foreign policies," who launched a "storm of denunciatory propaganda."[80] Ironically, after the conference Hoover wrote to Endicott Peabody to convey the "valuable work done by Mr. George Rublee as an adviser to the American Delegates." Hoover observed that Rublee's "efforts were directed largely toward…problems in relation to submarine activities, and to the actual drafting of the treaty." Hoover concluded by pointing out that Rublee's "wide experiences and abilities were indeed an important contribution to the success of the conference, and I felt you would be glad to know of the part played by the first graduate of Groton School at this historical conference."[81] Hoover's letter must have amused Peabody exceedingly. On 27 March Rublee had written to Peabody informing him that he "had a good deal to do with our Delegation's proposal to consider the entry of the U.S.A. into a consultative pact." He added, "If Washington permits us to do it we may yet succeed in reaching an agreement."[82] Rublee also paid a visit to Peabody in June during which the rector likely learned of the first graduate's exploits.

Like Hoover, Stimson may have never learned the role Rublee played in the affair. Following Hoover's order that he "send for Stone," Stimson did so on 26 March and reported: "I have sent for Stone and castigated him. He is a young man, not a regular correspondent, practically unknown to any of us. He confessed he had no information from any delegate but said the basis of his reports was from some other member of the staff whose name he would not disclose; probably no one of any importance."[83] Although Stimson may have been protecting Rublee, he may have simply been unsuspecting. Stimson's view of the entire ordeal, in fact, remains indiscernible. In his semiautobiographical *On Active Service in Peace and War*, Stimson asserts that American "newspapermen and private citizens" calling for a political agreement durıng the conference were "quite oblivious of the fact that no consultative pact which could be ratified in the American Senate would contain anything of the remotest value to France."[84] Stimson was able to make this assertion because in the end the agreement to consult was not written into the treaty. Although on 26 March Hoover capitulated and accepted the idea of a narrowly defined consultative pact, in the end it did not prove necessary for the U.S. government to make a formal commitment to consult.[85] The verbal agreement to do so had been enough to restart the negotiations and save the conference. In stipulating that the British and French had to reach an agreement on their own before the America delegation would draft with them wording for a consultative pact, the American announcement simply removed the obstacles to negotiation. Within a week the French and British were close to an agreement. On 2 April Stimson reported, "Since last week there has been a change in the entire spirit of the Conference."[86] During a meeting with Stimson the next day, Briand reported on the progress being made with the British and thanked the American delegation for "having given the push that broke the jam between" the two European powers.[87] Pearson, reporting French minister Jacques-Louis Dumesnil's exclamation that "[t]he Americans have changed everything," observed that "immediately the Conference started juggling…the naval puzzle…into something which began to resemble vaguely a five-power naval treaty."[88]

Although in the end France would not agree to sign a naval treaty that locked them in parity with Italy, the French government did agree to back off its former inflated tonnage demands so that the Anglo-American-Japanese figures could be committed to a treaty. The French did sign parts of the treaty and professed an earnest intention to reach an agreement with Italy that would later allow the two Mediterranean powers to become signatories to the London naval treaty. Of the conclusion of the conference, Pearson observed: "The end of the London Naval Conference came very quickly after that. George Rublee, on his own initiative, had been working on the draft of a three-power pact and after the decision to abandon a five-power treaty he quietly produced it."[89] It seems that although Rublee was zealot enough to conduct dangerous maneuvers against Hoover, he was pragmatist enough to have a three power treaty on hand to bring the conference to a swift conclusion.

In the end, the London naval treaty had no fixed provision for a consultative pact. Nevertheless, Hoover had a difficult time getting the Senate to ratify the treaty because news coverage of the conference indicated that some sort of American accommodation of European security interests had taken place, despite the absence of any such statement in the final treaty. Believing that some sort of secret agreement had been reached, throughout much of June the Senate Committee on Foreign Relations sought to obtain documents leading to the drafting of the treaty. Hoover successfully blocked the public disclosure of the "statements, reports, tentative and informal proposals" leading to the treaty and called the Senate into a special session in July to consider the treaty. It was ratified on 22 July.[90] Of the treaty and the diplomatic move that made it possible, Walter Lippmann observed: "To the American delegation must be given the credit for patience in negotiating and for the insight and courage which at the eleventh hour saved the Conference from moral disaster and brought out of it the first complete treaty of naval limitation in the history of the modern world."[91] While Rublee's success was not complete, it was substantial.

Drew Pearson, in a poignant conclusion to the section of his work dealing with the London Naval Conference, wrote that on the return trip to America Morrow spent his days

> with his feet propped on a chair, talking to George Rublee and dictating to his stenographer a personal diary of the [conference]. Perhaps the most important incident in the diary was Rublee's insistence that the United States offer the Conference a consultative pact. One day Henry L. Stimson dropped into Morrow's cabin. He also had been dictating his Conference memoirs. He also considered the Consultative Pact the high light of the Conference. "I've been trying to remember," he remarked, "how it was I happened to propose that Consultative Pact." Mr. Morrow did not reply.[92]

Stimson's usurpation, if it was one, likely would not have bothered Rublee. He had learned early on that the secret to great accomplishments was letting public figures take the credit.

Although Rublee did not achieve his aim of America extending explicit foreign commitments to the preservation of peace in Europe, his efforts did contribute to improved relations between the United States, Britain, and France that would prove important in the coming decade. On a more personal level, after having been pushed aside in London in 1918 by a determined and inflexible mining engineer posing as public philanthropist, Rublee was to some degree able to challenge the chauvinistic policies that Hoover had helped to establish a decade before.

NOTES

1. Ferrell, *American Diplomacy*, 518-522.
2. While the United States did not start any new submarine construction after 1922, it did complete forty-two that had been started before the Washington Conference. Ferrell, *American Diplomacy*, 523; Walter Lippmann, "The London Naval Conference: An American View" *Foreign Affairs* (July 1930), 500-501; and William Stone, "The London Naval Conference" (Foreign Policy Association) *Information Service* (May 28, 1930), 101.
3. Stephen Roskill, *The Period of Anglo-American Antagonism, 1919-1929,* vol. 1 of *Naval Policy Between the Wars* (London: Collins, 1968), 20.
4. Ferrell, *American Diplomacy*, 523.
5. Ibid.
6. Ferrell, *American Diplomacy*, 523; and William Starr Myers, editor, *The State Papers and Other Public Writings of Herbert Hoover* (New York: Doubleday, Doran & Company, 1934), vol. 1, 231.
7. Rublee, "Reminiscences," 232.
8. Lippmann, "The London Naval Conference," 510.
9. Ibid.
10. Ferrell, *American Diplomacy*, 515-516.
11. Henry Stimson, Memorandum of Conversation with Paul Claudel, French Ambassador, 10 October 1930, U.S. Department of State, Record Group 43, International Conferences, Records of the London Naval Conference [hereafter LNC records], file 200/Peace Pact Extension.
12. Ferrell, *American Diplomacy*, 521.
13. Henry Stimson, Memorandum of Conversation with Paul Claudel, 10 October 1930, LNC records, file 200/Peace Pact Extension.
14. Ibid.
15. Myers, *Writings of Herbert Hoover*, vol. 1, 239.
16. Drew Pearson and Constantine Brown, *The American Diplomatic Game* (New York: Doubleday, Doran & Company, 1935), 110, 111.
17. Felix Frankfurter, *Felix Frankfurter Reminiscences* (New York: Reynal and Company, 1960), 218, 223.
18. Rublee, "Reminiscences," 230-231.
19. Raymond O'Connor, *Perilous Equilibrium: The United States and the London Naval Conference of 1930* (New York: Greenwood Press, 1969), 54-56. O'Connor, whose central interest in the naval conference related to tonnage figures and strategies, noted the tentative development of a consultative pact but he does not appear to have understood the role of Rublee and Morrow in the success of that effort. Rublee does not appear in the work at all and Morrow's work is touched upon only in passing. Nevertheless, O'Connor's is the only scholarly study of the 1930 London Naval Conference.

20. It is interesting to note that George Rublee's father and Charles Francis Adams' grandfather worked together nearly sixty years earlier on the *Alabama* claims. While in 1930 the Anglo-American rivalry was not yet at an end, it was growing close.

21. "Memorandum of the First Meeting of Delegates to the London Naval Conference," 11 December 1929, LNC records, decimal file 110.0001/3.

22. Lippmann to GR, 20 December 1929, Yale-Lippmann, box 29, folder 1076.

23. GR to Lippmann, 25 December 1929, Yale-Lippmann, box 29, folder 1076.

24. Rublee, "Reminiscences," 232.

25. Ibid., 242.

26. Pearson and Brown, *American Diplomatic Game*, 157.

27. Rublee, "Reminiscences," 242-243.

28. GR to Juliet Barrett Rublee, 19 January and 28 January 1930, Juliet Rublee Papers, Dartmouth College, Baker Library Special Collections [hereafter JBR-Dartmouth].

29. GR to JBR, 28 January 1930, JBR-Dartmouth.

30. Stone, "The London Naval Conference," 103.

31. Ibid.

32. Ferrell, *American Diplomacy*, 523-524. See also Schulzinger, *American Diplomacy in the Twentieth Century*, 138.

33. Ferrell, *American Diplomacy*, 523.

34. Pearson and Brown, *American Diplomatic Game*, 123, 122.

35. O'Connor, *Perilous Equilibrium*, 72, 73, 89.

36. Joseph Cotton (for Herbert Hoover) to Stimson, 3 March 1930, *FRUS*, 1930, vol. 1, 40. Hoover worked on several drafts of this message. See Herbert Hoover Presidential Papers, Herbert Hoover Presidential Library, [hereafter HHPP] box 999.

37. Ibid.

38. Stimson to Hoover, 10 March 1930, HHPP, box 999 (also in *FRUS*, 1930, vol. 1).

39. Ibid.

40. GR to Lippmann, 1 March 1930, Yale-Lippmann, box 29, 1076.

41. Pearson asserted in *The Baltimore Sun*, 25 March 1930, that "it was the American decision not to enter any form of consultative pact that started the naval conference tobogganing to the abyss."

42. Stimson to Hoover, 12 March 1930, HHPP, box 999 (also in *FRUS*, 1930, vol. 1).

43. Ibid.

44. Telegram 198, Cotton to Stimson, LNC records.

45. Rublee, "Reminiscences," 239-241.

46. Pearson, "Manuscript for The American Diplomatic Game," 52, Drew Pearson Papers, Lyndon B. Johnson Presidential Library [hereafter Pearson Papers], box G 202.

47. Ibid., 52-53; and Pearson and Brown, *American Diplomatic Game*, 157-158.

48. Pearson and Brown, *American Diplomatic Game*, 158.

49. Ibid.

50. Pearson, "Manuscript for The American Diplomatic Game," 54, Pearson Papers, box G 202.

51. Unsigned and undated memorandum in French in the George Rublee correspondence of the Walter Lippmann papers. On the document's cover, Lippmann attached a note reading: "This is a statement of the French case at London Naval Conference, written by M. Aubert, special adviser to M. Tardieu, which belonged to Mr.

George Rublee, adviser of the American delegation and willed by him to me." Yale-Lippmann, box 29, folder 1076.

52. In his manuscript, Pearson identified Morrow as the author of Stimson's 23 March cable to Hoover. See Pearson, "Manuscript for The American Diplomatic Game," 54, Pearson Papers. Morrow is also identified as the author of the cable in Walter Lippmann to Norman Davis, 31 March 1930, Yale-Lippmann, box 7, folder 325.

53. Stimson to Cotton, 23 March 1930, cable 156, HHPP, box 984. This copy contains the original wording that Hoover received. The document in *FRUS,* 1930, 75-79, is paraphrased.

54. Ibid.; and Stimson to Cotton, 23 March 1930, *FRUS*, 1930, 78.

55. Ibid.

56. Stimson to Cotton, 23 March 1930, cable 156, HHPP, box 984.

57. Stimson to Cotton, 23 March 1930, *FRUS*, 1930, 79.

58. Ibid.

59. Ibid.

60. Stimson to Cotton, 25 March 1930, *FRUS*, 1930, 80-81.

61. Pearson, "Manuscript for The American Diplomatic Game," 56, Pearson Papers.

62. Laura Puffer Morgan to National Council for Prevention of War, 22 March 1930, enclosure in Gladys K. Gould Mackenzie to "Dear Friend," 25 March 1930, LNC records. The "Dear Friend" is Ray Wilbur, Secretary of Interior.

63. *Baltimore Sun*, 25 March 1930, in Pearson Papers.

64. Cotton (Hoover) to Stimson, 25 March 1930, *FRUS*, 1930, 81.

65. Thomas Lamont to Morrow, 26 March 1930, DMP.

66. Ibid.

67. "President's draft" of Cotton to Stimson, 25 March 1930, HHPP, box 999. See *FRUS*, 1930, 81-82.

68. Ibid.

69. Cotton to Stimson, 25 March 1930, number 260, *FRUS*, 1930, 83.

70. This is curious because Cotton's son, Joseph Cotton, Jr., was acting as Rublee's personal assistant in London. See GR to JBR, 19 January 1930, JBR-Dartmouth.

71. Pearson, "Manuscript for The American Diplomatic Game," 56, Pearson Papers.

72. Ibid.

73. *Baltimore Sun*, 28 March 1930.

74. Stimson Diary, 25 March 1930, reel 3, vol. 14, 24.

75. Statement contained in Stimson to Cotton, 26 March 1930, *FRUS,* 1930, 83.

76. *Baltimore Sun*, 28 March 1930, Pearson Papers.

77. Rublee, "Reminiscences," 240.

78. *Baltimore Sun*, 28 March 1930, Pearson Papers.

79. Pearson and Brown, *American Diplomatic Game*, 157. In his manuscript, Pearson included the title, "power behind the Crown Prince." This might have suggested that journalists thought that Morrow would (or should) be the next president, that is defeating Hoover in 1932.

80. Hoover, *The Memoirs of Herbert Hoover* (New York: Macmillan Company, 1952), 348.

81. Herbert Hoover to EP, 3 November 1930, GSA.

82. GR to Peabody, 27 March 1930, GSA.

83. Stimson to Cotton, 26 March 1930, telegram 163, LNC records. This portion of the telegraph was deleted in *FRUS,* 1930.

84. Henry Stimson and McGeorge Bundy, *On Active Service in Peace and War* (New York: Harper & Brothers, 1948), 170.

85. Cotton to Stimson, 26 March 1930, *FRUS 1930*, 85.

86. Stimson to Cotton, 2 April 1930, *FRUS,* 1930, 100.

87. Stimson to Cotton, 3 April 1930, *FRUS,* 1930, 101.

88. Pearson and Brown, *American Diplomatic Game*, 162.

89. Ibid., 169.

90. United States Senate, *Proceedings of Committee on Foreign Relations* (Washington, D.C.: Government Printing Office, 1930), 163-168; and Myers, *Writings of Herbert Hoover*, 357, 359. On the day the Senate passed the treaty Lippmann, wrote to Rublee observing that, from what he could tell, "nobody in the Senate really understood what actually went on in London" (Lippmann to GR, 22 July 1930, Yale-Lippmann). Quite interestingly, there are a number of documents from the conference that are missing in the official collection at the National Archives, II. For example, perhaps fifteen documents read like the following: "250.01 France-Great Bit./11. Filed in the safe in Mr. Salmon's room. April 15, 1930." The archivists at College Park have so far been unable to locate those documents and have expressed little hope of finding them. These documents, if found, might explain exactly what Stimson agreed to in London with regard to a consultative pact.

91. Lippmann, "The London Naval Conference," 518.

92. Ibid., 171.

11

The "Detached, Friendly Sage" (1930–1938)

While George Rublee had been forced off the world stage during much of the 1920s, throughout the 1930s he would be tapped for special assignments in international affairs as he was increasingly recognized as a wise man of foreign policy and a gifted technician in international finance. Yet while the decade began with much hope that he, Morrow, Cotton, and their internationalist cadre might yet reengage the United States on behalf of international peace and stability, by 1939 all hope of such a realignment had evaporated. What remained for Rublee was to seek international conciliation wherever he could bring his influence to bear and to continue to be an example to a younger generation of internationalists who might one day be in a position to set U.S. foreign policy.

Rublee returned to the United States with Dwight Morrow in April 1930 and was immediately asked to serve his good friend in a new capacity, as campaign adviser for Morrow's 1930 run for the U.S. Senate. In December 1929 New Jersey governor Morgan Larson appointed Morrow to complete the term of Walter Evans Edge, who had been named ambassador to France and whose term expired in 1930. In May 1930, coming off his great successes in Mexico and at the London Naval Conference, Morrow was prepared to move on to Washington and decided to stand for election. Rublee was interested in Morrow's campaign and, in fact, had helped convince Morrow to pursue the Senate seat.[1] During the early summer of 1930 Rublee moved into the Morrows' residence in Englewood and became Morrow's principal adviser during the primary.

The most significant aspect of Morrow's campaign was his call for a repeal of Prohibition. Rublee and Morrow were both against Prohibition on a federal level and believed that each state should be allowed to determine its own alcohol policy. Morrow and Rublee were assisted in crafting a Prohibition position by Walter Lippmann and Dean Acheson. In February 1930 Lippmann had written to Rublee in London to suggest that he induce Morrow to take a firm stance on Prohibition in the coming election. Lippmann believed "that the New Jersey primary will attract national attention and will become a national test of the wet-dry issue."[2] Rublee had recognized the importance of Prohibition in national politics since the 1928 presidential election and was likewise anxious for Morrow to take a stand. Toward the end of May Rublee and Dean Acheson helped Morrow draft a speech calling for a change in Prohibition laws.[3] Rublee later recalled that Morrow's speech "had country-wide circulation and influence."[4] Rublee believed that, as a Republican, "[i]t was a daring thing to do and it didn't please President Hoover." Hoover was, in fact, displeased with Morrow's speech and evidently expected more support from Morrow, having reappointed him as ambassador and having made him a delegate to the London Naval Conference. As a noted friend of Hoover's observed in a *New York Times* editorial, Morrow "virtually restates the Al Smith formula of 1928—a strange position for an administration Republican to take."[5] Rublee, Morrow, and Lippmann were correct in sensing that the nation's attitude toward Prohibition was fast changing with the deepening economic recession. Morrow's position evidently resonated with voters. As George reported to Juliet on 18 June, "We gained an overwhelming victory yesterday in the primary election," taking "about 70% of all the votes cast."[6] He pointed out, "This success makes [Morrow] about the most conspicuous man in the country. He is the rising star. People are thinking of him as a future president." Rublee believed that "his election as senator next Fall is I think assured and he will enter the Senate with a very great amount of prestige."

Throughout the summer Rublee continued to work with Morrow on the Prohibition issue. On 24 June Morrow sent for Rublee "to help him decide what should go into the platform in which he is to run in the fall."[7] For the next two months Rublee continued to consult with Lippmann and Acheson to lay out Morrow's approach. To help frame a definite plan, Lippmann related the essence of a number of schemes that had been proposed in Washington. The documents that Lippmann forwarded called for a rewording of the Eighteenth Amendment so as to authorize a federal role in local enforcement only if a state requested assistance. Lippmann liked this approach because it established a political formula that "recognizes the political principle of home rule, and the principle of federal assistance where states desire it," thereby leaving the state free not to pursue enforcement.[8] Rublee agreed in principle with Lippmann's proposals, but as he explained, "I don't think I want to leave the present 18th amendment operative anywhere." Rublee attended the New Jersey Republican Convention with Morrow and took as strong a stance against Prohibition as possible.

As Rublee surmised, Morrow easily won election to the U.S. Senate in November 1930, a victory that put him one step closer to the White House. It had been clear to Morrow's friends for a number of years that his popularity was moving him toward the presidency. As Walter Lippmann had reported in October 1928, Morrow was the leading candidate among notable New Yorkers. In his letter to Morrow, Lippmann observed:

> Incidentally, it might interest you to know that I was at a dinner on Monday night to Lady Astor, at which there were about twenty-five people, including, Tom Lamont, ...Well's of Harper's, Ruth Morgan, Oswald Villard, etc. Miss Morgan took a poll at the table in

which each person was asked to name not the person he was going to vote for, but the candidate he would have liked to have voted for. Smith got one vote; Hoover got one vote; George Norris got one vote; Hughes got one vote; Franklin Roosevelt got one vote; and you got, so far as I could count, fifteen votes.[9]

In addition to Morrow's friends and supporters, Herbert Hoover was evidently well aware that Morrow might mount a challenge in 1932 and kept a watch on the ambassador's blossoming career. Hoover likely knew that Morrow was a contender at the 1928 Republican Convention even without making a serious effort. As one article in Hoover's file on Morrow pointed out: "It may not be generally known that many Republican leaders wondered whether Morrow might not be a shining choice should the Kansas City convention fail to nominate Herbert Hoover."[10] Hoover's friends helped him monitor Morrow's political viability, sending him various news clippings and reports, including one lengthy study criticizing Morrow's work in Mexico. These clippings were likely not enjoyable for Hoover to read. Part of one article, for instance, asserted: "Here Morrow stands in marked contrast to the ineptitude of President Hoover. All in all, [Morrow] seems the great white hope of those who would like to see presidential timber which combines enlightenment, candor, competence and adroitness."[11] Another article dated 5 June 1930 reported that Morrow was no longer denying an interest in the White House. The article pointed out that Morrow's recent willingness to let such assertions stand might "infer rivalry between himself and President Hoover in 1932."[12] In March 1930 a Hoover disciple forwarded a circular letter authored by the "Morrow for President in 1932 Club." A scrap of paper accompanying the letter asserted: "Christ had his Judas, and Hoover has his Morrow."[13] It is clear that the Herbert Hoover and his friends considered Morrow a threat to his presidency.

Although Morrow did take the Senate seat without difficulty, beginning in the summer of 1930 his fortune began to turn, so that Hoover was never confronted with a Morrow challenge. His first setbacks in a series of them were significant because, as Drew Pearson pointed out, Morrow's "chances of reaching the White House, for which his friends are quietly grooming him, depend upon his present reputation as a super-diplomat."[14] Ironically, the trouble for Morrow began in Mexico, where his dazzling successes had given rise to great political fame. Morrow's distress, however, was not of his own making but rather of an assistant, Alexander McNab, who at a political event in New Jersey in April 1930 asserted that Morrow deserved all the credit for the success in Mexico and that the Mexican government was essentially made up of amateurs who relied on Morrow for guidance. As Rublee recalled, in his speech McNab, who had been Morrow's military attaché, indicated that "the Mexican officials were puppets in Morrow's hand" and "that the whole success of the reforms and everything that had been accomplished there" was due to Morrow alone.[15] Rublee called it "a very unwise, disastrous speech," and a State Department official called it "a diplomatic blunder of the first order."[16]

The enormity of McNab's misstep unfolded during July and August. Once Morrow's political enemies managed to get a copy of the speech, it soon found its way into New York and Mexico City newspapers.[17] Included in McNab's praise for Morrow was his assertion that "[t]here is no department of government in Mexico which [Morrow] has not advised or directed" and that Morrow had been obliged to take the "Finance Minister [Montes de Oca] under his wing" to teach him finance.[18] McNab also asserted that the religious crisis in Mexico came to an end "when Morrow finished writing letters to Morrow."[19] While there was substantial truth to what McNab said, these assertions led to an intense outburst of anger in Mexico. The embassy staff soon let Morrow and the U.S. State Department know that Calles and Oca were highly irritated and were calling for Morrow to make a statement denying McNab's assertions.[20] Although Calles was no longer president, he remained essentially in control of politics in Mexico, having hand picked his successor, Pascual Ortiz Rubio. Even more exposed was finance minister Montes de Oca, who still held office and came under a barrage of criticism and demands for his resignation.[21] Morrow did make a statement praising Calles and Oca and denying any improper influence in domestic political issues, but the statement did little to assuage the growing indignation of Mexicans. As one embassy official pointed out, anti-American feeling in Mexico "is always lurking under the surface and it does not require much to bring it into sight."[22] The official correctly warned that Morrow "will find himself very much handicapped in trying to accomplish much during his all to[o] short two months down here."

McNab's blunder proved a travesty for Morrow because it rendered impossible the successful conclusion of the international Mexican debt settlement that Morrow had been working toward since he arrived in Mexico in 1927. After years of work Morrow had at last convinced Mexico's European and American bondholders to accept a settlement to end Mexico's fifteen-year bankruptcy. The conference that was to be held in New York in August to ratify the debt agreement was scuttled because of the intervention of Thomas Lamont, who was able to take advantage of Morrow's diplomatic stumble in Mexico. As Ron Chernow points out in his *The House of Morgan*, a "heated feud" had developed between Morrow and Lamont over the proposed Mexican foreign debt settlement.[23] Lamont, who represented a great number of American and European bondholders, had agreed to join the general settlement only after much pressure from Morrow. Lamont evidently wanted out of the settlement following the October 1929 crash but could not see a way to withdraw with the U.S. State Department backing Morrow's settlement scheme. Taking advantage of Morrow's sudden weakness, however, on 25 July Lamont pulled his bonds out of the general settlement and reached a separate agreement with de Oca. This maneuver rendered Morrow's New York conference meaningless, thereby confounding his one remaining reform effort to stabilize Mexico. Upon learning of Lamont's sabotage Morrow quickly traveled to Mexico in an effort to stop the agreement between Lamont and de Oca. Although Morrow did block Lamont's program in the Mexican congress, according to Rublee, "[w]ith Monte de Oca's vanity so deeply hurt by McNab's speech," it was impossible for Morrow to salvage the situation.[24] Morrow was exceptionally deflated by the failure of his debt program. Sliding into deep despair, Morrow called for Rublee to join him in

Mexico. Writing to Juliet from Mexico on 26 August, George reported that Morrow suffered "a mental condition brought on by disappointment over the settlement made by Lamont and Montes de Oca in New York."[25] Rublee explained that prior to his arrival Morrow had been "on the verge of a nervous breakdown" and that the embassy staff were "anxious for me to come, as they thought I would have a better influence on him than anybody else could have." Rublee remained with Morrow until September 1930, when Morrow departed Mexico to prepare to take his seat in the U.S. Senate.

While Herbert Hoover may have been anxious about the political machinations of Senator Dwight Morrow, he had little to complain about the New Jersey senator once he arrived in Washington. Upon taking his seat, Morrow became the perfect administration senator, casting every vote with his Republican colleagues except on matters relating to Prohibition. Morrow's performance in the Senate during the first year of his term was disappointing to liberals, who had looked forward to Morrow's presence in Washington. Drew Pearson, for instance, wrote a lengthy criticism of Morrow which began by stating: "Dwight Whitney Morrow spent a life-time getting a reputation as a great liberal only to spend three months in the Senate blasting it."[26] Pearson complained that "in a session in which the issue between liberalism and conservatism was more clear-cut and harder fought than ever before in recent years, Dwight Whitney Morrow never on a single, solitary occasion failed to vote with the reactionaries."[27] In seeking an explanation for Morrow's waning liberalism, Pearson considered the absence of Rublee a critical element. Describing Rublee's influence on Morrow, Pearson observed that since 1918 "Rublee has been one of Morrow's most constant advisors and is responsible for many of the moves which have increased the latter's reputation as a great liberal." Pearson pointed out that before Morrow traveled to Mexico, Rublee had assisted him in a study of Mexico "by conducting long conferences with people of all walks of life—from labor leaders, to bankers, so that before Morrow arrived at this new post he knew more about the Mexican Government than the career diplomats of the State Department who had been there for years."[28] Pearson also noted Rublee's importance in the success of the London Naval Conference, explaining: "Constantly at [Morrow's] right hand during the London Conference was his old friend George Rublee. Rublee it was who drafted the treaty outlawing submarine warfare, and who drafted the preliminary text of the naval treaty long before any of the other delegates had thought about its necessity. Rublee it was also who sold Morrow the idea which Morrow later sold to Stimson that a consultative pact was absolutely essential."[29] Given Rublee's importance to Morrow's successes, Pearson concluded that the absence of Rublee, who had gone onto other international work for the State Department, was a factor explaining why Morrow "has fallen so flat."

Although Pearson believed that Rublee's influence was an important aspect of Morrow's liberalism, biographer Harold Nicolson notes that Morrow was simply ill equipped to function in the U.S. Senate. Nicolson found that "[t]he cynical superficiality of Parliamentary work filled him with a profound depression," and he points to a letter from Morrow to Reuben Clark in which the freshman senator complained: "I find the work in the Senate somewhat puzzling to me. It is very hard for one who has never had any legislative experience to be required to cast several votes a day on subjects which he feels he has not a chance to study, and as to which debates throw very little light."[30] Nicolson pointed out that, in the absence of expert knowledge, "During those initial months [Morrow] recorded his vote almost automatically according to party convention." Morrow was evidently not concerned that he at first was forced to act "artificial and unreal" since he had six years to build "a more solid and authentic" reputation. Time, however, was not on Morrow's side. On 5 October 1931, as his first year in the Senate neared conclusion, Dwight Morrow suffered a cerebral hemorrhage in his sleep and died that day. Morrow's death was a tragic blow for Rublee, who evidently believed that a Morrow presidency, with himself acting as an adviser, might help stabilize international relations and the reeling world economic system. In his oral memoir, Rublee observed that Morrow's death "was a very great loss to me and changed my general future plans."[31] Herbert Hoover, on the other hand, must have sighed a breath of relief.

As Drew Pearson observed, "All during Morrow's first session in the Senate, George Rublee, the reliable" was nowhere in sight. Having proved himself such a valuable adviser to Dwight Morrow, in the summer of 1930 Rublee began a steady stream of work as an expert on international legal and financial affairs. Although Rublee might have expected the work to serve as qualification for future cabinet-level work in a Morrow administration, it instead allowed him to become an independent adviser and troubleshooter for the U.S. State Department through 1942. This notable work began in the summer of 1930, when Rublee learned that the State Department had recommended him to act as an adviser to the president-elect of Colombia, who was facing the same sort of difficulties with U.S. oil companies that Calles had faced in Mexico. While negotiations for this work moved slowly forward, Rublee received a call from International Paper asking that he assist them in trouble that they were having with the Treasury Department in Washington. In late July 1930 Assistant Secretary of the Treasury Seymour Lowman announced an embargo against Russian pulpwood because he had received allegations that Russian pulpwood was being produced by convict labor. According to recent tariff legislation, the Treasury Department was authorized to embargo all products made in whole or in part by conscripted laborers. Such legislation had the backing of the American Federation of Labor and many large businesses that were suffering from the growing international economic collapse. In addition to economic concerns, the Treasury Department argued that the embargo was a defensive act of war in the struggle against communism. As Lowman argued: "Russia, having failed to conquer the world by propaganda, now seeks to achieve the goal of a world-wide Bolshevik state through a program of economic ruin."[32] According to the editors of *The New Republic*, however, the embargo of Russian imports and the legislation that allowed it "were not prompted by an inexplicable fear that somehow the Communists were about to overturn our government and corrupt our citizens" but rather "to act as protective coloration for an extension of the protective-tariff policy."[33]

George Rublee became involved in the Russian embargo issue when International Paper asked him to use his influence in Washington to get the embargo lifted. Attempting to undermine Canadian control of the supply of pulpwood, in 1929 International Paper had turned to Russia as its new chief supplier. When the embargo was announced, the company had six ships in U.S. ports and eleven others in transit. The company quickly contacted Rublee and other noted international lawyers, including Paul Cravath, who had worked with Rublee on the AMTC. Writing to Walter Lippmann on 1 August, Rublee explained his call to Washington to represent International Paper. Rublee reported, "I think we have succeeded in getting the Treasury Dep't to lift the embargo but we had to go outside to do it."[34] By going "outside," Rublee likely meant that he used his influence in the State Department with Stimson and Cotton to bring pressure on Hoover to force Treasury to rescind the embargo. According to *Time* magazine, representatives of International Paper "hustled to Washington" and "fairly swept Mr. Lowman off his feet with categorical denials that any of Russia's 1929 pulpwood had been produced by convict labor."[35] Being outmaneuvered in the cabinet, Treasury officials soon had to substantiate their claims against Russia. A few days later Lowman announced that the department had "gone off half-cocked" and that the evidence brought against Russia was, in fact, "conflicting and inconclusive…and not sufficient to establish the fact that the pulpwood was produced by prison labor."[36] In his letter to Lippmann, Rublee observed, "This story about this Russian embargo is a queer one. It is hard to believe that such things can happen in a grown up government."[37]

Although the abortive embargo on Russian pulpwood seemed somewhat comical to Rublee, the International Paper incident demonstrated that by 1930 Rublee's influence in Washington was substantial and increasing. Through his relations with Cotton and Reuben Clark in the State Department, Brandeis on the Supreme Court, a number of U.S. senators, and various relations through his law firm, Rublee was in a position to produce results, and his friends increasingly believed that he should be given a post in the State Department equal to his capacity. In the spring of 1931, eight months before Morrow's death, both Morrow and Felix Frankfurter attempted to get Stimson to tap Rublee for meaningful diplomatic work. Frankfurter seems to have started a personal letter writing campaign to get other notables to speak to Stimson. Among others, Frankfurter wrote to Lippmann asking that he speak to Stimson about Rublee's "qualifications for major problems of foreign relations."[38] While Morrow also believed that Rublee would be a "tremendous addition to the State Department," he was somewhat concerned that Rublee might not "work together happily" with Stimson.[39] Evidently, Rublee had kept himself so much in the background in London that Stimson, according to Morrow, "does not know George very well" and continued to believe that Rublee was "somewhat impractical." Attempting to disabuse Stimson of his assessment, Morrow "told him that George was not only a scholarly man but a very wise man, and had an unusual capacity for sensing the key-log that was holding up the jam." Nevertheless, as Morrow explained to Lippmann, "George's method of approaching problems is so very different from

Mr. Stimson's that in my opinion he would not want to tie himself down to a regular position." Instead, Morrow believed that Rublee could be "tremendously useful in the next two years in occasional jobs" dealing with Latin American problems.[40] While Morrow likely would have tapped Rublee as secretary or undersecretary of state in his own administration, Rublee instead would carry out only "occasional jobs" throughout the rest of his career. Rather than himself, his younger protégé Dean Acheson would become a noted secretary of state.

Rublee's first work for the State Department came to him in October 1930, when he traveled to Bogotá, Colombia, to serve as an adviser to newly elected president Enrique Olaya. Olaya had been ambassador to the United States for a number of years and committed his administration to restoring an amiable relationship with the United States, after twenty-five years of resentment following Theodore Roosevelt's virtual seizure of Panama. When Olaya took office, the Colombia government was in a dispute with U.S. oil companies that bore strong similarity to the U.S.–Mexican controversy. In 1926 the Colombian government canceled a generous concession granted by former leader General Barco, the so-called Barco concession, and in 1929 the Colombian congress began drafting new oil legislation that would force U.S. oil companies to reapply for titles on a basis that was more advantageous to Colombia. Although there was substantial distrust of U.S. oil companies in Colombia, as the global economic crisis began to spread, there was a general desire to come to an agreement with U.S. companies so that Colombia could receive an injection of U.S. foreign investment similar to what Venezuela was enjoying. President Olaya was committed to such a reconciliation and began working with the U.S. State Department early in 1930 to facilitate a better relationship between Colombia and U.S. oil companies. The new tone set by Stimson and Cotton in their evenhanded approach to the U.S.–Mexican crisis evidently earned them Olaya's trust. In May 1930 Olaya asked the U.S. State Department to name an American "who is in the confidence of the Department" and who can offer him "competent and disinterested advice."[41] Not surprisingly, Cotton turned to Rublee, who had his absolute confidence. In communicating its recommendation to Rublee that he act as Olaya's adviser, the department explained that Olaya asked for someone

> who would act somewhat more or less as a buffer between the oil companies and the Colombian Government; somebody who, the companies will know, if he tells them that they are too exacting in their demands or asking something which the country obviously can not give them, that his opinion will be respected by the Department, and that [the oil companies] will have to accept his decision because they will not get support from the Department over his head.[42]

That the Colombian government could even expect this kind of support from the U.S. Department of State was a clear indication that Morrow, Cotton, and Stimson had overcome the old interventionist attitude and had laid the foundation for the much lauded Good Neighbor Policy. Hoover's acceptance later in 1930 of Reuben Clark's 236-page legal opinion arguing that the

Roosevelt Corollary to the Monroe Doctrine was groundless and incorrect marks the official beginning of the Good Neighbor Policy, which some incorrectly associate only with Franklin Roosevelt's administration. However, Walter Lippmann asserted in 1943 that Morrow's Mexico mission actually established the policy. In a letter to Betty Morrow, Lippmann maintained: "I am very much concerned to have the historical fact established that Dwight was responsible for the reversal of policy which then became the Good Neighbor Policy."[43] Whether or not Lippmann actively worked to establish that historical fact is unclear.

Rublee met Olaya for dinner at the Savoy Hotel in New York on 24 June to discuss the issues confronting Colombia. Olaya was impressed with Rublee and wanted to hire him, but he was somewhat daunted at the request for $25,000 for a four-month assignment. While Rublee had been able to work nearly for free for Morrow for three years, he had lost what fortune he had left in the October 1929 stock market crash, and Juliet had lost her wealth making a film in Mexico that failed at the box office.[44] Given his new imperative to gain an income, Rublee was hoping to find more work with his firm, Covington, Burling, and Rublee, which negotiated his fee with the Colombian government. Olaya wanted Rublee but felt that "twenty-five thousand dollars and expenses…was a lot of money to spend now" and attempted to get Rublee to come for two months "for a lesser amount."[45] Rublee and his partners rejected that offer, and nearly two months passed before Olaya sent for him. Olaya's request came on 22 September, when he requested the U.S. minister, Jefferson Caffery, to "telegraph urgently to the Department of State asking George Rublee to come here at once."[46] Olaya thought it was urgent for Rublee to arrive because a bill had been introduced in a congressional committee, and Olaya wanted Rublee to come to Bogotá to act as an arbitrator between the government and U.S. oil companies on the final form that the bill would take. Acting strategically, according to Caffery, Olaya had arranged for the petroleum bill to be "presented to Congress before Mr. Rublee's arrival in order to avoid the charge that an American lawyer wrote it."[47] Although Rublee was apprehensive about acting as an expert on oil negotiations, he agreed to take on the work and sailed for Colombia on 14 October, the earliest date possible. Perhaps on Rublee's initiative, Drew Pearson wrote an article noting Rublee's appointment. Pearson explained that Rublee's contract with Colombia "practically" makes him "arbitrator between the American companies and the Colombian Government."[48] Noting the positive change in U.S.–Latin American relations, Pearson wrote: "Such an appointment by which a Latin-American nation virtually puts the fate of its oil resources in the hands of an American, is considered significant, since Colombia, which, ever since Theodore Roosevelt boasted of having looped Panama from Colombian soil, has harbored open and bitter resentment against the United States."[49] Pearson also noted that Rublee had already "won the confidence of Latin Americans" by "helping Mr. Morrow bring about an adjustment of the Mexican controversy which satisfied both the Mexican government and the State Department."

Although Rublee was pleased to have work that was both lucrative and exciting, he was apprehensive about the assignment because of his lack of technical expertise on the oil industry. Communicating his acceptance of the appointment, which would allow them "to live through next year," he complained to Juliet that he was "setting off ignorant, unprepared and unequipped" for the assignment.[50] Rublee was evidently able to disguise his anxiety, which at first was rather acute and led to an episode of self-doubt and depression. His lengthy journey to Bogotá allowed his nervousness to take hold so much so that he arrived in "a confusing, bewildering" frame of mind.[51] Twenty years later, when he recorded his oral memoir, Rublee still remembered feeling "rather startled when I realized what I had let myself in for because I was going to advise a government in regard to matters I knew nothing about, I went down there alone, I knew nothing about oil and the whole thing was new to me."[52] While Rublee was rather anxious about his unpreparedness for the assignment, he soon steadied himself and allowed those around him to think him an expert until he truly was one. An embassy dinner on his behalf shortly after his arrival and the enthusiasm of the Colombians, "most of all the President," helped him recover from strong feelings of "discouragement."[53] Rublee understood that the impression he made "on these people was important to my success."[54] For instance, writing to Learned Hand about his accommodations in the Hotel Granada, he explained, "It is expensive and for my prestige I occupy a larger suite than I require."[55]

Once Rublee arrived, he took up the first of his tasks, of advising the government on the form that the new petroleum bill was taking in Congress. The bill stripped foreign oil companies of their old concession titles and required them to apply for new ones that would have higher royalty rates for the Colombian government. Under some pressure to come up to speed because of his daily meetings with President Olaya, Rublee poured over voluminous materials relating to oil. As he complained to Learned Hand two months after his arrival, "I have nothing in my thoughts but oil...If the climate were warmer I believe I would sweat oil."[56] Rublee relied extensively on the U.S. minister, Caffery, for advice regarding the political situation and to identify the essential issues of contention between the oil companies and the government. He also worked closely with the president's advisers, Carlos Urueta and Luis Latorre, and with H. A. Metzger, representative of Standard Oil's regional Tropical Oil. Owing to the Tropical Oil Company's willingness to accept the government's new terms, it had the only existing concession in Colombia and was allowed to influence the oil bill as it was being formed in committee. Interestingly, Olaya evidently had more confidence in Caffery and Metzger than his own minister of industries, Dr. Chaux, who was unaware of the role that these Americans were playing in the drafting of the oil legislation.[57]

Rublee also overcame his lack of expertise in oil by relying on the experts surrounding him, regularly asking for memorandums that provided him with the essence of the issues to be resolved. Caffery reported to the U.S. State Department on 6 November, a week after his arrival, that "Metzger and Latorre have prepared for [Rublee], at his request, a number of memoranda on various articles of the bill."[58] Caffery also noted, "Yesterday he received visits from the representatives of all the American oil companies interested in the bill; requested them to state their objections to the bill; and asked them to furnish him with memoranda on all matters in that connection they considered important."[59] Relating his first month of work to Learned Hand, Rublee explained that he was pouring "over documents in Spanish relating to the last ten years of futile effort to pass a satisfactory oil law" and that he had sought out "people who I think can enlighten me."[60] Although Rublee did rely on American oil representatives for information, he was evidently wary of their reports and did not allow dubious assertions to stand. Caffery, for instance, reported how Rublee dealt with an American oil representative who was dissatisfied with Rublee's approval of the Colombian position that "in the case of disputed titles, all claimants shall submit their titles to the Supreme Court."[61] Replying to the oilman's objection, Rublee observed that "as he remembered it, when the United States took over Florida in 1819, all claimants to private property were compelled to exhibit their titles." Therefore, Rublee "could not advise the Colombian government to accept the principle that a mere two-year possession put the possessor in a privileged position."[62]

On digesting the various materials that he had received, Rublee soon identified where his skill as expert negotiator needed to be applied. It would be his responsibility to bring the parties together on a system of Colombian reserves, the procedure by which American oil companies would reapply for titles, and to reach a settlement on production levels, the government wanting production guarantees while the oil companies wanted to avoid compulsory production. In working out an equitable arrangement between the Colombian government and U.S. oil companies, Rublee faced a challenge in earning both sides' trust. Although the oil companies tended to believe that he was too liberal owing to his work in Mexico, he was also hampered with Latin Americans owing to his identity as a Washington and Wall Street lawyer.[63] Rublee understood that in order to succeed, it was critical for both parties, especially the Colombians, to believe that he was a disinterested arbitrator. Fortunately, along with an ability to make recommendations that brought vying parties together, Rublee had a real talent for gaining the trust of others in individual negotiations. Not surprisingly, as early as 6 November Caffery was able to report that "Mr. Rublee has made an excellent impression here: the Colombians he has met find him 'simpatico.'"[64] Rublee also gained the trust of Tropical Oil representative Metzger and other oil representatives so that within five weeks he was able to smooth the way to an accommodation between the two sides. Rublee gained both sides' confidence by understanding what each faced. In regard to the production question, for instance, Rublee believed that while "the Government is entitled to have an article put in the bill protecting them against sudden and precipitous loss of revenue through the companies suddenly suspending operations," he also recognized that "the companies should not be compelled to operate at full speed when the market does not justify it."[65]

Writing to Learned Hand on 15 December in what he called a "rather shamefully egotistic" letter, Rublee reported his success in Colombia and the method leading to his success. He began by stating: "I have good news to report. The President, the Council of Ministers and the Interparliamentary Committee...have all accepted and approved all of my recommendations."[66]

Rublee admitted, "I don't myself quite understand how it happened. Perhaps it was a case of worming in. I had four main conferences and at each one I got on a little further than I had before until at the end I got everything." Nevertheless, the seven-week effort was challenging, Rublee explained, because of the "concentration of mind and purpose" that had been required of him in "keeping the right mood of the uninsistent, detached, friendly sage in dealing with the different personalities."[67]

As usual, Rublee was careful not to let matters drift after he worked out a deal between the oil companies and government. As the bill came before the petroleum committee, he worked to smooth its way because "some of its members had been antagonistic in the past."[68] Rublee later recalled that he had to "use judgement in dealing indirectly with the Colombian Congress."[69] Writing to Hand at the time, Rublee explained that "a little quiet work in an unobserved quarter" helped him overcome the opposition of conservatives on the committee.[70] Rublee had found that the "chief difference between the parties is in regard to their attitude towards the Church. The conservatives are pro-Church." Rublee soon "learned that the Jesuit Father Sarasola had much political influence with the conservatives." Given the priest's influence, Rublee sought to win him over. In his letter to Hand, he explained his interesting experience converting the priest:

> [Sarasola] is interested in science, particularly meteorology and the perfection of the radio. He lives in a great room on the top of the Jesuit College of San Bartolome filled with scientific instruments, a telescope or two etc. It has the tranquil atmosphere of delightful studies and is the pleasantest spot I have found in Bogota. Well, I got acquainted with Father Sarasola and used to go to him and discuss the oil law. I told him my ideas and the reasons for them, why certain provisions in the pending measure were bad for the country, and why the changes I wanted to make would be good for the country.[71]

Once Rublee convinced him of the benefits of his recommendations, Sarasola became "sympathetic and wanted to help." The powerful priest soon "described who might make trouble" in Congress and, "[l]ittle by little he got well pepped up and well provided with material" that Rublee provided. Evidently hoping to make Sarasola feel a stake in the bill, Rublee allowed him to read his "reports to the President and the Minister of Industries." Once converted, Sarasola "did some good work with members of the parliamentary Committee," and Rublee believed he would "continue to help when the bill is before the Congress."

Rublee spent the first few weeks of January watching the bill as it was subjected to three readings in the Senate. Writing to Hand on 16 January, he noted that he was in "the very ecstacy and whirlwind of this experience."[72] Always energized by legislative struggles, Rublee was soon fully engaged, making adjustments to the bill as needed and attempting to ward off opposition. As Rublee explained to Hand: "I have to watch them closely, and once or twice, when they began to mess things up, I have had to get up a new formula to attain the same end, and they have swallowed the new formula though they gagged at the former one."[73] To Caffery's delight, he was able to report that the bill passed the Senate "as recommended by Rublee" on 28 January and passed the House on 23 February, despite meeting "considerable opposition" in mid-February.[74]

Although Rublee spent substantial time watching over the oil bill in Congress throughout January, he was also called upon to take up his second task, which was to arrange a settlement between Colombia and Gulf Oil's South American Oil Company over the disputed Barco concession near the Venezuelan border. While Standard Oil's representative, Metzger, had been willing to work with Rublee, Gulf Oil's Clarence Folsom at first tried to sabotage Rublee's role in the negotiation by suggesting that Rublee secretly represented the American-Maracaibo Oil Company.[75] Folsom's claims were quickly disproved, however, and on 15 January he began negotiations with Rublee, who had received the support of the U.S. State Department and Colombian government on the matter.[76] Despite earlier problems, Rublee and Folsom soon negotiated all issues relative to the Barco concession except for a final agreement on the royalty rate. While Standard Oil would agree to pay only 5.5 percent, Rublee was informed by minister of industries Chaux that Congress would not accept less than 6 percent. What followed for Rublee was a drawn-out negotiation to bridge the .5 percent difference and to prevent Chaux from adding additional requests each time Gulf Oil made a concession. Using his influence with both the State Department and Olaya, Rublee at last produced a final agreement, which was signed on 27 February with Gulf Oil agreeing to a number of concessions, including a 6 percent royalty. Letting Hand know of his final success in Colombia, on 4 March Rublee wrote: "The representatives of the Gulf Co. were most effusive in their thanks for my action in the Barco matter. They told me that they never could have put it through without me. The President and the Minister of Industry also thanked me. They seemed to be of the same opinion as the Gulf people."[77] On 5 March Secretary Stimson wired Caffery to offer his "[h]eartiest congratulations to you and Rublee!"[78]

Having completed his work in Colombia, Rublee passed back over the Andes and down to the Pacific Ocean where he boarded a steamer bound for America. Although very satisfied with his success in Colombia, Rublee returned home without definite work awaiting him and with a very heavy heart over the loss of a close friend. Early in 1931 Joe Cotton had learned that he had a tumor on his spinal cord and had undergone surgery to remove it. Although the tumor was successfully removed, Cotton developed blood poisoning and languished for a month. Learning of Cotton's illness in Colombia, Rublee acknowledged to Hand that he "was deeply distressed about him and think of him constantly."[79] To the distress of his many friends Cotton's rising influence and leadership as a public official came to a tragic end on 10 March when he died at Johns Hopkins in Baltimore. Although his friends were devastated at their fifty-six-year-old friend's death, Stimson was anxious from a professional point of view since Cotton had been useful to him in dealing with Herbert Hoover. At Cotton's funeral Stimson exclaimed to a friend: "You can't realize what a loss to the country Joe's death is. He is the only man who could do anything with the President."[80] For Rublee, the loss was a tragedy. In his memoir twenty years later

Rublee characterized Cotton as a "very wonderful man" and described his death "as a great loss."[81] Coupled with Morrow's death five months later, Rublee quickly lost "the two ablest men that I ever dealt with."

As Rublee traveled back to the United States heavy-hearted over the loss of Cotton and somewhat anxious about his future work, he was surprised one day to learn on a news bulletin board a statement asserting that it was expected that he would soon be named to replace Cotton as undersecretary of state. By the time he reached Washington, however, the situation had changed. When he returned, he learned that although "it had been the desire of Mr. Stimson to appoint me as Under Secretary," Senator Reed of Pennsylvania had intervened and succeeded in demanding that William Castle, who was then assistant secretary, be named to the position.[82] Stimson instead offered Rublee another post in the department, which he declined. Rublee later explained that he "could not have accepted either appointment" because he had lost his fortune and "could not afford to go into the public service" in a full-time capacity.[83]

Declining the position at the State Department, Rublee returned to his Washington firm, where he marked time. As the international economy slipped further into the abyss in the summer of 1931, Rublee soon had new work with the Colombian government, which was suddenly on the verge of bankruptcy when foreign lending precipitously came to an end. Beginning in March, Olaya had been confronted with a serious financial crisis when New York's National City Bank withheld an expected $4 million credit. Olaya complained to the State Department and asked that it exert pressure on City Bank to follow through with the loan. Informing Stimson of Olaya's position, Caffery reported, "The President holds that he has based his entire political program on cooperation and friendship with us, but now, in view of the action of the bankers, his confidence in American businessmen seems to be a bit shaken."[84] Owing to Olaya's unprecedented cooperation with American business interests, which he sold to Colombians with promises of large U.S. foreign investment, the State Department felt some obligation to assist him and did exert some pressure on the New York bankers to work with him. After lengthy negotiations and major cuts in the Colombian budget as directed by City Bank, Colombia received its final $4 million installment at the end of June 1931.[85] Hoping now to secure long-term financing at lower interest rates, Olaya was surprised when U.S. banks suddenly ceased foreign lending owing to the deepening recession.

Needing a representative in the United States with influence in financial markets, Olaya called upon Rublee, who operated both on Wall Street and in Washington. Before accepting the position, however, Rublee consulted Morrow, evidently to make sure that such work would not jeopardize Rublee's viability in a future Morrow administration.[86] Morrow cleared Rublee for the work a month before his untimely death, and Rublee soon set about the difficult task of finding financing for Colombia. Owing to the deepening world economic and financial crisis, however, Rublee could find no banks willing to take on the marketing of Colombia's foreign debt. Rublee began to make some headway with the Federal Reserve Bank, but it, too, proved ultimately unwilling to act as Colombia's banker. Paying a visit to Louis Brandeis in October, Rublee asserted that New

York bankers had told him that "no foreign govt could get a loan now—not even Holland."[87] Rublee announced his failure to Olaya in early October and learned that Olaya was threatening to suspend payments on his current indebtedness in the absence of an immediate $12 million loan. Evidently taken by surprise, Rublee let Stimson know of this situation on 2 October and asked if "any political developments have occurred to account for the latest move of President Olaya." The State Department, in turn, let Rublee know of the bitter negotiations between Olaya and National City Bank earlier in the year and of Olaya's belief that he had been betrayed. Rublee also learned that Olaya was baffled that the State Department could not simply insist that the Federal Reserve Bank or some other institution grant Colombia a loan after all that he had done for American interests. Attempting to calm Olaya, Stimson cabled explaining that the American response was "not a question of letting him down but of world conditions over which the Department has no control."[88] Stimson suggested that Olaya "continue to work through Rublee in New York to take advantage of any possible favorable turn, to keep cool, and not to take impulsive measures in a moment of despair which may seriously and adversely affect Colombia's future credit standing."[89] While Olaya did cool down and maintain at least interest payments on Colombia's foreign debt, Rublee was unable to secure a loan, and Olaya suffered some political fallout. Downcast by Morrow's and Cotton's deaths and his own now bleak political future, Rublee described the period of acting as Colombia's financial representative as "a winter of futile and depressing negotiations."[90] In the spring he terminated his representation of Colombia, having had no success.

Rublee, now sixty-three, was in a difficult and somewhat sadly ironic situation. While at age thirty-two Rublee had managed to largely retire from active work, with his wealth in stocks now worthless he was forced to reenter the workforce. In the fall of 1932 Rublee was in the unfortunate position of turning down a "judicial appointment" in New Hampshire owing to his need to produce a substantial income to support Juliet's and his somewhat grand lifestyle. Writing to Robert Bass, he explained that he would have liked to accept the position offered by Governor John Winant but could not "do with $7000 a year and retirement without pension at 70 if I live that long."[91] Nevertheless, Rublee confessed that he would have liked "the serenity of a steady and honorable job at my time of life."

Although Rublee's public work seemed to be grinding to a halt after having been revived with much optimism four years earlier with Morrow's call to join him in Mexico, in September 1932 a dramatic event in Colombia led to another flurry of activity and gave Rublee the opportunity to again practice diplomacy on a high level. The event that drew Rublee back into the international arena began as a bit of nationalistic turf warfare in an isolated town in the Amazon jungle but soon came to have serious implications for the postwar treaty system. On 1 September 1932, several hundred Peruvian nationalists seized the Colombian Amazon port town of Leticia, which had been part of Peru until a 1922 treaty transferred the municipality and its hinterland to Colombia. Shortly after learning of the takeover, Peruvian president Sanchez Cerro instructed his officials to communicate to the Colombian government that he had no prior warning of the act and that he did not support it. Calling for calm, Cerro asked that Colombia not react with hostility so that the situation might not escalate.[92]

In a world where nationalistic aspirations increasingly influenced domestic politics, Colombian president Olaya felt rather uneasy about making no effort to reestablish sovereignty over Leticia as Cerro had requested. Not fully trusting Cerro, Olaya decided to call upon the U.S. government to act as referee. On 9 September Olaya requested that the U.S. State Department speak to Peru about its apparent violation of the 1922 treaty. The State Department, however, had very little hope of influencing the Peruvian government, which was quickly becoming antagonistic. As the U.S. ambassador to Peru reported, "At the very first mention of our friendly hope [for a peaceful solution] the President became stubborn, defiant and uncommunicative" and "insisted that the matter was purely domestic."[93] Whether or not Cerro, was in fact, secretly behind the seizure of Leticia is unclear, but he soon backed away from his initial diplomatic communique that disavowed the seizure, and instead argued that the 1922 treaty transferring Leticia to Colombia was a deplorable mistake and must be rescinded. As Peru's foreign minister explained to the U.S. ambassador two weeks after the seizure, the Leticia "incident was like Fiume," and therefore the "withdrawal of Peruvians from Leticia could not be thought of."[94] Given their support for the sentiment behind the seizure, Peru could therefore not stand by in the event that Colombia attempted to reestablish control over the province. Having invoked the comparison to fascist Italy's seizure of Fiume, Peru evidently expected the United States to understand that feelings of irredentism superseded any legal document in the eyes of the Peruvian public. Like Colombia, however, the United States could not agree with that perspective, and Stimson reminded the Peruvian foreign minister that "[h]owever unpopular the Salomon-Lozano treaty may have been, it is a fact that it was ratified by both countries and has been in force for some years."[95] Stimson pointed out that if the Peruvian argument was accepted, it would "make all international treaties and agreements absolutely valueless." Trying to convince the Peruvians to adopt a peaceful course, Stimson cautioned, "The present is a time of great unrest and disquiet throughout the world and it is to the interest of all Governments to try to maintain order and stability not only internally but in their foreign relations as well." Stimson warned, "To start reopening these questions now by the use of force can only lead to chaos."[96]

Olaya hoped that Stimson's forthright appeal for a peaceful resolution would be heeded, but the Peruvian government refused to speak out against the illegal seizure. With pressure mounting for him to move against the Peruvian-backed aggression, Olaya began to prepare to send a flotilla of gunships on a lengthy journey up the Amazon River, even while he continued his diplomatic efforts to avoid what would be a costly confrontation. As it became clear to Olaya that he might soon be at war with Peru, the Colombian president contacted George Rublee in New York, who he believed would be helpful in working with the U.S. State Department. Rublee once again agreed to accept the representation of Colombia, and he immediately moved into action. Olaya's well-placed trust in Rublee was such that he made the American lawyer his proxy ambassador to the United States As Rublee later explained, "I was the real representative of Colombia in this country because the Minister of Colombia, Dr. Don Fabio Lozano, had instruction from Olaya to consult me and follow my advice in whatever he did. I was really dealing with the State Department....and then communicating through the Minister with Olaya in Colombia."[97]

Traveling to Washington to discuss the situation with State Department officials, Rublee soon learned that Secretary Stimson did not wish to see the United States act as the hemisphere's policeman by intervening in a dispute between two Latin American countries. Having recently rescinded the Roosevelt Corollary to the Monroe Doctrine, Stimson instead wished to see Colombia and Peru work out their impasse through a Pan-American committee of conciliation. As Stimson explained to the Peruvian ambassador, "We are willing to do what we can to assist in a friendly manner to keep this question within proper bounds, but we have no responsibility to act as sole guardian of the peace of Latin America nor do we desire to assume such responsibility."[98] Although Stimson hoped that Brazil might take the lead in procuring a settlement, Rublee believed that it was a dangerous precedent to allow Peru to effectively seize territory by force, and he wanted to see stronger U.S. and world criticism leveled against Peru's action. Given his understanding of the importance of world public opinion in such contests, Rublee evidently advised the Colombians to quickly organize a public relations campaign. As Rublee later recalled, "The first thing that it occurred to me to do was to try to establish the rightful claim of Colombia to Leticia."[99] While Peru attempted to present its own case in response to the Colombian initiative, its effort proved weak and ineffective. As one early historian of this affair notes, "Both countries tried to defend their respective positions in the eyes of world opinion by long series of newspaper statements and articles. Colombia seemed more adept and more successful in this sort of propaganda."[100] Although one might wonder if Rublee felt some misgiving over the use of high-stakes tactics to see Colombia win this dispute over a small town in one of the remotest sections of the Amazon, it is evident that he quickly understood that the incident had much wider importance. Since Colombia and Peru were both members of the League of Nations and signatories of the Kellogg-Briand Anti-War Pact, he realized that the Leticia incident offered an important test to the postwar international security system, which rested on legal compacts. The unabated Japanese invasion of Manchuria beginning in 1931 likely heightened Rublee's awareness of the opportunity that existed in this Latin American controversy.

A difficulty facing Rublee was that the case against Peru as an aggressor required some argument because the Peruvian government maintained that it was not involved in the initial seizure of the province, which may or may not have been true. For an expert opinion on the matter Rublee turned to John Bassett Moore, who, according to Rublee, had a "world-wide reputation" as America's "most distinguished international lawyer."[101] Rublee met with Moore at his vacation home on Long Island and presented the case to him. Rublee was especially interested in knowing whether or not Moore believed that, assuming the facts were correct, Peru's actions were "a violation of the Kellogg-Briand Pact." Although Moore agreed that Peru's actions could be deemed a violation of the antiwar pact in its threat to prevent Colombia from restoring its control over the province, he nevertheless "refused to get directly mixed up in it." Instead, Moore suggested that if Rublee would write him a letter asking his opinion, he would respond to him with his views. As Rublee recalled, Moore "wouldn't address it to the Colombian government but he'd write the letter to me." Once the letters had been exchanged, Rublee forwarded the correspondence to Olaya, who "was very much pleased" to have it. Olaya used Moore's letter "throughout Latin America and the world in general" to gain support.[102]

The legal case that Rublee helped put together against Peru was critical to Colombia's success in the matter. By January Colombia was able to publish—likely at Rublee's direction—a collection of opinions that showed the legitimacy of its cause and condemned Peru for violation of the Paris antiwar pact and the League of Nations Covenant, both of which Peru had signed. The eminent jurists who contributed to the collection included the noted Chilean Alejandro Alvarez, a founder of the American Institute of International Law; Francisco de la Barra, former president of Mexico; Raymond Poincare of France; Luis Anderson of Costa Rica; Eugene Borel of Switzerland; and Lester Hood Wolsey of the United States. Historian Robert McNicoll called the publication "an element of immeasurable importance in the formation of opinion favorable to Colombia."[103] McNicoll also noted that while Peru did "muster some authorities on its side," it "did not display quite the systematic zeal of Colombia in organizing propaganda in its favor."[104] Historian Orazio Ciccarelli, although he writes sympathetically of Peru's position in the contest, likewise pointed out that "[w]hile the contest for international diplomatic support was being won by Colombia, Peru's isolation was augmented by its rather tactless handling of foreign affairs."[105]

Although Rublee's efforts won overwhelming international public support for Colombia, he was still having difficulty winning the diplomatic contest owing to Stimson's continued reluctance to officially declare Peru in violation of the Kellogg pact despite the chorus of international jurists whom Rublee had enlisted. From October to December Olaya had agreed to withhold military action in hopes that a Brazilian conciliation effort would result in Peru voluntarily backing down. Having allowed Brazil and the United States months to bring Peru to the table, public outcry in Colombia was such that Olaya feared that he would be overthrown if he did not act to restore Colombia's legitimate control over Leticia. Bowing to public pressure in early January 1933, Olaya released the gunship flotilla that he had been holding some distance from Leticia so that it began its final, month long approach to the province.

With time running out, Rublee attempted a final gambit to win Stimson over to a declaration against Peru. While Stimson had privately admitted to Rublee that Peru "probably had…violated the Kellogg Pact," the secretary was hesitant because he "had no absolute evidence that they had."[106] Stimson was likely reluctant to invoke the Pact of Paris because he would be the first leader to do so and likely was apprehensive of the scrutiny he would come under. Stimson may also have been reluctant to take such weighty steps since it would bind the incoming Roosevelt administration to a course of action when it assumed control in March. Since Stimson would not move without clear evidence, Rublee devised a way to procure it. Having studied the diplomatic style of the Peruvian government for some months, Rublee believed that he "could get an admission from the Peruvian government that they had violated the Kellogg Pact," which they had thus far denied. Perhaps recalling lessons from his early readings on the diplomatic feats of Otto von Bismarck, Rublee crafted a lengthy letter to be delivered to Cerro, which he hoped would lead the Peruvian president into a subtle diplomatic blunder. Describing his efforts on behalf of Colombia, Rublee explained:

> There had been communications back and forth between the two governments which I, of course, had kept in touch with and had advised about. I proposed sending a note as a part of this international communication between the two countries which would state facts which, if true, would show that Peru had committed acts that were an infringement of the Kellogg Pact. I drew up quite a long note..., submitted it to Mr. Stimson [and] then cabled it to Olaya and asked him to send it without changing a word in it to the Peruvian government, which he did. They did just what we expected them to do. They said, "Sure, we did this, but we had a perfect right to do it."[107]

Rublee's note went to Cerro's government on 11 January, and the Peruvian reply, which admitted the action but disputed its meaning, was received in Bogotá on 14 January. In its response the Peruvian government admitted that the 1922 boundary was duly ratified and legally binding and admitted moving its military into the region to support the rebels who had seized the town in the name of Peru. The government argued, however, that it was justified in taking this step "in view of the motive of reintegration of the national territory that impelled them."[108] Because they were acting out of nationalistic sympathies, these patriots, Peru maintained, "could not be abandoned to the menacing uncertainty established...by [the] sending of Colombian military authorities [who have] the mission of subduing them."

Peru's ill-considered reply in light of international law was exactly what Rublee had hoped for. For the next week he worked with the Colombian government to set out a strategy to invoke international compacts against Peru's admitted aggression. On 23 January the Colombian minister in Washington delivered a copy of the diplomatic exchange and a statement to Stimson that asserted that Peru was in violation of the Kellogg-Briand Pact. In the statement, without doubt written by Rublee, the Colombian government argued that the Peruvian diplomatic note of 14 January had "re-affirmed the Peruvian Government's recognition of the validity of the Boundary Treaty of 1922, but insisted on the modification of the frontier established by that treaty so as to correct what it asserted was a grave injustice committed in separating Leticia from Peru."[109] Through Rublee's carefully chosen words the Colombian government asserted, "This note evinces the purpose of Peru to compel the revision of the Treaty by the use of military force and thus to use such force as an instrument of national policy." The note concluded by explicitly asking that

Stimson "call the Peruvian Government's attention to its obligations under the General Pact for the Renunciation of War, ...to [in fact] renounce war as an instrument of national policy and to urge [Peru to] not violate that Treaty."[110] This precise request for action is likely what Stimson requested of Rublee so that he might be compelled to act under mechanisms in the Kellogg-Briand Pact and thereby be cleared of any appearance of favoritism toward Colombia. While Rublee's strategy to compel a Peruvian withdrawal evidently envisioned a similar official complaint before the League of Nations, Peru beat Colombia to the punch in asking the league to intervene by advising the Colombian government to hold back its armed flotilla. Owing to this request, the two principal elements of the postwar security system were simultaneously invoked in an international dispute. It was a unique event in the history of the interwar period, and yet it remains generally ignored by historians of U.S. foreign relations.

After twelve years of Republican administrations' trying to distance the United States from international political compacts, Stimson soon found himself calling the ambassadors of Britain, France, Italy, Germany, and Japan to his Washington residence, where he announced that Colombia had invoked the Pact of Paris against Peru and that the United States intended to support Colombia in that effort. A memoir of the meeting describes the ironic moment when the U.S. secretary of state asked the major world powers to join the United States in invoking international law in the name of world peace and security. The document observes that, in siding with the Colombia position, "The Secretary said he thought it would be very unfortunate if the first time one of the Pact signatories invokes the support of the other signatories to prevent a violation thereof the call should go unheeded. The French and British Ambassadors said that they agreed and the German and Italian Ambassadors assented. The Japanese Ambassador made no comment throughout the meeting."[111] Within two weeks the British, French, Italian, and German governments joined the United States and almost all of Latin America in reminding Peru of its obligations as a signatory to the Kellogg-Briand Pact of Paris.[112] While this combined diplomatic effort invigorated internationalists and peace advocates, in the history of the interwar period it was a unique event that, although remarkable, did not portend a period of increasing cooperation through the application of the rule of law to international affairs.

While Rublee's gambit did succeed in leading the United States to launch the only constructive use of the Pact of Paris in the interwar period, it did not prevent war from breaking out between the two countries. On 14 February Peruvian military officials near Leticia launched an air assault on the Colombian flotilla while it was still in Brazilian waters. Although the war was not averted, it was short in duration and isolated because of Rublee's diplomatic strategy. Peru soon sustained a "barrage of diplomatic condemnations" and "world condemnation" for its action, and the League of Nations issued a report on 16 March calling for a "complete evacuation by the Peruvian forces" from Leticia and the "withdrawal of all support from the Peruvians who have occupied that area."[113] Interestingly, the new U.S. secretary of state, Cordell Hull, was hesitant about working too closely with the League of Nations to end the armed conflict. While he did send an observer to Geneva, his fears were confirmed when that observer pointed out that the league members "are anxious to establish a precedent based on the case of Leticia, which can be invoked in considering the much more serious Manchurian matter or future eventualities elsewhere."[114] Although the league hoped to bring Peru to heel with the arms embargo, thereby setting an important precedent, the Roosevelt administration, according to Bryce Wood, "did not favor the application of an arms or other embargo" on Peru because there was no U.S. legislation that could support it.[115] Had Hull, however, checked documents in a certain wall safe in the State Department, he might have found a 1930 document signed by Henry L. Stimson that stated that the United States was willing to consult with the European powers in the event of a league-sanctioned embargo.[116] Such a document may have paved the way for at least tacit U.S. approval of a precedent-setting league embargo.

Although the league missed its opportunity to utilize its powers of coercion, the Leticia dispute came to an end shortly after the assassination of Cerro at the end of April. By the end of May, the league, with the support of the U.S. State Department, had induced the new Peruvian president, Oscar Benavides, to accept a plan whereby Leticia would be handed over to a three-member league commission during what amounted to a yearlong armistice. In May 1934 Peru and Colombia signed the Protocol of Peace, Friendship, and Cooperation, which reestablished ties between the two countries. The document included a statement in its first article that read: "Peru sincerely deplores...the events which have taken place since September 1, 1932, which have disturbed her relations with Colombia."[117] The agreement confirmed the legitimacy of Colombia's position from the beginning, but the lengthy negotiation leading to it allowed Peru to rehabilitate its international image. The energetic support and wise strategies leading to this end earned George Rublee the gratitude of Colombia for some time.

While Rublee was in the midst of his effort to invoke the Pact of Paris and the league covenant against Peru's seizure of Leticia, new work came his way when he was asked if he would allow his name to be put forth as a possible arbitrator in a labor dispute in the U.S. anthracite coal industry. The coal operators informed Rublee that his would be one of three names that they would present to the labor union, which would select one of the three as representative for the management. To his "considerable surprise," the coal union selected him to represent the operators opposite Frank Morrison, then secretary of the American Federation of Labor, whom the operators had chosen from the union's list of candidates.[118] The union likely selected Rublee because of his friendly relations with labor leaders and his notoriety as an impartial mediator.

The dispute in which Rublee found himself stemmed from the growing economic depression, which, among other things, had greatly depressed the demand for coal. The coal industry also suffered from increasing competition with natural gas, which further undermined the price of coal. Since the miners were employed on a pre-1929 wage contract, the price of coal was fairly inelastic. The mine owners wanted the coal union to agree to a wage reduction so that demand might be stimulated through price reduction. As Rublee later explained, “The operators believed that if the miners would be willing to accept some reduction in wages, the price of coal could be reduced sufficiently to increase the demand so that mines which otherwise would be closed could be kept opened and some that had been closed could be reopened—so that more miners could be employed.”[119] The operators assured the miners that “all of the savings…would be applied to the reduction in the price of coal.” Despite such assurances, the miners’ union rejected the proposition but was forced to agree to an official arbitration because of the terms of the contract. The advantage, however, yet remained with the union because the contract called for two, rather than three, arbitrators. If these two did not agree, then there would be no change in the contract.

Since Rublee had little knowledge of the economics of the coal industry, “there was a considerable period of preparation” during which he “studied the matter very carefully” with the help of an expert whom he employed.[120] Upon studying the matter, Rublee agreed that the wage reduction might prove a benefit to the miners as a group and made a report to that effect. Having reached an opinion, Rublee joined Morrison and a number of technical experts and officials representing each party in Washington for the arbitration hearing. The miners’ representatives included labor leaders John Lewis, Philip Murray, and John Kennedy. According to Rublee, while the operators’ side relied on “a large mass of statistics,” the labor side, although it provided some data, relied more on passionate oratory. Not surprisingly, Rublee thought the operators “had much the best argument,” and he spent a considerable amount of time after the hearing going over the testimony with Morrison in an attempt to convince the labor leader of the soundness of the operators’ position.[121] Rublee recalled, however, that Morrison “didn’t yield in any way and it finally became apparent that there was no possibility of an agreement.” In the absence of an agreement between them the contract remained “unchanged.”[122] Although Rublee could not convince Morrison to accept his reasoned position during the negotiation, after the arbitration Rublee was surprised when Morrison “spoke very pleasantly to me and complimented me on my presentation of my side of the case.” Rublee was further surprised when Morrison admitted that “it was a pity that he couldn’t have agreed but he said, ‘It just wasn’t in the cards.’” Rublee, who thought that the negotiation had been in good faith, soon understood that “[w]hat he meant was that it was the rule of the union never to retreat from any past gain in the wage structure without regard to the effect upon the workers at the time.” This approach frustrated Rublee, who pointed out that “after we failed to reach an agreement, the result was the continued rapid closing of the mines and more and more men thrown out of work” and the eruption of serious labor strife in the industry. While Rublee admitted that he could not “say how successful our proposed remedy would have been, “ he believed that “it seemed well worth trying,” adding: “If it had been successful it would certainly have been in the interest of the mine workers.” Rublee criticized union leader John Lewis, who he believed was “determined to remain in control of the union and had a fanatical belief in maintaining the cause.” Rublee allowed that “[w]hether his own position and his own selfish interests were uppermost, or whether he was thinking most about the miners and their good, I really can't say."[123]

Although the election of Franklin D. Roosevelt in 1932 signaled the end of public work for a number of Republicans, Rublee's independent political orientation and noted liberalism made him a candidate for continued work in Washington. It appears that Rublee came to have influence in the Roosevelt administration early on, evidently in part through his friendship with Ray Stevens, of whom Roosevelt thought well. While Stevens had been acting as an adviser to the king of Siam (Thailand) for several years, he maintained an interest in domestic U.S. policy, especially with regard to antitrust measures and the tariff. Writing to Learned Hand in October 1933, Rublee reported his excitement that Stevens had "prevailed on the President to appoint two excellent men on the Trade Commission. Jim Landis of the Harvard Law School and [George] Matthews of Wisconsin."[124] Rather disappointed in the history of the FTC under three Republican administrations and in the wake of decisions by a conservative Court, Rublee confessed that he hoped that the appointment of noted legal experts "may transform the Commission into a useful body."

Like Stevens, Rublee, too, managed to have some influence on Roosevelt's administration. Through his work in Latin America, New York, and Washington Rublee had become acquainted with problems leading to the widespread default on U.S. bank loans to Central and South American governments. When the defaults came, Rublee believed that the U.S. banks should not act so terribly surprised. Rublee believed that "during the flush times" there had "been a great deal of high pressure salesmanship on the part of bankers in this country to sell South American bonds to investors here."[125] Rublee believed that U.S. banks were responsible for the existence of the bonds, as they had "sent their agents around in South America and really stimulated the issue of bonds there by municipalities and South American states who were, of course, glad to borrow."

Like Rublee, the new Roosevelt administration under the leadership of Cordell Hull was concerned about the antagonism arising from defaults and proposed to establish a committee to negotiate the resumption of payments based on what each country could afford. The State Department planned to pattern the committee on a British model that had for some time been successful in negotiating on behalf of British investors. In the autumn of 1933, Rublee was invited to the State Department, along with noted banker Pierre Jay and noted international lawyer Charles Howland, to form the nucleus of the new committee, which was called the Foreign Bondholders' Council. At the meeting Rublee learned that the council planned to call for American bondholders to deposit their various defaulted bonds with the committee. The work of the committee would be to negotiate the best possible terms of settlement with the debtor states and municipalities. While Roosevelt first hoped to put the committee "under the Securities Act," as Rublee reported to Hand, with the help of Ray Stevens he had persuaded Roosevelt to form instead a "private Council on the lines on which Pierre and I were working and with the men we had selected."[126] Having won Roosevelt's support, Jay, Howland, and Rublee worked with the State Department to craft the committee's powers. Through their influence they then, as Rublee recalled, “succeeded in forming a very high class committee of bankers and experts under the chairmanship of Francis White.” For the next several years Rublee acted as an adviser on the committee, which he believed was successful in concluding “substantially better settlements…than could have been reached if the bondholders had tried individually to come to an agreement with the debtors.”[127] Equally important to Rublee, this progressive approach to the default situation prevented further deterioration in U.S.–Latin American relations.

As the Depression years stretched on Rublee continued to look for work that was both lucrative and interesting. Writing to Juliet in 1933 he announced one hopeful development: “Chinese Minister came to-day with possible big job—nothing to be done for some months, however—said F. D. R. recommended me.”[128] While the Chinese assignment evidently did not materialize, opportunities of one sort or another continued to develop. In 1935 Thomas Lamont induced Rublee to return to Mexico to represent the International Committee of Bankers on Mexico. Although Rublee may have had some misgivings in working for Lamont in the wake of the man’s treatment of Dwight Morrow, at age sixty-seven Rublee was likely drawn to the work because of his personal interest in Mexico and the substantial income he would receive. While he would be away from Washington and New York for extended periods during his Mexican assignment, he maintained an active role in the life of his law firm, advising on various international legal issues and continuing his friendships with his younger partners, especially Dean Acheson. After three years of tedious negotiations that allowed plenty of time for golf, Rublee at last managed to get the Mexican government to agree to a settlement. On the eve of the settlement’s signing, however, the deal fell through when the Mexican government pulled out. Rublee returned to the United States in 1938 without success. With his seventieth birthday soon approaching, George Rublee seemed pretty certain that his days of high drama in public work were over. Ironically, the most important work of his life was about to come his way. While he was, in fact, likely the most qualified person in the world for the work, the task before him was monumental, and the stakes were the highest he had ever faced.

NOTES

1. Rublee, “Reminiscences,” 223-224. According to Rublee, he and J. Reuben Clark convinced a hesitant Morrow to seek the Senate seat. For Morrow’s reluctance see Elizabeth Morrow’s diary entries in Nicolson, *Dwight Morrow*, 352.
2. Lippmann to GR, 12 February 1930, Yale- Lippmann.
3. GR to JBR, no original date but later dated “May-June 1930", GRP.
4. Rublee, “Reminiscences,” 227-228.
5. *The New York Times*, editorial, June 5, 1930 by H. Alexander Smith, in HHPP, box 1054. Smith had worked in the Food Administration during the war and in 1930 was teaching at Princeton. He was elected to the U.S. Senate serving New Jersey in 1946 and 1952.
6. GR to JBR, 18 June 1930, GRP.

7. GR to JBR, 24 June 1930, GRP.

8. Lippmann to GR, 21 July 1930, Yale-Lippmann.

9. Lippmann to Morrow, 24 October 1928, Yale-Lippmann.

10. Outlook and Independent, 11 December 1929. The section quoted was underlined. See HHPP, box 1054.

11. *New York Telegram*, 23 May 1930.

12. *Louis Globe-Democrat*, 5 June 1930.

13. Enclosure from Lenna Yost to Mr. Richey, March 1930, HHPP, box 1054.

14. Pearson manuscript for a 7 January 1930 article in the *Baltimore Sun*, Pearson Papers, box F61.

15. Rublee, "Reminiscences," 225.

16. Ibid.; and Louis McBride to Arthur Springer, 11 June 1930, DMP.

17. Ibid.

18. Quoted in Chernow, *House of Morgan*, 298-299.

19. Louis McBride to Arthur Springer, 11 June 1930, DMP.

20. "Paraphrase of telegram no. 117, dated June 10, noon, from the American Embassy at Mexico City to the Secretary of State," DMP.

21. Ibid.

22. Louis McBride to Arthur Springer, 11 June 1930, DMP.

23. Chernow, *House of Morgan*, 297. I must here say that Ron Chernow's treatment of Morrow is rather dissatisfying. While earlier in his work Chernow goes to great lengths to rationalize Thomas Lamont's facilitation of European fascism, he gives the worst possible interpretation of Morrow's highly lauded work in Mexico, suggesting at every turn that Morrow's interest in Mexico was purely for political gain. I came away with the feeling that Chernow sacrificed Morrow to elevate Lamont. Unfortunately, to date, Dwight Morrow has never been the subject of a complete academic study. The only biography of Morrow was written by Harold Nicolson, whom the Morrow family employed to produce it. Incidentally, according to Chernow, Lamont "gave Nicolson a 125-page critique of a draft of Nicolson's biography of Morrow and reproached him for idealizing his subject" (297). It seems that Lamont's criticism worked. As Stephen Schuker points out, Morrow "was exceedingly ill served by" Nicolson. Schuker notes that "Morrow's achievements remain essentially unchronicled." See Stephen Schuker, "Dwight Morrow" in *American National Biography* (Cary, NC: Oxford University Press, 1998), vol. 15, 928.

24. Rublee, "Reminiscences," 226.

25. GR to JBR, 26 August 1930, GRP.

26. Drew Pearson, manuscript for article "Little Nemo, the Wonder Worker," 1, Pearson Papers, box G-204.

27. Ibid., 2.

28. Ibid., 16.

29. Ibid., 23.

30. Nicolson, *Dwight Morrow*, 391.

31. Rublee, "Reminiscences," 258.

32. *Time*, 11 August 1930.

33. *The New Republic*, 6 August 1930.

34. GR to Lippmann, 1 August 1930, Yale-Lippmann.

35. *Time*, 11 August 1930.

36. Ibid.

37. GR to Lippmann, 1 August 1930, Yale-Lippmann.

38. Lippmann to Morrow, 9 February 1931, Yale-Lippmann.

39. Morrow to Lippmann, 11 February 1931, Yale-Lippmann.

40. Ibid.

41. Francis White to GR, 23 May 1930, *FRUS*, 1931, vol. 2, 1.

42. Ibid.

43. Lippmann to Elizabeth Morrow, 14 October 1943, Yale-Lippmann, box 91, folder 1547. For the importance of Clark's memorandum, see Ferrell, *American Diplomacy*, 767-768. Walter LaFeber's *The American Age: U.S. Foreign Policy at Home and Abroad* is an example of the Good Neighbor Policy being associated only with FDR's administration (375-376). It must be admitted that a reluctance to credit Hoover with the Good Neighbor Policy is understandable, given his support of intervention as secretary of commerce in the Harding and Coolidge administrations. Furthermore, since the move originated with liberal Republicans such as Morrow, Cotton, Clark, and Stimson, it understandable that some might not wish to link the change in policy to Herbert Hoover. However, to associate the policy only with Roosevelt's administration is incorrect.

44. Rublee, "Reminiscences," 257.

45. Jefferson Caffery to Francis White, 3 September 1930, U.S. Department of State, National Archives II, box 5660, decimal file 821.6363 BARCO/284.

46. Caffery to Stimson, 22 September 1930, *FRUS*, 1931, vol. 2, 2.

47. Ibid.

48. *Baltimore Sun*, 10 October 1930.

49. Ibid.

50. GR to JBR, 11 and 13 October 1930, JRP-Dartmouth. These papers were presented to the Baker Library through an unusual set of circumstances, having been recovered from an old trunk discarded at a garbage dump near Hanover.

51. GR to JBR, 31 October 1930, JRP-Dartmouth.

52. Rublee, "Reminiscences," 246.

53. GR to JBR, 31 October 1930, JRP-Dartmouth.

54. Rublee, "Reminiscences," 248.

55. GR to Hand, 7 December 1930, HLS-Hand.

56. GR to Hand, 16 January 1931, HLS-Hand.

57. Caffery to Stimson, 9 October 1930, *FRUS*, 1931,vol. 2, 5.

58. Caffery to Stimson, 6 November 1930, *FRUS*, 1931,vol. 2, 8.

59. Ibid.

60. GR to Hand, 7 December 1930, HLS-Hand.

61. Caffery to Stimson, 11 November 1930, *FRUS*, 1931,vol. 2, 9.

62. Ibid., 10.

63. On the oil companies attitude see Rublee, "Reminiscences," 254.

64. Caffery to Stimson, 11 November 1930, *FRUS*, 1931,vol. 2, 10.

65. Caffery to Stimson, 11 November 1930, *FRUS*, 1931,vol. 2, 9.

66. GR to Hand, 15 December 1930, HLS-Hand.

67. Ibid.

68. Ibid.

69. Rublee, "Reminiscences," 251.

70. GR to Hand, 15 December 1930, HLS-Hand.

71. Ibid.

72. GR to Hand, 16 January 1931, HLS-Hand.

73. Ibid.

74. Caffery to Stimson, 28 January and 25 February 1930, *FRUS*, 1931,vol. 2, 11 and 14.

75. Caffery to Stimson, 20 November 1930, U.S. Department of State, National Archives II, Decimal file 821.6363 BARCO/408. This document is not printed in *FRUS*.

76. GR to Hand, 7 December 1930, HLS-Hand.

77. GR to Hand, 4 March 1931, HLS-Hand.

78. Stimson to Caffery, 5 March 1931, U.S. Department of State, National Archives II, Decimal file 821.6363 BARCO/464.

79. GR to Hand, 21 February 1931, HLS-Hand.

80. Elting E. Morison, *Turmoil and Tradition: A Study in the Life and Times of Henry L. Stimson* (Boston: Houghton Mifflin Company, 1960), 354.

81. Rublee, "Reminiscences," 256. Throughout the remainder of his life, Rublee kept portraits of Morrow and Cotton in his study in Cornish.

82. Rublee, "Reminiscences," 257.

83. Ibid.

84. Caffery to Stimson, 17 March 1930, *FRUS*, 1931, 30.

85. See documents in *FRUS*, 1931, 31-36.

86. Rublee, "Reminiscences," 257.

87. Louis Brandeis to Felix Frankfurter, 11 October 1931, Urofsky and Levy, *Half Brother, Half Son,* 469.

88. Stimson to Caffery, 6 October 1930, *FRUS*, 1931, 40.

89. Ibid.

90. Rublee, "Reminiscences," 259.

91. GR to Bass, 20 January [1933, erroneously dated 1932], RBP.

92. See *FRUS*, 1932, vol. 5, 271-272.

93. Fred Dearing to Stimson, 3 Sept 1932, *FRUS*, 1932, vol. 5, 272.

94. Dearing to Stimson, 13 September 1932, *FRUS*, 1932, vol. 5, 277.

95. Stimson to Dearing, 15 September 1932, *FRUS*, 1932, vol. 5, 277-278.

96. Ibid.

97. Rublee, "Reminiscences," 262-263.

98. Stimson to Dearing, 17 September 1932, *FRUS*, 1932, vol. 5, 280.

99. Rublee, "Reminiscences," 261.

100. Robert E. McNicoll, "The Leticia Controversy" (Duke University, 1935), 73.

101. Rublee, "Reminiscences," 261.

102. Ibid., 261-262.

103. McNicoll, "Leticia Controversy," 73, note 24.

104. Ibid., 74.

105. Orazio Ciccarelli, "The Leticia Dispute, 1932-1934: A Reconsideration of Peruvian Motivations," *Southern Quarterly*, 11, no. 4 (1973), 288.

106. Rublee, "Reminiscences," 263.

107. Ibid., 264.

108. Quoted in Stimson to the Peruvian Minister of Foreign Affairs (Manzanilla), 25 January 1933, *FRUS*, 1933, vol. 4, 425.

109. Colombian Minister (Lozano) to Stimson, 23 January 1933, *FRUS*, 1933, vol. 4, 419.

110. Ibid.

111. Memorandum by the Assistant Secretary of State, 25 January 1933, *FRUS*, 1933, vol. 4, 422.

112. See Ibid., 437-475.

113. Ciccarelli, "The Leticia Dispute," 286, 288; and "Dispute between Colombia and Peru: Colombia's Appeal Under Article 15 of the Covenant," (Geneva, Switzerland: League of Nations, 1933), 12.

114. Quoted in Bryce Wood, *The United States and Latin American Wars, 1932-1942* (New York: Columbia University Press, 1966), 220-221.

115. Wood, *The United States and Latin American Wars*, 221.

116. See note 90 in chapter ten.

117. Quoted in Wood, *The United States and Latin American Wars*, 247.

118. Rublee, "Reminiscences," 264, 266.

119. Ibid., 265-266.

120. Ibid., 266.

121. Ibid., 270.

122. Ibid., 271.

123. Ibid., 271-272.

124. GR to Hand, 6 October 1933, HLS-Hand. For Landis' noteworthy career see McCraw's *Prophets of Regulation*, chapter 5.

125. Rublee, "Reminiscences," 273.

126. GR to Hand, 6 October 1933, HLS-Hand. Rublee was evidently generally supportive of Roosevelt's New Deal, which he hoped would lead to economic recovery. Writing to Hand he observed: "I have no clearer view of the future than I had when we last talked. Yet I have a feeling that things are on the mend in spite of the N.R.A. and everything."

127. Ibid., 276.

128. GR to JBR, 15 August 1933, GRP.

12

The "Gaunt Prophet" (1938–1939)

George Rublee's public work climaxed with his six-month effort from August 1938 to February 1939 to find a workable solution to the Jewish refugee crisis that erupted in the wake of the March 1938 German-Austrian anschluss. The last major undertaking of his life, it became the most studied of his public contributions.[1] Rublee's selection as director of the Intergovernmental Committee on Political Refugees Coming from Germany was based on his long experience with European and Latin American governments, his expertise in international finance, and his good standing among influential circles in Latin America and Europe. In his effort to locate havens of refuge for German Jews and to secure funds to finance their emergency emigration, Rublee was required to rely on all that he had learned of domestic and international politics, high finance, and the art of negotiation. In carrying out his negotiation with the Nazis, he would accomplish much more than was thought possible, attempting perhaps more than the Western democracies had intended.

On 13 March 1938 Adolph Hitler sent troops into Austria to secure Nazi control of that state and to accomplish a German-Austrian anschluss, or union. The third in a series of maneuvers forbidden under the Versailles Peace Treaty, the Austrian anschluss provoked a Jewish refugee crisis as German and Austrian Jews fled Nazi-controlled areas. Following the 1935 Nuremberg laws that stripped Jews of their citizenship, terminated their access to professional occupations, and forbade interracial marriage, a great number of German Jews had secretly relocated to Austria, were they believed themselves safe from Nazis. As a result of the Nazi takeover of Austria in 1938, tens of thousands of German and Austrian Jews fled their homeland in search of refuge in neighboring countries to the west, chiefly France, Switzerland, Belgium, the Netherlands, Great Britain, and Scandinavia. Owing to restrictive immigration laws, continued economic stagnation, and varying degrees of anti-Semitism in those European countries (especially in France and Switzerland), Germany and Austrian Jews were unwelcome and were subject to expulsion. Making these Jews particularly unattractive for immigration was a Nazi flight tax, which rendered emigrating Jews virtually penniless in an economically—and spiritually—depressed world.

Although the Western world condemned Germany for its policies that provoked the Jewish flight and especially for its flagrant disregard for the Versailles Treaty, no world authority was immediately in a position to attempt a solution to the Jewish refugee crisis. Following Germany's withdrawal from the League of Nations in 1934 and the remilitarization of the Rhineland in 1936, the Nazi government was an international pariah with which no democratic government wished to work. The plight of the refugees was exacerbated when Neill Malcolm, the league's high commissioner for refugees coming from Germany, refused to recognize German Jews desiring to emigrate as falling under league jurisdiction.

Although Europe seemed ill-prepared to deal with the Jewish refugee crisis, evidently owing to pressure from influential Jewish and liberal Christian organizations in the United States, President Franklin D. Roosevelt at the end of March began sounding out Britain and France on a joint response to the crisis.[2] Toward that end, Secretary of State Cordell Hull instructed U.S. ambassador Joseph Kennedy to inquire whether or not the British government would be willing to join in "setting up a special committee…for the purpose of facilitating the emigration from Austria and presumably from Germany of political refugees."[3] Hull explained that his request related to "the urgency of the problem with which the world is faced and the necessity of speedy, cooperative effort [if] widespread human suffering is to be averted." Hull sent similar requests for participation on an international committee to France, Belgium, the Netherlands, Denmark, Sweden, and—somewhat surprisingly at first glance—twenty Latin American countries. In addition, FDR organized a special committee, the President's Advisory Committee on Political Refugees, to consider solutions to the Jewish refugee crisis. Believing that his effort would meet with success, on 25 March FDR announced his decision to call an international conference to meet the crisis and communicated his hope for broad participation.[4]

Both the British and the French were initially wary of the U.S. initiative. The British feared that any international conference focusing on locating refuge for German Jews would provide a forum for Zionists demanding increased Jewish immigration to Palestine, Britain's troublesome Versailles mandate. The French, suffering from high unemployment, feared that the proposed international committee would focus on the hundreds of thousands of Jews still in Germany awaiting an outlet for immigration and neglect to find areas of resettlement for German Jews illegally residing in France. An additional fear common to both Britain and France was that the United States would pressure them to raise their immigration quotas to accommodate more German Jews and, too, that there would be no end to Jewish emigrants fleeing Central and Eastern Europe. For instance, on 13 April, the Romanian government communicated its interest in attending the upcoming conference because it wished, in its words, to "dispose annually of a number corresponding to the Jewish birth rate."[5] The Romanians hoped that the Western democracies would not simply concentrate on German Jews but would also develop an international organization "to deal with Jewish or political refugee problems in" Romania, Czechoslovakia, Hungary, and Poland. With much of Europe east of the Rhine River intent on reducing its Jewish population, it is no wonder that France and Great Britain balked at the prospects of an international conference dealing with Jewish refugees for fear that it might open the floodgates.

During May and June the United States managed to convince both the French and the British that there would be no difference of viewpoints among them at the conference. The United States pledged to prevent the interjection of questions regarding Palestine, stipulated that funds for transporting and settling Jews would be the responsibility of private international organizations rather than governments, agreed that political refugees would be labeled as "persons who desire to leave Germany as well as those who have already done so," proposed that the conference would seek to facilitate Jewish immigration "within the existing immigration laws and regulations of the receiving countries," and stipulated that "no country would be expected to receive a greater number of emigrants than is permitted by its existing legislation."[6] The United States, it seems, was mostly intent on convening a conference at which the Western democracies would establish an ongoing committee based in Europe to "formulate and carry out, in cooperation with existing agencies, a long range program looking toward the solution or alleviation of the problem in a larger sense."

While it would seem that the United States had rendered the conference pointless through its preconference promises to Great Britain and France, the United States was counting on Latin American cooperation to make the international gathering a success. Of the thirty-two invited nations, only those of Latin America had no "existing" restrictive immigration quotas. When the conference convened in Evian, France, on 6 July, however, it soon became clear that the European democracies had illegal Jewish immigrants whom they did not wish to maintain, that U.S. would not relax its 1924 ethnically biased immigration quota system to receive more Jews, and that the Latin American governments were invited only so that they might be publicly pressured into providing havens of refuge. Perhaps not surprisingly, when the Latin American representatives were asked to demonstrate their willingness to aid destitute German Jews, each of them refused to commit his government to any specific number.[7] Making matters worse, following the Evian conference, each of these governments introduced new restrictions or completely altered its existing immigration laws to thwart Jewish immigration.[8] Rublee, who would serve as director of this ongoing refugee committee, later expressed the opinion that the United States championed the Evian conference because the Roosevelt administration "thought that some sort of gesture was necessary to assuage the indignation excited by the persecution of the Jews, but [had little] real hope of success in improving the lot of the Jews in Germany."[9] Rublee thought Roosevelt's conference "merely an impressive protest."[10]

Although the conference actually closed more doors to persecuted German Jews than it opened, the United States was satisfied that the final conference document established the ongoing body that the United States hoped would deal with the international Jewish question, the Intergovernmental Committee for Political Refugees Coming from Germany. A conference resolution established that "there should meet at London an intergovernmental committee consisting of" a chairman, four vice-chairmen, and "a director of authority."[11] The director was authorized to "undertake negotiations [with Germany] to improve the present conditions of exodus and to replace them with conditions of orderly emigration." The director would also "approach the governments of the countries of refuge with a view to developing opportunities for permanent settlement." To make the involuntary emigrants more attractive to potential host governments, an Evian conference resolution called for Germany to "make its contribution by" reducing the flight tax imposed on Jews so that they could leave with more of "their property and possessions."[12]

While the Evian conference was in no sense a success, the United States achieved a fundamental aim of compelling a reluctant world body, especially Britain and France, to create an authoritative and independent organization to work on behalf of German Jewish refugees. This accomplishment was no easy task. Concerned that the new committee would undermine the League of Nations' prestige, according to the U.S. representative, the British attempted to "reduce the Intergovernmental Committee to the role of advisory body to [the] League Commission" during the conference.[13] The United States, however, successfully thwarted that British effort. Evidently, the President's Advisory Committee on Political Refugees (PACPR) was largely responsible for formulating the U.S. position at the conference and viewed the creation of the Intergovernmental Committee (IGC) as the only hopeful scheme to achieve a solution to the Jewish refugee crisis. The PACPR, as Rublee explained in a letter to Learned Hand, was a mixed committee "composed of Jews, Catholics, and Nordics."[14] The most important members of the committee were James McDonald, Rabbi Stephen Wise, Joseph Chamberlain, George Warren, and Myron Taylor. Taylor, former president of the U.S. Steel Corporation, represented the United States at Evian, during which he had the rank of ambassador extraordinary and plenipotentiary.[15]

Although Rublee would not be selected as director of the IGC until its first meeting in London in early August 1938, he was approached about the post in early May. In a letter to Myron Taylor on 4 May, Thomas Lamont, then chief executive of J. P. Morgan, suggested Rublee for the role of director of the proposed committee. Lamont observed that Rublee, who was "closely conversant with State Department affairs" and who had "served Dwight Morrow on repeated missions in the same relationship that you have in mind," was the best man for the job.[16] Lamont described Rublee as "completely discreet, tactful, [possessing] excellent judgement, and [one] who would work in beautifully with that staff." Evidently, Rublee was interested in the work, and his name began to circulate in the press in late July as the likely IGC director. The final appointment seems to have come from Roosevelt, who had appointed Rublee to the Foreign Bondholders Committee in 1933 and who knew of Rublee's background in American politics and in European and Latin American affairs, not to mention his legendary status at Groton, from which Roosevelt had graduated. Rublee agreed to the appointment toward the end of July, but he felt some trepidation about the assignment. Writing to Endicott Peabody on 26 July, Rublee confessed: "It seems to me it might have been wiser for the President to select a younger and more vigorous man; but now that I am in, I'll do my best and I hope I can do some good, for the state of these refugees is pitiable."[17] While Rublee agreed to get the IGC off the ground by serving as the director in its infancy, he explained to Peabody, "I made it a condition that I should not be expected to hold the job permanently." Although Rublee thought himself up to the challenge of attempting to find a solution to a terribly thorny problem, he nevertheless believed that having, just turned seventy, he lacked the stamina to stay at the work indefinitely.

On 3 August the executive committee of the IGC met in London and selected Rublee as director general.[18] Prior to his departure for Europe, Rublee attended a meeting of the PACPR on 9 August, at which he was briefed on the restraints and conditions he would face as director. In a letter to Louis Brandeis, Stephen Wise reported that James MacDonald and George Warren had explained to Rublee "that Britain chiefly, and France secondarily, had sought throughout to minimize the Evian Conference" and that those countries would likely continue to prove reluctant partners. In addition to having little international support, Rublee also learned of U.S. constraints on his negotiations. Wise, for instance, made it clear to Rublee "that no relief to the refugees [can] justify any action on our part, which would imply that Hitler had done a good deed in permitting refugees to go with a very small fraction of their funds." By this Wise meant that the worldwide boycott on German products, a retaliatory international Jewish effort, would not be relaxed as a quid pro quo for any agreement Rublee reached with the Nazis. Wise observed that "G.R.'s response ran thus, 'Hitler isn't going to give us something for nothing. We have got to bargain with him, and he and his financial advisors are likely to drive a very hard bargain.'" Wise reported that Rublee "was quite understanding and sympathetic when I pointed out the danger of any action of the Democratic Governments which would give prestige and even economic support to Hitler. I must in all fairness add that the entire committee sided with me. G.R. said that he was too ignorant of the whole matter even to ask intelligent questions but he did ask very shrewd ones piercing to the heart of the thing, in his queries to MacDonald and Warren." Wise concluded by noting that "G.R. is aware of all the difficulties that face him" and added, "He made the best impression upon all of us."[19] The committee sent Rublee off with a rather thick dossier, and Wise gave him two volumes on the plight of German Jews because Brandeis had suggested that Rublee could digest books remarkably fast.[20]

Rublee left the meeting with a feeling that the task he had agreed to take on was nearly impossible of solution. Limited by German, American, British, French, and Latin American objections, Rublee confessed to Brandeis that he had "no illusions regarding the chances of success" but was yet "prepared to take the consequences...whatever they may be."[21] To Hand, he was more candid: "The waters closed over my head at about noon on Monday."[22] With manifest misgivings George Rublee stepped onto the *Queen Mary* to sail for London on

10 August, hoping that he could discover a way to help Germany's Jews. The mission would be both his last and most important, and he would have many occasions to question his decision to attempt it.

When Rublee arrived in London, he found that his freedom of action had been further curtailed. Although the United States had managed to pressure the British and French into creating the IGC at Evian, the American leadership seems to have blundered in the formation of the IGC's executive. That committee was to be composed of one chairman and four vice-chairmen representing the United States, Great Britain, France, the Netherlands, and Brazil. Agreeing that the British could hold the chairmanship, the United States apparently believed that with Rublee's acting as director and the Brazilian representative's naturally siding with the U.S. representative, Myron Taylor, a sort of transatlantic balance of power could be achieved. This balance, however, was rendered void when the Brazilians, in an effort to distance themselves from the IGC, replaced the statesman who had represented them at Evian with a commercial attaché in their London Embassy as their representative. The IGC executive (IGCE) ruled this substitution unacceptable.[23] With the Brazilians refusing to name an alternate, the Europeans were in a position to control the organization, which only the United States seemed to care existed.

During a meeting of the IGCE in London on 5 August, Rublee's options were effectively closed through a series of agreements. With Britain's Lord Winterton presiding as chairman, the committee agreed that Rublee would travel to Berlin only "upon an indication from the German government that it would receive him." If such an opportunity materialized, an unlikely development according to the British and French, Rublee was to begin with "exploratory conversations" with the German Foreign Office in Berlin and "then with appropriate party leaders aiming at Hitler," who the committee members "agreed would have to make the final decision."[24] It was also arranged that the preliminary communications with the German government would not take place in London, where Rublee would be, but in Berlin through the American, British, and French ambassadors, the American envoy leading the approach at the appropriate time. Further, Rublee was also not allowed to communicate independently with the press, as was his custom, but instead the committee insisted on "absolute secrecy" and stipulated "that no word should go to the press except through the Chairman." Relieved of any responsibility in securing his invitation to Berlin, the committee anticipated Rublee focusing on "negotiations with governments of the countries of settlement, notably the governments of Latin America." Owing to the fact that the Latin American governments had been "tightening up their immigration requirements" in the wake of the Evian conference, the committee expected that Rublee "would have to negotiate separately with each of these [twenty] governments in order to arrive at something concrete." Very adroitly, it seems, the Europeans had managed to restrain the American director's ability to act independently and focused his attention on Latin American governments as resettlement havens rather than their own large colonial empires. Always the maverick, however, Rublee would abide by these constraints until they proved fruitless and then would launch his own clandestine operations.

The second meeting of the IGCE was set for 23 August, but at the last moment it was canceled when the French government announced that Senator Henry Bérenger would not attend the meeting since the Brazilians had not yet provided an acceptable representative. Rublee and Taylor learned, however, that "the French have become concerned lest our activity which has to do with the emigration of persons still in Germany may thrust into the background" the refugees in France "who have not reached a place of final settlement."[25] With the meeting canceled, Rublee and Taylor planned to proceed to Paris, where they would meet Hugh Wilson, the U.S. ambassador to Germany, and William Bullitt, the U.S. ambassador to France, to discuss the diplomatic approach to Germany. Rublee evidently wanted to visit with Hugh Wilson, upon whose "initiative" he was "to a very great extent" dependent.[26] Rublee and Taylor communicated their intentions to Secretary of State Cordell Hull, who, with Assistant Secretary Sumner Welles, monitored their activities. In the cable announcing their intention to travel to Paris, Rublee also related his effort to arrange "for the coordination of the League Commission and the Intergovernmental Committee" to assuage British concerns that, as IGC director, he would denigrate or complicate Neill Malcolm's work as high commissioner for refugees.[27] Hull had "no objection" to Rublee alleviating British concerns, and he approved Rublee's intention to coordinate efforts with Wilson because, unlike the Europeans, Hull believed that "the Committee should undertake all negotiations with the German Government through its Director with the assistance of the principal diplomatic representatives in Berlin."[28]

Although Hull's approval of Rublee's plan to work with Hugh Wilson was somewhat liberating, the secretary's subsequent long cable regarding any eventual agreement with the German government had the opposite effect. Hull had since 1933 been attempting to undermine Nazi Germany's inroads into Latin American markets, and he feared that Rublee's effort to convince the Germans to allow Jews to leave with a greater portion of their wealth might lead to further German influence in the Latin American economies. Short of foreign exchange and international credits, Germany under the leadership of Reichsbank president and sometime economic minister Hjalmar Schacht had implemented a series of inventive trade initiatives centered on "export subsidies, blocked marks, barter deals and clearing agreements."[29] This innovative, state-organized approach, which undermined principles of free trade, had resulted by 1938 in a "spectacular expansion of German trade in Latin America and southeastern Europe" at a time when all the world was looking for domestic economic relief through exports.[30] In his communiqué to Rublee and Taylor, Hull asserted: "You are familiar with the fact that the broad trade policies of this Government are fundamental in our entire program. We cannot permit the German Government to use our Government's interest in the distress of German refugees as a lever to break up this policy or create additional spheres of bilateral trade influence through the medium of specially constructed currency or credit arrangements."[31] Hull realized that, owing to Germany's "particularly acute" foreign exchange crisis (a situation exacerbated by the international boycott of German goods), "the funds in question can be transferred from Germany only through increased German exports." Hull insisted, however, that Rublee not enter any agreement with the Germans that was "based on inequitable commercial practices tending to divert the course of trade into artificial bilateral channels." Hull was particularly concerned with the so-called Haavara system, by which Jews emigrating to Palestine received German-manufactured products in lieu of foreign exchange for their forfeited or confiscated property. Hull believed that while that program had "hitherto been of minor importance," if the Haavara scheme was "used for the transfer of even a small percentage of the funds of several hundred thousand refugees the result would have a very considerable effect on the course of international trade." Although Hull preferred that the flight tax be completely abolished and that Jewish emigrants "be permitted to take free foreign exchange out of the country," he knew that such an arrangement was likely "an impossibility." As a compromise that he thought favorable to both the emigrants and U.S. trade policy, Hull proposed that Rublee seek a plan by which Jews would be given special convertible marks that might be deposited in the Bank for International Settlements, through which the fund might be redeemed over a long period of time as Germany's foreign exchange position improved. Hull admitted that "this is merely suggesting that the refugees take what the German Government offers, leaving this with the Bank to act as holding agent in the hope that something may eventually be realized." Hull thought, however, that these deposits might serve "as a basis for resettlement loans made by relief organizations, ...thereby giving such organizations at least a chance of ultimately recouping part of their expenditures." In closing, Hull stipulated, "It should be borne in mind throughout the negotiations that Rublee is negotiating on behalf of the Committee rather than on behalf of this Government." Hull added, however, "[B]ut I need hardly assure you both of our full and entire support."[32]

Although Hull admitted that Rublee was supposed to be "negotiating on behalf of the Committee" and therefore on behalf of German Jews, it was clear to Rublee that the United States had weighed in with one more rather large constraint. Rublee found it frustrating that U.S. policy was evolving ad hoc. The administration first identified Latin America as the optimal choice for havens of refuge, and only subsequently did the State Department recognize the possible corresponding impact on U.S. trade policy in the region. Writing to Learned Hand on 29 August, Rublee complained: "The job is more difficult than I thought when I left home. Nobody has thought out anything. There is no plan yet. I have too much to learn to make one myself at present. The Evian Conference was called suddenly by FDR. The other countries came reluctantly and with no confidence in the idea. Taylor did a very good job in holding them together and getting them to agree to the permanent organization which they have formed. But that is all."[33] Describing Hull's "[l]ong cable...forbidding any plan with Germany which would interfere with principle of trade treaties," Rublee observed that the secretary "[d]oes not want the only arrangement for increasing German exports which seem feasible." Rublee found the situation "[v]ery difficult."

Making matters worse, Rublee explained, what work he had performed "may be frustrated by war." By a twist of fate, Rublee's final international mission allowed him to be in Europe when the remnants of the ill-considered Versailles Peace Treaty came crashing down. In piecemeal fashion Hitler since 1933 had steadily cast off the constraints placed on Germany in 1919 and had begun a final phase of dismantling the Versailles Treaty system in 1938, beginning with the Austrian anschluss and with demands on Czechoslovakia for the annexation of the strategically important Sudetenland, where ethnic Germans were a majority. During the summer of 1938 Germany kept up a media blitz charging Czech mistreatment of Sudeten Germans and Hitler put his country on a war footing. When Rublee arrived in Paris at the end of August, he learned from Ambassadors Wilson and Bullitt that war appeared imminent. Writing to Hand, Rublee observed that "everyone is worried and unsure." Rublee confessed to the emotional turmoil he was experiencing:

> [War] hardly seems possible on this lovely summer day. ...The city is peaceful and its beauty kindles the admiration I felt in the years that have gone. I have enjoyed a few walks about the streets that I found a little time for. Paris streets are much friendlier than London's. I feel more relaxed and at ease in them—a happier mood. Places I used to know and had forgotten—old memories—these have affected me deeply. It is a fine city and unchanged. But the German frontier is only 45 minutes away by air, and think what might happen![34]

Rublee admitted, "This is a very tense moment."

For the next month Rublee worked under the shadow of war while the well-intentioned yet enervated British prime minister, Neville Chamberlain, traveled repeatedly to Germany in an effort to forestall a German–Czech clash, which, by treaty obligation, would have brought France and Great Britain into a war that they lacked the will to wage. While Chamberlain sought with little apparent success to appease Hitler throughout September, Rublee continued searching for a plan to save German Jews despite the torrent blowing around him. Rublee's plan, however, was going nowhere. Writing to Dean Acheson on 9 September, he admitted, "The more I learn about this business the harder it looks," and he added: "Dwight Morrow used to say that for some problems there is no solution. Perhaps this is one of them."[35] From Ambassador Hugh Wilson, Rublee had learned that the Nazis would negotiate with him only if he secured specific commitments from the world community to take Germany's Jews.[36] On the other hand, Latin American countries were unwilling to accept penniless immigrants, and neither the United States, France, nor Great Britain was willing to open its overseas territories to the refugees. Even if the Germans agreed to negotiate, the American, British, and French constraints were such that a final agreement seemed unlikely. Making matters worse, reports coming from Eastern Europe indicated that millions more Jews were likely to become involuntary emigrants. A cable from U.S. ambassador Anthony Biddle in Poland to Cordell Hull confirmed that "acute anti-Semitism" exists "amongst the ranks of radical anti-Semitics not only in Poland but also in Rumania, Hungary and other countries where the Jewish problem [is] steadily becoming a more acute social-economic-political issue."[37] Biddle passed on a portentous warning from Polish foreign minister Josef Beck, stating "that a solution of the Jewish problem in a global sense was a matter for our generation to settle for the signs of the times held little promise of the oncoming generations' dealing with the problem with the same degree of tolerance, objectivity and liberalism as our own."[38] Hull, however, shot back warning that the United States, Great Britain and France were all agreed that their "efforts on behalf of German refugees must not...encourage persecution by other Governments aimed at forcing out unwanted sections of their populations and the dumping of these people onto the hands of international charity."[39] Hull added that the "reception which has so far met our efforts to meet the German problem...gives no encouragement whatever to any hope that a 'global' solution of the problem might be possible."

Added to the prospect of millions more Jewish refugees coming out of Eastern Europe was news from Latin America indicating further restrictions on immigration. On 2 September Rublee warned Hull that the "Argentine government has decreed new immigration laws which come into force on October 1st."[40] Rublee had learned that the Argentine consul in Berlin, having issued visas to 600 Jews who had liquidated their possessions (at an extreme loss), was now stipulating "that unless they arrive in Argentine before October 1st, which is impossible unless a special boat is chartered, they will not be admitted." Eager to intervene, Rublee asserted: "It seems to me that this is an opportunity to achieve something tangible for the Committee, and I should like you to instruct the Embassy at London to introduce me to the Argentine Chargé and to give me whatever support may be necessary at Buenos Aires."[41] Rublee added that he had asked the British to "arrange for me to meet the Argentine Chargé but they have sidestepped my request with the suggestion that the introduction should come through the American Embassy." Rublee needed help there because Joseph Kennedy was proving decidedly uninterested in the refugee crisis.[42] Rublee's intervention ultimately proved valuable and may have revived his spirits somewhat. On 3 September Hull sent a communiqué to Argentina indicating that excluding the German Jewish visa recipients "due to new immigration restrictions at this time would create a most unfortunate impression in this hemisphere and in Europe."[43] Hull informed Rublee later in September that "the Argentine authorities have now modified their regulations in order to permit all persons in Germany who have valid visas and who leave Germany before October 1 to enter Argentine."[44] Although Rublee must have been satisfied to know that he had helped 600 Jews get out of Germany, the difficulty of getting out only one-thousandth of the German population must have made the work before him seem more daunting.

In addition to troubles with Latin Americans and friction with the British and French over the workings of the IGC, the threat of war made the situation nearly untenable for Rublee and produced a surreal atmosphere full of rumor and portent. On 25 September Rublee related the stressful situation: "The threat of war, which has been waxing ever since we came here, now looms like a thunder cloud darkening the sky. Juliet and I were fitted for gas masks this evening at one of the many stations the government has opened for the purpose."[45] Rublee reported that so likely did war seem that he had "offered the services of myself and staff to Ambassador Kennedy" and that he had "joined the London Committee to help evacuate Americans."[46] While worried personally about the prospects of war because "[b]oth France and Britain fear the German air force…to be much stronger than theirs," Rublee seemed to think that appeasement was not the correct course.[47] Of the Anglo-German negotiations he observed: "Hitler has conceded nothing and has met every concession of the other side by stepping up his demands. We do not yet know just what terms are in the ultimatum he handed to Chamberlain day before yesterday, but if the reports are true, he demands that the Czechs get out of the Sudeten country before there is time to arrange for any of the safeguards necessary to protect them."[48] Rublee believed that "[i]t is hard to see how the Czechs can yield if they believe…that France and Britain will support them." Rublee was concerned that the "Germans appear to have taken Chamberlain's visits as a sign of weakness," but he hoped that the visits "proved to the British people that Hitler was not concerned with rescuing the Sudeten Germans, but with destroying Czechoslovakia in order to gain power that would be perilous to" Great Britain.

Although Rublee could be pragmatic about the situation, the prospect of war weighed heavily upon him owing to his love for European civilization. To Hand he confessed:

> I think you can imagine how painful this drama, like the unfolding of a Greek tragedy in the feeling of impending doom by fate, has been to me. You know my feeling about England and France and also about Germany. When it looked as if Hitler would get what he wanted without resistance, I could hardly bear it. I could not criticize because my country was on the side lines taking no part. How could I know what I would do if I knew all the facts and had the responsibility of decision? When you go to war you are entering a road to an unknown destination. Even if you win, the result may be contrary to what you went in for. But I felt and feel that the influence of France and Britain in the world is at stake. Nothing would grieve me more than to see them fall under the heel of Germany, and Hitler's Germany at that.[49]

Not only was the threat of war and its probable impact on Europe causing Rublee emotional pain, but the crisis situation also rendered his opportunity to negotiate with the Germans less likely. Earlier in September Hugh Wilson reported that the British ambassador in Germany stated "emphatically that he believes that the present is not the time to make the proposed *démarche* to Ribbentrop," adding that "while the Czechoslovak matter is in its present acute phase it would be a mistaken policy to bring up another big question, however important and urgent."[50]

Despite the tension he felt at the prospects of war, Rublee's reaction was mixed when Chamberlain returned to London and claimed to have secured "peace for our time." Writing to Acheson—who had asked that he write "about the world as you see it"—Rublee admitted that he was "naturally glad to have escaped the war" because he "didn't want to be bombed."[51] Nevertheless, while Rublee thought it possible that "[p]eace may last through my time," he admitted that "if I were an Englishman I should be distressed." Rublee lacked optimism because he had "heard nothing to convince [him] that Hitler" would agree to a general, lasting settlement and because he believed that "England has failed to preserve the balance of power in Europe." Rublee observed to the future secretary of state:

Hitler has added ten million Germans to his people without firing a shot and he commands the approaches to the East and Southeast. Who or what is there to stop him from going on? England and France have sacrificed Czechoslovakia. That country, it is likely, will feel more resentment against them even than against Germany. Poland and the Balkan countries will no longer put trust in England and France. Hitler has the greatest power in Europe since Napoleon. France has become merely a satellite of England.[52]

Despite his disgust, Rublee observed dryly:

Well it is done and is irrevocable. The best course now seems to me not to make a fuss and chide at Chamberlain, but to try to live in a friendly manner with Hitler, taking him at his word and seeking a reconciliation, but at the same time to proceed with re-armament much more thoroughly and rapidly than in the past—unless Hitler should consent to measures of disarmament. That of course should be tried for. As you may gather, I am rather deeply depressed as I look ahead. There is a chance of appeasement, but how much of a chance is it?[53]

Rublee hoped that the Munich conference, despite its failings, might provide an atmosphere in which an approach to Berlin regarding Jewish refugees might succeed. Even if the German government agreed to see him, however, Rublee admitted to Acheson that he was still having trouble with the Western democracies:

The problem seems to me about as hopelessly insoluble as it did. I have a number of financial schemes, but none in which I have confidence. Nor do I know whether the Governments will give me the effective support which I need. Kennedy tells me that the British will do nothing unless the American Government will contribute something positive. And they have contributed nothing yet but words. In what manner am I going to come out of this adventure? I don't know.[54]

Lacking support, Rublee admitted that his work had begun to resemble "a sort of detective thriller" owing to his conversations with a "mysterious Englishman from Berlin," by the name of Godman, "who claims to have enormous influence with the Nazis and that he can put through a financial scheme." Rublee asserted that he "should pay no attention to him," but "Lord Winterton and the treasury people tell me I must take him seriously" and profess "that this fellow was useful to the Prime Minister in his negotiations" at Munich. Rublee concluded, that "All these experiences would be very stimulating and exciting—I suppose they are so—but they are wearing and I should be more cheerful if I had my face card or trump in the hand I have to play."

After the Munich conference Rublee began to step up pressure on the American and British governments to move forward. He asked for, and received, support from the U.S. State Department to persuade the British that there could be no more delay in approaching the German government about his visit to Berlin. On 7 October the State Department communicated a letter from Roosevelt to Chamberlain asking that Chamberlain take up the refugee crisis with the German government. The letter also informed the British that the United States was prepared to begin an inquiry on its own at the German Foreign Office regarding a possible Rublee visit. Rublee, however, evidently felt that Roosevelt's letter was weak and phoned Sumner Welles, a personal friend, to complain about the lack of progress. A memorandum of the conversation between Rublee and Welles was preserved and indicates that Rublee was becoming rather frustrated. The following selections relate Rublee's intensity and hint at his preparing to take matters into his own hands:

Welles: The main point is that no step should be taken either by yourself or anybody in your organization until the Ambassadors in Berlin have an opportunity to sound out the situation.

Rublee: I agree with that but I think they ought to do it immediately.

Welles: I quite agree. That is our own point of view here. You can be positive that steps in that sense will be taken immediately.

Rublee: ...It is very important at this phase that the British Empire should make a real contribution. They have shown me in confidence a statement which they propose to submit [to the IGC]. They must be persuaded to take the matter more seriously. This can only be done through Ambassador Kennedy. I mean, I cannot do much with them. The President's message was very useful...but evidently [has] not made a very big impression. I want to say this very confidentially. I have the impression [that] the British Foreign Office is definitely against it. Lord Halifax thinks that the...[55] would like to smother it. We have that to counteract. My impression is that Ambassador Kennedy is not disposed to take a strong line. He feels that our undertaking is hopeless. ...I don't think its hopeless, but it is very difficult.[56]

Two days after his call to Welles, Rublee sent a long cable further explaining the reluctance of Britain to work to have him received in Berlin and relating other obstacles to his work. Rublee explained that he continued to make no progress with Latin American countries, which would "not commit themselves to receive even a small number of involuntary emigrants unless they are assured that [they] will not be...destitute persons who will become burdens" to them.[57] He also complained that the British proposal for accepting refugees "is wholly unsatisfactory in that it indicates no real effort to open up their colonies or to use their influence with their Dominions to take involuntary immigrants." Rublee believed that "[u]nder the circumstances, the negotiation with Germany is the key to the situation." He had learned, however, that the British Foreign Office officials wanted the question of German Jews to "be subordinated to high policy and [were] therefore not really anxious that I go to Berlin." Rublee, on the other hand, was "not as yet convinced that the Germans will refuse to talk" and added: "In fact, I have received communications through various intermediaries that some German authorities at least have been giving serious consideration to the problem and have gone so far as to formulate concrete proposals which they are said to be prepared to discuss."[58] It appears that Welles' 10 October instruction that "no step should be taken" to communicate with Berlin came after Rublee had already established informal contact with a number of Germans. In letters to Acheson and Hand a little later, Rublee related how he came to know several officials in the German Embassy in London. Rublee explained to Acheson, "I have managed to get into touch with the German Government. I have done this on my own without the knowledge of anybody except my little group." After Myron Taylor returned to America on 20 September, Rublee's "little group" consisted of Robert Pell, a State Department expert on European affairs assigned to work with Rublee, and Joseph Cotton Jr., who acted as Rublee's personal assistant.[59]

While Pell and Cotton would prove important to his negotiations with the German government, Juliet, as Rublee explained in a letter, was the first to establish contact with the Germans. Describing to a friend Juliet's role in his relations with German officials, George observed:

> It has come about in a curious way through Juliet. She met the wife of the air attache of the German Embassy at a luncheon and they talked sympathetically about the refugee question. Soon after this the air attache, Lieutenant General Wenninger, and his wife came to dine with us alone. I talked quite freely and unemotionally about the situation and let him know how I wanted to handle it. In the following week Wenninger invited me to dinner at his flat. The only other guest was the Counselor of the German Embassy, Dr. [Theodore] Kordt.[60]

Through Wenninger and Kordt, Rublee managed to get independent information on the German government's attitude toward his work. Rublee learned that a number of economically oriented nationalists under the leadership of Reich Marshal Hermann Göring and Reichsbank president Hjalmar Schacht, the latter not a member of the Nazi Party, desired a meeting with Rublee to arrange a solution to the Jewish question. His German sources also indicated that Joachim von Ribbentrop, the German foreign minister, opposed any negotiations with Rublee, who Ribbentrop thought was Jewish. Rublee was obliged to inform Hugh Wilson that he was actually of Huguenot descent and was not Jewish.[61] In a letter to Hand communicating his travails, Rublee recounted the incident questioning his lineage and related his response: "I began [the letter] by saying that the report of the rumor gave me the feeling that Anatole Franco ascribed to the angels and saints in heaven when they heard the news of the baptism of the penguins: 'neither joy nor sadness, but a sensation of extreme surprise.'"[62] While some of the information coming out of Germany may have been personally bothersome, understanding the situation in Berlin proved helpful in Rublee's effort to achieve a breakthrough. Although he knew that Ribbentrop was opposed to a negotiation, Rublee hoped to capitalize on the rift between leading members of the German government through continued diplomatic pressure.

Working with Wilson and the British ambassador Sir Neville Henderson, Rublee brought further pressure on the American and British governments in an effort to prompt them to proceed with some activity in Berlin. While the U.S. State Department and British Foreign Office had been working on a draft statement for their ambassadors, neither man had been informed to proceed. On 15 October Wilson wrote to Hull, "Both Henderson and I now feel that the time is advantageous" to make "soundings respecting proper moment for Rublee visit."[63] Later that day Hull replied that the department, too, felt that "the time has come for you to make an informal approach...paving the way for an eventual visit of Rublee to Berlin."[64] Although Rublee was pleased that a diplomatic effort was at last being launched, he found it necessary to correct the statement that the United States and Britain had agreed upon regarding the approach to the German Foreign Office. The statement asserted, "Mr. Rublee should be in a position to give the German Government authoritative information as to the number of refugees who might be admitted for settlement by various governments."[65] Rublee, who managed to see the document at the British Foreign Office, wrote to Wilson on 14 October stating:

> I have not wanted to enter into a discussion with the State Department with regard to wording, but I feel that I should at least tell you, in order that you may be somewhat guarded when the occasion arises for you to talk with the Germans, that I have not obtained very concrete information from the participating governments as to the number of involuntary emigrants which they would be willing to admit. Naturally, I should not tell the Germans this. I should wish to convey to them an impression that I know more than I can tell. But I should not want, at the first meeting with them, ...upon my inability to produce information with regard to numbers, to have the conversation break down.[66]

Rublee concluded, "I know that you will do the wise thing, whatever it may be, but I have felt in duty bound to inform you of the existing position." Intent on still making a success of his mission, Rublee was clearly willing to hazard a quiet redirection of official instruction to preserve his chances of success.

Wilson and Henderson made their separate calls upon the German Foreign Office on 18 October but found that "Ribbentrop as usual [was] out of town" and instead visited with state secretary Ernst von Weizsäcker.[67] Based on German documents, it seems that Wilson adjusted his remarks to reflect Rublee's request and may have compelled Henderson to do the same. According to a memorandum Weizsäcker sent to Ribbentrop following the interviews, Wilson simply pointed out that the United States had been providing "an annual quota of 27,000 persons for the admission of Jews and thus was willing to admit Jews."[68] Although Wilson expressed the American desire to see "an orderly procedure" for Jewish emigration, Weizsäcker discerned that Wilson "had no specific plan for such procedure; nor had Mr. Rublee." Weizsäcker informed both ambassadors that in his "personal opinion a journey by Mr. Rublee to Germany would be of no value." He asserted that if Rublee came to Berlin, "it would be ascertained that—for obvious reasons—we would not let the Jews take along any foreign exchange" and it would then be reported "that once more it was German obstructionism that was to blame for the misery of the Jews." Weizsäcker would "not help promote Mr. Rublee's journey merely in order to make Germany the scapegoat." While disapproving, the state secretary nevertheless sent the British and American memorandums to Ribbentrop, whose assistant would note on them: "No reply to be made, by direction of the Foreign Minister."[69]

On 19 October, the day after Henderson's and Wilson's less than promising interviews, Rublee wrote to Hull that British Foreign Office was arguing that because "Henderson's report was discouraging," it seemed that "the German reply to the request that I be received would be in the negative." Perhaps relying on Rublee's personal confidence, Hull replied, "We have no reason for sharing the pessimism expressed by the Foreign Office" and indicated a willingness for Wilson to continue pressing the request.[70]

With the critical moment of his mission possibly approaching, Rublee proceeded to formulate an initial plan to lay before the German government in the event that he was received. Rublee communicated his plan to Hull in a lengthy cable on 27 October. Although Stephen Wise had warned him in August that there could be no relaxation of the international boycott on German products, Rublee explained to Hull that his plan's "adoption will strongly tend to remove the existing boycott of German goods and resistance to their purchase by the public."[71] While the international Jewish community was satisfied that the boycott aiming at better treatment of German Jews had begun to bite and was intent on continuing it, Rublee and other American and British experts realized that Jews fleeing Germany had no chance of taking any of their wealth with them so long as the German currency crisis continued. Too, while the influence behind the international boycott was considerable, it was the least difficult obstacle to surmount on the international stage.

Although Rublee's plan was rather complex in its use of financial instruments and clearing arrangements, the principal feature was clear. As he explained to Hull, "The central idea of the plan is that Germany and the involuntary emigrant should share the proceeds derived from an increase in German exports consequent upon the reversal of the boycott and political appeasement resulting from the settlement of the non-Aryan question in Germany."[72] Rublee had essentially concluded that both sides would have to relax their stance. International Jewish organizations would have to abate the boycott, and the German government would, in turn, have to arrange "a political appeasement" of Jews remaining in Germany and allow emigrating Jews to recoup their property over a ten-year period through a bond retirement scheme. While Rublee did not explain what he meant by "political appeasement," his memorandum stipulated: "Preferably the Aryanization of non-Aryan property of potential emigrants would cease. Businesses and other property would be Aryanized only coincidentally with the individual holder's emigration." If the general confiscation did not stop, Rublee proposed that "the German government issue its bonds against transfer of all non-Aryan property other than personal belongings." Although he did not in October communicate it, Rublee would also aim for a new political classification for Jews that would mitigate to some extent the 1935 Nuremberg laws that stripped Jews of their citizenship and would also aim for a relaxation of the subsequent restrictions on Jews that approximated Jim Crow laws in the southern United States and the South African apartheid system. While he knew that the international Jewish community would resist terminating the boycott, Rublee seems to have viewed his hopeful negotiation with the Nazis as the fruition of the Jewish community's lengthy effort to bring about a change in German policy. Rublee likely believed that he was in effect reaching an accommodation that the Nazis and the international Jewish community could not conclude.

In addition to being problematic for Western Jews, Rublee's plan gave few safeguards that would satisfy Hull's concerns regarding Latin American trade. Taking up Hull's concern that Germany would "attempt to secure trade concessions" from countries providing refuge, Rublee asserted that he would answer such German efforts with the observation that he was "not authorized to negotiate on a basis which would involve such concessions" without the approval of the involved countries. In a statement that reflected his belief that the Latin Americans should answer for themselves, Rublee observed:

> You have made it quite clear to me that any such concessions are completely out of the question in the case of the United States. It is, however, possible that other countries may be prepared to grant trade concessions to Germany in order to contribute to the success of a transfer plan for the benefit of involuntary emigrants which, in measure, would tend to perpetuate and intensify the bilateral export character of the trade relations between Germany and such countries.[73]

Rublee allowed that he would "bear in mind the possible effect of such arrangements on the American trade agreement programme" and affirmed that he would keep Hull "informed as to any developments in this connection." Carrying on in the Morrow tradition, Rublee believed that Latin American republics could act independently of U.S. interests. At any rate, he certainly seemed unwilling to make the protection of a trade policy of uncertain merit a constraining condition in his effort to alleviate the plight of 600,000 people.

Not surprisingly, Hull did not condone Rublee's plan. After two days of "continuous thought" and "a general joint conference with Treasury" Department officials concerning Rublee's proposal, Hull could report only that "[a] number of serious technical difficulties are evident. We are giving further consideration to all aspects of the matter and will send you within a few days a comprehensive discussion of the whole problem and certain new suggestions.[74] While Hull would not send the department's "comprehensive" response for another eleven days, matters in Berlin relative to a Rublee visit went through a series of dramatic developments. On 2 November Wilson recounted the substance of his luncheon conversation with "one of the leading bankers of Berlin," likely Hjalmar Schacht.[75] Wilson reported:

> He informed me in the strictest confidence and begged me to see that no leak occurred, that both [Minister of National Economy Walther] Funk and Goering are convinced that Rublee's visit must be encouraged and that some kind of plan must be worked out with him. They see the great advantages to Germany of doing away with or mitigating this cause of international hatred. Goering...intends to speak to Hitler on the subject. Their apprehension is Ribbentrop's attitude which they fear will be exercised against the plan.[76]

Wilson's dispatch confirmed what Rublee had been hearing from his German sources and invigorated his hopes that the German schism might shift in his and the emigrants' favor.

The next day Rublee was able to state in a cable that "a responsible German source" had informed him that "Goering has the matter in hand, and that his final decision will be determined by the possibility of Germany obtaining economic and financial advantages in negotiation with the Intergovernmental Committee." Very likely Göring had learned the substance of Rublee's plan through air attaché Wenninger, who would have been in communication with Göring, who was also minister for aviation. Rublee's apparent intention to work against the international boycott and his ability to communicate that intention seem to have been critical to giving the economic coterie in Berlin leverage against Ribbentrop.

The first indication of a thaw in the German Foreign Office came on 8 November when Weizsäcker told Hugh Wilson, who had continued to press the issue, that "they did not want Rublee to go away without something [if he came] but that it had not yet been possible to solve the financial problem which was the main difficulty."[77] Weizsäcker indicated that the German government might be willing to begin a negotiation with Rublee if it seemed that a financial solution could be found and if Rublee could provide the specific number of immigrants whom foreign countries were willing to accept. This positive, though guarded, response was the break Rublee was looking for, and it seemed that he might go to Berlin almost any day. To his dismay, however, a dramatic event in Paris brought the hopeful situation crashing down.

On 28 October German soldiers had rounded up 12,000 Polish Jews living in Germany, dumped them on the Polish frontier without shelter or provisions, and insisted that they could not return to Germany. The Polish government, which approached the Nazis in their antisemitic views, refused to allow the Jews to enter Poland, so they remained on the frontier without support. On 7 November, seventeen-year-old Herschel Grynszpan, who lived in Paris but whose parents were among the 12,000 Jews on the Polish-German border, proceeded to the German Embassy in Paris, where he intended to shoot the German ambassador. Instead, Grynszpan shot the third secretary, Ernst vom Rath, whom he encountered first. When vom Rath died on 10 November, organized Nazi assaults on Jews and their property were carried out throughout Germany. The event became known as Kristallnacht, or the Night of Broken Glass.[78]

The Paris shooting and subsequent upheaval in Germany rendered Rublee's visit impossible in the short run and seemed at first to strengthen Ribbentrop's control over any negotiation with the IGC. Writing to Learned Hand on 10 November, Rublee vented his frustration, claiming, "This is the God-damnedest job I have ever been in."[79] Rublee related the opportunity that the schism between Göring and Ribbentrop seemed to offer and observed, "I felt that even if I went to Berlin the chances were greatly against my success, but still this was what I came for, and I wanted to have a go at it." Rublee believed that there "seemed to be a chance but now the way looks barred again,"explaining: "The German Secretary of Embassy, who the poor little Jew boy shot in Paris dies yesterday. And to-day terrible news has come of rioting all over Germany, pogroms, clubbing and beating of Jews, looting, burning of Synagogues, terrible, brutal madness." Rublee added: "There is a strange inconsistency in the German conduct. They order the Jews out, drive them out, force them across frontiers; and at the same time, they keep up continuous anti-semitic propaganda in other countries—South America for instance—directed at preventing those countries from admitting Jews. Perhaps they just want to torture them.[80] Rublee was depressed about his work, admitting that "There is the constant painful feeling that, if somebody else were in my place, he could see something to be done that I am missing."[81] He was also concerned about the prospects for European civilization if another war erupted. Although Rublee agreed with Hand's wife that the totalitarian systems could not last indefinitely, he feared that they "may last long enough to destroy what we care for."

Rublee did not confine his expression of frustration to close personal friends. On 14 November he sent a cable to Hull, the opening sentence of which read: "The attack on the Jewish community in Germany on the one hand and the indifference of the participating governments to the fate of the victims on the other has brought the affairs of the [IGC] to a critical stage where...immediate action is required if the President's initiative is to lead to a positive result."[82] Rublee requested that an emergency meeting of the IGC be called to demonstrate "to the German Government that its present activity is not a matter of complete indifference to the governments participating in the Intergovernmental Committee." During the proposed meeting Rublee planned also to bring pressure to bear on the IGC members by reporting the he had "discussed the possibilities of immigration with representatives of the Latin America Republics, with the commissioners representing the British Dominions, with spokesmen for the colonial empires, and have met with a negative response."[83] Rublee's only success to date was having managed to convince Western countries neighboring Germany to temporarily abate their policy of "*refoulement*" by which they "ship refugees back to Germany indiscriminately," where many "are thrust into prison camps." Rublee was able to procure this hiatus "somewhat on the understanding that I was about to go to Berlin." Likewise frustrated with the ongoing diplomatic impasse, Rublee wanted the member governments to continue "pressing the German Government for a definite 'yes' or 'no' to the request that [he] be received." Rublee planned to conclude his planned IGC report with the observation that "there can be no real appeasement" in Europe "so long as large numbers of people are kept in fear of their lives and uncertainty as to their fates."

The next day Rublee sent Hull a summary of a conversation regarding the future of the IGC with officials at the British Foreign Office. Rublee reported that the British had pointed out that the IGC was "set up at the request of President Roosevelt," that the "Director's office was organized as a result of the American effort at Evian," and "that therefore the British would not presume to offer suggestions as to what the future of the Committee would be." Nevertheless, the British added: "For instance, although the British would welcome the [re]constitution of the [IGC] as an advisory body to the League Commission, they would not propose this solution in any formal manner." A few days later Rublee reported that, in addition to British threats of detachment, the French had basically abandoned the IGC, the executive having "not heard from Bérenger since the meeting in August."[84] Through these reports Rublee let Hull know that time was running out on his mission and that pressure would have to be stepped up on Germany to receive him before the IGC disintegrated. Evidently owing to Rublee's cables, two days later Hull made an announcement at a press conference recognizing Rublee's months of effort and reproving Germany's lack of cooperation. Hull asserted that Rublee had "for some time been prepared to go to Berlin" but that "no definite reply has yet been received."[85]

Rublee's call for renewed pressure on Germany was timely, likely owing to information he had on the status of the schism within the German government. While at first it seemed that the vom Rath assassination had given Ribbentrop the upper hand, ending any chances Rublee had to negotiate a settlement, Hermann Göring had yet been able to slyly—if viciously—bend the destructive Kristallnacht pogroms to fit his purposes. On 12 November Göring held an interdepartmental conference at which he announced that Hitler had recently entrusted the direction of Germany's Jewish policy to him. A memorandum describing the meeting that circulated in the German Foreign Ministry stated:

> In the conference...which dealt with the Jewish question Field Marshal Göring had demanded that Jewish emigration be promoted and in this connection [envisioned] collaboration with trusteeships organized abroad. ...[T]he question had been discussed whether the offer of Director Rublee of the London Committee should not be accepted. All those present had been in favor of doing so. [Göring] believed that it might yet be possible to obtain practical results through Rublee.[86]

Göring proceeded to shrewdly encapsulate a plan for working with Rublee within a larger program that touted further denigration of Jewish life in Germany to encourage their emigration. Marginal, handwritten notes on a summary of Göring's meeting relate that his clique had taken control of German Jewish policy. The notes, written by Schumburg, a counselor in the German Foreign Ministry, and described as "partly illegible," read:

> As long as a Jew is engaged in export business he is *not* to be touched. We can link our interests with Jewish interests. The Jews are to be used in the export trade.... *Jews as sales representatives* to be decided according to individual cases. Better than new Aryan representatives. *Greatest caution* in replacing them. The Party point of view must be

eliminated; the business point of view must prevail...every concession involving ideological principles is possible.[87]

To prevent regional and local Nazi violence against Jews, a directive was adopted stating: "A strict prohibition of unauthorized action [against Jews] is to be issued immediately to...the Party authorities."[88]

Rublee's efforts to induce the U.S. State Department to step up pressure on Germany were likely based on information coming from Wenninger and Kordt relating Göring's success in displacing Ribbentrop. He did not, however, have immediate success. An interview that Wilson secured with Ribbentrop on 15 November resulted in the German foreign minister refusing to allow Rublee to come to Berlin, suggesting instead that "unofficial persons might explore this matter with Rublee perhaps in Holland and go into the question from the ground up."[89] This was Wilson's last effort in Berlin before he returned home to the United States for what began as a temporary visit but became a diplomatic recall protesting Kristallnacht.[90] In his absence, Prentis Gilbert, the chargé d'affaires, represented the United States in Berlin.

Although Ribbentrop seemed to be warming somewhat to a Rublee negotiation, Göring evidently worried that the foreign minister was feigning interest and would in the end block any change in policy toward German Jews. In an effort to secure support in the Nazi Party for his planned negotiation with Rublee, Göring on 9 December held a meeting with *Gauleiters*, regional party officials, to float the idea. As reported by Prentis Gilbert, Göring was said to have informed them that the Jewish question had become recently both an internal and external problem and warned them that "they must not be surprised if they should hear of his being in conference with groups of Jews." Göring added that he "could see no reason why Mr. Rublee if he felt inclined to do so should not shortly come to Berlin to talk things over." Undermining Ribbentrop's position and existing government policy, Göring stated that it would be "absurd to expect the emigrants from Germany [to be] completely lacking in funds." Lest they fear the new policy would relieve pressure on Jews, Göring informed the officials that his plan envisioned the "elimination of all Jews within a period of 3 years." Göring affirmed that Germany had much to gain from settling the issue, pointing to the example of an I. G. Farben official who complained that the giant chemical company "estimated that it was facing a curtailment in its foreign orders of about forty percent." Finally, Göring was reported to have privately told intimate friends that "Hitler had a few days previously conveyed to [him] the liquidation of the Jewish problem."[91]

Over the next two weeks, the two German factions struggled for control over access to Rublee, creating what Gilbert described as a "highly charged political atmosphere [in] Berlin."[92] The result of the contest was that a planned clandestine meeting in Holland between Rublee's assistants Pell and Cotton and a German economic expert was terminated at the last moment. While Ribbentrop had it in mind that Rublee would meet the Englishman Godman, whom Ribbentrop felt he could control, Göring and Reichsbank president Schacht had initiated a separate rendezvous to establish contact with Rublee through Pell and

Cotton.[93] Rublee related the potential breakthrough and subsequent failure in private letters to friends on 8 December. He began by explaining, "There are two factions in Germany. One headed by Göring, Funk [the Minister of Economics], and Schacht [who] want to stop the world rumpus by settling the Jew question with me if they can do so cheaply enough. The other led by Ribbentrop, Himmler, and Goebbels want to exterminate the Jews."[94] Relating the episode involving the secret meeting, Rublee explained that Wenninger and Kordt "emphasized the need of secrecy and speed in order to keep the other faction from knowing that contact with me was on foot."[95] To Rublee's great irritation, however, the French, who "knew nothing about the intended meeting in Brussels," wrecked the secret encounter. Rublee explained that

> there was a leak in Paris, not about me, but about the plan of settlement which the Germans had got up. So the bright idea occurred to [Foreign Minister Georges] Bonnet that he should take the matter up with Ribbentrop—the very man who was not to know—when he came to Paris. Bonnet did so and Ribbentrop reacted violently. He said that the Jews were all pickpockets, thieves and murderers, that their property had been stolen and Germany meant to take it all away and to treat them like criminals.[96]

Rublee observed, "This happened the day before Pell and Joe were to go to Brussels and the next day the German intermediary 'fell ill.'" Rublee complained that, Bonnet having "forced Ribbentrop to take a position, …the matter of the [planned] meeting had become difficult." Highly irritated, he spouted: "All the results of my careful maneuvering undone by this God-damned bonehead gaffe of the French!"[97]

While it seemed that all was lost, Reichsbank president Hjalmar Schacht emerged out of the chaos in Berlin on 12 December, when he secured Hitler's approval authorizing him to travel to London, where he would openly meet with Rublee. Schacht would officially be traveling in response to an invitation from Bank of England president Montagu Norman that the two discuss monetary and credit policies. An ardent nationalist, but not a member of the Nazi Party, Schacht was on record as early as 7 July 1938 of warning of the consequences of an effort to rid the German economy of Jewish businesses. In a letter to minister of interior Wilhelm Frick on that day, Schacht denounced Frick's plan for "the final elimination of Jews from German economic life" and warned that "vital foreign trade and foreign exchange would be lost by the sudden closing of Jewish firms with business connections abroad."[98] Schacht "suggested instead that the Jews be allowed over a 5- to 10-year period to dispose of their holdings in German industry in an orderly fashion, possibly in accordance with agreements with foreign governments and Jewish organizations abroad." Schacht, who would be tried (and acquitted) at the Nuremberg Trials for managing the German economy so as to allow Hitler to rearm for an aggressive war, was central to Rublee's success in negotiating with the German government.

Schacht arrived in London on 14 December and met with Rublee, Lord Winterton, Norman Montagu, chief economic adviser Sir Frederick Leith-Ross, and British foreign secretary Viscount Halifax on 15 December. Prior to leaving

Germany, Schacht visited first with Göring, who reported, according to a German memorandum, that he had visited with Hitler about steering the Jewish question "away from the field of politics into that of the purely economic."[99] Göring asserted that he had "an express directive to that effect from the Fürher." Nevertheless, Schacht traveled to see Hitler before going to London, where he "had had the Fürher expressly repeat the instruction to him personally during a half-hour conference in Munich." Although Hitler approved of Schacht communicating a plan to Rublee while in London, he did not give Schacht "plenipotentiary powers" or authorize him to negotiate a final settlement.[100]

Following the early evening meeting with Schacht, Rublee sent a cable informing Welles of the interview. Rublee wrote:

> Schacht presented his plan orally saying that it had the approval of Göring and was the best that could be put forward, although it did not necessarily exclude other plans, if a better could be found. The atmosphere of the meeting was extremely agreeable and it concluded by Schacht assuring me that I would be welcome in Berlin if it was found that the plan presented a basis for discussion. Schacht did not say that the plan was a "take it or leave it" proposition but said that whatever observations we might have should be presented quickly because otherwise he did not know what would happen to the Jewish community in Germany.[101]

Schacht began the substance of his proposal by pointing out that there were 600,000 Jews in Germany based on the 1935 Nuremberg race laws. Of that population, his plan envisioned the emigration of 150,000 adult males over a three-year period. Following their settlement, they would be joined by 250,000 women and children. The remaining 200,000 "were old people and would have to remain in Germany." Schacht estimated that Jewish property in Germany amounted to 6 billion marks, and he proposed that German Jews deposit 1.5 billion marks of their property in a trust fund and that an additional 1.5 billion marks' worth of foreign exchange be raised by international Jewish organizations and lent to the German government, which would then distribute the funds for Jewish emigration. The German government would pay 4 percent interest and amortize the loan at 2 percent annually. Those payments would be made in credits to be spent on German goods to be exported to the areas of resettlement, something closely akin to the Haavara program. Rublee concluded, "Schacht said that Germany would not concede one cent out of the proceeds of its exports. He also said that as a condition of the plan persecution of Jews would cease."[102]

Schacht's proposal was not very close to Rublee's, but Rublee believed it reflected a basis for continuing negotiation. The next day he let Hull know that he and Winterton had "decided that two committees should be set up immediately with me as chairman."[103] The first would "consist of governmental financial experts" from the United States, Great Britain, France, the Netherlands, and "possibly Sweden." The second committee would consist of "prominent Jews representing the American, British, French and Dutch Jewish communities, to which might be added representative of the church groups who [are] particularly interested in the fate of the non-Aryans." Rublee wanted Hull to quickly name a U.S. representative to the first committee, and he thought it "essential that some representative of American Jewry" be found for the second. Rublee concluded reminding Hull that "Schacht impressed upon me the importance of reaching a decision as soon as possible in view of the uncertain situation in Germany."

Although Rublee evidently thought that Schacht's proposed plan was workable as a basis for negotiation, he soon found resistance mounting against it. Hull quickly replied that he "strongly" thought it "inadvisable" for a U.S. official to sit on the first committee, instead thinking an American banker more suited.[104] While Hull did request the PACPR to "designate a representative" for the second committee, he would soon find the committee opposed to the idea. Reporting the difficulties he was likewise encountering in Europe, Rublee reported on 18 December that French Jewish leaders were "categorically opposed to the setting up of a private committee which would lend an air of credulity to the idea that there is such a thing as world Jewry."[105] They instead believed "that the matter should be considered exclusively by the governments."

Hull, too, had met Jewish resistance in the United States and informed Rublee that, first, no one "believes that it would be possible to raise the sum mentioned, or even an appreciable part of it," and, second: "The plan is generally considered as asking the world to pay a ransom for the release of hostages in Germany and to barter human misery for increased exports."[106] Hull also pointed to other problems in the plan, which in sum rendered it void of "any hope of acceptability." So as not to add to "the plight of Jews in Germany," however, Hull decided against "summary rejection" and asked Rublee "merely" to emphasize to "all groups that subscriptions to these bonds would not be forthcoming on the basis of Schacht's plan." Hull believed that "far more money would be subscribed as a straight loan to some central committee" that would "have no connection with Germany, German exports or the liquidation of refugee property in Germany." Such a loan would "be repaid ultimately by the individual refugees when they are in a position to do so." On 21 December Hull sent a cable detailing the State and Treasury Departments' preferred plan, which reflected Hull's preference for a "straight loan" that would avoid the issue of German exports and foreign exchange.[107] Such issues would have required the United States to work against the international Jewish boycott of Germany, "which was wholly unofficial" and therefore difficult to control.

Rublee was frustrated with the resistance of Western European and American Jews to participation in a loan to German Jews and to the idea of relaxing the boycott. He did not believe that they sufficiently realized the impending violence awaiting Jews in Germany and that, although any arrangement with Germany would be distasteful, it was necessary to save lives. Writing to Dean Acheson on 21, December he related his concerns and frustrations:

> I gather that there has been much heat and fury at home over Schacht's scheme as reported (quite inadequately and inaccurately) in the press.... I sometimes wonder whether people in their indignation against Germany do not altogether lose sight of the

dreadful predicament of the Jews in Germany and what more may happen to them if we do not succeed in making a settlement which will enlist Germany's cooperation. They forget, or do not know, that there are two factions in the Nazi party, one of which is intent on exterminating the Jews, while the other wishes to conciliate world opinion and stop the persecution. At the moment we have the chance to deal with the moderate faction who have won Hitler's consent. If we fail to settle, the pendulum will swing the other way and the extreme radical wing will regain control.[108]

Likewise, Rublee warned Hand that those joining in the "outcry in America against Schacht's proposal...don't realize that by attacking the Nazi moderates they are playing into the hands of the Nazi extremists who want to exterminate the Jews." Rublee complained, "The plight of the wretched Jews in Germany seems to be the last thing these Americans think of. They appear to want to give themselves the pleasure of taking a crack at Germany without regard to what may happen to Germany's victims.[109] Although at first concerned that the public outcry would doom his negotiation, "which a little while ago...seemed impossible to have at all," Rublee had managed to calm various interested parties and thought that the "way is now clear for me to go to Berlin early in January."[110] He hoped "it may remain clear."

While Rublee was excited to at last have a chance to carry out the high-level negotiation on behalf of German Jews, he was also ready for the work to be completed. Earlier in December to a friend he had confided, "I am thinking of how I can detach myself from this job without getting in bad with the president and the State Department."[111] "Do it I must," he believe, "but it cannot be before the meeting of the full committee in January." The Schacht visit and Rublee's now cleared mission provided him a chance to bring his work to an end either as a success or as a failure. Rublee evidently informed Myron Taylor of his plans, who wrote to Hull on 28 December, stating: "Rublee made it plain to you and to me when he accepted the office of Director that he could only occupy this function for a limited period. He will wish to withdraw at the end of the German negotiation, that is to say after he has presented his report to the full Committee."[112] Myron reported that the IGC committee would meet toward the end of January, when Rublee "will record success or partial success or no success." Rublee's last public mission was coming, as he wrote to Acheson, to "the critical and interesting stage."[113] As he stepped onto a train heading for the English Channel in early January, Rublee was aware that he was taking part in a world historic moment and that the fate of hundreds of thousands of people stood in the balance.

Rublee arrived in Berlin on 13 January 1939 and immediately resumed negotiations with Schacht at the Ministry of Economics, seemingly demonstrating the continued strength of the Göring-Schacht-Funk cadre over Ribbentrop and the Foreign Office. After three days of negotiations Rublee and Schacht began formulating a written proposal on the points to which they had agreed. Although Rublee was disturbed that Schacht's position "represented a hardening of the German position on several points," Rublee did not think that they were at an impasse.[114] Too, while he knew that the plan would elicit strong resistance in the Jewish community—even Brandeis had communicated his disapproval to Rublee through Acheson—Rublee believed the plan would offer many dramatic improvements for German Jews.[115]

Because Schacht had pledged to do so, he sent a memorandum to Ribbentrop on 16 January updating him on the status of the negotiations. Evidently, Schacht did not take Nazi invectives against Jews seriously enough. If he had, he would have edited his and Rublee's memorandum extensively for Ribbentrop's digestion. The financial arrangement was straightforward enough, providing that the German government would take over all Jewish property, 25 percent of which would go into a "trust fund" to be returned to emigrating Jews over a period of time, the remaining 75 percent remaining "at Germany's disposal in so far as it is not needed to support the Jews until they emigrate, or to maintain until their death those who are aged or not suited for emigration."[116] Jewish emigration under the new agreement would be financed by international organizations and governments rather than through a loan to the German government from "international Jewry." While these features of the agreement were likely viewed as relatively innocuous, Rublee's requests aiming at improving conditions for Jews remaining in Germany were evidently highly inflammatory. Of Rublee's requests Schacht observed: "It is desired that Jews now in the concentration camps (information requested as to their numbers) should be given priority in the matter of emigration in so far as they are not criminals. In this connection, it is proposed that a camp be opened abroad in which these Jews may be quartered temporarily."[117] Rublee apparently wanted these Jews out of Germany as quickly as possible. Schacht next reported: "So far as the Jews concerned who do not come under the category eligible for emigration, they are to be assured satisfactory living conditions—not only economically (housing, food, etc.) but also in the sense that they be permitted to lead a normal life free from molestation."[118] Partly because Rublee had found that Latin American governments believed that Jews would make poor pioneers since most were urban professionals until Nazi laws stripped them of professional occupations, he requested that "Until they actually emigrate, the Jews eligible for emigration are, so far as possible, to be employed in some way, either on model or other farms or in factories.... Mr. Rublee would consider it very desirable if such farms and factories could be set up by the Jewish community in Germany."[119] Hoping to prevent the reintroduction of Jewish ghettos in Germany, Rublee also asked, according to Schacht, that "[t]he relatives of the emigrating Jews, as well as the Jews who cannot emigrate, shall, so far as possible—this is Mr. Rublee's wish—be left were they are, and not be segregated. In other words, Mr. Rublee would like to see the pressure upon these Jews to abandon their present apartments and houses eased."[120] Schacht may have believed that with Hitler seeming to support the negotiations, Ribbentrop would accept the proposed dramatic shift in Jewish policy. Instead, Schacht would be out of office within forty-eight hours.

On 20 January Rublee sent a cable to Hull, the opening sentence of which began: "I was informed officially over the phone this morning that Dr. Schacht had been relieved of his functions and that as a consequence he would be unable to continue the conversations or even to see me again."[121] Rublee later explained that after he and Schacht had "had about three or four sessions" during which they "were getting along well[,] there occurred a strange incident":

> At the last meeting I had with [Schacht] he asked Pell to stop behind a moment. We waited until Pell came out and as we drove home, Pell said that Schacht had drawn him aside into a window where he spoke in a low voice and said that the Gestapo had reported that "Mr. Rublee and you have stated that I'm disloyal to the regime. Can this be denied?" Of course we…had no knowledge whatever about it. It surprised us a good deal. The next morning before I was up Dr. Schacht had telephoned that it would be impossible for him to meet me or see me again. We telephoned the Ministry and found that he had left the Ministry and every Schacht person was out of the Ministry—they didn't know anything about it or where he was. They had nothing to say to us.[122]

Although Schacht was important enough to the regime to have his life preserved, his unguarded memorandum reflecting his negotiations with Rublee was evidently enough to spur the opposition to action. The day before Schacht's ejection, Ribbentrop circulated a memorandum countermanding the Schacht–Rublee statement that Schacht had shared at an interministerial meeting. Reasserting control, Ribbentrop ordered that

> 1. Initialing of any agreements with Mr. Rublee is out of the question.
> 2. Among the agencies, the Foreign Ministry is to have primary responsibility in this matter, but must not give this impression vis-a-vis foreign countries.
> 3. No promises are to be made to Mr. Rublee concerning the future treatment of the Jews in Germany.[123]

As Rublee had feared in December, an untoward step had caused the "pendulum to swing" toward "the extreme radical wing."[124]

Owing to Schacht's abrupt removal, Rublee was suddenly in a disastrous position. He was scheduled to be in Paris three days hence for a meeting of the IGCE, which was to be a preliminary meeting for a gathering of the full IGC scheduled for 26 January, at which he was to give his final report. To return to Paris in time, he had to catch the last train out of Berlin the next day, roughly thirty-six hours. Suddenly, however, he had no one with whom to negotiate in Berlin. Schacht had been appointed to meet with Rublee only in his capacity as Reichsbank president, his tenure as economic minister having ended a few years before. With Ribbentrop insisting that the Foreign Office could not receive Rublee because the German government did not recognize the body he represented, his negotiation was effectively terminated. Rublee was in a very difficult position, as he later recalled: "I knew that if I went back to Paris without having renewed negotiation with the German government, my committee would never let me go back to Berlin."[125] He realized that "it was necessary to do something and we had only two days."

Rublee, of course, was unwilling to let Ribbentrop outmaneuver him even in Berlin. In his communication to Hull on 20 January he announced his intention to "satisfy myself that there is no intention on the German part to continue the discussion through some other channel before I leave Berlin."[126] Rublee first attempted to solicit help from Prentis Gilbert and Sir George Ogilvie-Forbes, the British chargé d'affaires, but neither was able to speak with anyone at the Foreign Ministry. On the morning of the day that he was to leave, Rublee took a bold step. Having determined that he needed to get into touch with Göring, Rublee asked Gilbert to arrange a meeting between the two. Gilbert, however, felt that this would be inappropriate according to diplomatic convention and regretfully refused. Unwilling to give up, Rublee next pressured Raymond Geist, the American consul-general, to get involved. Geist agreed to call on General Karl Bodenschatz, who was Göring's assistant. Working through Bodenschatz, to Rublee's relief, Göring granted him an interview early that afternoon.[127]

Rublee's meeting with Göring lasted about an hour, during which Göring did most of the talking. Although Göring insisted that emigrating Jews could take no foreign exchange with them, he did not otherwise touch upon the negotiation details. Instead, Göring named Helmuth Wohlthat, an adviser in the German Ministry for Economic Affairs, to carry on the negotiation where Rublee and Schacht had left off. This was all that Rublee had sought. Following the meeting Göring and Rublee issued a statement that read:

> Mr. Rublee had a private conference with Field Marshal General Goering this afternoon. Mr. Rublee is therefore in a position to state that the negotiations commenced with Dr. Schacht have not broken down but will be continued with Ministerial Direktor Wohlthat, an official designated for these negotiations.[128]

Immediately after the meeting, Rublee departed for Paris. There he secured approval for his immediate return to Berlin and a postponement of the full IGC meeting pending his return.[129]

While Rublee was in Paris, Göring seems to have reasserted his control over the Jewish question. Although Rublee did not believe that Göring "was actuated by humane feelings" but rather a belief "that the persecution was damaging Germany," he was nevertheless delighted that Göring had risked Ribbentrop's, Himmler's, and Goebbels' wraith. Upon his return to Berlin, Rublee met steadily with Wohlthat and produced a memorandum that both signed on 3 February after nine meetings. The document promised a surprising reversal of Jewish policy. It began:

> It has been ascertained that Germany is disposed to adopt a policy which will in every way facilitate and encourage the organized emigration of Jews. A program along the lines hereinafter outlined will be put into effect when Germany is satisfied that countries of immigration are disposed to receive currently Jews from Germany in conformity with this program.[130]

The introduction also stipulated that if Germany implemented the program and the result was an "improvement in the international atmosphere—the emigration will take place in a uniform and orderly manner." By this the Germans asserted that the program would continue if the international boycott was relaxed—the quid pro quo that Stephen Wise had warned against.

Surprisingly, Rublee was able to secure most of the aspects that Schacht had agreed to before his downfall. Those elements included the following points:

> 10. Conditions which have led to the retention of Jews…in camps should automatically disappear if a program of organized emigration is put into effect. […]
> 13. It is the intention on Germany's part to assure that persons [unfit for emigration] and persons awaiting emigration may live tranquilly, unless some extraordinary circumstance should occur. There is no intention to segregate the Jews. They may circulate freely. Persons fit for work shall be given the opportunity of employment so as to earn their living;[131]

The plan provided that those unable to work would be supported by a trust fund established out of confiscated or forfeited Jewish wealth. The financial aspects were likewise essentially the same as those worked out with Schacht. The plan provided for the transfer of the trust fund to the emigrant beneficiaries "whenever a change in conditions may render transfer possible," that is, when Germany's foreign currency position improved. It was agreed, however, that emigrants could meanwhile exchange their holdings in the fund for German-manufactured goods in the "Haavara method of transfers," the system that the State Department did not wish to see extended to Latin America.

In his report to Hull at the close of his negotiations, Rublee pointed out that he had "pressed the Germans throughout the conversations to state with the maximum of clarity how they proposed to organize the emigration, how they intended to care for the person who would remain behind in Germany permanently or while awaiting emigration, and how they proposed to deal with the Jewish property which would be set aside in trust while awaiting transfer."[132] These appear to have been Rublee's fundamental concerns. Although the Germans would not recognize the IGC, they did agree to work with the IGC director and agreed to implement the plan independently "when they are satisfied that the countries of immigration are disposed to receive currently Jews from Germany in conformity with the program." Satisfied that he had pressed the Nazi government as far as possible, Rublee pointed out to Hull that the plan "represents a substantial departure from their previous policies and an entirely new attitude towards the Jewish problem which cannot be welcome to the radical elements which are opposed to Goering."[133]

Rublee returned to London to prepare his final report for the full IGC meeting, rescheduled for 13 February at the Quai d'Orsay in Paris. While on 17 January Rublee had received the admonition of a leading American Jew that he not "identify" himself "as an advocate for any suggestion which may come out of your Berlin visits,"[134] upon his return to London he received an encouraging word from Hull, who observed: "Rublee appears to have accomplished more in Berlin than we had reason to expect, and we wish to congratulate him and to express appreciation of the energy and determination with which he carried out his mission in Berlin."[135] It seems that Rublee throughout his tenure as director had pushed the Americans, British, and French to do more than they were willing to do. They may have expected Rublee to be less energetic and resourceful. They may have even at times wished they had not selected him. The French senator Bérenger, at least, verbalized his annoyance at Rublee's unyielding determination to call attention to imperiled Jews, deriding him the "gaunt prophet."[136]

Although Hull was pleased with Rublee's work and recognized that the plan represented "the maximum obtainable" from the German government, he was nevertheless apprehensive about several aspects of the agreement.[137] Hull was concerned that the Germans would not proceed until the resettlement lands had been secured. Since no havens of refuge had emerged, he believed that this would permit Germany "to drop or change the program at any time on the excuse that other governments were not acting in accordance with it." Hull determined that rather than accepting the plan, the committee should only take cognizance of it so that the document could not be used against the IGC governments should no country step forward to help Germany's Jews. Concerning this point, Hull stated: "The distinction between raising no objection to, and actively accepting, a project may seem a fine one, but it is none the less real."[138]

At the 13 February meeting in Paris Rublee gave his final report. All thirty-two participating nations sent representatives. Rublee told them what he had accomplished with the Germans and let them know that it was up to them to take the next step, to open their countries to the desperate emigrants. Having carried out the directives established at the Evian conference, his work was finished. A few days later Rublee resigned and returned to America. Endicott Peabody welcomed him home, observing: "What a good work you have done in London and Berlin! We have been bragging about you ever since 1886 with increasing enthusiasm as the years have gone by."[139] Peabody was glad to know that "the shores of this country of ours are being brightened by the approach of the Queen Mary with my friend the oldest living graduate of this School." Aware of the controversy surrounding Rublee's work, however, Peabody added: "Hitler and his crew are so devoid of conscience that their promises are in themselves of little worth, but it may be that they will find it expedient to stand by the agreements to which you were clever enough to win their consent."

On 2 March Rublee received a letter from two leading German Jews, Dr. Leo Baeck and Dr. Otto Hirsh, who wrote:

> We fully realized the greatness of the sacrifice you offered when you declared your readiness to assume this difficult thorny duty. We have seen the way you displayed the qualities people praised you for: wisdom, straightforwardness, patience, endurance, and we understood that all these spring from one common source: humanity and willingness to help. The work you have achieved—mankind will learn it from the annals of history.[140]

Acheson, who remained close to Rublee in the years that followed, noted that the effort to save German Jews was the last movement in the symphony of Rublee's life. Acheson observed:

> Once again the magnitude of the cause fired George Rublee to overcome towering obstacles. One difficulty after another was met, as conference followed conference up the

Nazi hierarchical scale. At last the impossible seemed to be accomplished. ...The Red Sea seemed to have parted to open the way to a new deliverance. Then came the war, and the deaths of six million people in the concentration camps and gas chambers of Germany and the ghettos of Poland. This was the last passion; the fire, even in the inner recesses of his nature, had gone out.[141]

NOTES

1. Rublee's work figures prominently and sympathetically in Henry Feingold's *The Politics of Rescue: The Roosevelt Administration and the Holocaust, 1938-1945* (New Brunswick, NJ: Rutgers University Press, 1970); in David S. Wyman's *Paper Walls: America and the Refugee Crisis, 1938-1941* (Amherst: University of Massachusetts Press, 1968); in Ari J. Sherman's, *Island Refuge: Britain and Refugees from the Third Reich, 1933-1939* (Berkeley: University of California Press, 1973); and in Arthur D. Morse's *While Six Million Died: A Chronicle of American Apathy* (NY: Random House, 1967).

2. Feingold, *Politics of Rescue*, 17-19.

3. Cordell Hull to Joseph Kennedy, 23 March 1938, *FRUS,* 1938, vol. 1, 740-741.

4. Feingold, *Politics of Rescue*, 22.

5. Minister in Rumania (Gunther) to Secretary of State (Hull), 13 April 1938, *FRUS,* 1938, vol. 1, 742.

6. *FRUS,* 1938, vol. 1, 748, 751.

7. Feingold, *Politics of Refuge*, 32.

8. Myron Taylor to Cordell Hull, 5 August 1938, *FRUS,* 1938, vol. 1, 760.

9. Rublee, "Reminiscences," 284.

10. Ibid., 285.

11. Taylor to Hull, 14 July 1938, *FRUS,* 1938, vol. 1, 756.

12. Ibid., 755.

13. Taylor to Hull, 12 August 1938, *FRUS,* 1938, vol. 1, 764.

14. GR to Hand, 9 August 1938, HLS-Hand, box 107, folder 6.

15. *FRUS,* 1938, vol. 1, 743.

16. Lamont to Myron Taylor in E.T.S. to William Fitch, 4 May 1938, HBS-Lamont, box 133, folder 7.

17. GR to EP, 26 July 1938, GSA.

18. Myron Taylor to Cordell Hull, 3 August 1938, *FRUS,* 1938, vol. 1, 758.

19. Stephen Wise to Brandeis, 9 August 1938, LBP.

20. Ibid. Wise wrote: "[Rublee] laughed when I told him of your estimate of his reading power and reading taste and insisted that you greatly overrated him."

21. GR to Brandeis, 10 August 1938, LBP.

22. GR to Hand, 9 August 1938, HLS-Hand, box 107, folder 6.

23. Hull to the Chargé in Brazil (Scotten), 3 August 1938, *FRUS,* 1938, vol. 1, 758.

24. Chargé in the United Kingdom (Johnson) to Hull, 5 August 1938, *FRUS,* 1938, vol. 1, 760.

25. Taylor and Rublee to Hull, 23 August 1938, *FRUS,* 1938, vol. 1, 770.

26. Rublee would make this observation in Rublee to Taylor, 14 October 1938, John Mendelsohn, editor, *The Holocaust: Selected Documents in Eighteen Volumes* (New York: Garland Publishing, 1982), vol. 6, 4.

27. Taylor and Rublee to Hull, 23 August 1938, *FRUS,* 1938, vol. 1, 770.

28. Hull to Taylor and Rublee, 24 August 1938, *FRUS,* 1938, vol. 1, 769; and Hull to Taylor, 16 August 1938, *FRUS,* 1938, vol. 1, 769.

29. "Latin America, Germany and the Hull Program," *Foreign Affairs* (January 1939), 380.

30. Ibid., 374.

31. Hull to Taylor and Rublee, 27 August 1938, *FRUS,* 1938, vol. 1, 775.

32. Ibid., 776.

33. GR to Hand, 29 August 1938, HLS-Hand, box 107, folder 6.

34. Ibid.

35. GR to Acheson, 9 September 1938, Yale-Acheson, box 27, folder 340. Morrow died of a stroke in October 1931. Rublee had helped plan Morrow's successful Senate campaign in 1930 and planned to assist Morrow in challenging Herbert Hoover's reelection for president in 1932. A Morrow-Roosevelt contest would have been interesting.

36. Taylor and Rublee to Hull, 29 August 1938, *FRUS,* 1938, vol. 1, 777.

37. Biddle to Hull, 30 August 1938, *FRUS,* 1938, vol. 1, 778.

38. Ibid., 779.

39. Hull to Biddle, 1 September 1938, *FRUS,* 1938, vol. 1, 783.

40. Rublee to Hull, 2 September 1938, *FRUS,* 1938, vol. 1, 784.

41. Ibid.

42. In his oral memoir, Rublee asserted that "The United States Ambassador, Joseph P. Kennedy, did not seem interested and never gave me any real support or assistance." Rublee added that "I gathered that President Roosevelt was not seriously interested himself." Rublee, "Reminiscences," 284. Henry Feingold reached the same conclusion regarding Roosevelt. See *Politics of Refuge*, 17-18.

43. Hull to the Ambassador in Argentina (Weddell), 3 September 1938, *FRUS,* 1938, vol. 1, 786.

44. Hull to Weddell, 24 September 1938, *FRUS,* 1938, vol. 1, 791.

45. GR to Hand, 25 September 1938, HLS-Hand, box 107, folder 6.

46. GR to Acheson [1938 ca. Oct 4—editors note], Yale-Acheson, box 27, folder 340.

47. GR to Hand, 25 September 1938, HLS-Hand, box 107, folder 6.

48. Ibid.

49. Ibid.

50. Wilson to Hull, 3 September 1938, *FRUS,* 1938, vol. 1, 785.

51. Acheson to GR, 23 September 1938 and GR to Acheson [1938 ca. Oct 4—editors note], Yale-Acheson, box 27, folder 340.

52. GR to Acheson [1938 ca. Oct 4—editors note], Yale-Acheson, box 27, folder 340.

53. Ibid. While Acheson may have learned the rapid rearmament lesson, he does not seem to have remembered Rublee's admonition regarding an earnest effort at reconciliation, even with a loathsome tyrant and demagogue. Acheson, however, may have lost faith in disarmament negotiations after the poor history of the effort during the interwar period.

54. Ibid.

55. Omission in *FRUS*, which asserts: "Apparently a break in telephone connection at this point." Rublee could have said "Foreign Office," "Prime Minister,"or even the "French."

56. Memorandum of Trans-Atlantic Telephone Conversation, *FRUS,* 1938, vol. 1, 795-796.

57. Rublee to Hull and Welles, 12 October 1938, *FRUS,* 1938, vol. 1, 797.

58. Ibid., 798.

59. Son of Rublee's close friend Joseph Cotton, who died in January. Rublee took on Joe, Jr. as an understudy but it is not currently known how Cotton applied what he learned from Rublee.

60. GR to Frances Hand (Learned Hand's then somewhat estranged wife), 4 December 1938, HLS-Hand, box 107, folder 6. Kordt was later involved in an assassination effort against Hitler. See John Toland, *Adolf Hitler* (New York: Doubleday, 1954), 495.

61. See Wilson to Hull, 15 November 1938, *FRUS,* 1938, vol. 1: 824.

62. GR to Frances and Learned Hand, 10 November 1938, HLS-Hand, box 107, folder 6.

63. Wilson to Hull, 15 October 1938, *FRUS,* 1938, vol. 1, 799.

64. Hull to Wilson, 15 October 1938, *FRUS,* 1938, vol. 1, 799.

65. Ibid., 800.

66. GR to Wilson, 14 October 1938, Hugh Wilson Papers, HHPL, box 3.

67. Wilson to Hull, 18 October 1918, *FRUS,* 1938, vol. 1, 800.

68. Memorandum by the State Secretary, 18 October 1938, *Documents on German Foreign Policy, 1918-1945*, Series D, 1937-1945 (Washington: U.S. Government Printing Office, 1953) vol. 5 [hereafter *German Documents*], 900.

69. Note 2, *German Documents*, 900.

70. Hull to Rublee, 19 October 1918, *FRUS,* 1938, vol. 1, 802.

71. Rublee to Hull, 27 October 1918, *FRUS,* 1938, vol. 1, 809.

72. Ibid.

73. Ibid., 812.

74. Hull to Rublee, 29 October 1938, *FRUS,* 1938, vol. 1, 813.

75. Wilson to Hull, 2 November 1938, *FRUS,* 1938, vol. 1, 814.

76. Ibid.

77. Wilson to Hull, 8 November 1938, *FRUS,* 1938, vol. 1, 815.

78. Wyman, *Paper Walls*, 71.

79. GR to Hand, 10 November 1938, HLS-Hand, box 107, folder 6.

80. Ibid.

81. Ibid.

82. GR to Hull, 14 November 1938, *FRUS,* 1938, vol. 1, 820.

83. Rublee even attempted to get the Soviet Union to accept German Jews. See United States, Department of State, *Records of the German Foreign Office received by the State Department, Auswärtiges Amt (1920-1945*), microfilm, E90, roll 126, frame 191269.

84. GR to Hull, 19 November 1938, *FRUS,* 1938, vol. 1, 834.

85. Hull to Rublee, 18 November 1938, *FRUS,* 1938, vol. 1, 832.

86. *German Documents*, 905-906.

87. *German Documents*, 904, note 2. The italics may indicate that words were underlined.

88. *German Documents*, 904-905.

89. Wilson to Hull, 15 November 1938, *FRUS,* 1938, vol. 1, 824.

90. Wyman, *Paper Walls*, 73.

91. Gilbert to Hull, 9 December 1938, *FRUS,* 1938, vol. 1, 864-65.

92. Gilbert to Hull, 30 November 1938, *FRUS,* 1938, vol. 1, 845.

93. Ibid.

94. GR to Frances Hand, 8 December 1938, HLS-Hand, box 107, folder 6.

95. GR to Acheson, 8 December 1938, Yale-Acheson, box 27, folder 340.

96. Ibid.

97. Rublee was especially irritated at the French because, after months of abandoning the IGC, their representative, Senator Bérenger, made a declaration, at the long postponed executive meeting held on 4 December, stating that the officers "no longer needed to bother about the questions on the agenda" because Chamberlain "had entrusted to M. Bonnet the further handling of this difficult problem." According to a memorandum in the German Foreign Ministry, "Rublee, who is naturally somewhat uneasy about this development because he is afraid that the matter could be jeopardized by clumsy handling on the part of the French, gave the Committee no hints as to the contacts he had meanwhile established." Instead, Rublee "urgently requested the French delegation to avoid anything that might prejudice the success of his future negotiations with Germany" since "his possibilities of negotiation with Germany had not yet been exhausted," *German Documents*, 910.

98. See *German Documents*, 912, note 3.

99. Memorandum by the State Secretary, 20 December 1938, *German Documents*, 913.

100. GR to Welles (then Acting Secretary), 15 December 1938, *FRUS,* 1938, vol. 1, 871.

101. GR to Welles, 15 December 1938, *FRUS,* 1938, vol. 1, 873-874.

102. Ibid.

103. GR to Hull, 16 December 1938, *FRUS,* 1938, vol. 1, 873-874.

104. Hull to GR, 16 December 1938, *FRUS,* 1938, vol. 1, 875.

105. GR to Hull, 18 December 1938, *FRUS,* 1938, vol. 1, 876.

106. Hull to GR, 18 December 1938, *FRUS,* 1938, vol. 1, 876-877.

107. Hull to GR and Taylor, 21 December 1938, *FRUS,* 1938, vol. 1, 878-879. In early December, Roosevelt sent Taylor back to London in an effort to demonstrate renewed U.S. interest.

108. GR to Acheson, 21 December 1938, Yale-Acheson, box 27, folder 340.

109. GR to Hand, 21 December 1938, HLS-Hand, box 107, folder 7.

110. Ibid., and GR to Acheson, 21 December 1938.

111. GR to Frances Hand, 8 December 1938, HLS-Hand, box 107, folder 7.

112. Taylor to Hull, 28 December 1938, *FRUS,* 1938, vol. 1, 883.

113. GR to Acheson, 21 December 1938, Yale-Acheson, box 27, folder 340.

114. GR to Hull, 20 January 1939, *FRUS,* 1939, vol. 2, 71.

115. Acheson to GR, 17 January 1939, Yale-Acheson, box 27, folder 340. Acheson let Rublee know that he had informed Brandeis that Rublee "felt a tremendous responsibility for the people for whose benefit you were carrying on these negotiations and in fact you seemed to have a greater feeling of responsibility for them than anyone else."

116. Memorandum by the President of the Reichsbank, 16 January 1939, *German Documents*, 921.

117. Ibid., 922.

118. Ibid.

119. Ibid.

120. Ibid.

121. GR to Hull, 20 January 1939, *FRUS,* 1939, vol. 2, 71.

122. Rublee, "Reminiscences," 292-293. No work that I have seen on Schacht ties his negotiations with Rublee to his downfall in January 1939. Instead, they all point to his continued rejection of Hitler's rearmament program, which he believed would undermine the German economy. See for instance, Hjalmar Schacht, *Confessions of "The Old Wizard": The Autobiography of Hjalmar Horace Greeley Schacht*, translated by Diana Pike (Boston: Houghton Mifflin Company, 1956); John Weitz, *Hitler's Banker: Hjalmar Horace Greeley Schacht* (Boston: Little, Brown and Company, 1997); and Eugene Davidson, *The Trial of the Germans: An Account of the Twenty-Two Defendants before the International Military Tribunal at Nuremberg* (New York: Macmillan, 1966).

123. Memorandum by the State Secretary, 18 January 1939, *German Documents*, 926.

124. GR to Acheson, 21 December 1938, Yale-Acheson, box 27, folder 340.

125. Rublee, "Reminiscences," 294.

126. GR to Hull, 20 January 1939, *FRUS*, 1939, vol. 2, 71.

127. Rublee, "Reminiscences," 295.

128. Gilbert to Hull, 21 January 1939, *FRUS*, 1939, vol. 2, 73.

129. Taylor to Hull, 25 January 1939, *FRUS*, 1939, vol. 2, 74.

130. Rublee to Hull, 3 February 1939, *FRUS*, 1939, vol. 2, 77-78.

131. Ibid., 79.

132. GR to Hull, 6 February 1939, *FRUS*, 1939, vol. 2, 82-83.

133. Ibid., 83.

134. The advice was from Ben Cohen and was communicated in Acheson to GR, 17 January 1939, Yale-Acheson, box 27, folder 340.

135. Hull to Taylor and Rublee, 8 February 1939, *FRUS*, 1939, vol. 2, 84. 87.

136. Quoted in Feingold, *Politics of Rescue*, 75.

137. Hull to Taylor and Rublee, 8 February 1939, *FRUS*, 1939, vol. 2, 84.

138. Ibid., 84-85.

139. Peabody to GR, 22 February 1939, GSA.

140. Leo Baeck and Otto Hirsch to GR, 2 March 1938, Rublee Papers, Covington and Burling Law Firm, Washington, D.C.

141. Acheson, "George Rublee," 4.

13

Conclusion (1940–1957)

While Dean Acheson described George Rublee's effort to save German Jews as "the last passion," Rublee continued to be an influence in leading circles and contributed further to his period. Recognizing Rublee's penetrating understanding of world events, Cordell Hull asked him early in 1940 to join the State Department's Advisory Committee on Problems of Foreign Relations, for which Rublee served as the chairman of the subcommittee considering the political problems that would follow the war that had engulfed Europe.[1] Fittingly, the Advisory Committee was to analyze the "mistakes of the past" and to consider "the possibilities of the future" to enable the United States "to play a constructive part in the post-war era."[2] Worried about the lack of U.S. preparedness and the constraints of the Neutrality Acts, in May 1940 Rublee wrote Franklin Roosevelt to advocate "a large increase in the appropriations for national defense" and "every possible economic aid that we can give the Allies and whatever change in the laws that may be necessary to that end."[3] In August 1940 Rublee signed with Dean Acheson, Charles Burlingham, and Tom Thacher a legal opinion in support of the Roosevelt administration selling aged American destroyers to Great Britain. Aimed at demonstrating to both the public and a hesitant administration that the Neutrality Acts were not a deterrent to such a transfer, the opinion, published as a letter to the editor of *The New York Times*, argued that "the release of fifty of our over-age destroyers for sale to Great Britain is not only compatible with, but is vitally important to, the safeguarding of our own national defense."[4] Henry Stimson believed the role these lawyers "played in world politics" reflected "real genius in statesmanship."[5] Early in the war Rublee gave some assistance to a group attempting to promote the immigration of English and French children and he also lent some influence to the Non-Sectarian Committee for German Refuge Children, which aimed at securing nonquota entry of German children, Jewish and Christian, into the

U.S.[6] Always the internationalist, toward the war's end Rublee was a member of the Emergency Campaign Committee of the American Association for the United Nations and in December 1947, during the height of congressional debate over the Marshall Plan, Rublee wrote an editorial in *The New York Times* urging support for the massive European assistance program.[7]

When Dean Acheson became secretary of state in January 1949, he wrote to Rublee and confided: "You must know that your own career in behalf of the public at various times has always been an inspiration to me and I doubt very much if I would ever have had so much of it without your example."[8] Acheson hoped that he would continue to "have the benefit of your understanding of the problems and your advice." When Acheson's often troubled tenure as head of the State Department was completed, Rublee complimented him on his "dignity and patience" in bearing "some outrageously unfair criticism and abuse" and predicted that he would "take very high rank among our Secretaries of State."[9]

Rublee retired from Covington and Burling in 1945 and thereafter spent most of his time at Crossways, where his days were full of reading in his library, visiting friends, and playing golf.[10] As Acheson observed, with his days of struggle over, Rublee "turned more and more to his beloved classics (in the original, with a handy trot), to his friends, [and] to his walks at Cornish, New Hampshire."[11] After twelve years of reflection and likely some concern about where the world was heading, on 26 April 1957, at age eighty-nine, George Rublee died in New York City.[12]

In surveying the world in 1898, at age thirty, George Rublee had cautioned Juliet Barrett that "a multitude of important events occurring everywhere" seemed "to portend changes and crises involving the vastest consequences."[13] Believing that they would "live to see some great things done," he hoped that they would "understand and appreciate them if" they could. Over the next fifty-nine years George Rublee did live to see the world's most profound changes and greatest crises and understood only too well the implications of the events.

Dean Acheson thought Rublee "a great gentleman" who "added something unique from himself" to his time, a "brave man" who not only did "not know fear" but "conquered the urge to run away."[14] Rublee's profound interest in his world, and his desire to understand it and to see an improvement in human life led him to insert himself in public affairs to seek solutions to problems that tended to threaten destabilizing conflict. His penetrating observation of his times led him first to conclude that the American laissez-faire political-economic model would have to be substantially altered. Observing both extremes of life at the turn of the century in New York—working in Wall Street's most celebrated firms during the week and teaching immigrant children on Sundays—Rublee recognized the need for a regulated capitalist society. Through his various illuminating experiences, especially those with Cornish colony pundits and mergers such as the one creating U.S. Steel, Rublee by 1910 was prepared to enter the tumultuous and conflicted field of American politics and bring his considerable wisdom to bear in the national struggle, first to help shape Theodore Roosevelt's New Nationalism and the Progressive Party platform, and then to convince Woodrow Wilson and eventually Louis Brandeis of the importance of large corporations to the nation's domestic and international well-being. Creating the Federal Trade Commission and struggling to set its course, Rublee contributed importantly to the nation's acceptance of a government-regulated economy. Eyeing at home and abroad the growing conflict between labor and capital, appreciating the fear of unregulated corporate power, sympathetic to the suffering of the urban masses yet appreciative of the importance of sanctity of property in societal progress, Rublee felt compelled to contribute to the establishment of a salubrious middle way, a new synthesis frustrating the prognostications of both David Ricardo and Karl Marx.

Like other visionaries of his period, Rublee foresaw grave conflict on the international stage and advocated the development of a harmonizing international policy to establish an era of peace and security. Believing that human progress was linked to enlightened self-interest and cooperation among nations, Rublee worked at the close of World War I to establish an innovative, barrier-toppling international organization and struggled without success to secure U.S. support for it. During the interwar years he worked first with Dwight Morrow in Mexico and then on his own in Colombia to rectify U.S.–Latin American relations and to establish equitable relationships between Western capital and developing systems. At the 1930 London Naval Conference he sought to restore European security after America's abortive 1917–1918 intervention, and, on the eve of the world's most horrific war, he persevered against insurmountable odds in a hopeless struggle to establish a program to save German Jews. During each of these pivotal episodes Rublee did "understand and appreciate" the momentous consequences of public policy. Discerning what politicians failed to see, however, he was thought an unintelligible idealist in 1919 and an implacable alarmist in 1939. A witness to human folly to the end, behind his serene eyes the tragic history of the period was quietly chronicled.

NOTES

1. Cordell Hull, *The Memoirs of Cordell Hull* (New York: Macmillan Company, 1948), 1627. According to Hull, Rublee did remain on the committee for more than a year because of illness. While he served, Rublee was only one of two members of the committee who were not State Department officials.

2 Draft of AP article in Hugh Wilson to Sumner Welles, 25 April 1940, Hugh Wilson Papers, Herbert Hoover Presidential Library, box 1.

3. GR to Franklin D. Roosevelt, 21 May 1940, Rublee Papers, Covington and Burling Law Firm, Washington, D.C.

4. Chace, *Acheson*, 79-80; and *The New York Times*, 11 August 1940. According to Leonard Mosley, in his work *Dulles: A Biography of Eleanor, Allen and Foster Dulles and their Family Network* (New York: Dial Press, 1978), Rublee was asked to replace Allen Dulles who withdrew his name from the editorial (104).

5. Henry Stimson to Charles C. Burlingham, 25 August 1940, Yale-Acheson, box 4, folder 53.

6. GR to Peabody, 5 June 1940, GSA; and Wyman, *Paper Walls*, 76-77.

7. Undated article and clipping in GRP. His letter to the editor was written 22 December 1947.

8. Acheson to GR, 18 January 1949, Yale-Acheson, box 27, folder 340.

9. GR to Acheson, 19 January 1952, Yale-Acheson, box 27, folder 340.

10. GR to Hand, 5 July 1945, HLS-Hand, box 107, folder 7.

11. Acheson, "George Rublee," 4. Greek and Roman classics dominated the bookshelves closest to Rublee's reading chair in his library at Crossways (author's visit to Cornish, New Hampshire, May 1995. Remarkably, Rublee's library was left almost undisturbed for nearly forty years. Crossways was owned by Rublee's great nephew, George Rublee, after Juliet's death in 1966 until 1997.

12. George Rublee's ashes were spread at a small cemetery near his home at Cornish, New Hampshire. A headstone bearing witness to his life is erected there.

13. GR to JB, 22 February 1898, GRP.

14. Acheson, "George Rublee," 2.

Selected Bibliography

UNPUBLISHED MATERIALS

Acheson, Dean. Papers. Sterling Library Special Collections, Yale University, New Haven, Connecticut.

Ames, James Barr. Papers. Harvard University Archives, Harvard University, Cambridge, Massachusetts.

Baker, Phillip Noel. Papers. Churchill Archives Center, Churchill College, Cambridge, England.

Bass, Robert Perkins. Papers. Baker Library Special Collections, Dartmouth College, Hannover, New Hampshire.

Bowers, Jane E. "'Oceans of Love': An Introduction to and Excerpts from Juliet Barrett Rublee's Letters to Margaret Sanger." Ph.D. diss., University of Texas at Austin, 1994.

Brandeis, Louis. Papers. Brandeis Law Library, University of Louisville (microfilm), Louisville, Kentucky.

Bring, Danny. "The Origins of the Federal Trade Commission Act: A Public Choice Approach." Ph.D. diss., George Mason University, 1993.

Cravath, Paul. Papers. Herbert Hoover Presidential Library, West Branch, Iowa.

Eliot, Charles. Papers. Harvard University Archives, Harvard University, Cambridge, Massachusetts.

Gay, Edwin. Papers. Houghton Library Special Collections, Harvard University, Cambridge, Massachusetts.

Great Britain. Public Record Office. Cabinet Papers. Cab 23: War Cabinet, June 1917–March 1918, and April–May 1918 (microfilm).

Hand, Learned. Papers. Harvard Law Library Special Collections, Harvard University, Cambridge, Massachusetts.

Harvard University Archives. Houghton Library, Harvard University, Cambridge, Massachusetts.

Hoover, Herbert. Presidential Papers. Herbert Hoover Presidential Library, West Branch, Iowa.

House, Edward. Papers and Diaries. Sterling Library Special Collections, Yale University, New Haven, Connecticut.

Hudson, Manly O. Papers. Harvard Law Library Special Collections, Harvard University, Cambridge, Massachusetts.

Lamont, Thomas. Papers and Diaries. Baker Library Special Collections, Harvard Business School, Harvard University, Cambridge, Massachusetts.

Lane, Arthur Bliss. Papers. Sterling Library Special Collections, Yale University, New Haven, Connecticut.

Leffingwell, Russell. Papers. Sterling Library Special Collections, Yale University, New Haven, Connecticut.

Lippmann, Walter. Papers. Sterling Library Special Collections, Yale University, New Haven, Connecticut.

McNicoll, Robert E. "The Leticia Controversy." Ph.D., diss., Duke University, 1935.

Morrow, Dwight W. Papers. Amherst College Library, Amherst College (microfilm), Amherst, Massachusetts.

Peabody, Endicott. Papers. Groton School Archives, Groton, Massachusetts.

Pearson, Drew. Papers. Lyndon B. Johnson Presidential Library, Austin, Texas.

Progressive Party Archives. Theodore Roosevelt Collection, Houghton Library Special Collections, Harvard University, Cambridge, Massachusetts.

Roosevelt, Theodore. Presidential Papers. U.S. Library of Congress (microfilm), Washington, D.C.

Roosevelt, Franklin. Presidential Papers. U.S. Library of Congress (microfilm), Washington, D.C.

Rublee, George. Papers. Covington and Burling Law Firm, Washington, D.C.

———. Papers [from Crossways, Cornish, New Hampshire]. Currently with author. To be placed with the Baker Library Special Collections, Dartmouth College, Hannover, New Hampshire.

———. "The Reminiscences of George Rublee." New York: Columbia University Oral History Research Office, 1972.

Rublee, Horace. Papers [from Crossways, Cornish, New Hampshire]. Currently with author. To be placed with the Wisconsin Historical Society, Madison, Wisconsin.

Rublee, Juliet. Papers. Baker Library Special Collections, Dartmouth College, Hannover, New Hampshire.

Rublee, Juliet. Papers [from Crossways, Cornish, New Hampshire]. Currently with author. To be placed with the Baker Library Special Collections, Dartmouth College, Hannover, New Hampshire.

Stimson, Henry L. Papers and Diaries. Yale University Library (microfilm), New Haven, Connecticut.

Strauss, Lewis. Papers. Herbert Hoover Presidential Library, West Branch, Iowa.

United States. Department of State. Record Group 43, International Conferences, London Naval Conference Records. National Archives II, College Park, Maryland.

———. Record Group 59, Decimal File. National Archives II, College Park, Maryland.

United States. *Records of the German Foreign Office received by the State Department. Auswärtiges Amt, 1920-1945* (microfilm).

Wilson, Woodrow. Presidential Papers. U.S. Library of Congress (microfilm), Washington, D.C.

Wilson, Hugh. Papers. Herbert Hoover Presidential Library, West Branch, Iowa.

Wise, Stephen. Papers. American Jewish Historical Society, Brandeis University, Waltham, Massachusetts.

PUBLISHED MATERIALS

Acheson, Dean. "George Rublee." *The Groton School Quarterly* (Summer 1957).

———. *Morning and Noon.* Boston: Houghton-Mifflin, 1965.

Ambriosius, Lloyd E. *Wilsonian Statecraft: Theory and Practice of Liberal Internationalism during World War I.* Wilmington, DE: Scholarly Resources, 1991.

Ashburn, Frank Davis. *Fifty Years On: Groton School, 1884-1934.* New York: At the Sign of the Gosden Head [privately printed], 1934.

———. *Peabody of Groton: A Portrait.* Cambridge: Riverside, 1967.

Baker, Ray Stannard. *Woodrow Wilson: Life and Letters.* Volume 6, *Facing War, 1915-1917.* Garden City, NJ: Doubleday, Doran & Company, 1937.

Bellush, Jewel. "Reform in New Hampshire: Robert Bass Wins the Primary." *The New England Quarterly,* 35 (December 1962).

Bane, Suda Lorena and Ralph Haswell Lutz. *The Blockade of Germany after the Armistice, 1918-1919.* New York: Howard Fertig, 1972.

Becker, William and Samuel F. Wells Jr., editors. *Economics and World Power: An Assessment of American Diplomacy since 1789.* New York Columbia University Press, 1984.

Brandeis, Louis D. "The Solution of the Trust Problem." *Harper's Weekly* (8 November 1913).

———, George Rublee, and Joseph P. Cotton. *On Hearings Before the Joint Committee of Congress, Investigation of the Department of the Interior and of the Bureau of Forestry, Brief on Behalf of L.R. Glavis.* June 13, 1910.

Browning, Christopher. *The Final Solution and the German Foreign Office.* New York: Holmes & Meier Publishers, 1978.

Carls, Stephen. *Louis Loucheur and the Shaping of Modern France, 1916-1931.* Baton Rouge: Louisiana State University Press, 1993.

Chace, James. *Acheson: The Secretary of State Who Created the American World.* New York: Simon & Schuster, 1998.

Chandler, Alfred D., Jr. *The Visible Hand: The Managerial Revolution in American Business.* Cambridge: Belknap Press of the Harvard University Press, 1977.

Chernow, Ron. *The House of Morgan: An American Banking Dynasty and the Rise of Modern Finance.* New York: Simon & Schuster, 1990.

Chesler, Ellen. *Woman of Valor: Margaret Sanger and the Birth Control Movement in America.* New York: Doubleday, 1993.

Chiappinelli, Eric. "Victor Morawetz." *American National Biography.* Volume 15. Cary, NC: Oxford University Press, 1998.

Ciccarelli, Orazio. "The Leticia Dispute, 1932-1934: A Reconsideration of Peruvian Motivations." *Southern Quarterly,* 11 no. 4 (1973): 272-296.

Concise Dictionary of American Biography. New York: Charles Scribner's Sons, 1964.

Cooper, John Milton, Jr. *Pivotal Decades: The United States, 1900-1920.* New York: W.W. Norton, 1990.

Cooper, John Milton, Jr. *The Warrior and the Priest: Woodrow Wilson and Theodore Roosevelt*. Cambridge: Belknap Press, 1983.

Cotton, Joseph and Dwight Morrow. "International Cooperation During the War." *Atlantic Monthly* (June 1919).

[Covington & Burling Law Firm]. *Permanent Court of the Arbitration at the Hague: United States-Norway Arbitration, The Argument of Norway*, 22 June 1922.

Craig, Gordon and Francis Loewenheim, editors. *The Diplomats: 1939-1979*. Princeton, NJ: Princeton University Press, 1994.

Croly, Herbert. *The Promise of American Life*. New York: Macmillan, 1909.

Davidson, Eugene. *The Trial of the Germans: An Account of the Twenty-Two Defendants before the International Military Tribunal at Nuremberg*. New York: Macmillan, 1966.

Davis, Cullom. "The Transformation of the Federal Trade Commission, 1914-1929." *The Mississippi Valley Historical Review* (December 1962).

Democratic Party. *National Democratic Platform—Progress in Every Plank*. New York: Democratic National Committee, 1912.

Dryfhout, John H. "The Cornish Colony." *A Circle of Friends: Art Colonies of Cornish and Dublin*. University Art Galleries, University of New Hampshire, and the Thorne-Sagendorph Art Gallery, Keene State College. Durham, NH: University of New Hampshire, 1985.

Duchéne, François. *Jean Monnet: The First Statesman of Interdependence*. New York: W.W. Norton & Company, 1994.

Duncan-Clark, S.J. *The Progressive Movement: Its Principles and Its Programme*. Boston: Small, Maynard & Company, 1913.

Fayle, Ernest. *The War and the Shipping Industry*. Volume 18. Carnegie Endowment for International Peace, Economic and Social History of the World War, British Series. New Haven, CT: Yale University Press, 1927.

Feingold, Henry. *The Politics of Rescue: The Roosevelt Administration and the Holocaust, 1938-1945*. New Brunswick, NJ: Rutgers University Press, 1970.

Ferrell, Robert. *American Diplomacy: A History*. 3rd edition. New York: W.W. Norton & Company, 1975.

Foner, Eric and John Garraty, editors. *The Readers Companion to American History*. Boston: Houghton Mifflin Company, 1991.

Forcey, Charles. *The Crossroads of Liberalism: Croly, Weyl, Lippmann, and the Progressive Era, 1900-1925*. New York: Oxford University Press, 1961.

Frankfurter, Felix. *Felix Frankfurter Reminiscences*. New York: Reynal and Company, 1960.

Gable, John Allen. *The Bull Moose Years: Theodore Roosevelt and the Progressive Party*. Port Washington, NY: Kennikat Press, 1978.

Gardner, William Amory. *Groton Myths and Memories*. Concord: Rumford Press for Groton School, 1928.

Gaskill, Nelson. *The Regulation of Competition*. New York: Harper & Brothers Publishers, 1936.

Gordon, Sarah. *Hitler, Germans and the "Jewish Question*." Princeton, NJ: Princeton University Press, 1984.

Great Britain. *The Allied Maritime Transport Council*. 2 volumes. [London: H.M. Stationery Office, 1919]

Gunther, Gerald. *Learned Hand: The Man and the Judge.* New York: Alfred A. Knopf, 1994.

Gurney, George. *Sculpture and the Federal Triangle*. Washington, D.C.: Smithsonian Institution Press, 1985.

Hall, Linda B. *Oil, Banks, and Politics: The United States and Postrevolutionary Mexico, 1917-1924*. Austin: University of Texas Press, 1995.

Heaton, Herbert. *A Scholar in Action: Edwin F. Gay*. Cambridge: Harvard University Press, 1952.

Hoftstadter, Richard. *The Age of Reform: From Bryan to F.D.R.* NY: Vintage Books, 1955.

Hoover, Herbert. *An American Epic*. Volume 2, *Famine in Forty-Five Nations: Organization Behind the Front, 1914-1923*. Chicago: Henry Regnery Company, 1960.

———. *The Memoirs of Herbert Hoover*. New York: Macmillan Company, 1952.

Howland, Harold. *Theodore Roosevelt and His Times: A Chronicle of the Progressive Movement.* New Haven, CT: Yale University Press, 1921.

Hull, Cordell. *The Memoirs of Cordell Hull.* 2 volumes. New York: Macmillan, 1948.

Hurley, Edward. *A Bridge to France*. Philadelphia: J.B. Lippincott, 1927.

Isaacson, Walter and Evan Thomas. *The Wise Men: Six Friends and the World They Made: Acheson, Bohlen, Harriman, Kennan, Lovett, McCloy*. New York: Simon and Schuster, 1986.

Iriye, Akira. *The Cambridge History American Relations.* Volume 3, *The Globalizing of America, 1913-1945*. New York: Cambridge University Press, 1993.

James, Henry. *Transatlantic Sketches*. Boston and New York: Houghton-Mifflin, 1875, 1903.

Kenwood, A.G. and A. Lougheed. *The Growth of the International Economy 1820-1990.* New York: Routledge, 1992.

Kloppenberg, James. *Uncertain Victory: Social Democracy and Progressivism in European and American Thought, 1870-1920*. New York: Oxford University Press, 1986.

Knock, Thomas. *To End All Wars: Woodrow Wilson and the Quest for a New World Order*. New York: Oxford University Press, 1992.

LaFeber, Walter. *The American Age: United States Foreign Policy at Home and Abroad.* Volume 2. New York. W.W. Norton & Company, 1994.

LaForte, Robert. *Leaders of Reform: Progressive Republicans in Kansas, 1900-1916.* Lawrence, KS: University of Kansas Press, 1974.

Lamont, Edward M. *The Ambassador from Wall Street: The Story of Thomas W. Lamont, J. P. Morgan's Chief Executive*. Lanham, Maryland: Madison Books, 1994.

Langsam, Walter Consuelo. *The World Since 1914*. New York: Macmillan Company, 1940.

League of Nations. "Dispute between Colombia and Peru: Colombia's Appeal Under Article 15 of the Covenant." Geneva, Switzerland: League of Nations, 1933.

Levy, David W. *Herbert Croly of the New Republic: The Life and Thought of an American Progressive*. Princeton, NW: Princeton University Press, 1985.

Link, Arthur et al., editors. *Papers of Woodrow Wilson*. 68 volumes. Princeton, NJ: Princeton University Press, 1966-1993.

Link, Arthur and Richard McCormick. *Progressivism.* New York: Harlan Davidson, 1983.

Link, Arthur. *Wilson: The New Freedom.* Princeton: Princeton University Press, 1956.

———. *Woodrow Wilson and the Progressive Era, 1910-1917.* New York: Harper & Brothers Publishers, 1954.

Lippmann, Walter. "Church and State in Mexico: the American Mediation." *Foreign Affairs* (January 1930).

———. "The London Naval Conference: an American View." *Foreign Affairs* (July 1930).

Martin, Albro. *Enterprise Denied: Origins of the Decline of American Railroads, 1897-1917.* New York: Columbia University Press, 1971.

Marrus, Frederick. *Lessons of Allied Co-Operation: Naval, Military and Air, 1914-1918.* New York: Oxford University Press, 1942.

McClure, Marc. "George Rublee." *American National Biography.* Volume 19. Cary, NC: Oxford University Press, 1998.

———. "Joseph Potter Cotton," *American National Biography.* Volume 5. Cary, NC: Oxford University Press, 1998.

———. "Robert Perkins Bass," *American National Biography.* Volume 2. Cary, NC: Oxford University Press, 1998.

McCraw, Thomas K. *Prophets of Regulation.* Cambridge: Belknap Press of the Harvard University Press, 1984.

McFarland, Gerald. *Mugwumps, Morals & Politics, 1884 -1920.* Amherst: University of Massachusetts Press, 1975.

Melzer, Richard. "The Ambassador Simpatico: Dwight Morrow in Mexico, 1927-1930." *Ambassadors in Foreign Policy: The Influence of Individuals on U.S.-Latin American Policy.* C. Neale Ronning and Albert P. Vannucci, editors. New York: Praeger Publishers, 1987.

Mendelsohn, John. *The Holocaust: Selected Documents in Eighteen Volumes.* New York: Garland Publishing, 1982.

Miller, David. *The Drafting of the Covenant.* 2 volumes. New York: G.P. Putnam's Sons, 1928.

———. *My Diary at the Conference of Paris, with documents.* 21 volumes. New York: Printed for the author by the Appeal Printing Co., 1924 (microfilm).

Monnet, Jean. *Memoirs.* Translated by Richard Mayne. New York: Doubleday & Company, 1978.

Morawetz, Victor. *The Banking and Currency Problem in the United States.* 2nd edition. New York: North American Review Publishing Co., 1909.

Morison, Elting E. *Turmoil and Tradition: A Study in the Life and Times of Henry L. Stimson.* Boston: Houghton Mifflin Company, 1960.

Morrow, Dwight. *The Society of Free States.* New York: Harper Brothers Publishers, 1919.

Morse, Arthur D. *While Six Million Died: A Chronicle of American Apathy.* New York: Random House, 1967.

Mosley, Leonard. *Dulles: A Biography of Eleanor, Allen and Foster Dulles and their Family Network.* New York: Dial Press, 1978.

Mowry, George. *The Era of Theodore Roosevelt.* New York: Harper and Row, 1958.

Mowry, George *Theodore Roosevelt and the Progressive Movement*. Madison: University of Wisconsin Press, 1946.

Muhlen, Norbert. *Schacht: Hitler's Magician*. New York: Alliance Book Corporation, 1939.

Murras, Michael. *The Unwanted: European Refugees in the 20th Century*. New York: Oxford University Press, 1985.

Myers, William Starr, editor. *The State Papers and Other Public Writings of Herbert Hoover*. 2 volumes. New York: Doubleday, Doran & Company, 1934.

Nash, George. *The Life of Herbert Hoover*. Volume 3, *Master of Emergencies, 1917-1918*. New York: W.W. Norton, 1996.

Nicolson, Harold. *Dwight Morrow*. New York: Harcourt, Brace and Company, 1935.

Noble, Ransom E. *New Jersey Progressivism before Wilson*. Princeton, NJ: Princeton University Press, 1946.

O'Connor, Raymond. *Perilous Equilibrium: The Unites States and the London Naval Conference of 1930*. New York: Greenwood Press, 1969.

Paper, Lewis. *Brandeis*. Englewood Cliffs, NJ: Prentice-Hall, 1983.

Pearson, Drew and Constantine Brown. *The American Diplomatic Game*. New York: Doubleday, Doran & Company, 1935.

Pershing, John. *My Experiences in the World War*. 2 volumes. New York: Frederick A. Stokes Company, 1931.

Porter, Glenn. *The Rise of Big Business, 1860-1920*. Wheeling, IL: Harlan Davidson Inc., 1992.

Roberts, Pricilla. "The Anglo-American Theme: American Visions of an Atlantic Alliance, 1914-1933." *Diplomatic History*, 21 no. 3 (Summer 1998).

Robertson, William. *Soldiers and Statesmen, 1914-1918*. 2 volumes. London: Cassell and Company, 1926.

Rodgers, Daniel. *Atlantic Crossings: Social Politics in a Progressive Age*. Cambridge: Belknap Press of the Harvard University Press, 1998.

———. "In Search of Progressivism." *Reviews in American History* (December 1982).

Roskill, Stephen. *Naval Policy Between the Wars*. Two volumes. London: Collins, 1968 and 1976.

Rublee, George. "A Handicap to Business," *Collier's Weekly* (October 1907).

———. "Government Rate-Making," *Collier's Weekly* (6 January 1906).

. "Inter-Allied Machinery in War-Time," In *The League of Nations Starts: An Outline By Its Organizers*. London: Macmillan and Company, 1920.

———. "The Original Plan and Early History of the Federal Trade Commission." *Proceedings of the American Academy of Political and Social Sciences*, 11 (January 1926): 114-120.

Safford, Jeffrey. *Wilsonian Maritime Diplomacy, 1913-1921*. New Brunswick, NJ: Rutgers University Press, 1978.

Salter, James Arthur. *Allied Shipping Control: An Experiment in International Administration*. Carnegie Endowment for International Peace. Economic and Social History of the War, British Series. James T. Shotwell, general editor. London: Oxford University Press, 1921.

———. *Memoirs of a Public Servant*. London: Faber and Faber, 1961.

———. *Personality in Politics: Studies of Contemporary Statesmen*. London: Faber and Faber, 1948.

Salter, James. *The United States of Europe*. London: George Allen and Urwin, 1933.

Schacht, Hjalmar. *Confessions of "The Old Wizard": The Autobiography of Hjalmar Horace Greeley Schacht*. Translated by Diana Pike. Boston: Houghton Mifflin Company, 1956.

Schewe, Donald, editor. *Franklin D. Roosevelt and Foreign Affairs, January 1937-August 1939*. New York: Garland Publishing, 1979.

Schlup, Leon. "Consistent Conservative: Jacob Gallinger and the Presidential Campaign of 1912 in New Hampshire." *International Review of History and Political Science* (1984).

———. "Jacob Harold Gallinger." *American National Biography*. Volume 8. Cary, NC: Oxford University Press, 1998.

Schwabe, Klaus. *Woodrow Wilson, Revolutionary Germany, and Peacemaking, 1918-1919: Missionary Diplomacy and the Realities of Power*. Translated from German by Rita and Robert Kimber. Chapel Hill: University of North Carolina Press, 1983.

Schuker, Stephen. "Dwight Morrow." *American National Biography*. Volume 15. Cary, NC: Oxford University Press, 1998.

Schulzinger, Robert. *American Diplomacy in the Twentieth Century*. 3rd ed. New York: Oxford University Press, 1994.

Sedgwick, Ellery. *The Happy Profession*. Boston: Little, Brown and Company, 1946.

Sessions, Gene. *Prophesying Upon the Bones: J. Reuben Clark and the Foreign Debt Crisis, 1933-39*. Urbana, IL: University of Illinois Press, 1992.

Shattuck, Gardiner. "William Stephen Rainsford." *American National Biography*. Volume 18. Cary, NC: Oxford University Press, 1998.

Sherman, Ari J. *Island Refuge: Britain and Refugees from the Third Reich, 1933-1939*. Berkeley: University of California Press, 1973.

Siney, Marion. *The Allied Blockade of Germany, 1914-1918*. Ann Arbor, MI: University of Michigan Press, 1957.

Smith, Darrell and Paul Betters. *The United States Shipping Board: Its History, Activities and Organization*. Washington: Brookings Institution, 1931.

Sproat, John. *"The Best Men": Liberal Reformers in the Gilded Age*. New York: Oxford University Press, 1968.

Stimson, Henry and McGeorge Bundy. *On Active Service in Peace and War*. New York: Harper & Brothers, 1948.

Stone, William. "The London Naval Conference." *Information Service* (28 May 1930).

Strum, Philippa. *Louis D. Brandeis: Justice for the People*. Cambridge: Harvard University Press, 1984.

Tillman, Seth. Anglo-American Relations at the Paris Peace Conference of 1919. Princeton, NJ: Princeton University Press, 1961.

Todd, A. L. *Justice on Trial: The Case of Louis D. Brandeis*. New York: McGraw-Hill, 1964.

Toland, John. *Adolf Hitler*. New York: Doubleday, 1954.

Tuck, Jim. *The Holy War in Los Altos. A Regional Analysis of Mexico's Cristero Rebellion*. Tucson: University of Arizona Press.

United States. Department of State. *Papers relating to the Foreign Relations of the United States*, 1871, 1875, 1917, 1918, 1919, 1921, 1930, 1938, 1939. Washington, D.C.: Government Printing Office, 1871-1957.

United States. Department of State. *Department of State Bulletin.* "Meeting of the Intergovernmental Committee on Political Refugees: Proceedings of the Meeting." Washington, D.C.: Government Printing Office, 1939.

———. Department of State. *Documents on German Foreign Policy, 1918-1945.* Series D (1937-1945). Volume 5: *The Smaller Powers — June 1937–March 1938.*

———. Federal Trade Commission. *Report on Cooperation in American Export, Part One, Summary and Report.* Washington, D.C.: Government Printing Office, 1916.

———. House of Representatives. *To Promote Export Trade, and for Other Purposes, Hearings before the Committee of the Judiciary, House of Representatives, Sixty-fourth Congress, First Session on H.R. 16707, Serial 46, July 18 and 20th, 1916.* Washington, D.C.: Government Printing Office, 1916.

———. *Permanent Court of the Arbitration at the Hague: United States-Norway Arbitration, Appendix to the Counter-Case of the United States of America: Documentary Evidence.* Washington, D.C.: Government Printing Office, 1922.

———. Senate. *Hearings Before a Subcommittee of the Committee of Interstate Commerce, United States Senate, Relating to the Fitness of the Members of the Federal Trade Commission, February 25 and 26, 1915.* Washington, D.C.: Government Printing Office, 1915.

———. Senate. *Hearings Before a Subcommittee of the Committee of Interstate Commerce, United States Senate, Relating to the Fitness of the Members of the Federal Trade Commission, Part II, March 1, 1915.* Washington, D.C.: Government Printing Office, 1915.

———. Senate. *Proceedings of Committee on Foreign Relations.* Washington, D.C.: Government Printing Office, 1930.

———. 63rd Congress, 2nd Session, *Brief by the Bureau of Corporations Relative to Section 5 of the Bill to Create a Federal Trade Commission.* Washington, D.C.: Government Printing Office, 1914.

———. 63rd Congress, 2nd Session, *Brief by George Rublee Relative to the Court Review in the Bill to Create a Federal Trade Commission.* Washington, D.C.: Government Printing Office, 1914.

———. 63rd Congress, 2nd Session, Committee on Interstate and Foreign Commerce, *Interstate Trade Commission . . . Minority Views.* Washington, D.C.: Government Printing Office, 1914.

———. 63rd Congress. *Congressional Record.* Washington, D.C.: Government Printing Office, 1915.

Urofsky, Melvin. *A Mind of One Piece: Brandeis and American Reform.* New York: Charles Scribner's Sons, 1971.

———. "Brandeis, Louis D." The Reader's Companion to American History. Edited by Eric Foner and John A. Garraty. Boston: Houghton-Mifflin Company, 1991.

———. "Wilson, Brandeis and the Trust Issue, 1912-1914." *Mid-America: An Historical Review.* 49, no. 1(January 1967): 3-28.

——— and David W. Levy, editors. *"Half Brother, Half Son:" The Letters of Louis D. Brandeis to Felix Frankfurter.* Norman, OK: University of Oklahoma Press, 1991.

——— and David W. Levy, editors. *Letters of Louis D. Brandeis.* 5 volumes. Albany, NY: State University of New York Press, 1972.

Vincent, Paul C. *The Politics of Hunger: The Allied Blockade of Germany, 1915 -1919.* Athens: Ohio University Press, 1985.

Weinberg, Gerhard. *The Foreign Policy of Hitler's Germany: Starting World War II, 1937-1939*. Chicago: The University of Chicago Press, 1980.

Weitz, John. *Hitler's Banker: Hjalmar Horace Greeley Schacht*. Boston: Little, Brown and Company, 1997.

Wood, Bryce. *The United States and Latin American Wars, 1932-1942*. New York: Columbia University Press, 1966.

Wright, James. *The Progressive Yankees: Republican Reformers in New Hampshire, 1906-1916*. Hanover, NH: University Press of New England, 1987.

Wyman, David S. *Paper Walls: America and the Refugee Crisis, 1938-1941*. Amherst: University of Massachusetts Press, 1968.

Index

Acheson, Dean, 173, 219–20, 226, 242, 272, 280 n.115, 283–84; his interpretation of Rublee's life, 33, 61, 277; and importance of AMTC, 154; Rublee's influence on, 3, 15, 173–74, 257, 284
Alabama claims, 8–9
Allied Maritime Transport Council (AMTC): activities, 142–48, 150–54, 156–57, 160–62; influence on League of Nations structure, 154, 162, 169 n.161, 174; origins, 139–42
Ames, James, 24–26, 29
Anthracite coal strike, 239–41
Argentina, 256
Attolico, Bernardo, 143–44, 151
Ayer, Walter, 41

Baker, Newton D., 152–53, 155, 159, 167 n.15
Baker, Philip, 203, 211
Balfour, A. J., 139
Ballinger, Richard, 50–52
Ballinger-Pinchot Controversy, 49–52
Bank for International Settlements, 254
Baruch, Bernard M., 149, 164 n.24
Bass, John, 16, 49–50, 53
Bass, Robert, 16, 50, 53–60, 65–67, 69–70, 76, 86, 98–99, 105–6, 110–14, 127 n.15; Rublee's role in his governorship, 55–60, 65, 110–11
Beck, Josef, 256
Bérenger, Henry, 253, 266, 276, 280 n.97
Biddle, Anthony, 255–56
Billings, Sherrad, 15, 27
Bismarck, Otto von, 39, 237
Boston and Maine railroad (B&M), 52–57, 59–60
Brandeis, Louis, 49–52, 54–56, 61, 65, 70, 85–86, 98, 101 n.13, 101 n.19, 107, 110–11, 122, 171–73, 180, 182, 225, 232; and the FTC, 109, 112–15, 124, 132 n.144; and the Jewish refugee crisis, 251, 272, 280 n.115; relinquishes anti-trust program to Rublee, 89, 92–96, 99–100, 102 n.43; Supreme Court nomination, 116–18, 123; and Woodrow Wilson's anti-trust program, 76–77, 87–88, 91
Brazil, 252–53
Briand, Aristide, 200, 204, 208, 211, 213
Bullitt, William, 253, 255

Bureau of Corporations, 88, 93, 95, 99, 109, 112–13
Burke, John, 189
Burling, Edward, 16, 27, 29, 41, 46 n.38, 115, 129 n.63, 137–38, 172–73

Caffery, Jefferson, 227–29, 231–32
Calles, Plutarco, 176–77, 180–82, 184, 187–90, 222, 224
Cecil, Robert, 143, 148, 152, 160, 174
Cerro, Sanchez, 233–34, 237, 239
Chamberlain, Neville, 250, 255, 257–59, 280 n.97
Chernow, Ron, 222, 243 n.23
Churchill, Winston, 52–53, 74, 119
Clapp, Moses, 98
Clark, Reuben, 191, 223, 225–27, 242 n.1
Claudel, Paul, 200–201
Clayton Act, 88–92, 94, 99
Cochran, Tom, 186
Colby, Bainbridge, 142
Colombia: Leticia controversy, 233–39; oil concession settlement, 226, 228–29, 231; relations with the U.S., 227, 229, 232–35, 239
Commercial Economy Board, 137–37
Coolidge, Calvin, 175, 178–79, 186, 191
Cooper, John Milton Jr., 93, 133 n.145
Cornish Colony, 40–41
Cotton, Joseph P., 16, 49, 54, 56, 60, 66, 69, 76, 80, 85–86, 117, 127 n.25, 171; advisor to Robert Bass, 53–55, 58; advisor to Theodore Roosevelt (1912), 70–71, 78, 80; death of, 231–33; public work during World War I, 137–38, 149, 154–55, 158, 161–62, 173; Under Secretary of State, 191–92, 201, 206, 209–11, 217 n.70, 219, 225–26
Cotton, Joseph P. Jr., 215 n.70, 260, 267–68, 279 n.59
Council on Foreign Relation, 172
Covington, J. Harry, 46 n.38, 124–25, 172–73
Covington, Burling and Rublee law firm, 172–74
Cravath, Paul, 144, 175, 225

Croly, Herbert, 16, 40–41, 49, 96; editor of *The New Republic*, 85, 110, 162; influence on progressive politics, 44, 65, 70, 76–80, 89

Davies, Joseph, 99, 109, 112–15, 126, 129 n.60
Davison, Henry, 161
Dawes, Charles, 199, 202
Denman, William, 138
Diaz, Porfirio, 176, 188
Dow, Louis, 16, 188
Dyer, Louis, 18

Eliot, Charles, 13, 24, 26
Emergency Fleet Corporation, 137–38, 173
Evian Conference, 248–50

Federal Reserve System, intellectual origins, 42–43, 80, 86
Federal Trade Commission (FTC), 109–10, 112–15, 119–26, 135
Federal Trade Commission Act, origins, 88–100
Ferrell, Robert, 7, 203–4
Fish, Hamilton, 10
Folsom, Clarence, 231
Foreign Bondholders Council, 241–42
France, 9, 18, 33–34, 136, 188, 238; and the Allied Maritime Transport Council, 139, 141–47, 150, 152; and the London Naval Conference, 197–200, 202, 204–8, 210, 213–15; postwar foreign policy, 156, 159, 161
Frankfurter, Felix, 52, 73, 117, 119, 191, 201, 225; writes editorial in support of Rublee's nomination to FTC, 111
Franklin, George, 137
Funk, Walther, 264, 268, 271

Gallinger, Jacob, 72, 105–13, 115–19, 121, 123, 135
Gardner, Gilson, 115, 117, 129 n.60
Gaskill, Nelson, 93
Gay Edwin, 136, 138, 172, 193 n.2; and the Allied Maritime Transport Coun-

cil, 143, 153, 166 n.91, 167 n.112; and the FTC, 115
Geist, Raymond, 274
George, David Lloyd, 139, 156
Germany, 33–34, 121, 160–61, 179, 199–200, 204; and the Jewish refugee crisis, 247–53, 256, 259–61, 263–65; Nuremberg laws, 247, 263; political economy of, 39, 49; political schism regarding Jewish policy, 260–61, 264; overthrows the Versailles Treaty, 255, 257–58; trade policy, 254–55, 262, 264; in World War I, 136–39, 141, 146–47, 154, 160–61
Gibson, Hugh, 199
Gil, Portes, 190
Glavis, Louis, 50–52
Goethals, George, 137–38, 164 n.19
Good Neighbor Policy, liberal Republicans role in shaping, 176, 191–92, 226–27, 244 n.43
Göring, Hermann, 260, 264–69, 271, 274–75
Great Britain, 34, 136, 238, 283; and the *Alabama* claims, 8–9; and the Allied Maritime Transport Council, 139, 141–47, 151–52, 167 n.111; and the Jewish refugee crisis, 247, 252, 255–57, 259–61, 269; and the London Naval Conference, 197–200, 202, 204, 206–8, 215; political-economy of, 39, 49; postwar foreign policy, 155–57, 160
Greenback Party, 9–10
Greer, Benjamin, 106–8
Grynszpan, Herschel, 264

Hand, Learned, 16, 27, 41, 49, 56, 85–86, 129 n.63, 150, 179, 279 n.60; advisor to Theodore Roosevelt, 65–67, 69, 71, 73–74, 76, 78–80, 82 n.11, 83 n.54, 84 n.88; critiques Rublee, 16–17, 119–20,131 n.97; his views on anti-trust and the FTC, 94–95, 100, 104 n.75, 119–20
Hapgood, Norman, 16, 27, 32, 39–41, 49–50, 76, 117, 130 n.81, 144, 165 n.53, 171, 180; involvement in anti-trust policy, 85–88, 91–92, 95; Rublee ally on FTC issues, 109, 119–22, 127 n.15, 127 n.25
Harris, William, 109, 112, 119–22
Henderson, Neville, 261–62
Hepburn Act, 41–42
Hill, Arthur D., 49, 67, 69–70, 75, 78
Himmler, Heinrich, 268, 274
Hitler, Adolph, 247, 251–52, 255, 257–58, 266–69, 271–72, 276
Hollis, Henry, 92, 95–96, 111, 118–19, 122
Holmes, Oliver Wendell, 67–68, 82 n.11
Hoover, Herbert, 137, 168 n.158, 190–93, 225, 231; considers Dwight Morrow a political rival, 220–21, 223–24, 278 n.35; and the Good Neighbor policy, 226, 244 n.43; influence on Harding administration's foreign policy, 174–75; and the 1930 London Naval Conference, 197, 199, 201–2, 205–15; opposes Rublee's call for closer cooperation with Allies, 149, 154–62; Rublee critical of, 149, 155–58, 175, 192–93, 202, 212
House, Edward, 109, 113, 141–42, 144, 147, 157–58; involvement in FTC feud, 120–24; Rublee critical of, 158
Houston, Davis, 136
Hughes, Charles Evans, 54, 175, 221
Hull, Cordell, 283; and the Jewish refugee crisis, 248, 253–56, 261–63, 265–66, 270, 270, 275–76; response to Leticia controversy, 238–39
Hurley, Edward: on the FTC, 109, 112, 119–24, 126; and U.S. cooperation with the AMTC, 145, 147–49, 155–56, 161, 166 n.91, 168 n.148; U.S. Shipping Board chairman, 138, 145

Intergovernmental Committee for Political Refugees Coming from Germany (IGC), 250–53, 256, 265–66, 271, 275–76
International Paper Company, 224–25
Interstate Commerce Commission, 41–42, 54, 87, 97, 99, 120, 137
Italy, 9, 188, 234, 238; and the Allied Maritime Transport Council, 139–40,

142, 145, 147; and the London Naval Conference, 197–200, 202, 204, 214

Japan, 235, 238; and the London Naval Conference, 197–200, 202, 214
Judicial recall, 65–72

Kellogg, Frank, 176–77, 185
Kellogg-Briand Anti-War Pact, 200, 205, 235–39
Kennedy, Joseph, 248, 256–59, 278 n.42
Kirkland, David, 184
Kordt, Theodore, 260, 267–68, 279 n.60
Kristallnacht, 264–65

La Follete, Robert, 10, 47 n.78, 52, 65, 70, 74, 76, 88, 92, 98, 108, 192; defends Rublee's FTC appointment, 110–11, 116
Lamont, Thomas, 144, 148, 172, 210–11, 220, 250; evaluation of Rublee's personality, 17; and Mexican foreign debt, 186–87, 222–23, 242, 243 n.23
Lane, Franklin, 91, 96, 136
Lansing, Robert, 152
League of Nations, 156, 161–62, 168 n.152, 169 n.159, 171–72, 174, 183, 195 n.70, 199, 248; and international security, 200–201, 212; and the Jewish Refugee Crisis, 250, 253, 266; and the Leticia controversy, 235–36, 238–39
Leffingwell, Russell, 185–86
Lincoln Republicans, 52–53
Lindbergh, Charles, 184
Lippmann, Walter, 89, 110, 117, 123, 128 n.41, 199, 200, 202, 214, 216 n.51, 218 n.90, 219–20
Littell, Philip, 16, 29, 41, 100, 110
London Naval Conference: background, 197–202; consultative pact controversy, 205–14, 223; French diplomatic aims, 200–202, 204
Loucheur, Louis, 143, 150
Low, Seth, 24, 37
Lowman, Seymour, 224–25

MacDonald, Ramsay, 199–200, 203–4, 206, 209, 211
Malcolm, Neill, 248, 253
Marshall, Thomas, 118
Mazzini, Guiseppe, 67–68
McCarthy, Charles, 92, 95
McCraw, Thomas, 89, 93, 99, 101 n.20, 102 n.30, 126
McDonald, James, 210
McNab, Alexander, 221–22
McReynolds, James, 91, 94
Mellen, Charles Sanger, 55, 58–61
Metzger, H. A., 228–29, 231
Mexico: Church-state controversy, 185–91, 221–23, 242; Cristeros rebellion, 190–91, foreign debt settlement, 185–87; relations with the U.S., 176–82, 184, 187–88
Monnet, Jean, 171, 174–75, 203; co-architect and leader of the AMTC, 139–44, 146–47, 150–51, 153, 157, 161, 165 n.50
Moore, John Bassett, 235–36
Morawetz, Victor, 27–32, 35–37, 39–40, 44, 47 n.78, 48 n.115, 84; and the Federal Reserve System, 42–43, 80, 86– 87, 101 n.8; influence on development of corporation law, 29, 36, 46 n.35;
Morgan, John Pierpont, 24, 28–29, 31, 36
Morgan, Laura Puffer, 209
Morones, Luis, 182, 195 n.64
Morrison, Frank, 239–41
Morrow, Dwight: and the Allied Maritime Transport Council, 143–46, 149, 158, 164 n.45, 164 n.50, 169 n.161; ambassador to Mexico, 176, 180–91, 201, 243 n.23; campaign for U.S. Senate, 219–22, 242 n.1; death of, 224, 232; describes Rublee's attainments, 185, 225–26; ends Church–state crisis in Mexico, 185–91; feuds with Thomas Lamont over Mexican debt settlement, 222–23, 242; genius of the Good Neighbor policy, 171, 175–76, 179,182, 184, 191, 226–27, 244 n.43; and the London Naval Conference, 201–5, 207–9, 211–12, 214, 215 n.19; opposes Hoover at London Naval

Conference, 207–9, 211–12, 215 n.19, 217 n.52; opposes Hoover's presidency, 193, 217 n.79, 219–21, 224; record as senator, 223–24; *The Society of Free States,* 162
Morrow, Elizabeth, 227, 242 n.1, 244 n.43
Mugwumps, 11
Munich Crisis, 255, 257–58

New Freedom, 76–77, 87–89, 99–100
New Nationalism, 44, 76–77, 81, 96, 100
Newlands, Francis, 95, 98–99, 111, 119
Nicolson, Harold, 175, 223–24, 242 n.23
Norman, Montagu, 268
Norris, George, 116, 191–92
Norton, Charles, 27, 137–38
Nye, Gerald, 180

Oca, Montes des, 187, 222–23
Olaya, Enrique, 226–28, 231–37
Orlando, Salvatore, 143, 156

Paris Commune, 7
Parker, Gilbert, 179, 185
Parry, William, 109, 112, 119
Peabody, Endicott: disapproves of Theodore Roosevelt's 1912 campaign, 72–73; headmaster of Groton and Rublee mentor, 5, 13, 15, 18–19, 23–27, 31, 37, 45 n.28, 61, 213; skeptical of Rublee's negotiations with Nazis, 276;
Pearson, Drew, 201, 203–4, 206–9, 211–14, 216 n.41, 217 n.52, 221–24, 227
Pell, Robert, 260, 267–68, 273
Pershing, John, 144–45
Peru, Leticia controversy, 233–39
Pinchot, Gifford, 50–53, 76, 78
Poindexter, Miles, 116
Prentis, Gilbert, 267, 274
President's Advisory Council on Political Refugees (PACPR), 248, 250–51, 270
Progressive Party, formation and early history, 72, 74–76, 78–81
Prohibition, 219–20

Rainsford, William, 31–32, 46 n.51
Reading, Lord, 152
Record, George, 109, 127 n.23
Reed, David, 202
Reed, James, 98, 110
Renan, Ernst, 19
Ribbentrop, Joachim von, 257, 260–62, 264–68, 271–74
Rich, Edgar, 59
Robinson, Joseph, 202, 205, 207
Rogers, Will, 184–85, 195 n.79
Roosevelt, Franklin D., 221, 227, 237, 239, 241–42, 244 n.43; and the German Jewish refugee crisis, 248–51, 259, 266, 278 n.42, 280 n.107; Rublee critical of, 249, 254, 258, 278 n.42
Roosevelt, Theodore, 38, 41, 44, 50, 110, 226–27; criticizes Gallinger, 108, 117; 1912 campaign to unseat William Howard Taft, 53, 65–78, 81, 85–86, 93, 96
Rublee, George: and the Allied Maritime Transport Council (AMTC), 143–54; AMTC, and U.S. cooperation, 145–50, 153–54; and the anthracite coal strike, 239–41; article on federal banking and monetary policy, 42–44; article on the Hepburn Act, 41–42; assistant to Louis Brandeis, 50–52, 87–88, 101 n.13; and the Ballinger-Pinchot controversy, 49–52; becomes national symbol of progressivism, 115–18, 123; civic mindedness of, 5–6, 30, 33, 37, 56, 61, 86; and the Commercial Economy Board, 135–37; courtship of Juliet Barrett, 27–28, 32, 35–36; critical of Franklin Roosevelt's handling of the Jewish refugee crisis, 249, 254, 258, 278 n.42; critical of Herbert Hoover's foreign policy, 149, 155–58, 175, 192, 202, 212; criticizes Woodrow Wilson's lack of cooperation with allies, 158; critiques Neville Chamberlain's handling of Munich crisis, 257–58; early financial success, 35–36; early interest in international affairs, 33–35, 37–38; education of, 12–16, 20, 23–24; and the Eight-Hour Commis-

sion, 123; and the Emergency Fleet Corporation, 137–38; extracts Jean Monnet from French army, 150–51; Federal Trade Commission Act, author of, 88–100, 125; FTC, attempts to shape, 108–9, 112–15, 120–22; FTC, criticizes Woodrow Wilson's appointments, 113–14; FTC, nomination blocked by Jacob Gallinger, 109–12, 115–18, 123; FTC, resigns from, 123–24; and the Foreign Bondholders Council, 241–42; formative European experiences of, 7, 12, 18–20, 37–40; German Jews, his unsuccessful search for havens of refuge, 252, 255–56, 259, 261; German Jews, forms plan to ransom, 262; German Jews, negotiates with German government to end refugee crisis, 268–75; German Jews, warns of extermination of, 271; intercedes in diplomatic approach to Germany, 253–54, 258–62, 264–68; Intergovernmental Committee for Political Refugees (IGC), accepts directorship of, 250–52; IGC, makes final report to, 275–76; and the International Committee of Bankers on Mexico, 242; legal expertise of, 23–25, 29–31, 36–37, 131 n.97; legal profession, attitude toward, 16, 19–20, 25, 27, 32–34, 40, 56; and Louis Brandeis' Supreme Court confirmation, 117–18; and origins of the Lend-Lease Act, 283; political advisor to Theodore Roosevelt, 66–74; political advisor to Robert Bass, 53–61, 65; political views of, 11, 39, 41–44, 49, 52, 55, 57–58, 66–68, 70, 72, 77–81, 110–11, 246 n.126; and the Progressive Party, 74–81, 105–8; regulatory commissions, evolving attitude toward, 41–42, 55, 77–79, 89–90; retirement and death of, 284; teaches at Harvard Law School, 24–26; Versailles Treaty, critical of, 160–62; and the Webb-Pomerene Act, 121–22; works to unseat Senator Jacob Gallinger, 105–8

Rublee, Horace, 5, 13, 15, 17, 19, 21 n.21, 21 n.34, 38, 65, 127 n.28; influence on George Rublee, 5–7, 10, 12, 24, 26, 33, 61, 72; minister to Switzerland, 7–10; political views of, 6–7, 9–11; and the Republican party, 6

Rublee, Juliet, 27–28, 128 n.45, 172, 183, 257; and the birth control movement, 183, 195 n.69; contributions to George Rublee's public work, 56, 91, 172, 260; courtship and early marriage, 27–28, 31–32, 34–40; produces film, *The Flame of Mexico*, 184, 227

Rublee, Katherine Hopkins, 17, 22 n.57, 45 n.28,

Russia, 224–25

Saint-Gaudens, Augustus, 40

Salter, James Arthur, 171, 174–75, 182, 203; co-architect and leader of the AMTC, 139–44, 150–51, 153, 157, 160, 163 n.50

Sanger, Margaret, 183

Santayana, George, 16, 32, 40

Saulsbury, Williard, 119

Schacht, Hjalmar, 253, 260, 263; negotiation with Rublee, 267–75, 281 n.122

Shaw, Arch, 136

Sherman Anti-Trust Act, 29, 77–78, 86, 89, 94, 96–97, 121–22

Spooner, John, 24, 44, 53–54, 87

Stettinius, Edward R. Jr., 145–46, 150, 152

Stevens, Raymond, 49, 56–57, 61, 76, 85, 91, 111, 115, 173, 241; and the AMTC, 138, 143–45, 147–53, 158, 161, 165 n.52, 166 n.99, 167 n.106; and the FTC Act, 91–92, 95, 101 n.19; 105–8, 110, 136 n.4, 127 n.15; advisor to the King of Siam, 165 n.52, 191, 241

Stimson, Henry, 191, 225–26, 231–33, 244 n.43; and the London Naval Conference, 200–14; and the Leticia crisis, 236–39

Stone, William, 203, 209–11, 213

Straight, Willard, 38, 85

Strum, Phillipa, 93

Switzerland, 5, 7, 9–10, 247

Taft, William Howard, 66, 69, 72–75
Tardieu, Andres, 204, 208
Taylor, Myron, 250, 252–54, 260, 271
Teal, Joseph, 118
Tumulty, Joseph, 119, 138, 164 n.18

Urofsky, Melvin, 102 n.43, 118, 138
U.S.-Norway arbitration, 173–74
U.S. Shipping Board, 137–38
U.S. Steel Company, 36–37, 77

Versailles Treaty, 160–63, 169 n.161, 172, 197–99, 202, 206, 247–48, 255
Villard, Oswald Garrison, 51

Warren, George, 250–51
Webb-Pomerene Act, 121–22
Weizsacker, Ernst von, 261–62, 264
Welles, Sumner, 253, 259–60, 269
Wenninger, General, 260, 264, 267–68
William, Denman, 134
Wilson, Hugh, 253, 255, 257, 260–64, 267
Wilson, Woodrow, 81, 85–86, 98, 105, 108–9, 112–17, 135, 137–38, 164 n.18, 164 n.45, 168 n.159; adopts Rublee's approach to anti-trust, 91–97, 99–100; anti-trust program, 76, 87–88; criticism of his management of FTC, 124–26, 132 n.144, 132 n.145; indecisive leadership during FTC feud, 120–22; and international cooperation during World War I, 141–43, 147–49, 152–59, 161–63; uses Rublee's FTC nomination to attract Progressive voters, 118, 122–23
Winterton, Lord, 252, 258, 268–69
Wisconsin Idea, 10–11, 52
Wise, Stephen, 250–51, 262, 274
Wohlthat, Helmuth, 274
Wood, Bryce, 185, 239

Zayas, Alfredo, 175

ABOUT THE AUTHOR

MARC ERIC MCCLURE is Assistant Professor of History and Coordinator of the International Studies Program at Lees-McRae College in North Carolina. His areas of expertise include U.S. diplomatic history and U.S. business history. He was a 1999 Hoover Presidential Scholar and a recipient of the Alfred D. Chandler Jr. Traveling Fellowship from the Harvard University Business School. His current research interests include a reappraisal of Ambassador Dwight Morrow and an examination of diplomat and financier Joseph P. Cotton.

Recent Titles in
Contributions in American History

"Like Fire in Broom Straw": Southern Journalism and the Textile Strikes of 1929-1931
Robert Weldon Whalen

Purity and Hygiene: Women, Prostitution, and the "American Plan," 1900-1930
David J. Pivar

Brand of Infamy: A Biography of John Buchanan Floyd
Charles Pinnegar

Expectations for the Millennium: American Socialist Visions of the Future
Peter H. Buckingham, editor

In the Affairs of the World: Women, Patriarchy, and Power in Colonial South Carolina
Cara Anzilotti

Cadwallader Colden: A Figure of the American Enlightenment
Alfred R. Hoermann

The Tormented President: Calvin Coolidge, Death, and Clinical Depression
Robert E. Gilbert

Bulwark of the Republic: The American Militia in Antebellum West
Mary Ellen Rowe

Uncommon Americans: The Lives and Legacies of Herbert and Lou Henry Hoover
Timothy Walch, editor

The Eliot Tracts: With Letters from John Eliot to Thomas Thorowgood and Richard Baxter
Michael P. Clark, editor

Harvesting Freedom: African American Agrarianism in Civil War Era South Carolina
Akiko Ochiai

Unions, Radicals, and Democratic Presidents: Seeking Social Change in the Twentieth Century
Martin Halpern